Contents

Introduction
    ANTHONY BRADLEY AND MARYANN GIALANELLA VALIULIS   I

Queering the Irish Renaissance: The Masculinities of
Moore, Martyn, and Yeats
    ADRIAN FRAZIER   8

Cathleen ni Houlihan Writes Back: Maud Gonne and
Irish National Theater
    ANTOINETTE QUINN   39

Nationalism, Pacifism, Internationalism: Louie
Bennett, Hanna Sheehy-Skeffington, and the Problems of
"Defining Feminism"
    MARGARET WARD   60

The Fionnuala Factor: Irish Sibling Emigration at the
Turn of the Century
    MAUREEN MURPHY   85

"Oh, Kathleen Ni Houlihan, Your Way's a Thorny Way!":
The Condition of Women in Twentieth-Century Ireland
    MARY E. DALY   102

The Posthumous Life of Roger Casement
    LUCY MCDIARMID   127

Gender, Sexuality, and Englishness in Modern Irish
Drama and Film
    ELIZABETH BUTLER CULLINGFORD   159

"Our Bodies' Eyes and Writing Hands": Secrecy and
Sensuality in Ní Chuilleanáin's Baroque Art
  DILLON JOHNSTON   187

"The More with Which We Are Connected": The Muse
of the Minus in the Poetry of McGuckian and Kinsella
  GUINN BATTEN   212

Godly Burden: The Catholic Sisterhoods in
Twentieth-Century Ireland
  MARGARET MACCURTAIN   245

The Changing Face of Cathleen ni Houlihan: Women and
Politics in Ireland, 1960–1966
  CATHERINE B. SHANNON   257

"Hello Divorce, Goodbye Daddy": Women, Gender,
and the Divorce Debate
  CAROL COULTER   275

Language, Stories, Healing
  ANGELA BOURKE   299

Notes on Contributors   315

Index   319

GENDER
AND
SEXUALITY
IN
MODERN
IRELAND

Edited by

. . . .

ANTHONY BRADLEY AND
MARYANN GIALANELLA VALIULIS

UNIVERSITY OF MASSACHUSETTS PRESS / AMHERST

Published in cooperation with the
American Conference for Irish Studies

Copyright © 1997 by
American Conference for Irish Studies
All rights reserved

Printed in the United States of America
LC 97-26859
ISBN 1-55849-130-9 (cloth); 131-7 (pbk.)

Designed by Dennis Anderson
Set in Sabon by dix! Typesetting, Inc.
Printed and bound by Braun-Brumfield, Inc.

Library of Congress Cataloging-in-Publication Data
Gender and sexuality in modern Ireland / edited by Anthony Bradley and
Maryann Gialanella Valiulis.
p.   cm.
". . . in cooperation with the American Conference for Irish Studies.
Includes bibliographical references and index.
ISBN 1-55849-130-9 (cloth : alk. paper).—
ISBN 1-55849-131-7 (pbk. : alk. paper)
1. Sex role—Ireland.   2. Sex—Ireland—Religious aspects—Catholic Church.
3. Women—Ireland—Social conditions.   4. Women—Ireland—Sexual behavior.
5. Heterosexuality—Ireland.   6. Homosexuality—Ireland.   7. Sex in literature.
8. Irish literature.   I. Bradley, Anthony, 1942– .
II. Valiulis, Maryann Gialanella, 1947– .
HQ18.I73G45   1997
305.3'09415—dc21   97-26859
CIP

British Library Cataloguing in Publication data
are available.

Acknowledgments for material under copyright
appear on the last printed page.

GENDER AND SEXUALITY
IN MODERN IRELAND

ANTHONY BRADLEY AND
MARYANN GIALANELLA VALIULIS

Introduction

OUR DECISION to focus this first annual ACIS collection of essays on the subject of gender and sexuality, rather than on a more traditionally accredited theme or area of Irish studies, is in part a recognition that academic discourse is struggling to keep up with recent, fairly sudden social change in Ireland that is directly concerned with gender. It is also in recognition of the new and interesting perspectives afforded to Irish studies by the example of American and French theorists and critics in the area of gender and sexuality. To what extent rapid if overdue social change in Ireland may have been facilitated by such an international discussion of the implications of gender and sexuality is a matter for debate. In the Republic of Ireland the recent reform of laws affecting divorce, the availability of contraception, the decriminalization of homosexuality, the sensational events around what has become known as the X case, the fall of an Irish government over the extradition of a pedophile priest, the revelation of a bishop's and priests' actual rather than figurative paternities, and the various pathologies of misogyny that have come to light—all these, whether progressive social changes or disturbing revelations, have given an urgency to the issues of gender and sexuality, and have been accompanied by a growing intellectual awareness of the extent to which social experience, past and present, is gendered.

These changes and revelations are summarized with somewhat different emphases in several essays included here, most fully perhaps, in Carol Coulter's essay on the divorce referendum, which also exposes the international ideology of "family values" at the same time as it argues that the outcome of the referendum depended less on the persuasive power of rhetoric on either side than on prior social and demographic change. Others (such as Catherine Shannon in her essay on women and politics in Ireland) would argue that both progressive social legislation and an academic discourse more responsive to gender issues are consequences of challenges from the margins in Ireland.

They would argue that challenges to the status quo by women's groups, gay and lesbian groups, and dissenters from the Catholic ethos of the state, as well as a self-awareness prompted in part by affiliation with other European countries, and a crisis of identity about what it means to be Irish at the end of the twentieth century, have altered the social and cultural nature of contemporary Ireland.

We understand gender to be culturally constructed, and to be, like class, race, and nation, susceptible of analysis from a variety of critical and theoretical vantage points; it is also, like those terms, interestingly fluid and problematic, indeed often intertwined with them in an active matrix, at the same time as it is, again like those other terms, defined historically, socially, and culturally. The theorizing of gender has done much to unsettle ideas of sexual identities, and of what constitutes masculine and feminine, as being fixed and ordained by nature. The study of gender is accordingly not limited to feminist accounts and critiques—though it certainly includes them, and indeed probably originated in feminist theory—but rather recognizes that if the feminine is a social/historical/cultural construction then so also (however implicated in the patriarchy) is the masculine. If sexual identity and predilections are arguably more related to culture than nature, and more fluid and nuanced than they have traditionally been considered, then one sees historical and fictional characters, their behavior, and relationships (both the historical and the imaginary), in a different light than before. The study of sexuality, and especially homosexuality, in the culture at large, as well as in individuals, has become an urgent area of concern for critics and scholars, especially after Foucault and subsequent theorists. The clear, self-evident lines of demarcation between heterosexuality and homosexuality have, moreover, been challenged by a number of influential theorists and critics.

The study of gender in Ireland has been suppressed, with some notable exceptions, in the dominant male-centered discourses of historiography and literary criticism, which have until very recently assumed an understanding of culture that marginalizes gender in revising nationalism or in analyzing Ireland's postcolonial status. Not only that, but recognition of the contributions of women historians, writers, and critics, has, as a consequence, been slow to come. It has been left mainly to a small number of women historians, such as Margaret MacCurtain, to work against prevailing trends in historiography; the projected volume 4 of the *Field Day Anthology of Irish Writing*, edited by women scholars, will undoubtedly also be a major corrective in the representation of women's writing. Women historians have challenged both the nationalist and the revisionist accounts of Ireland's past by expanding what is understood by "political" to include women's activities in a broad range of voluntary and other areas. (It is in this context, perhaps, that one should read MacCurtain's essay on women religious.) Or, less frequently, women historians have challenged the assumptions of the dominant, revisionist school of Irish historiography, which presumes to debunk nationalism, and they have argued for an affiliation between nationalism and feminism: Margaret Ward sees her purpose as contributing toward "the development of an Irish feminist historiography that interrogates and rejects a politically loaded 'revisionist' enterprise aimed at discrediting the entire nationalist agenda." It is clear from our essays that a focus on gender does not imply a particular theoretical or ideological point of view. The differences in point of view, for example, of those essays that deal with the vexed relationship between feminism and nationalism in Ireland are quite apparent. Despite their differences, however, these essays collectively suggest that it may be more useful and productive to think in terms of the various strands in Irish nationalism and feminism than in terms of internally consistent, monolithic entities, and to understand both in the context of particular historical moments.

By analyzing the ways in which the simultaneous affiliations and contradictions between nationalism and feminism were embodied in Maud Gonne and the Daughters of Erin, and by suggesting how the spectacle of theater and not just the medium of print was important in achieving the imagined community of nation, Antoinette Quinn enhances and meaningfully complicates our understanding of Irish theater at the turn of the century. The strains between nationalism and feminism are most apparent in Maud Gonne's play *Dawn*, which she intended to represent famine and oppression realistically, as a kind of docudrama, in contrast to the more symbolic Yeatsian drama; the play is, however, gendered according to a nationalist ideology in which women suffer and men are politically active. This, of course, directly contradicts Maud Gonne's own political activism. And while she herself went against bourgeois morality—in her extramarital sexual relations, in giving birth outside marriage (twice), in her separation from her husband after a short and unhappy marriage—and was personally convinced of the rightness of the feminist cause, she nonetheless felt that it was not desirable to represent Irish women, as J. M. Synge did, as oppressed by Irish husbands, in unhappy marriages, or having sexual desires. (There is a bizarre contemporary echo of this conflict in the rhetoric of the anti-divorce lobby which, as Carol Coulter tells us, divided women into figures of the Madonna or Eve.) Contradictory though this may have been, one can appreciate Gonne's dilemma, which seemed to her to pit liberation from colonialism against liberation from an oppressive patriarchy.

Margaret Ward's essay highlights the opposition in Ireland's suffrage movement between an internationalist and pacificist group, and a group whose pacificism was qualified by its nationalism. The careers of Louie Bennett and Hanna Sheehy-Skeffington, respectively, are taken to embody these groups and, Ward suggests, continuing problematic tensions between feminism and nationalism in Ireland today. Recent Irish feminism has, in large part, so Angela Bourke notes in her essay, rejected the Irish language because it has seemed too intimately connected with a patriarchal and repressive nationalism; revisionist historians, too, in discrediting that nationalism, have inevitably discredited the language. Bourke's autobiographical essay eloquently revises these assumptions in the light of her own experience and suggests that the differences between feminism and the Irish language may be assuaged in narratives—such as the traditional story she translates as part of her essay (and, one might add, the narrative of her essay itself) —which are in the nature of healing meditations on change and are markedly relevant to Ireland's present and future.

Two essays, in particular, revise notions of the uniqueness of Irish women's historical experience. Mary E. Daly's essay cautions us against the danger of present-mindedness, or the unexamined assumption of continuity between past and present in the matter of Irish women's history. Daly sees the present interest in women's history as fueled by the contemporary women's movement and an explicitly feminist agenda; this agenda should not, she argues, be projected onto the Irish past. Indeed, her representation of Irish women's experience in the earlier part of this century explicitly challenges such projection and raises questions that suggest the need for more research. In pointing out the importance of activist women religious, for example, and of "maternal feminism" in the interwar years in Ireland, Daly demonstrates the need to complicate the contemporary feminist model. Her comparison of Irish women's experience with that of women in other modern states also challenges that model in its suggestion, essentially, that Irish women have not been appreciably more oppressed than women in other countries, and that Irish women's historical experience is probably not unique. An emphasis on uniqueness, paradoxically, may lead to an undervaluing and underestimation of the real achievements of Irish women in the past.

In an analogous spirit, Maureen Murphy's essay on Irish female emigration to the United States at the turn of the century challenges the nationalist representation of that phenomenon, which characterizes it as part of a catastrophic past, filled with the pain and suffering of a diaspora. Murphy revises this idea of emigration as involuntary exile, suggesting instead the positive consequences of opportunity and empowerment. The Irish women who "sojourned" in the States, mostly as servant girls, were able to dower themselves by means of their earnings; whether they came back to marry in Ireland or returned to the States, they had a greater choice of a husband because of this degree of economic independence. If they returned to the States, these female sojourners frequently became the nucleus for a family of emigrant siblings (male and female). Murphy's essay marries emigration statistics and passenger lists with the representation of the sister in Irish lore and legend as a powerful force for reconstituting the dispersed family and transforming women's experience of diaspora and exile.

Another group of essays deals with connections between sexuality and nationalism, both cultural and political. The essays by Adrian Frazier and Elizabeth Cullingford are concerned with masculinities in the form of homosocial and homoerotic relationships. Frazier sharply revises the history of the Irish Literary Revival in the light of the history of sexuality in the late nineteenth century, revealing the complexities and variabilities of male-male desire in Moore, Martyn, and Yeats, and showing how that desire gets mapped onto the literature and cultural politics of the period. Cullingford sees a recurrent intertext in Irish drama (and film) from Boucicault and Shaw to Jordan and McGuinness, in which the colonial allegory is inscribed in homosocial/homoerotic relations between Irish and English characters. The anticolonialist politics of such humanist rapprochements, and their undermining of fixed gender roles, may also be, ironically, oppositional to both feminist and republican viewpoints. Lucy McDiarmid's essay on Roger Casement, one in a series of political figures whose sexuality proved difficult for Ireland to accept, suggests that the rich afterlife of Casement in Ireland has been a way of projecting and coping (or not coping) with sexual issues and has until very recently amounted to a sort of national bad conscience about sexuality and especially homosexuality.

The essays on contemporary Irish poetry (by Guinn Batten and Dillon Johnston) intervene in an ongoing discussion of gender in Irish poetry, and they seek to deconstruct a poetics of identity based on an appeal to the experience of oppression and to reveal some of the more complex and problematic ways in which poetry may be gendered. Dillon Johnston's essay on Ní Chuilleanáin is prompted by the relative neglect of a woman poet whose work does not thematize oppression or appeal to the politics of identity; his subtle analysis focuses on the affiliation with baroque painting of Ní Chuilleanáin's art, its particular mixture of the spiritual and the sensual. Guinn Batten's essay, surprisingly at first sight, brings together the two poets in contemporary Ireland whose work has been identified in terms of the extremes of masculine and feminine (Thomas Kinsella and Medbh McGuckian), and she subverts this identification by revealing startling symmetries and mutualities in these poststructuralist poets: Kinsella feminizes law and structure, McGuckian depicts paternity as caring and nurturing, and both are significantly concerned with the maternal body.

Ireland has, of course, long been gendered—by the political nationalist metanarrative and the cultural nationalism of traditional history and literature—as a woman victimized by the colonizing English male. For an equally long time, the lives of actual Irish women were arguably colonized by Irish men, at the same time as both genders were colonial subjects of England. The point of gender studies is, among other things, to reveal in what ways the gendering of Ireland—not just in the personification of the nation, and not only in the case of women—is a matter of culture and ideology, and not "natural." Until very recently, Irish studies scholars had, for the most part unconsciously, elided gender and sexuality from their concerns and spoken of it only in their silences on the subject. As a self-conscious perspective on Irish experience, gender and sexuality make possible a series of interweaving narratives that are pluralizing and inclusive, fuller and more accurate in their reflection of the diversity and multiplicity of what it means to be Irish than can be afforded by any single, dominant narrative. Our collection of essays makes no pretense to being exhaustive or definitive in its treatment of gender and sexuality in modern Ireland, but we would maintain that, individually and collectively, these essays advance our understanding of the area and open up rather than close off further discussion. What they do, in Adrian Frazier's words, is "to cross the national narrative with counternarratives . . . of genders [and] sexualities." This collection is just one sign of the increasing awareness of the significance of gender in Irish studies, an awareness which will surely transform the field; the future possibilities for rewriting Ireland, in the analysis of Irish culture viewed through the lens of gender and sexuality, are many and inviting.

Queering the Irish Renaissance

The Masculinities of Moore,
Martyn, and Yeats

SOMETHING INTERESTING has been happening in recent years in Victorian studies that has not until lately made much of a dent in studies of the Irish Literary Revival. Scholars engaged in women's studies, accustomed to defining emergent forms of modern female identity against a patriarchal norm, began to question the unity of that norm, and moved from the construction of female identities to the study of the forms and transformations of Victorian male identities. At the same time, scholars engaged in gay or queer studies, often inspired by Foucault's *History of Sexuality,* tried to document the shift Foucault places in the late nineteenth century from *sexe* to *sexualité:* the historical moment of the medicalization of sexuality with its typologies of "inversion," and the criminalization of something now for the first time called "homosexuality." In the wake of Foucault's *History* have come studies by Ed Cohen, Christopher Craft, Richard Dellamora, Jonathan Dollimore, Linda Dowling—an entire A-to-Z of guidebooks to the "higher sodomy," "the Dorian Mode," "the Urnings," and so on. Central to most of these studies are the figures of Walter Pater, Oscar Wilde, and Havelock Ellis: the first created the theory, the second the practice and art, and the third the pathology of new ways of being male.

Now, it seems, an explanation is needed as to why these present academic interests of Victorian scholars have not hitherto been taken into account by those of us in Irish studies.[1] George Moore, Edward Martyn, W. B. Yeats, and James Joyce all found themselves out in reading Pater. It is fair to say that each of these Irish writers styled himself more on the figure of Wilde than that on, let's say, Thomas Davis. And Havelock Ellis lived in the Temple when Moore, Martyn, and Yeats all lived there; while working on *Sexual Inversion,* he shared rooms with Arthur Symons, "boon companion," to use Moore's term, of GM and WBY. In short, those males most identified with the deliberate creation of an "Irish Renaissance" were well schooled in the creation of alternative male identities.

Evidently the two features are connected: it is often remarked that cultural nationalism was an offshoot of London "Decadence" as much as of the Dublin "Irish Party"; begotten by an inflow of Wilde upon an upwelling of John O'Leary, Yeats's conception was of an elitist, aesthetic, and nonparliamentary movement. The way in which the dainty five-foot-three figure of Lionel Johnson floated on the arm of Yeats from the cells of Urnings to those of Fenians is emblematic: Johnson was at the center of homosexual circles at Oxford, where he was friends with Simeon Solomon in 1888[2] and fell in love with Wilde in 1890.[3] By 1891 he had shifted to London and the Rhymers' Club, from which he became a leading "Celtic" poet who traveled four times to Dublin, on the last to speak at a 23 May 1898 rally celebrating the centenary of the 1798 rebellion.[4] This aesthetic invasion of the Irish movement was obvious enough to people at the time: the veterans of the Irish movement, the O'Duffys and Morans, spoke sourly of the effeminate character of the new Irish literature: in the current code of deprecation, these poets "crooned" or "lisped"; real men, the implication was, shouted and argufied. Nineties cultural nationalism was, after all, susceptible to being thought of as an appropriation of the female sphere, "culture"; nationalism pure and simple, and mid-nineteenth-century Irish cultural nationalism, was male—a matter of guns behind the hedge, cigars in the lobby at Westminster, and ballads to Mother Ireland. The Celtic mist was often created by cigarettes in a parlor near the Strand.

While there is material for making the history of these Irish writers part of the history of sexuality as expressed in late nineteenth-century English literature—indeed, they are crucial to that history—to do so would not fit "naturally" into the larger narrative of Irish literary studies: the emergence and later fortunes of a national identity, as it is created or critiqued by Irish writers, in such a fashion as to make a marked difference between Irish literature and English literature (traditions, subjects, genres, styles peculiar to Ireland); in short, the national narrative. For this reason, though Victorian scholars and queer theorists such as Alan Sinfield can now speak of our age as *The Wilde Century,* Wilde hardly fits into the national narrative of Irish literature at all unless, as in *The Field Day Anthology,* Wilde and Shaw are roped back into the narrative by calling them the "London Exiles" (if the first Home Rule Bill had passed in 1886, would Wilde have found fulfillment in late Victorian Dublin?). One could put issues of male sexual identity, in the case of Moore, Martyn, and Yeats, into the nationalist master-narrative, but this should not be necessary, nor may it be desirable: is sexual desire a figuration of politics, or politics a displacement of sexual desire? The question can only be answered case by case.

Shaw says that a conquered nation is like a man with a broken arm; he doesn't like having it set, but it has to be done, and he can think of nothing else until it is put right, while "a healthy nation is as unconscious of its nationality as a healthy man of his bones."[5] While this pained obsession with national identity was the central fact of life for many Irish people in the late nineteenth century, it wasn't the only pain, the only obsession, of everyone. At any rate, would it be a sign of health if it were the obsession of all scholars today? A literary history that was complicit in earlier decades in the sexualization of power is now more ready to recognize the power of sexuality, and thus to cross the national narrative with counternarratives, not of nations, but of genders, sexualities, localities, and congeries of extra-national interests. Partly this dispersal of scholarly interest is the result of the ordinary scholarly desire to provide a map of the past that better fits the contours of fact, contours beyond the broad national highway so often traveled, and partly, no doubt, it results from the desire to multiply possibilities for the future by showing the multiplicity of the past. The nationalisms that seemed in the late nineteenth century to be liberationist, in the late twentieth often seem oppressive, inelastic, violently cyclical, and xenophobic.

Part of each of the forms of European nationalism after the French Revolution was an attempt to control sexuality, to establish "national" norms of sexuality, and to create a sexual dimension of its own, as George Mosse explains, "through the advocacy of beauty, its stereotypes of ideal men and women."[6] As nationalism was a quasi-military movement, which had to create unity by crushing forms of diversity within its borders and by entering into rivalries for spheres of power beyond those borders, it also promoted only certain kinds of masculinity: "manliness" involved excellence in the propagation of new citizens, in combat against aliens, in the expansion of an industrial economy, and in the regulation of respectability in the home—these were the duties of citizen; they went with the vote. It is this version of manliness in England, whether created by Thomas Arnold at Rugby School or Charles Kingsley in his campaign for "muscular Christianity," that Swinburne, Pater, Wilde, and company rebelled against. The popular and political side of Irish nationalism often simply received and reinforced this rhetoric of militant manliness characteristic of other national movements, even though many of the individual nationalists, especially those in the cultural movement, might be better understood in terms of the rebellion against the Protestant, respectable, no-nonsense, muscular, married, procreative manliness of Kingsley. Like the other Decadents, some of the Irish aesthetes were "engaged in a 'passive protest' against an imperialist ethic that championed the principles of duty, sacrifice, and self-sufficiency."[7] There is consequently a richness in the possibilities of masculinity during this period—when there were multiple forms of sexual practice (and nonpractice) and shifting ways of acting out gender—before the emergent model of sexual identities (as hetero-, homo-, or bi-sexual) came into force in the early twentieth century, that makes our categorical identities inadequate: the more one studies the lives of certain particular authors, the more one concludes that the categories underdetermine the life studied; they fail in explanation, and succeed in distortion. There are the gay Irish patriots like Wilde, Hugh Lane, and Roger Casement; the aesthetic, donnish revolutionaries like Joseph Plunkett and Thomas MacDonagh; and also the specific, uncategorical masculinities of Moore, Martyn, and Yeats, which are the subject of this paper.

Moore's own writing will be at the center of the following outline of the subject for two reasons, one an accident, the other a necessity. The accident is that I am writing a biography of Moore, and consequently have more to say about him. The necessity is the result of the fact that Moore was famously indiscreet: he left behind confession after confession, in which he outed himself, then outed Martyn, and finally made intriguing insinuations about Yeats. Martyn, on the other hand, in his last will and testament, delivered his bodily remains to a teaching hospital and his literary remains to the Carmelites in Clarendon Street, who employed the carefully Catholic Edward

Gwynn to write a biography sanitized of names, dates, and, as much as possible, facts. And once the biography was finished by Gwynn, the Carmelites lost Martyn's papers. About Yeats, there is a great deal more to be known, but the subject is so large that it is possible here only to make a few suggestions and to direct readers to books like Elizabeth Cullingford's *Gender and History in Yeats's Love Poetry,* while they await R. F. Foster's forthcoming biography of the poet.

2

George Moore has left several accounts of his first reading of Pater's *Marius the Epicurean,* "the book to which I owe the last temple of my soul."[8] He had come up to Moore Hall in February 1885, after the "Castle Season" in Dublin, where he was doing research for *A Drama in Muslin.* He had promised his mother to stay with her until the buds came to the beech trees in spring, before returning to his Strand lodgings in London. While she knitted and he read reviews of *A Mummer's Wife,* he came across a notice for Pater's book, and having heard of Pater as a writer of beautiful books, and seeing himself despised in London as a writer of ugly Zolaistic ones, he sent off for it. Its first lesson for him, he says, was that "by helping one's mother with her white and purple wools . . . it was possible to win . . . an urbane and and feminine refinement."[9] He was so excited that he wanted to write to Pater, or short of that, to get back to London and hear what was said of the book in the little salon held every Tuesday afternoon by Mary and Mabel Robinson. By late April, he had broken loose from his mother, and gotten back to London.

When he went to the Robinsons, he found Vernon Lee and Henry James with Mary and Mabel. GM steered the conversation around to *Marius,* one of the greatest books ever written, he blustered.[10] What most excited Moore in the ensuing discussion was not James's assessment that the center of consciousness was wrongly placed, but the news that Pater himself had recently become a neighbor of the Robinsons, just a few doors down at 12 Earl's Court Terrace; indeed, he often called for tea. Tuesday after Tuesday GM returned, but it was probably not until July that he finally met the author he so adored.[11]

Lawrence Evans is correct in saying Pater met Moore's "assaults on his acquaintance with studied reserve":[12] it was characteristic of the man. Pater had an "unhappy and even furtive timidity (so excessive that he could never look another man in the eye)."[13] But Moore managed to get himself invited to Pater's home, and on the third visit, Pater took him for a walk in Kensington Gardens. GM was "spying on Pater," trying to get him to drop his mask. But despite his "genius for intimacy," GM could not get the "Vicarage Verlaine" to share his "real self," except for a moment in the street, when he told Pater that his "Prince of Court Painters" was "the most beautiful thing ever written";[14] then Pater sighed with pleasure, " 'My dear Moore!' He put his hand upon my shoulder and the mask dropped a little."[15]

What was behind the mask of the beautiful stylist? A man who had strange desires—who conceived as a most beautiful moment the last night in the life of Flavian, when, to keep the dying man warm, Marius slept in his bed—desires, that is, not to be safely satisfied except in death, or in intimacies of understanding between men, exchanged through the perfection of phrases and sensations refined from grosser forms of fulfillment.[16] After the interception of an 1874 letter to his student William Money Hardinge, signed "Yours Lovingly" (which led to Hardinge's being sent down), Pater conducted himself in life with caution, but in his work, he continued to make beautiful certain forms of masculinity and types of affection that were a great stimulus to his readers. They found that what they had done, or wished to do, was not ugly, but aesthetic, antique, refined, the very mark of an artist. And Moore was one of those inspired by Pater to believe that a boy more comfortable helping his mother with her needlework than following after his father in dueling, Arabian caravanning, and electioneering might have the true makings of the highest culture. Moore was grooming himself to become like the man addressed in Tennyson's poem "On One Who Affected an Effeminate Manner."[17]

After completing *A Drama in Muslin* (a reviewer shocked by the lesbian ecstacies of Hilda scornfully asked, "Is George Moore a man?"), GM began a novel that was effectively an offering to Pater, *A Mere Accident*. The hero of the novel, John Norton, is modeled on Edward Martyn, as will be evident later in this essay. Norton had among his books at college Walter Pater's studies of the Renaissance, though *Marius* had been banned by the school authorities for its "realistic suggestion."[18] John Norton later reads it anyway, and recommends it to a clergyman, William Hare, for the depiction of beautiful altar boys. Norton confesses to Hare its effect on him: "It seemed to me I was made known to myself . . . the rapture of knowledge came upon me that our temporal life might be beautiful; that, in a word, it was possible somehow to come to terms with life."[19] It was inconceivable that anything could be more beautiful than the death of Flavian. While Norton adores altar boys and dying adolescents, he finds women hateful. There is "something very degrading, something very gross" in the idea of sexual relations with women;[20] besides that, they are "cunning and mean."[21] But his mother takes very seriously her duty to get John married, and his duty to propagate an heir. It is not good enough for her that John makes a will leaving something to all the tenants. Out of dread of his mother's plans, John considers entering the priesthood, except that he would then have to listen to women in the confession, "a kind of marriage bureau";[22] instead, he contemplates becoming a Carmelite monk—he likes the dress, the dangling rope belt, and the tonsure. Anything but marriage.

Putting aside the question of sexual proclivities, for Martyn, Norton, and, indeed, Moore, marriage meant that life had no other meaning than the perpetuation of life. In Schopenhauer's terms, it was surrender to the world as will, loss of the world as idea. In Pater's terms, it was an unbeautiful, merely natural life; the aesthetic life was against nature, above nature. For similiar reasons, Yeats sometimes envied homosexuals like Verlaine, while still conceiving them to be defective or immoral. "Without some vice or deficiency," he worried that it might not be possible to make that "complete renunciation of the world" necessary for complete self-expression.[23] Creation was set against procreation, art against nature, and perversity against normality. To be an artist, it was perhaps necessary to explore other ways of being male.

However, Norton like Martyn is really no artist; he has no "spiritual procreancy," to use a Paterian term.[24] He does not have quite the same aesthetic alibi for his aversion to matrimony as Moore and Yeats possessed. Norton has scholarly, architectural, and literary projects, but they "always met with failure, with disapproval."[25] As a result Mrs. Norton is able, in the course of the plot, to so contrive matters that Kitty Hare, the daughter of John's closest male friend and his confidante, is placed constantly in the propinquity of her son, until at last a kiss occurs, followed by a then-obligatory proposal: there is nothing in life for him to do, it seems, but marry. Now the crisis anticipated by readers is, What will a homosexual man actually do in a heterosexual marriage? This eventuality is astonishingly prevented when Kitty Hare is raped by a tramp on the road. She commits suicide, and John Norton, rescued by mere accident from marriage, resolves that he shall become a secular celibate: "the world shall be my monastery."[26]

The climactic incident of the rape, which gives the novel its title, is totally unforeshadowed on the literal level: the rapist appears and disappears from the cast of characters and from the plot with the rape. On a nonliteral, symbolic level, it may be that the rape is foreshadowed by Norton's feeling that sexual intercourse is "something very degrading, something very gross."[27] Whether this feeling about penetration also covers the case of male-male relations, and Norton feels himself to have been raped, one cannot say, because not only does Moore in this hitherto naturalist novel suddenly project symbolistically Norton's feelings about sexual intercourse, but Moore also at this point shifts the center of consciousness from the hero to the violated heroine. We enter her nightmarish hallucinations; we depart from Norton's high-principled, dogmatic, but passion-driven mind.

In spite of its interesting premise, the novel has so many tedious and inept passages in addition to these awkward surprises that there could be no argument for its success, but in a 31 December 1887 letter Moore still objected after Shaw wrote in a *Pall Mall Gazette* review that GM invented the psychology of John Norton. No, Moore complained, he had known the original of Norton since he was a boy; Martyn/Norton had confided to him "his most secret thoughts." Yes, the rape was improbable, but GM chose it because it was "the most violent blow to [Norton's] character that could be imagined" (one might ordinarily have thought the violent blow was to Kitty).[28] By the time of Shaw's review, Moore had accepted that the novel was not the great breakthrough he imagined,[29] but earlier, upon its publication in the spring, he sent it to Pater, with a request for a review in *The Guardian*.

Pater was not about to associate himself with such a thing, neither discreet nor beautiful. In a letter of August 1887 he made GM understand that "descriptions of violent incidents and abnormal states of mind do not serve the purpose of art."[30] After reading this letter, GM held out no further hope for the book: it had failed both as a gift and as a novel. And he despaired at having disgraced himself before Pater. Here Pater had revealed, by means of *Marius,* his desire for intimacy with men. GM had tried to show, through his own answering novel, that he was sympathetic—in fact, enthusiastic—and Pater basically acted as if he was shocked at the thought that Moore might be homosexual or might broach that unmentionable subject in print. Pater would identify himself aesthetically *as* a homosexual, without identifying publicly *with* homosexuals. Moore countered by identifying with homosexuals, but stopped short, he thought, of identifying himself as homosexual.[31] It was a wretchedly embarrassing impasse on both sides—two men lodged in a doorway, unable to come out, or go back in.

However, *A Mere Accident* was not the only book Moore was stimulated to write by the disclosure of new possibilities in *Marius.* Within a week of writing his dismissive reproof in August 1887, Pater was reading an article in *Time* by Arthur Symons on Pater's recent *Imaginary Portraits,* and noticed in the pages of that journal some chapters of *Confessions of A Young Man.*[32] These were chapters about the young GM in Paris, how he loved his fellow student in Julien's atelier, Lewis Marshall, of the ample shoulders and soft violet eyes, who lived off the earnings of Alice Howard, a young English prostitute. Unable to bear his failure to compete with Alice for the love of Lewis, or with Lewis for prizes in painting, GM began to think, he says, of love and death, and retreated to his mother's house in London. Returning months later, now dressed like Lewis, with manners like Lewis, he wanted only to find Lewis. They moved into an apartment together, GM paying the rent. But GM's impotent defeat as an artist left him in despair.

Having read these chapters, Pater wrote a second time to Moore, and admired his appreciation of French poets and his account of himself.[33] After the book was published, Pater wrote "My dear audacious Moore" a third time, praising GM's "Aristophanic joy" but wondering at the "questionable shape" in which GM presented himself, " 'shape'—morally I mean."[34] Once again Pater was trying to disclaim his followers, but there can be little doubt that GM was trying to follow Pater and go him one better.

The portrait Moore presents of himself in this remarkably influential book is as one who came into the world "bearing no impress, like a smooth sheet of wax."[35] Is he alluding to the uncertainty of his sexual identity, which he later confessed to his brother? That seems to have been the story as he develops it in the volumes of *Hail and Farewell*. His mother thought he was ugly; his father concluded he was stupid. He could hardly believe anyone could love him. When at a Catholic school in England, a tall, bald-headed priest, on pretense of helping him after classes with a Latin translation, tried to put his hand in George's trouser pocket; young George was irritated, older George says, and took revenge by telling tales in the confessional (a secret not kept from the headmaster: the Latin teacher soon vanished from the faculty). Later his uncle Jim Brown, a painter of vast canvases of naked goddesses, walked the streets of London teaching the boy which women were beautiful. George wanted to be like Jim Brown, a painter and amorist. GM went to Paris as soon as he reached his twenty-first birthday, and there fell in with the Lewis Marshall about whom Pater read in *Time*. Lewis and Alice go on a summer outing with him to Bas Meudon. Lewis is a glorious swimmer, and Alice is not, so GM remains in the shallows with her, admiring Lewis "disporting himself in midstream."[36] George then nearly drowns Alice— just meant to be a friendly ducking, he pleaded afterwards. Later, tiring of the studio, he stayed in with Alice, watching her bathe and dress after Lewis went off to sketch. In the autumn GM foots the bill for a trip to a hotel in the Barbizon woods, where they all stay in one bedroom. While Lewis goes off to sleep, George poses a curious question to Alice: would it make any difference whether she had to swallow "something incredibly nasty" from the body of Lewis or from the body of George? A great deal, she said, and woke up Lewis to see if he would not feel the same way about her effluvia vis-à-vis that of George. No, a "crap was the same all the world over, and he would prefer to swallow a pinch rather than a pound."[37]

Eventually GM struggles out of this hopeless entrancement by Lewis. First, in a grand bivouac in Alice's apartment, with Lewis present, GM has sex with "la belle Hollandaise," a grand *demi-mondaine*. Second, he wins the friendship of Manet, a far greater painter than Lewis (whose skill as a painter was as inferior to that of Manet as it was superior to that of Moore). And third, having won the attentions of a great lady of the world and a great artist, GM is confident enough to kick Lewis out of his apartment. By GM's last evening in Paris before being forced back to Ireland by the rent-strike some time in late 1879, he takes Lewis out to dinner, along with Lewis's latest amour, the model Marie. Lewis, we are told, still has his "beautiful, slim, manly figure." In the course of the dinner, GM, with his genius for intimacy, draws Lewis into conversation, and soon they were "absorbed in one another and in art." Marie is bored. Moore is triumphant: he has for once stolen Lewis from a woman. "It was always so," he says.[38] By his own account, it never had been. But henceforth GM would not be quite so fatally enthralled with one man, and while he might continue to circulate his desire for men through women, he managed to keep the men and the women in separate pairings.

Part of the agony of this Paris period of undecided sexuality comes out in GM's imitations of Swinburne in *Flowers of Passion* (1877). A number of the poems have the same themes, and even the same titles, as Swinburne's most transgressive works: "The Hermaphrodite," "Laus Veneris," and "The Triumph of Time."[39] It is a polymorphously perverse book. There are poems with straightforward references to incest, necrophilia, cunnilingus, lesbianism, and, not to be forgotten, the drowning of a woman-lover. The poems are ineptly obvious. Consider the dialogue called "Hendecasyllables," in which Carmen and Eliane in the "absolute love time" say, basically, it is that time of day, let us go into the garden together and get away from these men; they are false anyway; we'll find someplace where there's a bed and lots of flowers; then let's have sex.[40] No wonder Edmund Yates warned readers of the *World* (28 November 1877) not to leave the book lying around the house; in fact, he recommended it be "burnt by the common hangman, while its writer was whipped by the cart's tail."[41] For all that, the Sapphic poems serve that function Isabelle de Courtivron discovers in the lesbian lyrics of French poets like Gautier and Baudelaire: "men whose sexual investments are in women use representations of lesbian sexuality to express dissatisfaction with conventional male gender norms,"[42] though GM, with part of his "investments" banked in men, used them also as a currency of gender exchange, to play with the possibilities of same-sex desire.[43] But while androgyny and homosexuality might pass as fashionable in Paris, and—in a highly classicized, prosodically complex Swinburnean form—get by as tolerable in London, Moore's rather more gauche projections, his

cheerfully enthusiastic imitation perversities, were assaulted by reviewers as "dirty, emasculate, loathsome." This was a side of himself
he had to rein in upon his return to England in 1880, at least until
after reading a novel by the professor at Brasenose College. Once he
had studied Pater's *Marius the Epicurean,* he was able to approach
the subject with an ironically tender sympathy for the troubles of his
own youth, now safely past.

One of the formal features of *Confessions* GM may have picked up
from Pater is its mode of address, its attempt to call into being a new
community of men. Thais Morgan borrows a term from Eve Sedgwick
to describe this feature in Pater's prose: an "aesthetic minoritizing
discourse," a system of subcodes by which male beauty is "preferred
and validated," and thus a readership within the general readership is
"presupposed and invoked at the same time it is being constructed in
the discourse itself."[44] This double-voiced rhetoric—art criticism for
the masses, homoerotic self-affirmation for the minority—proved
rather too emphatically audible in the famous conclusion to the first
edition of Pater's *Studies in the History of the Renaissance* (1873),
with its urgent message to be sure to spend life in passionate moments,
"for those moments' sake." In the 1877 edition, Pater was pressured
into deleting it, "because it might possibly mislead some of those
young men into whose hands it might fall."[45] Moore was much more
explicit still: he deliberately addressed himself, as a former young
man, to other young men. He divides his readers into two groups: the
hypocrites (clubbable, married men, who never acknowledged instinctual desires) and "young men."[46] To the latter he recommends the
pleasures of the "woman of thirty" as a great teacher in life: it was
such a woman that finally taught him how to be a man. And once he
knew, he discovered that the later nineteenth century in England was
a paradise for the single young man of means: he is "feted, flattered,
and adored," women drop at his feet.[47] One may continue to contem-
plate the slim-hipped perfections of the male ephebe, whom GM calls
"Lovelace"—not GM's subjective self-presentation, as some have
thought, but the male sex object of his dreams: "clean about the hips
and his movements must be naturally caressing."[48] In 1886, a year or
so before the composition of *Confessions,* Marc-André Raffalovich, at
the time Oscar Wilde's young friend, published a plausibly homoerotic
poem called "Lovelace": in the poem, Lovelace once said "No" but

now has come to love all things dangerous.[49] GM, while possibly using the name of the cavalier poet as a symbol for the male love-object, was not so in love with danger: he preached the risqué, not the risky, life.

At this point, GM's formation of his own masculinity was, by his own reckoning, more or less complete, and the despondencies of the artless, unlovable youth were gone. He was still fighting to be something other than a husband, a worker, and a dutiful subject, but his chosen form of perversity would be to see women as objects of pleasure, the intellectual always leading to the bodily pleasure; and men as associates in intimacy, the bodily desire always leading to the intellectual pleasure. Far from being ashamed of where he had come from, sexually speaking, or where he had arrived at, GM was (like Pater at least in this) setting up himself up as a teacher in the aesthetics of passionate masculinity. And the text he chose most to explicate was a liberating motto of Manet: "To be ashamed of nothing but to be ashamed."[50]

3

What were the relationships among George Moore, W. B. Yeats, and Edward Martyn? In *Ave* Moore gives a description of his friendships that makes them sound more than homosocial, less than homosexual: they were his "boon companions," a term he takes curious pains to define.[51] A famous woman of fashion (Mery Laurent or Marie Pelligrini) had been expounding to Moore the difficulty of finding an *amant de coeur* (perhaps suggesting that Moore might try his luck in filling the post with credit) when he admitted he had the same problem —it was so hard to find a man who lived up to one's standards, someone who was not married, not too old or too young, someone who would stay up all night and into the morning smoking cigars and "aestheticizing," someone who could say unexpected things. Any one of Mery's lovers would do for him as well (though the trade of George Moore for Mery Laurent may have startled the gentlemen in question), but in the British Isles finding a talented, pleasing, and devoted *bon ami* was harder going.

Martyn, he concedes, was a single man of means who smoked, and he had some taste in art, but not much. Furthermore, he was a clumsy, overweight person, "obsessed with a certain part of his person which he speaks of as his soul."[52] More seriously still, one could not talk with him about women. Symons and Yeats, however, were delicate, refined men of temperament—no gross clumsy maleness there, and no dogma. The defect of Symons was that while the good fairy blessed him in his cradle with all the literary gifts, the bad fairy took away his power to express them in conversation: he wrote beautifully of French poetry, but his talk was "as commonplace as Goldsmith"—so he failed the test of being able to say unexpected things. Yeats, on the other hand, would rise from sleep at any hour to aestheticize, and, his raven lock falling over his forehead and his beautiful white teeth showing, he talked with genius (the scene of an importunate GM waking Yeats in his bed, only to aestheticize is interesting). WBY could not get himself into his poetry, owing to the restrictions of his style, Moore claimed. But if Yeats withheld himself and his mysteries from readers, that was fine, since he kept nothing from GM, who wanted him only for blessings of male companionship.[53]

There is a strong current of male-male desire in these relationships, expressing itself in praise not only for the beauty of the boon companion, but for his sense of the beautiful in art and life. Desire expresses itself through emulation of the style of maleness of the male beloved. Martyn, for instance, will pattern himself on many of Moore's tastes: he will collect Degas and Corot, and learn to aestheticize about them, somewhat convincingly in the opinion of Yeats.[54] He will write plays after GM writes plays, under the direction of GM. It was not an emulation in one direction only. If Martyn learned art and literature from man of culture Moore, Moore was taught music by Martyn, who dragged him to his first Wagner concert. At the time, only months after the first trial of Oscar Wilde, Moore featured his new submission to the "great sensualist" Wagner as a homosexual seduction by a dark-eyed Bohemian violinist in a European cafe: "a strange germination progressing within me, thoughts and desires that I dread . . . repudiation is impossible."[55] From August 1893 onward, Moore and Martyn made several trips together to Bayreuth, as hilariously recalled in *Hail and Farewell!* The book portrays the two as ill-assorted art lovers, Moore always wanting to chase after women met in hotels and on trains, and Martyn trying to head him off, and keep him within the vicinity of a Church and a good breakfast. One infers the attraction between them from all the evidence of things that should drive them apart and don't; one sees how alike they are, or have become through friendship, by all the ways their differences prove annoying.

In the case of Yeats and Moore, the spirit of emulation was also at work on both sides. Moore's recruitment into the Irish cause was assisted by his desire to emulate Yeats, to collaborate in plots and be of service to him. By Yeats he was led—astray, he finally judged—into the pursuit of a "style," in the Yeatsian sense of a single personal filter through which only some parts of life would pass. And Yeats, on his side, while finding no beauty in Moore or Moore's style, hungered after GM's power of public certainty, what he later dismissively called GM's "demagogic virtues": his logic, courage, honesty, and ability to defy public opinion and turn it in a new course.[56] Defeated in love for Maud Gonne, ashamed of his "womanish dreamy introspection," Yeats wanted to cultivate these "masculine" features at the end of the Nineties:[57] they certainly proved useful in the later course of the Irish dramatic movement. Yeats was always remarkably acquisitive of attributes of other men. His *Autobiography* is in part not only the story of the great but incomplete artistic personalities of the "Tragic Generation," but also the story of how WBY, coming to know Wilde, Symons, Mathers, and others, came to possess their attributes and to complete their artistry in himself. In the same fashion, he was attracted to Moore, or something in him, and acquired that attribute of polemical manliness and brusque domineering public style.

This emulative form of ego identification is the way in which contemporary literary influences effectively occurred. The psychodynamics of literary influence may center on the father/son relationship when one speaks of the tradition, as Bloom does, but perhaps we need an erotics of literary influence to cover the case of contemporaries. Love of the man led to imitation of the work; the imitation revealed to the beloved one's love. Surely this is one of the dynamics behind male canon formation during the late nineteenth century, when there was a large and talented group of women writers appearing to rival males. Men with an ambition to write Literature generally did not imitate the styles of women (or at least admit to doing so) but used women to procreate images of their styles. Yeats's employment of Lady Gregory to write plays he inspired and then signed is a complicated instance of such self-transmission; Moore's coaching of Julia Davis in the composition of the naturalist *Dr. Phillips* (1887) is another. In any case, the homosocial bonds of the "boon companions" insured that the Masters would be men.

4

Edward Martyn was the only one of the three Irish writers under consideration who loved men only. Not far from Coole, Martyn had a large unencumbered estate with a twelfth century tower and, by the early 1880s, a twenty thousand-pound gothic-style annex, erected at his mother's insistence in order to suit Edward's future bride. She could not admit to herself, as Moore puts it, "any more than you can, reader, or myself, that we come into the world made as it were to order." Edward was "averse to women from the time he was born. It was not her fault; it was not his. Education could do nothing. His will to be different was helpless."[58]

When Edward went up to Oxford in 1879, many undergraduates were under the spell of Pater. They admired with Pater the beauty of the Catholic ritual; they followed Pater in believing that the wisest spend their life in art and song. But what most caught Edward's ear in the Paterian moment at Oxford was the celebration of Greek ideals of male beauty and Greek relations among men. John Addington Symonds could have been speaking about Martyn when he reproached Benjamin Jowett with the "dangers" of an education in the Greats at Oxford: the boys "discover that what they had been blindly groping after was once an admitted possibility—not in a mean hole or corner —but that the race whose literature forms the basis of their higher culture, lived in that way . . . derived courage, drew intellectual illumination, took their first step in the paths which led to great achievements and the arduous pursuit of virtue";[59] in short, that homosexuality in the greatest of Western cultures was not a crime but a cultural ideal. Edward took a tour to Greece, collected replicas of Greek statues, came to believe Greek the most beautiful of all languages (including Irish), and began a poem with a Greek setting. After the ministrations of Edward Gwynn and the Carmelites, there is little evidence remaining by which one could make an informed guess about whether Martyn entered into any "Greek" relationships himself at this time.

It is true, possibly during his time at Oxford, that he made friends with another student, Count Stanislaus Eric Stenbock, an eccentric Estonian homosexual, who kept a toad for a pet, carried a golden vial of perfume, and, as early as 1881, published love poems to boys:[60]

> And if some maiden beautiful
>   Become thy love and joy,
> Think on that passionate male heart
>   That loved thee when a boy.

When he received the down-and-out homosexual artist Simeon Solomon, Stenbock appeared at the door in a "magnificent blood-red silk robe embroidered in gold and silver."[61] Inside, he began swinging a censer before an altar covered with lilies. Then he played religious music on the harmonium. Finally Solomon was sent off with a five-pound note. This spectacular man became Edward's close friend right up to Stenbock's death in 1895. Yeats recalls a dinner with Stenbock, "scholar, connoisseur, drunkard, poet, pervert, most charming of men," and, previous to GM, Edward's "close friend."[62]

Gwynn's vigilance failed in one respect in his biography: he quotes a letter to illustrate Edward's regrettably unorthodox attitude to women and love-making that at the same time shows his preference for Stenbock. In autumn 1892 an old friend and relative planning a visit to Tillyra had written to ask Edward if he would arrange to invite at the same time "Mrs. and Miss L."[63] No, Edward replies, a person of his "modes of life or oddities" could not "turn his philosophic abode into a temple of Hymen." Surely, however, his friend would come over to meet "Stenbock and Bond."[64] Edward had by then begun to play religious music on the organ and to collect pictures by Simeon Solomon, though not to wear Chinese silk robes; still he could, as well as the ladies, provide entertainment for his kinsman.

After Edward failed out of Oxford, his mother placed him under the manly wing of George Moore, whose only recommendation must have been that he was the oldest son of her best friend Mary Blake Moore.[65] After 1880 GM then began to spend part of his annual autumn visit to Ireland with Edward at Tillyra. When Edward confided that he could not, being what he was, marry, and so what would he do with this huge annex under construction, GM told him to leave it unbuilt and follow his instinct—Edward was "startled by the idea." [66] Edward was despondent: "I am too different from other people, he used to say, ever to be a success." [67] Back in London, GM tried to help him along: he brought him to the Robinsons, the haunt of Pater; and he recommended to William Rossetti the poems Edward was writing ("totally different from anyone else's poetry"). [68]

It is not certain that these were the poems with Greek settings that Edward, after a terrible crisis, burned in late 1885. He told his friends poems like "Pheidas" and "Pericles," harmless though they might seem, were dangerous to faith and morals; at least they did not "conduce to the glory of God"—and no doubt they did not. [69] At this point Edward became fanatical about his Catholicism. Within weeks he withdrew his subscription from his friend Henry Barnett's *Court and Society Review* because his friend George Moore might publish there a novel harmful to the faith. [70] He began to write to his bishop for permission to read books on the index—perhaps Voltaire, lampooned in his next literary work, *Morgante*. In GM's opinion, things had come to such a pass that "when there is any question of religion, he ought to be under lock and key." [71] In burning his poems, it was as if he tried to burn himself at the stake: the good celibate Catholic punished the bad homosexual pagan.

It is not possible to know exactly what provoked the crisis in Martyn in 1885. GM delighted in "outing" his friend, and in the last narration of the *donnée* at the heart of *A Mere Accident,* written after his friendship with Martyn had ended, GM makes the crisis not the rape of a woman but a crush on a man. In "Hugh Monfret," the hero, pressured to marry, invites a trusted older man, the headmaster from his school, and a convert to Catholicism, to visit his home in order to intercede on his behalf with Mrs. Monfret. The schoolmaster does what he can, but he also urges Hugh to keep an open mind—perhaps he will see something different in the schoolmaster's own daughter, now at a convent. He is first joined, however, by his aesthetic son Guy, and Hugh quickly begins to fall in love. After some delightful travels with Guy, Hugh finds that the sister has become his mother's houseguest. Together Hugh and the sister translate a medieval poem for Guy to illustrate. As a result of their long hours together, and their appearance at a county ball, Mrs. Monfret tells Hugh that the girl is in a compromised position. Hugh does what he thinks is his duty, and proposes, sealing his engagement with a brotherly kiss. But, in a Calais hotel, he finds himself utterly unable to go through with what a wife expects of a husband. In despair, Hugh goes to her father and confesses the nature of his attachment for the son Guy, rather than for the daughter he married. Hugh Monfret even half-heartedly argues for the rightness of the feelings nature gave him—they spring from admiration and true affection. No other feelings were possible for him, much as he might esteem the daughter. But the father—a clergyman, one must recall—tells the unhappy, honest young man that he may never fulfill his desires; they are forbidden by the Church. While accepting that decree, Hugh suggests that lapses from what the law expects (that all sexual intercourse shall be for the sake of propagation) should not in theory be any worse for homosexuals than for heterosexuals, and, Lord knows, the latter's adulteries were common enough, both with prostitutes and within the ranks of the married and respectable. He even imagines, as the story ends, that there was probably a time in the life of the schoolmaster, perhaps in North Africa, where he could not resist the attractions of an Arab boy.[72]

I don't know that Martyn fell in love with an aesthetic young man like Guy, or was pushed toward marriage with the sister of a boy he loved, or ever confessed to same-sex desire to such a clergyman, or what he did on his many travels in the Mediterranean. But whatever the actual events were in the crisis in Martyn's life, Martyn appears, after 1885, to have regarded himself as one who, for all his wealth, was *"never* able to do what [he] lik[ed],"[73] and perhaps he never did.

Many things about his friend fascinated GM. His "intelligence . . . eager as a wolf prowling for food, . . . ran to and fro, seeking and sniffing in all [Martyn's] interests and enthusiasms."[74] What a testament it was to the power of literature to incite and shape desire when Martyn burned poems, canceled subscriptions, abided by the restrictions of the *Index*, and tried to cancel the Irish Literary Theatre performances because of *The Countess Cathleen*! And was it possible to renounce instinct altogether? What after all were Martyn's instincts?

Moore did discover and divulge the specific nature of Martyn's desires for men. In the always transgressive *Hail and Farewell*, GM portrays himself standing below Edward's window in Dublin, his heart "faint as a lover's," whistling a Wagner motif as his secret signal for "dear Edward" to descend, touch, and allow him to enter. Alarming as this regular serenade was to the men leaving the pub opposite Martyn's, GM soon makes it clear that Edward, sitting on the couch in all his fat, is not really GM's type; nor does Edward care for men like George. What then? Inside, Edward keeps a small harmonium, *Salve* continues—"one can only think it serves to give the keynote to a choir-boy." [75] Every Saturday night, before the Sunday performance of his Palestrina choir, Edward takes a boy home to listen to his singing.

In his first publication of an essay on the beauty of Palestrina's music as performed at Cologne, Edward had drawn particular attention to "the little altar-boys flitting hither and thither like the child angels of Meister Stephan" (*The Speaker*, 23 February 1895). He began to study the work of choirmaster Charles Bordes in Paris, and claimed that all the beauty of his services at St. Gervaise was owing to the exclusion of women and the beauty of the boys' voices. [76] By 1900 Martyn had begun a campaign in the *Leader* to rid the Catholic churches of Dublin of all female singers. It was "unecclesiastical and unaesthetic" to allow women to sing the liturgy: their voices were too passionate; only boys had that "short-lived," "evanescent" beauty in their voices that gives the listener "cerebral fervour exalted above earth." [77] For this extraordinary project to eliminate women from choirs and bring in prepubescent boys, Martyn found complete support in Archbishop Walsh. It appears that the plain-chant movement in Europe was, for some, an expression of a widespread antimodernist, antifemale movement in the Church. By November 1901, Edward had created a ten thousand-pound trust establishing in perpetuity a Palestrina choir at the central Catholic church in Dublin, with the specific proviso that "on no occasion shall females be employed." [78] Edward was pleased, but the parishioners were not: receipts from the collection plate plummeted.

GM believed it was not only wrong to renounce instinct, but impossible. [79] In *Ave,* Moore provided a way to read Martyn's plays as involuntary coming-out stories. In Martyn and his plays, one could find "a Greek marble . . . enfolded in a friar's frock," Martyn's Catholicism serving him—as it served Gray and Raffalovich—as an aesthetic male sanctuary from the persecutions of a homophobic world. [80] Moore reads *The Heather Field, Maeve,* and *An Enchanted Sea* as centered on a "craving" for a love beyond the love of women—expressed in Carden Tyrrell's love of his younger brother, Maeve's longing for a faerie, and, especially, Lord Mark's despair after the drowning of "the beautiful boy Guy." One wonders if Moore ever saw the poems Martyn published in *The Leader* in 1910, such as "The Singing Angels of the Nativity": "You choristers of God . . . How strange, unearthly are your charms. . . ." Or the sonnet on the young acolyte, where part of the charm of the prepubescent boy seems to be that he is preheterosexual: "He passes, like an apparition, white, / And stepless through the sanctuary's space . . . Such grace / Of shape and movement haunts the acolyte . . . Child of earth or heaven, mysterious child / Oh would thou couldst live on undefiled! / Gross manhood with such angel genius wars. / Thou'lt change—alas! Yet thy boy memory / Fair-haired and white, will flutter to the sky—/ A beauty among the children of the stars!"[81] These Uranian verses would have fit quite nicely in the pages of the homosexual coterie literary magazines of the Nineties, such as Lord Alfred Douglas's *The Spirit-Lamp* or Charles Kain Jackson's *The Artist and Journal of Home Culture.*

Martyn put up with a lot from Moore, but he could not put up with *Hail and Farewell.* Nevill Geary, Martyn's Temple roommate, seems right when he says that "Every word Moore wrote of Martyn makes one love Martyn more, and that is a noble tribute to a friend."[82] However, the way one takes the outing of Martyn may be homophobic for homophobes and sympathetic for those who sympathize. Edward took himself seriously as Sinn Fein's first president, as Gaelic League board member, and, especially, as perfectly pious Catholic; no reader of *Hail and Farewell!* will be unlikely to laugh at "dear Edward," and the laughter of men at the homosexual in the closet cannot be good to hear. Years after Martyn's death, Yeats might rhetorically ask, "What drove him to those long prayers, those long meditations, that stern Church music? What secret torture?"[83] But how could Martyn's old friend George Moore show off Martyn's secrets in that way during Martyn's lifetime?

Martyn tried to take his revenge by his satirical portrait of "George Augustus Moon" in *The Dream Physician* (performed in 1914). Moon is a hideously unpleasant character, egotistical, vain, ugly, rude to servants, stupid, delighting in annoying other people, pompous, and gullible (when his typist says, "Your genius is as great as your beauty," he's flattered). One cannot read it without disliking Moore, and Martyn too. Some say the performance, with Thomas MacDonagh's brother John playing GM, was funny; the text is not—there is too much hate, too little design. And Martyn could say nothing worse about Moore than Moore, with greater art, had said about himself.

One feels sympathy for Martyn. Prevented by his sexual formation from begetting an heir to Tillyra and by his religion from fulfilling his desires for young men, Martyn spent and spent and spent again on what he saw to be improvements of Irish "culture." He endowed an Ireland of his desire—Catholic, masculine, and aesthetic. He funded churches, choirs, nationalist journals, Irish craft workshops, concerts by Irish composers, and several Irish literary theaters. While he was not much of a writer, these sublimations were a generous form of "spiritual procreancy" in their own right.[84]

5

In Elizabeth Cullingford's subtle account of Yeats's relations with women, the adolescent poet took a passive role and projected on the woman (first Laura Armstrong, then Maud Gonne) the active part in life. Aware of the woman in himself, he seeks the man in his Beloved, conceived of as a courageous, virile, warrior-woman. He was caught up, by his own account, in a style of heterosexual love inherited from the Romantics—a sort of doomed devotion to the Muse, embodied in an unattainable woman—a Romanticism qualified by Yeats's male anxieties: he was sufficiently insecure to be unable to employ, Cullingford says, "the sexually cynical poetics of the *carpe diem* mode." [85] That is the early Yeats; the middle Yeats, praiser of Don Juan and his sweaty thigh, achieves that missing sexual confidence and shuns his youthful effeminacy. One thing that precipitated this transition was his reading of Nietzsche in 1902.[86] I would like to be able to supplement this account of Yeats and women with a tale about Yeats and men during the 1890s up to the important transition in 1902, but the forthcoming volume 2 of Yeats's *Collected Letters* edited by John Kelly, Warwick Gould, and Deirdre Toomey, and the much-awaited biography by Roy Foster will add so much to our knowledge of this phase of Yeats's life as to make any account now given obsolete. What

I would like to add, however, are a few remarks about the role of
Moore's *Evelyn Innes* and the Moore/Yeats collaborations.

Evelyn Innes is a story about a Wagnerian diva with two lovers,
and one of those lovers, Ulick Dean, is a portrait of Yeats, recognizable
to London reviewers—one of them pointed out that the only difference between Yeats and Ulick Dean is that the first is a poet and the
second is a composer of operas.[87] Moore wrote the novel at the height
of his infatuation with Yeats, and he often sees the poet through the
eyes of his heroine Evelyn. After Evelyn has begun to desire Ulick, she
leads him into a conversation about chastity: if he were to become her
lover, would he have to surrender his spiritual life? Dean says that a
sect of mystics in which he is involved advises the married state, but
for partners "to aid each other to rise to a higher spiritual plane."[88]
This is not what Evelyn had in mind. She is not sure he likes women
at all, but he is very sympathetic to her, and his magic arts, mental
abstractedness, and spiritual airs fascinate her. Carried away by the
"strange rhythmical chant of his about the primal melancholy of man,
and his remote past always insurgent in him," she wonders, why won't
he kiss me? He could kiss me now. But Ulick was "a thousand miles
away."[89] Finally, they do make love when she seizes the initiative
between the acts of *Tristan and Isolde*. He assumes that once they
have made love, she will be his and his only, forever. That is not her
plan.

When Moore read to Symons and Yeats from the proofs in April
1898, they told him his latest novel was wonderful, on even a higher
plane than the phenomenally successful *Esther Waters*.[90] However,
early in June, after Moore gave them presentation copies of the published novel, Yeats (who knew that he was the model for Ulick Dean,
and would be understood by many as the original for this character)
indicated that there was a flaw in the narrative: how could his heroine
have loved someone so effeminate and unassertive as Ulick Dean? The
moment was propitious for throwing Moore into a panic . . . it was
just before the reviews arrived, and Moore never had the least idea
whether he had written a masterpiece or a laughable flop. He had
been thinking that with *Evelyn Innes* he had run Balzac a close second
and knocked Huysmans into a cocked hat, but now he immediately
agreed with Yeats. Yes, surely he had failed to come up to his original,
and he had made the narrative simply illogical: no one like Evelyn

could have fallen in love with anyone like Ulick. Although when the reviews did come out, they were really very good and sales were excellent, Moore immediately set about revising the novel and demanding of his publisher, Fisher Unwin, that the changes to Ulick go into the second printing. Next he demanded a complete resetting for another edition with still more changes made with the help of Yeats, at last changing Ulick entirely and remodeling him on George Russell instead of Yeats.

There never was anything wrong with the novel that the correction of Ulick, making him more passionate and less mystical, would fix. Almost all the revisions, therefore, were useless and damaging. The problem was not with Ulick as a character; it was with Yeats as a man. GM had shown up the poet in prose, revealing, as only a talented realist novelist could, just how the mystifications of WBY's personality beguiled women, and men too. Yeats comes off as the consummate sexual tease, attractive to many of both sexes, but unable to satisfy the one woman he loves. When it came to love, he was a young boy in the arms of Evelyn—frightened before, doting afterward, and ultimately lovelorn. This is not how Yeats wished to be seen; thus, the advice and Moore's wild goose chase.

Later, Yeats and Moore collaborated on two and a half plays: *The Tale of a Town, Diarmuid and Grania,* and the abortive plan for a play that became Yeats's *Where There Is Nothing.* An analysis of this period of collaboration along the lines of Wayne Koestenbaum's *Double Talk: The Erotics of Male Literary Collaboration* would be useful. More generally, one can say that the construction of the first play—which Moore took over from Martyn and rewrote with Yeats, leaving Edward brokenhearted, is an emblem of a particular male love triangle in which Edward is the loser. In *Diarmuid and Grania,* there is a struggle about sex roles between Yeats and Moore, focused on who will do what when: Yeats finally concedes to Moore's experience, constructive power, and stage logic, but allocates to himself beauty, style, Irishness, and the final edit. And who would have the last word is what finally mattered most; it signified dominance for the one, passivity for the other. After the implied insult to the older author's virility, a general breakup was inevitable.

AE offered both of them a plot he could not finish in May 1901, a real apple of discord. In July 1901, WBY and GM had a plan for

collaboration on the scenario.[91] A year later, after the success of Lady
Gregory's *Cathleen ni Houlihan,* Yeats wanted to avail himself of the
still undeveloped scenario for the new Irish National Dramatic Society,
with the Fays as actors, Yeats as president, and Moore as odd man
out. Moore threatened an injunction—"engaged in one of his little
jokes at Willie's expense," as AE put it. Yeats went off to Coole, and
with the help of Lady Gregory and Douglas Hyde, rushed out a play
that John Quinn had copyrighted for him. Through a flurry of letters,
Yeats put together a conspiracy among their set to keep Moore in
ignorance. The play was published in *The United Irishman* 1 November, and Moore "was beaten."[92] Friends took sides as they do in a
divorce: was Yeats right that Moore was a "plagiarist" and a bully?
Or was Moore right that Yeats had behaved like one who is invited to
dinner and then steals your spoons?[93] The immediate victory went to
Yeats, who isolated Moore socially by his conspiracy to pirate the
scenario and keep Moore in the dark. In the long term, however, Yeats
regretted the incident: he and Moore "were never cordial again; on
my side distrust remained, on his disgust. I look back with some
remorse . . . but I was young, vain, self-righteous, and bent on proving
myself a man of action."[94]

It seems possible, after a review of *Evelyn Innes* and the collaborations with Moore, that Yeats's new masculinity is not just the effect of
reading Nietzsche, or losing Maud Gonne for the umpteenth time, or
wanting to be more the man of the house at Coole. As novelist and
mentor in the art of controversy, as first friend and then enemy, Moore
provoked Yeats to a reinvention of himself as "a man of action."

6

One of the most common ways of writing as a homosexual or about
homosexuals is through a "coming out" story, in which the subject/
author tells his or her life story as the discovery of a gay identity, a
type of social identity that is both produced and reproduced, as Ed
Cohen says, just by the author/subject "pronouncing this story to be
his or her own."[95] A late Victorian example of such a story would be
The Memoirs of John Addington Symonds, now much discussed.
What gets somewhat less attention are the stories of those who do not

come out, those who, either for instinctual reasons or reasons having to do with historical phases of oppression, cannot come out as homosexuals. In fact, a homosexual is what they are not. It could be said that one was only homosexual in feeling and maybe never so in practice, that another sometimes posed as a homosexual but wasn't that only, and that the third only inspired homosexuality in others. But such a formulation in terms of clinical categories of sexual identity conceals more than it reveals of the complex and mobile temperaments of these three authors. Their specific sexualities are underdetermined by the categories: something over and above, across and around these categories is left unexplained by the insistence on fixed models of personality determined by certain specified sexual practices. There is no evidence that Moore, Martyn, or Yeats kissed one another, on the lips or elsewhere; there are no dirty sheets like those displayed in the trial of Oscar Wilde. But that does not mean that there is no story here. The sexological terms "heterosexual," "homosexual," and "bisexual" are, to put it another way, deceptively exhaustive: the significant varieties of masculinity within and across these categories remain for the most part unnamed. Nonetheless, the uncategorical vagaries of male-male desire tell upon the urgencies of each author's life; they feed the lyrics and narratives of their works; they structure the collaborations in a literary movement; they sometimes dictate the character of literary influence; and they may even affect the nature of Irish cultural nationalism.

It was hard work for an Irish author to get accepted in England, though not as hard as for a homosexual. Still, the difficulty of qualifying, the demand to meet an alien standard, the condition of always being regarded with doubt, was an accusation against one's manhood: one wasn't, if Irish, a man of quite the right type. So it was attractive to enter into a cabal with men equally estranged, with the aim of interrogating the justice of the whole manly military rule of Ireland. One could aim to create a new republic where one would be at home, whether it was the high-cultured Catholic Greece of Martyn's imagining; Yeats's castle of heroes, romance, and primal mystery; or Moore's deCatholicized, deVictorianized Paris of the mind. Ireland would be that place, for each, where one could be as unconscious of one's manhood as a healthy man is of his bones.

Notes

1. One exception known to me is Declan Kiberd's essay in the 16 December 1994 *Times Literary Supplement,* "Wilde and the English Question" (13–15). Kiberd writes of how Wilde "inveighed against the specialization deemed essential in men fit to run an empire, and showed that no matter how manfully they tried to project qualities of softness, poetry and femininity on to their subject peoples, these repressed instincts would return to take a merry revenge."

2. Ian Fletcher, ed., *The Collected Poems of Lionel Johnson* (New York: Garland, 1982), xxii ff.

3. Richard Ellmann, *Oscar Wilde* (New York: Vintage, 1988), 308.

4. Fletcher, *Collected Poems of Johnson,* xxxi.

5. George Bernard Shaw, *John Bull's Other Island* with *How He Lied to Her Husband* and *Major Barbara,* rev. ed. (London: Constable, 1931), 40.

6. George Mosse, "Nationalism and Respectability: Normal and Abnormal Sexuality in the Nineteenth Century," *Journal of Contemporary History* 17 (1982): 223.

7. Joseph Bristow, *Effeminate England: Homoerotic Writing after 1885* (New York: Columbia University Press, 1995), 21.

8. George Moore, *Confessions of a Young Man,* ed. Susan Dick (Montreal: McGill-Queens University Press, 1972), 165.

9. George Moore, *Avowals,* rev. ed. (London: Heinemann, 1924), 170.

10. Ibid., 172.

11. Peter Gunn, *Vernon Lee: Violet Paget, 1856–1935* (London: Oxford University Press, 1964), 125.

12. Lawrence Evans, ed., *Letters of Walter Pater* (Oxford: Clarendon Press, 1970), 79.

13. Richard Aldington, ed., *Walter Pater: Selected Works* (New York: Duell, Sloan, and Pearce, 1948), 3.

14. Moore, *Avowals,* 183.

15. Ibid.

16. For Tennyson's similiar fantasies of homosexual release after death, see Christopher Craft, *Another Kind of Love: Male Homosexual Desire in English Discourse, 1850–1920* (Berkeley: University of California Press, 1994), 170–71, 178–79.

17. Discussed in Bristow, *Effeminate England,* 7.

18. George Moore, *A Mere Accident* (London: Vizetelly; New York: Brentano's, 1887), 65.

19. Ibid., 66.

20. Ibid., 103.

21. Ibid., 111.

22. Ibid., 147.

23. William Butler Yeats, *Autobiography*, rev. ed. (New York: Collier, 1965), 347.

24. Linda Dowling, *Hellenism and Homosexuality in Victorian Oxford* (Ithaca and London: Cornell University Press, 1994), 154.

25. Moore, *A Mere Accident*, 172.

26. Ibid., 282.

27. Ibid., 103.

28. Robert Becker, ed., "The Letters of George Moore, 1863–1901" (Ph.D. diss., University of Reading, 1980), 482.

29. Ibid., 444.

30. Moore, *Avowals*, 196.

31. Ibid., 62.

32. Ibid., 197.

33. Evans, *Letters of Pater*, 81.

34. Ibid., 75.

35. Moore, *Confessions*, 49.

36. George Moore, *Vale*, vol. 3 of *"Hail and Farewell!"* (London: Heinemann, 1914), 56.

37. Ibid., 500.

38. Moore, *Confessions*, 129.

39. Jean C. Noel, *George Moore: L'Homme et L'Oeuvre* (Paris: Marcel Didier, 1966), 47–49.

40. George Moore, *Flowers of Passion* (London: Provost and Co., 1877), 90.

41. [Edmund Yates], "A Bestial Bard," *The World* (28 November 1877): 18.

42. Richard Dellamora, *Masculine Desire: The Sexual Politics of Victorian Aestheticism* (Chapel Hill: University of North Carolina Press, 1990), 69–70.

43. Moore told a story of going to visit Swinburne in 1879. He found a naked man lying on the bed whom he thought for an instant was his other self; he blurted out, "Does Mr. Jones live here?" and ran away [Joseph Hone, *The Life of George Moore* (New York: Macmillan, 1936), 76]—a classic case of homosexual desire and homophobia wedded, and confessed with a kind of giddy awareness of all that is implied.

44. Thais Morgan, "Reimagining Masculinity in Victorian Criticism: Swinburne and Pater," *Victorian Studies* 36 (1993): 316.

45. Walter Pater, *N. Renaissance: Studies in Art and Poetry*, ed. Donald Hill (Berkeley: University of California Press, 1980), 217.

46. Moore, *Confessions*, 25–26; Jean C. Noel, "George Moore's 'Pluridimensional Autobiography,' " *Cahiers du Centre d'Etudes Irlandais* 5 (1979): 49–65.

47. Moore, *Confessions*, 176.

48. Noel, "Pluridimensional Autobiography," 55.

49. Brian Reade, *Sexual Heretics: Male Homosexuality in English Literature from 1850 to 1900* (London: Routledge and Kegan Paul, 1970), 199.

50. Moore, *Avowals*, 266; *Vale*, 103–4. After Lord Alfred Douglas's poem "The Two Loves" became an article of evidence in the Wilde trial, the term "shame" took on a specifically homosexual connotation. Of the "two loves" in a garden, one says the other is not named "Love" but "Shame." Sighing, the accused imposter says, "Have thy will / I am the love that dare not speak its name" (Reade, 362). When Moore gave a 1904 lecture on Hugh Lane's impressionist pictures and declared their principle was "to be ashamed of nothing but to be ashamed," Martyn told him that "detestable phrase" was like a "pin in the very quickest part of my body"; it ruined his pleasure in the paintings. Moore and Martyn had completely opposed attitudes toward the instinctual life.

51. George Moore, *Ave*, vol.1 of *"Hail and Farewell!"* (1912; London: Heinemann, 1937), 43.

52. Ibid., 47.

53. Ibid.

54. Yeats, *Autobiography*, 259.

55. Moore, "A Reaction," *The Speaker* (13 July 1895): 43.

56. William Butler Yeats, *Memoirs: Autobiography — First Draft, Journal*, ed. Denis Donoghue (London: Macmillan, 1972), 270.

57. Elizabeth Butler Cullingford, *Gender and History in Yeats's Love Poetry* (Cambridge: Cambridge University Press, 1993), 78; William Butler Yeats, *The Letters of W.B. Yeats*, ed. by Allan Wade (London: R. Hart-Davis, 1954), 434.

58. Moore, *Ave*, 183.

59. John Addington Symonds, *The Letters*, Vol. 3 ed. Herbert M. Schueller and Robert L. Peters (Detroit: Wayne St. University Press, 1969), 346.

60. Timothy D'Arch Smith, *Love in Earnest: Some Notes on the Lives and Writings of English "Uranian" Poets from 1889 to 1930* (London: Routledge and Kegan Paul, 1970), 36.

61. Reade, *Sexual Heretics*, 37.

62. William Butler Yeats, ed., *The Oxford Book of Modern Verse, 1892–1935* (Oxford: Clarendon Press, 1936), x; Yeats, *Memoirs*, 118.

63. For the probable date of this letter, I am grateful to Gerald Nolan, a postgraduate scholar of Trinity College Dublin writing a study of the works of Edward Martyn, and planning a biography of Martyn as his country's benefactor. He gave me a copy of Martyn's brief diary of travels and life events, covering the years from 1859 to 1921, and pointed out that Stenbock had been one of Martyn's visitors. Nolan, I should add, finds no proof that there was "anything between them," or between Martyn and any other man. Should daguerrotypes turn up of Martyn and Stenbock, or Moore, or altar boys, caught in the act of anal or oral intercourse, that most unlikely event

would certainly add to our knowledge, but it might also have the unfortunate effect of making us think our knowledge complete. A whole life would be categorized because of a single act. What is sufficiently interesting and worthy of study is the way in which Martyn took pleasure in traveling with men, in having men of a certain kind pay long visits to Tillyra, in listening to opera with men, in collaborating with men on plays about his own frustration of desire; it is also interesting that Martyn took no pleasure at all in the company of women. The nature of the pleasures we know he took, and did not take, are fundamental to who he was, and who he must be represented as being, if we are to understand the man.

64. Denis Gwynn, *Edward Martyn and the Irish Revival,* rev. ed. (New York: Lemma Publishing Corporation, 1974), 50–51.

65. Marie Therese Courtney, *Edward Martyn and the Irish Theatre* (New York: Vantage Press, 1956), 18–19.

66. Moore, *Ave,* 181.

67. Moore, *Salve,* vol. 2 of *"Hail and Farewell!"* (London: Heinemann, 1913), 94.

68. Becker, "Letters of Moore," 284.

69. Gwynn, *Edward Martyn,* 76.

70. *Drama in Muslin,* admittedly, contains a devastating portrait of the Martyns' parish priest, for which Mrs. Martyn banished Moore from Tillyra for as long as she was alive.

71. John Eglinton, trans., *Letters from George Moore to Ed. Dujardin, 1886–1922* (New York: Crosby Gaige, 1929), 21–22.

72. George Moore, *In Single Strictness* (New York: Boni and Liveright: 1923), 47–201.

73. Gwynn, *Edward Martyn,* 70.

74. George Moore, *Mike Fletcher* (London: Ward and Downey, 1889), 4.

75. George Moore, *Salve,* 129.

76. Moore twitted Edward about this obsession: on their visit to Paris for the Christmas Eve Mass in 1893, after Edward praised the boys' singing of the plain chant "Adeste Fideles," Moore says Bordes replied that it was not a plain chant and it was sung by a woman of fifty. There was no boy in the choir at all (Moore, *Vale,* 182–83).

77. Gwynn, *Edward Martyn,* 182–86.

78. Ibid., 207–8.

79. In the irresolvable debate over whether sexual orientation is something we are born with or something we learn, whether gender is something we perform or something we are, Moore had a slightly dodgy but persistent answer: we come into the world made to order, not as either homosexual or heterosexual, but with extremely individualized instincts. There is something that it is "natural" for each of us to be; if we are taught, it is simply to be taught not to be what we are; if we try to behave, we can only act against ourselves. In any case, our instinctual being will make its appearance, either

beautifully as what it naturally is, or ugly as made by education or social convention.

80. Moore, *Ave,* 149.

81. Gwynn, *Edward Martyn,* 323ff.

82. Hone, *Life of Moore,* 122.

83. Yeats, *Autobiography,* 259.

84. Martyn's misogyny and sectarianism (more acceptable to the Church than his homosexuality) not infrequently played a part in his cultural interventions, so his philanthropy was not entirely positive in its consequences.

85. Cullingford, *Gender and History,* 24

86. Ibid., 78.

87. A.M., "*Evelyn Innes,*" *The Bookman* (July 1898): 103–4.

88. George Moore, *Evelyn Innes* (London: Fisher Unwin, 1898), 338.

89. Ibid., 263.

90. Becker, "Letters of Moore," 1132–33.

91. John Kelly and Ronald Schuchard, eds., *The Collected Letters of W. B. Yeats,* Vol. 3 (Oxford: Clarendon Press, 1994), 86–87.

92. Ibid., 228ff.

93. Ibid., 243–44.

94. Yeats, *Autobiography,* 305.

95. Ed Cohen, "The Double Lives of Man: Narration and Identification in the Late Nineteenth Century Representation of Ec-Centric Masculinities," *Victorian Studies* 36 (1993): 355.

Cathleen ni Houlihan Writes Back

Maud Gonne and Irish Nationalist Theater

"CATHLEEN NI HOULIHAN is not a playwright," Victoria White declared, lamenting the paucity of women dramatists in the contemporary Irish theater.[1] Though the original embodiment of the Cathleen ni Houlihan figure in Irish theater, Maud Gonne, did in fact write a one-act play, *Dawn*, this anticipated the fate of much Irish women-authored drama today in that it remained an unstaged script.[2] The recuperation of Gonne's almost forgotten play will not add another mistress-piece to the Irish repertoire. To reread it in its historical context, however, spotlights the interplay between the new Irish theater movement and the newly founded nationalist women's organization, Inghinidhe na hEireann (Daughters of Erin),[3] with regard to the staging of Irish women, especially peasant women.[4] In the combined roles of president of Inghinidhe na hEireann and vice president of the Irish National Theatre Society, actress, audience, reviewer and playwright, Maud Gonne was at the centre of the nationalist debate surrounding the representation of peasant women in the emergent Irish theater at the turn of the twentieth century.[5]

Three one-act dramas in three successive years, which Maud Gonne and Inghinidhe na hEireann were involved in, focus on the plight of a woman and are set in, or in the environs of, a peasant cottage: Lady Gregory and W.B. Yeats's *Cathleen ni Houlihan* (April 1902), John Millington Synge's *In the Shadow of the Glen* (October 1903),[6] and *Dawn* (October 1904). Inghinidhe na hEireann sponsored the premiere of *Cathleen ni Houlihan* in 1902; its president, Maud Gonne, created the title role, and the other actresses were also drawn from its ranks; the Inghinidhe banner, a sunburst on a blue background, was conspicuous near the stage during the first performances.[7] The following year, the president and an honorary secretary of the Inghinidhe, Maire Quinn, withdrew in protest from the premiere of *In the Shadow*

of the Glen; Maud Gonne criticized the play in the columns of the
United Irishman and resigned as vice president of the Irish National
Theatre Society. *Dawn,* published in the *United Irishman* a year later,
dialogues with both *Cathleen ni Houlihan* and *In the Shadow of the
Glen,* returning to the issue of the staging of Irish peasant women in
both plays and implicating the nationalist women's organization in its
revisioning of their role. The title, *Dawn,* alludes to the symbolic
sunburst device on the Inghinidhe banner; its heroine, Bride, derives
her name from Brigid who, in her dual character of goddess and saint,
was the organization's patron; the lyrics for the play were composed
by an Inion, Ella Young;[8] and acting rights were reserved for Inghinidhe na hEireann.[9]

Nationalism and Gender

Inghinidhe na hEireann (Daughters of Erin), a political and cultural
nationalist organization, was founded in October 1900 in reaction
to the exclusion of women from politically nationalist societies.[10] Its
gendered title and adoption of sisterhood as an organizational model
signify the women's conscious defiance of the current male monopoly
of political activism and of the homosocial bonding promoted in nationalist ballads and songs.[11] Hitherto, a corollary of the customary
representation of the nation as female was the gendering of the political activist as male. Apart from their subversive claim to agency within
militant nationalism, the Inghinidhe were ideologically orthodox.
They were liberal feminists asserting equal metaphorical rights within
the existing tropes of nationalism where the figuration of Ireland as
a mother, and the nation as a family, were established signifiers of
community and common lineage.

However, the inscription of femininity within the nationalist movement was contested. While the Inghinidhe's adaptation of the familial
metaphor, which served to naturalize the idea of the nation and represent it as an organic unity, appears ideologically orthodox, it con-
flicted with the prevalent Victorian middle-class family ideology
adapted by the largely middle-class Gaelic League founded in 1893.
Though the League included some women activists among its ranks,
it idealized mother and home as the repository of spiritual, moral, and

affective values and it constructed women as the bearers and cultural reproducers of the future nation:

> the characters of the future citizens of the country are built up in the chimney corner, where a woman tells stories in the twilight to wide-eyed listeners.
> ... the spark struck on the hearthstone will fire the soul of the nation.
> If we make our hearthsides Irish we make Ireland Irish. . . .
> If the Gaelic League could get a thorough grip of the cradles all over the country, and keep that grip, its work would be assured. . . .[12]

Home for the League was the site of a nationalist pedagogy, an Irish alternative to the official colonial system of education designed to make "a happy English child" of every pupil. The Irish language, still spoken along the western seaboard, was presented as a home language, a mother tongue, transmitted to the nation's children along with an Irish cultural heritage of history and folklore. A nationalist pedagogy which conflated women's roles with their maternalism could prove unaccommodating to political activists such as the Inghinidhe who positioned themselves as daughters rather than mothers. Mary Butler, author of the Gaelic League pamphlet, *Women and the Home Language,* contrasted the "gentle, low-voiced women" inculcating nationalism at the hearth with the "shrieking viragoes or aggressive amazons" who seek a public platform.[13]

Some contemporary feminists would object to Inghinidhe na hEireann's choice of nomenclature because, in colluding with the iconization of Ireland as a mother, they were helping to deflect attention from the very real distress of many Irish women.[14] In their journal, *Bean na hEireann,* launched in 1908, the Inghinidhe did protest against the romanticization of the "pretty barefooted, red-petticoated cailín" whose "picturesque" appeal derived from her poverty, and they attributed the large-scale emigration of rural women to their "bleak and colourless life of endless drudgery."[15] Their involvement in the three plays under consideration here, however, reveals that a clear demarcation between the responsibilities of pastoral feminism and cultural nationalism was not apparent to them when peasant women and peasant homes were first represented in the national theater.

Intent on giving women public agency in the nationalist project,

Inghinidhe na hEireann were almost immediately drawn into controversy over the representation of women in Irish drama. *Dawn,* written
for the sisterhood, is Maud Gonne's experiment with a dramatic mode
designed to reconcile the pastoral, familial, and nationalist concerns
which had become disjoined in *Cathleen ni Houlihan* and *In the
Shadow of the Glen.*

Toward a Nationalist Women's Theater

Recent emphasis on print culture in the dissemination of nationalist
ideology has distracted attention from the importance of spectacle in
the creation of the imagined political community.[16] Almost from the
outset of the new Irish dramatic movement, nationalists perceived the
potential of theater as a mode of inventing and performing cultural
difference. In the early twentieth-century debate between those who,
like W. B. Yeats, championed the dramatist's artistic rather than ethnic
responsibilities and those who, like Arthur Griffith,[17] favored a repre-
sentatively national drama, the new theater's importance as successor
to the popular *Spirit of the Nation* ballad in nationalist consciousness-
raising was among the issues discussed.[18] Inghinidhe na hEireann were
in the vanguard of those who perceived the cultural importance of
constructing an Irish alternative to the imported popular culture of
theater and music hall. Among the organization's principal aims was:
"To discourage the reading and circulation of low English literature,
the singing of English songs, the attending of vulgar English entertain-
ments at the theatres and music hall. . . ."[19]

In their attempt at countering colonial popular entertainment, the
Inghinidhe experimented with inventing an Irish popular theater,
mounting *ceilidhes,* magic-lantern shows, *tableaux vivants* and one-
act plays, and sometimes combining all these in a single evening's
performance. The *ceilidhe,* an innovative theatrical form, was a concert where the repertoire of music, songs, and recitations was exclusively Irish and the stage set was an Irish peasant kitchen. The peasant
home was thereby recruited as an ideological site in urban theater.
Magic lantern shows were often devoted to realist propaganda: based
on photographs of political prisoners, evictions, British burning of
homesteads in the Boer war. (This coincides with the inclusion of silent
film as part of music hall entertainment in Ireland.) By contrast, the

spectacles staged in the *tableaux vivants* were a selection of symbolic images representing scenes from Ireland's pagan or Christian past or from nationalist ballads or Moore's *Melodies,* and were accompanied by the reading of a narrative or poem, the singing of a ballad, or the playing of instrumental music. The *tableau* form, in which Alice Milligan, a member of the Inghinidhe, had achieved considerable expertise during the 1798 centenary celebrations, marked a significant progression toward the emergence of a national drama, translating an existing nationalist iconography onto the stage or inventing new visual symbolism and amalgamating both with such established forms of nationalist discourse as historical narratives, legends, and ballads.[20] Alice Milligan herself made the transition from *tableau* to drama proper with her one-act plays on Irish historical and legendary themes, including *The Last Feast of the Fianna* (1900), the first play to use Irish saga material. Inghinidhe na hEireann, who had drawn on the talents of Alice Milligan to design and produce *tableaux vivants*,[21] was the first nationalist organization to recognize the desirability of training an Irish theater troupe to perform specifically Irish plays and to co-opt the talents of the Fay brothers to provide training and direction. Some of the future leading ladies of Irish theatre—Maire Quinn, Maire Nic Shiubhlaigh and Sara Allgood—learned their craft with the Inghinidhe. A sympathy with the language movement, signified by their choice of a Gaelic name, also led the Inghinidhe to pioneer the production of Gaelic drama in Dublin. Under their auspices Father Dinneen's *An Tobar Draoideachtha* (The magic well) was first publicly performed in 1900; the following year saw the first Dublin production of P. T. MacGinley's *Eilis agus an Bhean Deirce* (Eilish and the Beggarwoman) and of Alice Milligan's *The Deliverance of Red Hugh* in which she experimented with both Gaelic and English speaking parts to highlight the colonial intervention in Irish history.[22] Yeats, whose own plays were still being played by English actors, left the performance of *The Deliverance of Red Hugh* with his "head on fire," excited by a concept of Irish theater that staged specifically Irish themes in Irish accents.

It is probable that Inghinidhe na hEireann's experimentation with a theater that amalgamated Irish music, poetry, history, and iconography influenced a play such as *Cathleen ni Houlihan,* which includes all these features. Its dramatic incarnation of Ireland as Shan Van

Vocht and queenly maiden may well have derived from the genre of the nationalist *tableau*. To Maud Gonne and the Inghinidhe, the Gregory-Yeats play must have seemed a continuation of their own theatrical experiments and they were happy to sponsor the first performances.

Cathleen ni Houlihan

Cathleen ni Houlihan, set in a cottage kitchen in Killala at the time of the French landing in 1798, stages two conflicting narratives of Irish peasant womanhood. Mrs. Gillane and, potentially, Delia, her son's pretty, well-dowered bride-to-be, represent a realist, maternal order, the values of hearth and home; the Poor Old Woman, Cathleen, also dressed as a peasant,[23] represents a contrary order of being—symbolic, nomadic, virginal, sacrificial rather than procreative, not subject to the imperatives of generational replacement, metamorphosing magically from age to youth. Two forms of continuity are opposed: continuity in the corporeal dimension expressed through reproduction and inheritance; continuity at an ideological level in which an old symbol (Sean Bhean Bhocht/Cathleen) is revitalized through her success in obtaining adherents in the dramatic present (1798) and in the present tense of the play's production, just over a century later. *Cathleen ni Houlihan* concludes with a diptych of Irish peasant womanhood. The notorious transformation scene—in which the old crone who has lured away the bridegroom turns into a beautiful young girl with the walk of a queen—occurs offstage;[24] onstage, two bereft women, mother and jilted bride, comfort one another.[25] Inghinidhe members played both sets of contrasting female roles: the charismatic Cathleen who subverts the values of cradle, hearth, and smallholding, and the realist peasant women who lose out to the symbolic woman-nation. Nationalists, far from being perturbed by this dramatization of the split between the materialist and familist priorities of peasant conservatism and the abandonment of *kinder* and *kuchen* advocated by physical-force nationalism, were elated by the triumph of the woman-nation. *Cathleen ni Houlihan*, which subordinated the interests of women to a sacrificial paradigm of male patriotism and invoked a literary tradition of political allegory, was enshrined as the exemplary nationalist play. It was appropriate that a scheduled performance at the Abbey Theatre during Easter Week had to be canceled because the Rising, which the play adumbrated, had actually occurred.

It is now well attested that Lady Gregory scripted the roles of the realist peasants in *Cathleen ni Houlihan,* the Gillane family and Delia,[26] but to what extent was the role of Cathleen, which was authored by Yeats, authorized by Maud Gonne? All the part of Cathleen really needed, Lady Gregory famously quipped, was "a hag and a voice."[27] Would the play have proved as successful if the part had originally been played by any old hag? Or was it Maud Gonne's creation of the title role that was largely responsible for the play's mystique?

Cathleen ni Houlihan, now probably the best-known female symbol of Ireland, was by no means as familiar as Dark Rosaleen in 1902. She derived from a much less popular poem by Mangan, "Kathleen-ny-Houlihan," a translation of William Heffernan The Blind's eighteenth-century poem "Caitilin ni Uallachain." Her accessibility in the play as a personification of Ireland was largely due to her conflation with the Shan Van Vocht from the popular 1798 ballad. She appears as The Poor Old Woman, not as Cathleen, in the list of "Persons in the Play," and the authors toyed with the idea of using "The Poor Old Woman" as the title. Lady Gregory feared that audiences might confuse Cathleen ni Houlihan with the Countess Cathleen from Yeats's earlier play.[28]

The first-night audience had difficulty negotiating the transition from the play's realist representation of peasantry to the figurative role of Cathleen. Yeats reported that they were slow to turn from "delighted laughter" to an appreciation of the "tragic meaning" of Cathleen's part. By the third performance they had been educated, and crowds were being turned away from the packed theater.[29] Yeats's report betrays the risk that he and Lady Gregory were taking in staging Ireland as a female symbol in a realist setting. Without Maud Gonne's collaboration they might not have pulled it off. Edward Martyn comments that "her sheer talent saved the disaster which otherwise must have come to destroy the high poetic significance of the play by reason of the low comedy-man air adopted by another actor." That other actor was Willie Fay and Yeats, in his reply to Martyn, pointed out that the reason for the laughter that greeted him was that Dublin audiences associated him with comedy and were "ready to laugh before even he speaks." [30] Fortunately, Fay's associations with comedy, which almost ruined the play, were more than compensated for by Maud Gonne's considerable notoriety in Dublin as an exceptionally ardent and beautiful nationalist. It was her credentials on both counts that authenticated the role of Cathleen, making the final transformation credible.

In 1902 Maud Gonne was at the apogee of her career as an Irish nationalist. A public speaker who was much in demand, she had undertaken lecture tours in France and the United States as well as speaking at many Irish venues. She was a prolific journalist, a prominent pro-Boer campaigner, one of the organizers of the 1798 centenary celebrations, and she was generally prominent in anti-British demonstrations in Dublin. In the role of Cathleen, Maire Nic Shiubhlaigh recalls, she appeared to the young people in the theater as "the very personification of the figure she portrayed on the stage." [31] The *All-Ireland Review* noted the connection between Maud's theatrical role and her more customary role of nationalist orator, making her performance continuous with her politics: "The well-known nationalist orator did not address the other actors as is usual in drama, but spoke directly to the audience, as if she was addressing them in Beresford Place . . . she can scarcely be said to act the part, she lived it." [32] How much of the play's success in translating a female symbol of the nation from balladry and iconography onto the stage was due to Maud Gonne's charisma and her political "street cred."?

As George L. Mosse observes, theater which creates "sexed bodies as public spectacles" helps "to instill through representational practices an erotic investment in the national romance." [33] Maud Gonne brought to the part of the *femme fatale* an erotic charge all the more potent for being covert, her disguised beauty colluding with the dialogue, titillating by its promise of a final unveiling. Her late arrival for the premiere, sweeping through the auditorium in her costume when the audience was already seated, consciously or unconsciously anticipated the play's conclusion, preempting Yeats's script. [34]

Moreover, Maud Gonne, who like Yeats was a member of the mystical order of the Golden Dawn, invested the role of Cathleen with occult power. Yeats was not alone in attributing a "weird power" to her characterization of Cathleen; Maire Nic Shiubhlaigh described her appearance as "ghostly"; Joseph Holloway applied the adjectives

"mysterious," "weird," "uncanny," "strange" to her playing and remarked that she "realised" the role "with creepy realism."[35] Through
her personal alliance of nationalism and the occult Maud rendered the
woman-nation *unheimlich*, antithetical both to material values and to
the home.

The upstaging of real women by the nationalist female icon, which
contemporary feminists decry, was not only thematized in the script
of *Cathleen ni Houlihan* but was inseparable from its first production.
Lady Gregory's co-authorship was ignored on the playbill and neither
her co-authorship nor the Inghinidhe's sponsorship was acknowledged
in Yeats's postperformance speeches. That the nationalist cause was
privileged over the claims of sisterhood is evidenced by the fact that
the play went ahead despite the death of Anna Johnston (Ethna Carbery), a vice president of the Inghinidhe and the first of its members
to die.[36] A year later, the Inghinidhe broke away from the newly
formed Irish National Theatre Society because they disapproved of
the Society's denationalized attitude to female representation as mani-
fested in its staging of *In the Shadow of the Glen*.[37]

In the Shadow of the Glen

The peasant cottage of *In the Shadow of the Glen* is a private domestic
space, unaffected by nationalist politics, and the drama focuses on the
personal angst of the unhappily married Nora Burke. In its writing of
the body, the play voices a peasant woman's confrontation with sexuality, aging, physical decay, and death. Nora, who had pined for talk,
company, sexual fulfillment, and financial security, finally sees through
social and material comforts to the ultimate futility and horror of
being human. Within and without the cottage, life is menacing, but
the shadow that overhangs all the characters' lives is not that of British
imperialism.

At its first stagings in October 1903, *In the Shadow of the Glen*
was played with *The King's Threshold* and *Cathleen ni Houlihan*.
Its inclusion in a triple bill with *Cathleen ni Houlihan* normalized
the play as part of the emergent national theater repertoire. Maud
Gonne's exit from the premiere of Synge's play was as conspicuous as
her entrance at the premiere of *Cathleen ni Houlihan* the previous
year. In her ostentatious symbolic exit, she was accompanied by Maire

Quinn who, as well as being an honorary secretary of the Inghinidhe, was one of the cast of the first *Cathleen ni Houlihan* and by Dudley Digges, who had created the role of Michael Gillane, the peasant turned patriot. Their walkout was a demonstration by the cast of the original *Cathleen ni Houlihan* and its sponsors against the displacement of the woman-nation's troubles and their replacement by the personal distress of Synge's Nora Burke. It was also an attempt to uncouple *In the Shadow of the Glen* from *Cathleen ni Houlihan* as an acceptable national theater offering.[38]

The Inghinidhe were not alone in their opposition to Synge's play. Nationalist commentators immediately perceived its staging as a significant theatrical event and regarded it as an unwelcome rival to *Cathleen ni Houlihan;* the new theater was pulling in two directions and would have to choose between Cathleen and Nora. The controversy over *In the Shadow of the Glen,* in which the right to artistic freedom was pitted against the demand for a nationalist art, turned on the representation of the Irish peasant woman's sexuality. When *The Doll's House* had been mounted in Dublin's Queen's Theatre in June 1903, the audience, according to Joseph Holloway, reacted to Ibsen's Nora with utter indifference, chattering out loud, banging doors, and wandering in and out of the bar at the most inopportune moments, completely impervious to Nora's marital plight or departure from her husband.[39] However, Synge's Irish Nora outraged nationalists such as Maud Gonne, Maire Quinn, Douglas Hyde, James Connolly, and Arthur Griffith, because its construction of Irish peasant femininity was considered either untruthful or otherwise inappropiate in a national theater.

Primitivism was positively evaluated by nationalism as part of its anti-imperialist and anti-metropolitan agenda. "The peasantry," as constructed by the Gaelic League pamphleteer Mary Butler, for instance, were "by far the most attractive section of the community, by far the least vulgarised and anglicised . . . The language is still theirs in many districts, and native customs and characteristics are not yet wholly obliterated among them in any part of the country."[40] Even when peasant women's sexuality was not co-opted for a nationalist agenda of physical and cultural reproduction, the notion of extramarital peasant sexuality was offensive to puritanical nationalists. Adultery was a particularly touchy topic in post-Parnell Ireland.

The controversy over *In the Shadow of the Glen* conducted in the columns of the *United Irishman* in October 1903 bypassed the complexity of this troubling play and focused on its representation of peasant marriage. Nationalists were intent on closing off alternative configurations of Irish peasant womanhood, and Nora, who did not live up to their expectations of the virtuous, maternal peasant, was dismissed as "a libel on womankind." The play was denounced as "a corrupt version" of the "Widow of Ephesus" and "no more Irish than the Decameron."[41] While the play's opponents as well as its advocates accepted that the arranged and loveless marriage was a fact of Irish life, they differed as to whether marital unhappiness was a suitable theme for the national theater, and they clashed angrily over its representation of Irish peasant women's sexuality. James Connolly, who later described Irish women suffering under the double yoke of colonialism and patriarchy as "the slaves of slaves,"[42] considered that Synge's play was unsuited to a national theater whose purpose was to restore "our proper national pride."[43] Maud Gonne argued that "it is for the many, for the people, that Irish writers must write," and that "if the Irish people [did] not understand or care for an Irish play" she was "very doubtful of its right to rank as national literature." *Cathleen ni Houlihan,* her exemplary national play, "would be understood and loved by the simplest Irish peasant."[44] The negative reaction of the peasantry to *In the Shadow of the Glen* could only be hypothesized; Wicklow cottagers were unlikely to have been theatergoers. Mary Butler, without alluding directly to the childless Nora, reminded "The Daughters of the Motherland" that the onus of nationalizing Irish life falls on mothers and that "the best of all Irish schools is an Irish mother's knee."[45] Arthur Griffith, the play's most vehement opponent, maintained that Synge's characterization of Nora was a misrepresentation and that such a lie would neither "serve Ireland" nor "exalt Art." However unhappy the Irish housewife may be, according to Griffith, "she does not go away with the Tramp." "Irishwomen," he asserted, "are the most virtuous women in the world."[46]

Griffith was most probably the author of the dramatic riposte, *In a Real Wicklow Glen,*[47] carried by the *United Irishman* on 24 October, a one-act play in which a "town bred girl" learns the truth about peasant women's sexuality and marriage. Once again, the setting is a cottage. Here the townswoman encounters an elderly widow and a younger married woman, Nora, and is informed that young women forced into loveless marriages with older peasants for the sake of material security achieve some degree of amity with them, busy themselves with their maternal role, and, when their elderly husbands die, marry the sweethearts they were originally compelled to renounce, both partners by then being sufficiently prosperous to marry for love. Griffith's Nora, as a married woman, is insulted and outraged when her former sweetheart wants to kiss her: peasant women in a real Wicklow glen are shown to be paragons of marital virtue.

JOHN BUTLER YEATS appealed to Maud Gonne MacBride to allow her womanly empathy with Nora Burke's plight to prevail over her nationalism,[48] but she did not relent. Maud, who had a longstanding extramarital relationship with the French political journalist Lucien Millevoye and had borne two children out of wedlock before her marriage to the Irish Boer war hero John MacBride, cannot have been as preoccupied with Irish women's sexual virtue as Griffith. She considered that 95 percent of married women were less than happy with their lot and was sympathetic to the stance of the New Woman, believing that "any woman with independent instincts, with the dream of making her individual personality count for something in the world, might just as well shun marriage."[49]

Moreover, few women in Synge's first audience probably had as much first-hand experience of unhappy marriage as Maud Gonne. In May 1903, just a few months after her wedding to John MacBride, she was already confiding in Yeats about her marital unhappiness. Indeed, she may have been resident in Ireland rather than in France in October 1903 in order to avoid her husband. Her own conjugal drama was soon to receive a public airing when the *Irish Independent*'s reporting of her divorce case in France in 1905 was followed up by the reports of MacBride's suit against that paper for libel. MacBride was revealed as an alcoholic; he was insanely jealous of Maud's past and present friendships with other men; Maud was a battered wife. Close friends such as W. B. Yeats learned that MacBride had sexually molested other women in her household, including her ten-year-old love child, Iseult.[50] Nora Burke had it easy with Dan Burke by comparison. Maud Gonne's opposition to *In the Shadow of the Glen* would appear to have been political and strategic, not moral.

Dawn was primarily a theatrical response to *In The Shadow of the Glen*. Unlike *In a Real Wicklow Glen* which limited itself to marital mores, it was an experiment in combining realism with nationalist political allegory in a play focusing on a peasant heroine. Cathleen ni Houlihan was writing back.

Dawn

Dawn is a woman-centered play focusing on three generations of an Irish family who have recently been evicted from their home: Bride, a widowed grandmother; her daughter, Brideen, whose husband has emigrated; and Brideen's son, Eoin. It is a plotless drama that traces the increasing immiseration of a family and community through eviction and famine to the point where they decide to rebel against their colonial oppressor. The setting is outdoors, a desolate bog, instead of the snug domestic interior of the other two plays. Bride's evictor is a cruel landlord, not, as with Nora, a cruel husband. She and her family live outside the ruin of their former cottage to maintain the connection with their home and land, and life in the open is never romanticized as it was by Synge's Tramp. Lady Gregory, Yeats, and Synge had occluded the problem of peasant poverty; *Dawn* foregrounds it. Bride and her family are destitute and Brideen dies on stage of hunger and exposure. The term, stranger, repeatedly used by Synge to dichotomize the nomad from the "lady of the house" is now applied to construct the landlord as a foreigner, an oppressive other to the Irish peasant. Maud had refused the part of the Countess Cathleen, the eponymous good landlord, in the play Yeats had dedicated to her.[51] That was not the story about landlordism and famine that she wanted to tell. Her landlord is rendered as a heartless villain, an evictor responsible for peasant misery and hunger who, it is hinted, wishes to exercise his *droit du seigneur* on the dying Brideen.

   Dawn is realist in so far as it is factual. It is partly based on scenes its author had observed as an aid organizer during evictions in Falcarragh, Co. Donegal, in 1890 where among the hundred and fifty evictions scheduled to be carried out in one week she had witnessed that of an old woman, her daughter, and two children.[52] Although she resented the presence of foreign visitors who had come to witness the evictions in Falcarragh, angry that peasant misery should be a spectator sport, Maud Gonne was quick to grasp the propagandist power of eviction. She used slides and magic lantern shows of evictions to document her numerous lectures on English misrule in Ireland and, during the Boer war, juxtaposed slides of Irish evictions with those of the burning of Boer homesteads. A photograph of a battering ram at work on a cottage is the only illustration, apart from the author's portrait, in her autobiography, *A Servant of the Queen*.

In *Dawn* the slides, with which Maud illustrated her script on lecture tours, provide the backdrop to the dramatic dialogue. These scenes, in which the same isolated wrecked cottage in a bog is pictured in three different lights—at evening, night, and dawn—are referred to in the stage directions as three *tableaux*, an extension of Inghinidhe theatrical experimentation with *tableaux vivants*. The customary relation between *tableaux* and slides was that the *tableaux* were photographed so that a technology associated with realism and documentary would bestow a quasi-documentary status on imagined scenes from the Irish past. Maud Gonne reversed this process, converting photographs into *tableaux* in an experiment with staging docudrama.

The cottage on stage throughout *Dawn* is a roofless ruin, a continual visual reminder that domestic space has been violated and destroyed by eviction. The play appeals both to the English middle-class cult of the family and to the Irish nationalist cult of the peasant home by representing eviction as an "unhoming," primarily a crime against women and children. In her diatribe against Queen Victoria, "The Famine Queen," Maud Gonne had portrayed her as a hypocritical bourgeoise claiming to uphold family values while condemning Irish peasant women to emigration and possibly prostitution.[53]

For the most part, *Dawn* draws on Maud Gonne's experiences of Famine and Relief Works in North Mayo in 1898 when she was actively involved as an aid organizer and fundraiser.[54] Her own leadership in mobilizing local resistance against the horrific conditions in Mayo, recorded in *A Servant of the Queen*, is omitted from the play, which instead empowers the peasants themselves. The script records facts that she had personally observed or had had reported to her, such as: only the head of household was eligible for employment on Relief Work construction schemes even if she were an old woman or a female single parent, a child almost burned to death while its mother was so employed, and the pay was a grossly inadequate three shillings a week per household. Mrs. Ryan, the good gombeen woman in the play who gives credit to her starving customers, was based on a local shopkeeper, Mrs. Kelly, and was not a fantasy of peasant solidarity.

In her contemporary newspaper coverage of the Mayo famine Maud represented it as a familial disaster and gave a harrowing account of the plight of mothers and children. Her description of the relief works suggests that the treatment of the labor force bore some similarities to that meted out in Nazi concentration camps: "What shocked [her] most on the relief works was that women should be employed on them. There they were; old bent women of sixty; young, slight girls of sixteen working away with pickaxes and spades under the pouring rain, or worse, carrying great stones or sods of turf on their backs." Their food was a piece of Indian cornbread twice a day. Some had no boots on and their feet were bleeding.[55] Her newspaper articles end with an appeal to the women of Ireland: "Oh my sisters, women of Ireland, it is time we shake off our indifference and realise that we have duties of solidarity to each other. It is a slight to all of us that it should be possible to treat any Irish women as these helpless, uncomplaining starving peasant women of Erris are being treated."[56] Such feminization of famine and the appeal to a common womanhood against the barbarity of official relief schemes made it peculiarly appropriate that *Dawn* should be dedicated to Inghinidhe na hEireann.

During the Mayo famine of 1898 Maud Gonne undertook to be "the voice of these helpless victims of England's policy."[57] *Dawn* is a dramatic experiment in giving a voice to the emaciated, depressed victims themselves. Whereas both *Cathleen ni Houlihan* and *In the Shadow of the Glen* had modulated from the comic to the serious, *Dawn* is unrelievedly gloomy. The dialogue, which recounts the hardships endured or witnessed by Bride's family and the local community, dwells relentlessly on peasant misery, and the drama topples into melodrama by telescoping too many disasters into too few lines. Ostensibly, the play concludes on an upbeat note with the local men mustering for rebellion and the son who had joined the British army deserting to support the Irish cause, but its rebels are ragged, pathetic, and few in number and seem doomed to fail despite their brave words. The play's revolutionary optimism is undermined by its realism, by

Maud's memories of famine-stricken Belderrig where, when people attempted to cheer, it sounded more like a cry.[58]

In *Cathleen ni Houlihan,* in which peasant and patriotic values were in conflict, the realist and symbolic dimensions of the drama were dichotomized. *Dawn,* on the contrary, continually negotiates between the micropolitics of a local situation and the macropolitics of nationalism. Though based on a near-contemporary Mayo famine it gains much of its resonance from memories of the Great Famine of the mid-1840s. Timing and stage lighting are exploited to ensure that familial and local events are endowed with symbolism, charting a progression from evening to dawn, despair to revolutionary hope. Bride and Brideen carry the cultural weight of the nationalist idealization of rural family life. They represent two versions of nationalist womanhood: the elderly desexualized mother figure (a grandmother, but not as old as might be expected), who represents the successful outcome of maternal ideology, and the youthful sexualized victim of the Aisling tradition who, though also a caring mother, is associated, through the apple-blossom bouquet placed in the hands of her corpse, with pretty, flowery femininity. Bride also combines the roles of realist victim and nationalist icon, of Mrs Gillane and Cathleen: in addition to being associated with the values of family, nurture, continuity, home, and land, she is represented as an inspirational figure and a visionary. A convert to Catholicism, Maud Gonne is sensitive to the conflation of Catholic devotion to the Virgin Mary with a female Ireland; this is suggested by the Marian titles bestowed on Bride: Bride of the Sorrows *(Mater Dolorosa)* and (the concluding aspiration that she will become) Bride of the Victories *(Notre Dame des Victoires).* The issue of land and land ownership so central to the colonial situation was dealt with at a symbolic level, only, in *Cathleen ni Houlihan,* where the dramatic conflict partly derived from the sacrifice of the family farm for the "four beautiful green fields" of Ireland. Innes rightly remarks of that play: "the nationalism . . . has little to do with the aims of the Land League, which implied the creation of a bourgeois peasantry."[59] Instead of being a disruption of peasant life as in *Cathleen ni Houlihan,* the rebellion with which *Dawn* concludes arises out of communal peasant resistance against the misrule of the colonial landlord. It is a collective response to individual exploitation, not a "lonely impulse of delight." The rebels defend peasant family values rather than flouting them. *Dawn* is forthrightly propagandist, appropriating eviction and famine for a militant nationalist agenda. Disappointingly, in a play written for the Daughters of Erin, it genders political activism as masculine. The daughter, Brideen, dies; it is her son who rallies the all-male group of revolutionaries.

That Maud Gonne felt a sense of personal involvement in the role of Bride is signaled by the nearness of their respective ages: Maud, almost thirty-eight years old at the time of publication, Bride, a forty-year-old. Like Bride, Maud had been regarded as the subject of Brian Ruadh's prophecies.[60] Most obvious is the connection through nomenclature. The name Bride may have alluded to Brigid, patron of the Inghinidhe, but it carried the more immediate reminder of Maud's own married name, Maud Gonne MacBride, with which she signed the play. The young insurrectionary hero, Eoin, Bride's grandson, is virtually a young MacBride, perhaps a tribute to Maud's infant son, Sean. Had she not been preoccupied with sorting out her marital affairs from December 1904, it is probable that she would have acted the role of Bride in an Inghinidhe production of *Dawn*. Might her play then have enjoyed something of the nationalist cult status attaching to *Cathleen ni Houlihan*?

Maud Gonne MacBride's personal circumstances, in particular her legal separation from her husband in July 1905, probably had considerable bearing on the fate of her play. As the ex-wife of the Boer war hero, Major John MacBride, she was no longer the nationalist heroine she had formerly been. When she attended Lady Gregory's *The Gaol Gate* at the Abbey Theatre on 20 October 1906 there were shouts of "Up John MacBride" from some male nationalists in the audience.[61] Cathleen ni Houlihan had flouted the nationalist code for Irish womanhood and gone part of the way with Nora Burke. Having missed its moment, *Dawn* languished in the obscurity of the *United Irishman* journal for sixty-odd years before being republished—as one of the "Lost Plays of the Irish Renaissance"—in 1970, its only re-publication to date.[62]

Notes

An earlier version of this paper was read at the Synge Summer School in Co. Wicklow, July 1995.

1. *Theatre Ireland,* no. 30 (1993).

2. *Dawn* was first published in the *United Irishman* on 29 October 1904; it was reprinted in *Lost Plays of the Irish Renaissance,* ed. Robert Hogan and James Kilroy (Dixon, Calif.: Proscenium Press, 1970). It is not mentioned in Margaret Ward's otherwise excellent biography, *Maud Gonne, Ireland's Joan of Arc* (London: Pandora, 1990). In order to focus exclusively on Gonne's involvement in nationalist theater I have avoided elaborating on biographical information which is readily available in Ward's book.

3. The inaugural meeting took place in Dublin in October 1900. Many of this talented group were already well-known or were soon to become known as writers, actresses, editors, intellectuals: Jenny Wyse-Power, Anna Johnston, and Alice Furlong were joint vice presidents, and members included Alice Milligan, Ella Young, Maire Quinn, Maire Nic Shiubhlaigh, and Sara Allgood. They adopted the names of famous Irish women from history and myth; Maud Gonne was Maeve. For a full account of Inghinidhe na hEireann, see Margaret Ward, *Unmanageable Revolutionaries* (London: Pluto Press, 1983).

4. Throughout this essay I am using the term *peasants* for the small-farming class who lived in cottages, because it was the term commonly used by both Literary and Gaelic Revival writers at the time.

5. The role of Alice Milligan in the Irish theater movement has not yet been fully assessed. I hope to consider this on a future occasion. Though she was far more involved in theater than Maud Gonne, Milligan's contribution is not as relevant for my present purposes.

6. Synge's play was thus titled for the first performances; I use the now customary spelling of the Yeats-Gregory play, originally spelt *Kathleen ni Houlihan.* I am presuming that readers will be familiar with both these plays, but not with *Dawn.*

7. Maire Nic Shiubhlaigh, *The Splendid Years* (Dublin: Duffy, 1955), 17.

8. Ella Young, *Flowering Dusk* (London: Dobson, 1945), 102.

9. *United Irishman* (24 October 1904).

10. The Gaelic League, which did recruit women, was still in 1900 a cultural rather than a political organization.

11. Two such well-known refrains from *The Spirit of the Nation* (1843) collection of nationalist ballads, which ran to fifty-five editions between 1843 and 1896, were "Steady, boys, and step together" and "But a true man, like you man / Will fill your glass with us." Pearse also drew on such fraternal imagery, e.g., "The Nation is a great household, a brotherhood of adoption as well as of blood. . . ." *An Claidheamh Soluis* (5 October 1907). Quotations

throughout this paper from *An Claidheamh Soluis,* the organ of the Gaelic League, were supplied by Elaine Sisson.

12. The first two quotations are from Mary E. L. Butler, *Irishwomen and the Home Language,* Gaelic League Pamphlets, no. 6 (Dublin: The Gaelic League, 1901); the third and fourth are from Patrick Pearse's editorials in *An Claidheamh Soluis* (11 April and 28 November 1903, respectively).

13. Butler, *Irishwomen and the Home Language.*

14. One of the most persuasive critics of the feminizing of the nation is Eavan Boland in *A Kind of Scar* (Dublin: Attic Press, Lip Pamphlet, 1989).

15. *Bean na hEireann,* no. 16 (1910).

16. See Benedict Anderson, *Imagined Communities* (London: Verso, 1991).

17. Arthur Griffith, founding editor of the nationalist weekly, the *United Irishman* (1899), was paid an editorial subvention of twenty-five shillings a week by Maud Gonne. In return, the journal publicized the activities of the Inghinidhe. Samuel Levenson, *Maud Gonne* (London: Cassell, 1976), 150.

18. *United Irishman* (10, 17 October 1903).

19. Ward, *Maud Gonne,* 65. The importance of theater to the Inghinidhe may be gauged from the perception of one of the first members, Maire Nic Shiubhlaigh, that it was primarily a dramatic society. She writes: "its object was to encourage young Dubliners to write for the stage and to establish the nucleus of a national dramatic company . . ." (*The Splendid Years,* 3).

20. Holloway was critical of the production he attended in 1901, noting that apart from the "the excellence of the occasional solo and the novelty of the Irish ceilidh" the show was amateurish and ill-managed and the music dirge-like. Robert Hogan and James Kilroy, *The Irish Literary Theatre, 1899–1901* (Dublin: Dolmen Press, 1975), 90. This would have been among the Inghinidhe's earliest productions.

21. Maud Gonne and Maire Quinn each wrote to Milligan at the end of December 1900, requesting her assistance with St. Patrick's Day tableaux for 1901. Letters to Alice Milligan, ms. 5048, The National Library of Ireland.

22. Hogan and Kilroy, *The Irish Literary Theatre,* 85, 135.

23. "I have a beautiful untidy grey wig, a torn grey [flannil] flannel dress *exactly* like the old women wear in the west, bare feet and a big hoooded cloak." *The Gonne-Yeats Letters 1893–1938,* ed. with introductions by Anna MacBride White and A. Norman Jeffares (London: Hutchinson, 1992), 151.

24. The *Daily Express* review makes it clear that the rejuvenated Cathleen was not seen by the audience.

25. Delia and Bridget's final embrace was suggested by the Inghinidhe and the Fays during rehearsals. *The Gonne-Yeats Letters,* 150.

26. See James Pethica, " 'Our Kathleen': Yeats's Collaboration with Lady Gregory in the writing of *Cathleen ni Houlihan,*" *Yeats Annual,* no. 6 (1988).

27. Lady Gregory, *Selected Writings,* ed. Lucy McDiarmid and Maureen Waters (Harmondsworth: Penguin, 1995), 436.

28. Pethica, " 'Our Kathleen,' " 14.

29. Robert Hogan and James Kilroy, *Laying the Foundations, 1902–1904* (Dublin: Dolmen Press, 1976), 15.

30. Ibid., 17–18.

31. Nic Shiubhlaigh, *The Splendid Years,* 19.

32. Ibid., 195.

33. George L. Mosse, "Nationalism and Sexuality" in *Nationalisms and Sexualities* ed. Andrew Parker et al. (London: Routledge, 1992), 12.

34. "Her beauty was *startling . . .,*" Nic Shiublaigh, *The Splendid Years,* 19. For Mary Colum too "her beauty was startling in its greatness, its dignity, its strangeness . . .," *Life and the Dream* (Dublin: Dolmen Press, 1966), 124. Her late arrival is from *The Splendid Years,* 17.

35. Yeats quoted in Hogan and Kilroy, *Laying the Foundations,* 15; Nic Shiubhlaigh, *The Splendid Years,* 17; Holloway in Levenson, *Maud Gonne,* 195.

36. Anna Johnston died on 2 April 1902, the date of the premiere. Jenny Wyse-Power wrote to Alice Milligan: "it pained me more than I can tell to think they went on with the plays the night of the day she passed away—out of respect for her memory they should have been postponed that evening. . . ." She continued, "Mr Russel and Mr Yates [sic] each made speeches . . . and never once referred to the Society that had financed the whole affair." Letters to Alice Milligan, ms. 5048, The National Library of Ireland.

37. In her letter of resignation from the recently formed National Theatre Society to which she had been elected vice president following her success as Cathleen ni Houlihan, Gonne reveals that she had joined because she thought it shared the same theatrical aims as the Inghinidhe. *The Gonne-Yeats Letters,* 178.

38. Synge and Gonne had met regularly in Paris and were on friendly terms from December 1896 until the row over his play. See *The Collected Letters of John Millington Synge,* Vol. 1, ed. Ann Saddlemyer (Oxford: Clarendon Press, 1983), 41, 47. Nora Burke was played by Sara Allgood, a member of Inghinidhe na hEireann but not an officer in the society.

39. Hogan and Kilroy, *Laying the Foundations,* 65.

40. Butler, *Irishwomen and the Home Language.*

41. *United Irishman* (17 October 1903).

42. James Connolly, *Selected Writings,* ed. P. Beresford Ellis (Harmondsworth: Penguin, 1975), 190–91.

43. *United Irishman* (24 October 1903).

44. Ibid.

45. *United Irishman* (17 October 1903).

46. *United Irishman* (24 October 1903).

47. The play was signed with the pseudonym, Conn. I attribute the authorship to Griffith because in his first attack on Synge's play he had misnamed it *In a Wicklow Glen.*

48. *United Irishman* (31 October 1903).

49. Levenson, *Maud Gonne*, 230–31.

50. *The Gonne-Yeats Letters*, 183–5.

51. Ibid., 30.

52. Maud Gonne MacBride, *A Servant of the Queen* (London: Victor Gollancz, 1938). New revised edition by A. Norman Jeffares and Anna MacBride White (Gerrards Cross: Colin Smythe, 1994), 113. All page numbers are from the revised edition.

53. First printed in her Paris-based paper, *l'Irlande Libre* as "Reine de la Disette" and reprinted in the *United Irishman* (7 April 1900), it is included in *In Their Own Voice, Women and Irish Nationalism,* ed. Margaret Ward (Dublin: Attic Press, 1995), 10–13.

54. MacBride, *A Servant of the Queen*, 241–258.

55. *Freeman's Journal* (9 March 1898).

56. Ibid. and *Irish Daily Independent* (10 March 1898).

57. *Irish Daily Independent* (10 March 1898).

58. See MacBride, *A Servant of the Queen*, 255–6: "starving people are not the best material for a fight."

59. C. L. Innes, *Woman and Nation in Irish Literature and Society, 1880–1935* (Harvester: Wheatsheaf, 1993), 50.

60. In Mayo, Maud was told that Brian Ruadh had prophesied the coming of a "woman who is to bring war and victory," MacBride, *A Servant of the Queen*, 252–3.

61. Colum, *Life and the Dream*, 124.

62. *Dawn* is to be reprinted in the forthcoming fourth volume of the *Field Day Anthology of Irish Writing*.

Nationalism, Pacifism, Internationalism

Louie Bennett, Hanna Sheehy-Skeffington, and the Problems of "Defining Feminism"

IN HER SEMINAL article "Defining Feminism: A Comparative Historical Approach," Karen Offen based her analysis upon the history of the word and upon evidence from comparative history regarding its usage. She concluded that three criteria were necessary before an individual could be defined as feminist. The first two concern recognition and consciousness of the institutionalization of injustice toward women. The third focuses on the political consequences of this understanding of oppression: consciousness must lead to action. A feminist, therefore, is one who:

> advocate(s) the elimination of that injustice by challenging through efforts to alter prevailing ideas and/or social institutions and practices, the coercive power, force, or authority that upholds male prerogatives in that particular culture. Thus, to be a feminist is necessarily to be at odds with male-dominated culture and society.[1]

This broad definition needs to be placed in context. The characteristics of a "male-dominated culture and society" will differ according to circumstances and, consequently, movements challenging "male prerogatives" will not necessarily share the same political agenda. For historians concerned with understanding the origins of feminism and how that movement has adapted to different sets of circumstances, Offen makes clear the importance of research based on a specific context:

> . . . in order to fully comprehend the historical range and possibilities of feminism, we must locate the origins and growth of these ideas within a variety of cultural traditions, rather than postulating a hegemonic model for their development on the experience of any single national or sociolinguistic tradition . . .[2]

For those concerned with expanding the historical understanding of the origins of Irish feminism, this provides a useful point of departure, a rationale for the historical enterprise. We need to draw upon evidence not only from within feminism, but from areas where the feminist movement touches on other movements. We need also to insist on the specificity of the Irish national experience and to criticize historians who fail to realize that feminists cannot share the same views on every issue. What is defined as "the coercive power . . . that upholds male prerogatives"[3] may be different in various situations and may require different strategies to ensure its defeat.

This essay is an examination of the political assumptions underlying the automatic coupling of feminism with pacifism, and internationalism with anti-nationalism. Historians who argue for a "value-free" profession, while weighting their evidence to minimize the adverse effects of the colonial relationship between Britain and Ireland, have had considerable influence, particularly during the past decade. For feminist historians, uncomfortable with the manifestly masculine and militaristic tendency within Irish republicanism (historically and in the present), the political thrust of revisionist history appears to accord with their desire to develop a sustained critique of the patriarchal nature of Irish society.[4] The evidence presented in this essay challenges that "feminist-revisionist" conjunction through the development of an Irish feminist historiography that interrogates and rejects a politically loaded "revisionist" enterprise aimed at discrediting the entire nationalist agenda.

Within the Irish feminist movement there are two dominant strands. One emphasizes the centrality of the colonial relationship and links the struggle for women's emancipation to the movement for national liberation. The other emphasizes what it considers the essential qualities of feminism, to the exclusion of external political issues. There are great differences of strategy, not only *between* these two tendencies, but also *within* each,[5] but we shall leave aside these nuances of emphasis in order to concentrate upon the two polarities: "nationalist feminism" and "essentialist feminism." Cliona Murphy has said that different types of feminist movements reflect and react to the national situations in which they find themselves.[6] This is a helpful point from which to begin. However, the emphasis here is that while feminism reacts and adapts, nationalism remains some monolithic entity, impervious to outside influence, and unwilling to consider policies put forward by other movements. I will argue that, depending on the level of dialogue engaged in by both parties, there can be constructive exchanges of views that allow for a degree of feminization of the nationalist program.

Unquestionably, the two most significant figures in the early feminist movement in Ireland were the suffragists, Hanna Sheehy-Skeffington and Louie Bennett.[7] Both were feminists, in the sense defined by Offen, but each had diametrically opposing views on issues concerning militancy, nationalism, pacifism, and internationalism. I see Sheehy-Skeffington as a nationalist feminist and Bennett as an essentialist feminist. One of the issues to be explored is the impact these differing political views had on their other political beliefs. With regard to the specific Irish context in which both women operated, and which remains of political relevance today, there are a number of other questions to be considered. Can an internationalism, which is in part based upon hostility to nationalism, be considered a progressive stance in a colonial context? Can feminists contribute to a nationalist-defined agenda and retain their critical independence? Can we, in brief, even speak of feminism without some additional elaboration of the term?

Brief outlines of the political careers of Hanna Sheehy-Skeffington and Louie Bennett will help to establish the political and historical framework of this study. Sheehy-Skeffington, daughter of an Irish nationalist member of Parliament, university graduate, and founder-member, in 1908, of the Irish Women's Franchise League, was a suffrage militant who served two prison sentences for her part in the campaign for the Irish woman's right to vote. During the Easter Rising of 1916 she assisted those fighting against British rule in Ireland by carrying supplies to several outposts. Following her pacifist husband's murder at the hands of a British army officer, Sheehy-Skeffington went to America for eighteen months before returning to Ireland to join Sinn Fein. She remained a prominent figure on the republican side and an effective propagandist for the cause, while maintaining her commitment to women. She opposed the Treaty in 1922 but tried to prevent the outbreak of civil war. In her later years she again became a prominent advocate of feminism, leading the opposition to the 1937 Constitution and standing for election on an independent, pro-woman platform in 1943, three years before her death.[8]

Louie Bennett came from a wealthy Protestant family in Dublin. She had not worked for a living, but wrote two novels before abandoning writing. Social issues concerned her and she was sympathetic to the aims of the suffrage movement. In 1911 she established the Irish Women's Reform League and the Irishwomen's Suffrage Federation as nonmilitant suffrage organizations to provide cohesion for those who did not support militancy. Initially antagonistic to the nationalist cause, her hostility lessened as a result of the horror of the murder of Frank Sheehy-Skeffington, whose work as editor of the suffrage journal, the *Irish Citizen,* she greatly respected. Bennett, like Francis Sheehy-Skeffington, was a convinced pacifist. She became secretary of the Irish section of the Women's International League for Peace and Freedom and, in the post-1916 era, organizing secretary for the Irish Women Workers' Union. Disliking confrontation, she attempted to achieve her goals without resorting to strike action. It has often been remarked that she came from the same social class as the majority of the employers, and was at ease in negotiations.[9]

It is obvious, from this brief summary, that the two women occupied very different positions within the broad parameters of feminism. The issue of militancy was one of the most contentious of all controversies within the international suffrage movement, making cooperation between opposing groups fraught with difficulty. In Ireland, militancy had greater political ramifications in the sense that supporters of militancy often had fewer objections to (or at least had more sympathy with the reasons for) the use of militant tactics by extreme nationalists. Equally, nonmilitant suffragists tended to be consistent in their opposition to nonconstitutional forms of activity. The rigidity of this distinction is well-expressed in criticism of militarists made by the British pacifist, Catherine Marshall, a nonmilitant suffragist and a member of the Women's International League and the No-Conscription Fellowship. In Marshall's view, any form of vigorous argument could be classified as militarist:

> The mark of your militarist is that he would rather get what he wants by fighting than by any other way. He wants to force his enemy to yield, so that he may have him at his mercy and be able to impose what terms he chooses. I have heard trade unionists talk like this of trade union

rights. I have heard socialists, who were ardent pacifists on international questions, talk like this of class warfare. I have heard suffragists talk like this of the struggle for sex equality. They were all talking pure militarism—they were all moved by the desire to dominate rather than co-operate, to vanquish and humiliate the enemy rather than to convert him to a friend.[10]

If this line of argument was extended to the Irish situation, presumably Irish nationalists should have attempted to convert Britain "to a friend." British Conservatives had been notoriously unsuccessful in their attempt to "kill Home Rule by kindness" in the late nineteenth century and one could hardly argue that a campaign from the other side of the Irish sea would have had any more positive outcome. Hanna Sheehy-Skeffington made plain her opposition to militarism (which she regarded as an institutionalized response by authority to neutralize challenges to its power) but she was not opposed to the weak using whatever means at their disposal to win their battle. It was one of the reasons she was a suffrage militant. In an article written on the eve of her first imprisonment in 1912, she expressed her belief that the militant campaign had done more for the women's cause than decades of peaceful pleading. She also saw suffrage militancy as part of a long tradition, in Ireland, of oppressed groups fighting their oppressors:

> Now that the first stone has been thrown by suffragists in Ireland light is being admitted into more than mere government quarters and cobwebs are being cleared away from more than one male intellect. As to the method, no one has much to say in Ireland: at the Siege of Limerick the women gathered aprons and stockings full of shards, glass and flints, which they hurled upon the Williamites, in Land League times Tipperary stone-throwers became proverbial . . . so the stone and the shillelagh need no apologia, they have an honoured place in the armoury of argument. So, too, men applaud the stone-thrower as long as the missile is flung for them and not at them.[11]

In contrast, Louie Bennett's attitude, described by Ellen Hazelkorn as "hardline pacifism," was very different. She argued that "no real victory has ever been gained by force or coercion" and believed that if suffrage was won by militancy, it would taint and spoil the final victory.[12] This insistence upon a feminism that eschewed any hint of a male-derived method of campaigning was rooted in a belief in the superiority of female qualities. Louie Bennett held the view, common to many feminists, that women, when they won the vote, would bring a "mother element" to government, transforming the "ordering of the world."[13] This essentialist equation—that feminist equals pacifist—has been accepted by historians writing on the career of Hanna Sheehy-Skeffington. However, when Sheehy-Skeffington appears to deviate from this rule, they are forced into attempting to resolve an issue which cannot easily be dismissed. Biographers Levenson and Natterstad, unwilling to pursue the matter too deeply, are forced to conclude that "Hanna was beset by the intellectual conflicts that beset many pacifists."[14] Maria Luddy, author of a recent monograph, sums up the relationship of her biographical subject to the 1916 Rising in the following sentence, "As pacifists, neither Hanna nor Frank took an active role in the Easter Rising in Dublin."[15] These contradictions require greater elucidation.

The impact of international affairs upon the internal politics of the Irish suffrage movement illuminates the ambiguities inherent in Irish pacifism. Although historians of suffrage have researched the importance of the formation of alliances between women from different countries,[16] there has been little consideration of the analysis advanced by Vellacott in her study of women's participation in the Women's International League for Peace and Freedom. In this, Vellacott states that women who took part in the League (formed in 1915 by feminists attempting to bring the First World War to an end) had certain defining characteristics: they refused to be limited by national boundaries; many were at odds with the mainstream activities of their nations; some even proclaimed that they felt no loyalty to their nations, feeling instead, part of a much wider international community.[17] It is a conclusion that has a certain validity, but as a generalized overview it fails to take into acccount differences between women from imperialist nations and women from countries dominated by imperialism. In specific terms, can this conclusion apply equally to British and Irish women, given the context of the British-Irish relationship in the 1914–1918 period?

Feminists who wanted to participate in the Hague Congress were certainly anxious to demonstrate their detestation of war and their belief that the granting of citizenship to women would contribute a civilizing influence to the world stage, helping to prevent any repetition of such male aggressive behavior. This was common to all. Hanna Sheehy-Skeffington explained why her organization was sending delegates to the Hague:

> The Irish Women's Franchise League regards war as the negation of the feminist movement . . . the essence of war . . . is the destruction of human life and the devitalising of the human race in the pursuit of property . . . we are naturally keenly interested in the various peace movements which have been instigated by suffragists and which specifically recognise the citizenship of women as an essential condition of any lasting peace.[18]

However, Irish feminists divided into two very different groups when it came to formulating their demands for the Hague agenda. In the struggle to ensure that the rights of small nations to self-determination would be included in peace negotiations at the end of the war, the imperative of the feminists of the Irish Women's Franchise League was to ensure that Ireland be recognized as a "small nation," independent from Britain, its imperial ruler. Therefore, while both groups opposed war, one approached participation in the conference from the perspective of national identity: as women from a subject nation, their agenda included reference to Ireland's unresolved status as a nation. The other side, articulated by Louie Bennett, conformed to the internationalist, anti-national perspective outlined by Vellacott: support for pacifist principles revolved around devising a mechanism to prevent any future pursuit of war. It was not concerned with the right of Ireland to be regarded as a small nation. In opposition to this, Sheehy-Skeffington argued that the war, which was being fought ostensibly for the rights of small nations, could provide an opportunity for feminists from Ireland to stake a claim for the nation and for the women of that nation. So insistent was she on this, and so hostile to this insistence were Irish feminists from outside the Irish Women's Franchise League, that in the end there were two separate Irish contingents. One was allied to the British delegation, one was entirely separate. Louie Bennett, not unsympathetic to the desire of Irish women to appear in the international arena as separate from the British, suggested that she continue to work with the British delegation while Sheehy-Skeffington organized an independent contingent. Sheehy-Skeffington hailed the existence of the separate Irish Women's Franchise League delegation as a victory for the nation, as well as a victory for Irish women:

> For the first time Ireland has a separate entity and Irish delegates take their place as representatives of their own country. It is the hour of small nationalities. Long live the small nationalities of the earth![19]

In addition, the IWFL had its own, quite separate resolution to put to the Congress, one which was not endorsed by the other Irish delegates:

> This International Congress of Women, recognising that Peace, to be permanent, must be founded on Justice and Liberty, and that the government of one nation by another is a frequent cause of war, urges that Subject Nationalities should be offered a path to freedom not involving war or war-like preparations and that to this end international machinery should be provided under the auspices of a world-wide International Council, whereby all subject people shall have the power, by plebiscite of their men and women effectively to declare whether they are contented with their lot or would prefer a change of government.[20]

In this resolution, woman's right to citizenship and Ireland's right to self-government were clearly inseparable. The IWFL hoped to use this opportunity to make Ireland's claim on an international stage. The British government did not want peace advocates or Irish nationalists embarrassing them. Of the Irish delegates, only Louie Bennett was granted a permit to travel. She was unable to reach the Hague however, as the government closed the North Sea to all civilian shipping. Despite all the discussion and planning, in the end, only one British woman was able to participate in the Hague Congress.[21]

During the internal negotiations on the policy of the Irish women, Sheehy-Skeffington and Bennett were in constant communication. In terms of the world war being waged, both defined themselves as pacifist and had no difference of opinion. Sheehy-Skeffington was clear that "a terrible war for reasons of commercial jealousy admits of no defence." However, she made a distinction between her position and that of the Tolstoyan pacifist:

> There are pacifists who hold with Tolstoi that resistance to all violence is wrong—I quite see the extreme logic of the position and if you hold that view of course all war is equally hateful to you. But there are other pacifists (and I am one of them) who hold that while war must be ended

if civilisation is to reign supreme, nevertheless there may still be times when armed aggression ought to be met with armed defence.[22]

That view had underpinned Francis Sheehy-Skeffington's support for the arming of the Irish Citizen Army during the 1913 Lock-Out, a time when a defenceless working class was confronted with the armed might of the state and the economic power of the employers. He believed that the Dublin workers had had no other choice. He drew the line when the same Citizen Army later, in the 1916 Rising, used arms to engage in confrontation that was not defensive.[23] I think he and his wife differed on this issue. Hanna Sheehy-Skeffington's definition of armed aggression included the presence of the British state in occupation in Ireland. An armed uprising, in her eyes, could therefore legitimately be defined as "armed defence." It is important also to stress that her espousal of the cause of international pacifism reveals that she was robustly on the side of radical political activism, as is demonstrated in a telegram to Jane Addams, one of the leading American feminists to support the pacifist cause:

Greetings American pacifists
Believe world peace only securable by scrapping capitalism and imperialism and outlawing armament-makers. Consider League of Nations merely a shield for the victors . . .[24]

Louie Bennett's very different views on what, if any, relationship could exist between pacifism and other political causes, was clearly revealed in a letter written after a meeting held in the Dublin Trades Hall to protest against government refusal to allow the Irish Peace Delegation to travel to the Hague. The meeting, chaired by Meg Connery of the IWFL, was attended by many of the most advanced nationalists as well as by representatives from different women's organizations. It took place in May 1915, less than one year before the Rising. Hanna Sheehy-Skeffington took the opportunity to make some gibes at the expense of Bennett, . . . who had been given permission to travel to the Hague, making her the only Irish woman to have been deemed acceptable by the British government: "The selected twenty included Miss Bennett, who was discreet, she notoriously was not (laughter)."[25] The protestors agreed to send Prime Minister Asquith and Home Secretary McKenna a message that "Ireland was still alive; and apt to kick them now and then." An ill-considered message of support from Patrick Pearse was read out: he hoped that the "present incident will do good if it ranges more of the women definitely with the national forces." Meg Connery protested at what she condemned as this "very masculine inversion" and, to loud applause, she reworked this to state "the incident ought to have the effect of ranging the national forces on the side of women." An embarrassed Thomas MacDonagh was forced to accept her criticism. MacDonagh (Director of Training for the Irish Volunteers) added, enigmatically, that as a Volunteer he hoped he would have a better opportunity than voting to show that by "people" he meant the women as well as the men of Ireland. He was explicit on the type of military training he was organizing. Connery again intervened, "She had considerable sympathy with the Irish Volunteers but she objected intensely to bloodshed." In her eyes, it was a "finer patriotism to live and fight for your country than to die for it." [26]

Louie Bennett, outnumbered by nationalists, had not felt able to express her feelings openly during the meeting. Instead, she wrote a strongly worded protest to Hanna Sheehy-Skeffington. She felt that the meeting had equated pacifism with an anti-militarism that was motivated by nationalist sympathies. In her eyes, its tone had revealed a concern, not for pacifism, but for encouraging anti-English sentiments:

> The impression I gathered was that the present World War was reckoned barbarous and immoral but that a war for Ireland would find justification. That seems to me a thoroughly superficial form of pacifism —hardly worthy of the name. I do not care for a pacifism which is not truly international, which is not tolerant towards all nations. . . . This letter . . . is to let you know that I shall in future take no part in peace meetings which put Irish nationalism above international tolerance and which are embittered by anti-England feuds. [27]

Sheehy-Skeffington understood that there was a considerable difference in the type of peace propaganda that would be effective in Ireland, and the type of political appeal that could be made in England. Many Irish people hoped that Germany would defeat Britain in the war, providing an opportunity for Ireland to claim its independence. To organize, in Ireland, an effective opposition to the war between Britain and Germany, Irish sentiments had to be stirred up. She explained to Bennett: "That is why a protest meeting succeeds where a purely peace meeting would not . . ." There could be no pure ideal regardless of context. In discussing the dilemmas facing pacifists, Sheehy-Skeffington went on to consider the Irish situation. Her argument overturns what many, erroneously, have supposed to be her attitude toward the Rising:

> If I saw a hope of Ireland being freed for ever from British rule by a swift uprising, I would consider Irishmen justified resorting to arms in order that we might be free. I should still be radically opposed to war and militarism. This is of course my personal view and in no way represents the League. But I hold no such hopes. I think that freedom for small nations lies in Justice by Arbitration and there is one of my strongest motives in standing for Peace.[28]

Sheehy-Skeffington was therefore not a pacifist when it came to consideration of the Irish situation. She believed that an uprising against British rule in Ireland could be justified. This view is completely independent of any traumatic reaction to Frank Sheehy-Skeffington's murder. It has been suggested that her later support for the insurgents was a consequence of her justifiable anger.[29] However, her private correspondence makes it clear that she believed support for armed struggle to achieve Irish self-determination was entirely consistent with her feminist beliefs. Equally clearly, she acknowledged that not all members of her organization shared these views.

Further comparison between the attitudes held by Bennett and Sheehy-Skeffington on the interlinking issues of pacifism and nationalism can be made when considering their different responses to a debate between Constance Markievicz and Frank Sheehy-Skeffington on the question "Do We Want Peace Now?" held in Dublin on 15 February 1916. Constance Markievicz declared she did not want the war stopped until the British Empire was smashed. It was, as Greaves puts it, a mechanistic formulation of Connolly's views on the possibilities that the war opened up for Ireland.[30] In contrast, Francis Sheehy-Skeffington urged people to support the Peace Crusade at the Hague. Louie Bennett's account of this meeting reveals a refusal to accept any difference between a war engaged in by imperialist powers and an insurgent struggle to gain national independence:

> The Countess had the meeting with her. Skeffington's supporters numbered 26. Her supporters spoke in a bitter and sinister vein. I gathered

they were willing to watch the war continue, with all its dreadful losses and consequences, if only it led to the overthrow of England and consequent release of Ireland. I broke out at the cowardice of that. I spoke pretty strongly and was listened to with civility. Then Connolly stood up and spoke at some length, claiming extra time from the chairman. As well as I can remember he spoke strongly in favour of seizing the moment to fight now against England. I gathered he regretted that more were not ready to do it. As always, one felt the tremendous force of the man, with his big, powerful body, and powerful face and head, and it came home to me that here, in this man, was the centre of danger at this time, and that he would be relentless in the carrying out of a purpose. This meeting depressed me unutterably. The spirit of it was bad, sinister, lacking in any idealism to redeem its bitterness.[31]

We can compare the sentiments in that intensely anti-nationalist and unambiguously pacifist account, with a description of the same event, written by Hanna Sheehy-Skeffington:

He [Skeffington] was pro-peace, she [Markievicz] for a longer war, as she held Britain was being beaten. After a warmly-contested word-duel, just before the vote was taken, James Connolly, who had been a quiet on-looker, suddenly intervened, on Madame's side, swinging the meeting round. When Skeffington laughingly reproved him for throwing in his weight at the end, he replied, with twinkling eyes, "I was afraid you might get the better of it, Skeffington. That would never do."[32]

The feeling is benign, a description of friends in disagreement, without the malignant force felt by Bennett. The reason is obvious. Louie Bennett profoundly disagreed with the outcome of the debate and regretted the fact that the pacifist case was defeated. Hanna Sheehy-Skeffington did not.

With regard to the question of whether or not the Rising should have been embarked upon, we have evidence that there was a significant difference of opinion between the two Sheehy-Skeffingtons. The Easter Rising was an attempt to establish an Irish Republic through force of arms. The odds against a successful rising were such that some have labeled it a "blood sacrifice," as defeating the British in battle was never considered a possibility. Instead, the insurgents hoped to take advantage of Britain's involvement in the battlefields of Europe for a sufficient length of time to enable Ireland to make a claim to be included as a small nation when the war ended and peace negotiations

began. Despite the confusion of Eoin MacNeill's countermanding
order (jeopardizing the plans of the leadership) the day before the
rising was to begin, Hanna felt that James Connolly was right to
continue once they had reached that point, while her husband remained utterly opposed to any shedding of blood. He thought any
attempt at a rising was foredoomed. He had hoped to organize an
anti-taxation movement as a safety valve for antigovernment feeling,
but that was not to be.[33] At some stage during the weekend before
Easter, Hanna Sheehy-Skeffington met Connolly, and was told by him
"if you are interested in developments, I would not advise you to go
away on holiday just now." He added that women had been given
equal rights and equal opportunities in the Proclamation, with only
one dissenter.[34] The confidence the leadership of the Rising placed in
Hanna Sheehy-Skeffington can be verified in that they selected her to
act as member of a civil provisional government that would come into
effect if the rising was a prolonged affair.[35]

Connolly had been trying, unsuccessfully, to persuade Louie Bennett to take over the task of organizing the Irish Women Workers'
Union. This she refused to do, in part because she disliked the close-
ness of the relationship between the women's union and Liberty Hall,
which was also home to the Irish Citizen Army. Her pacifism found
the notion of an armed body anathema to her beliefs regarding the
role of a labor movement. It did not matter that the Citizen Army
accepted women as members. Her description of Connolly, written
during the week of the Rising, shows her struggling to understand his
motivation:

> It has been difficult for those who knew him only as a Labour leader to
> understand how so hard-headed and practical a man could lead an
> enterprise which seemed to carry with it inevitable disaster and loss.
> But Connolly had as much of the fanaticism of the patriot as any poet
> in that rebel crowd. It seemed that he faced the probability of failure
> and yet thought the effort worth the risk.

She deeply regretted his loss to the labour movement, blaming "passion for Ireland and the freedom of Ireland" for ruining his life.[36]

The reaction of Hanna Sheehy-Skeffington was different. The loss
of husband and close friends was a tragedy that almost overwhelmed
her, but she remained positive in her emphasis on the contribution

that those who signed the Proclamation of the Republic had made to the cause of women's emancipation: "It is the only instance I know of in history where men fighting for freedom voluntarily included women."[37]

Her husband had spent the first day of the Rising walking around the streets, watching events, and attempting to organize a citizen's militia to prevent the widescale looting that he feared would discredit the ideals of the insurgents. On the second day, he continued with this. He and his wife walked into the center of Dublin, and Hanna went to the headquarters of the Rising, to offer supplies of food and to give her assistance in acting as messenger between the outposts. One of the first people she saw at the General Post Office was Eugene Sheehy, her uncle, towards whom she had always been closer than to her father. He was an old Fenian, a believer in physical force, exulting that the day had arrived while he was still alive to witness it. A priest, he had volunteered his services as confessor to the insurgents.[38] His niece was sent by Connolly to the College of Surgeons where Constance Markievicz was a member of the garrison. Markievicz later recalled the arrival of Sheehy-Skeffington along with other members of the Irish Women's Franchise League:

Just then the leading figure approached and asked for Commandant Mallin. Some of us recognised the voice. It came from the lips of Mrs Sheehy-Skeffington who was struggling under the weight of a huge sack bulging out into queer shapes and completely concealing her. She was followed by more laden figures. They proved to be members of the IWFL . . . and had collected a store of all manner of eatables from their friends . . . to bring them to us through the bullet-swept streets. We had great fun unpacking the parcels and hearing who had contributed this ham or that tin of salmon or soup before we sat down and had a glorious meal. . . . I have nothing but pleasant and happy memories of the Sheehy-Skeffingtons. They always instinctively took the right side and were always ready to help.[39]

Although Bennett became more sympathetic toward Connolly and the ideals of the Rising, she never deviated from her pacifist convictions. The senseless murder of Frank Sheehy-Skeffington had a profound effect upon her, and she had to face, for the first time, the reality of British militarism. After that watershed she realized that, unless Ireland was granted the right of a small nation, further blood would

be shed. In the aftermath of the rising, in her capacity as secretary of
the Irishwomen's International League, she added the weight of her
organization to the pressure for Irish representation at the Peace Conference. Her attitude at this period echoed that of Sheehy-Skeffington
at the time of the Hague debate:

> We have done all in our power to keep this point [representation of
> Ireland at the Peace Conference] to the fore in the ensuing months.
> And we have gained a small moral victory by securing for our League
> representation on the International Committee of Women for Perma-
> nent Peace as a *national* organisation enjoying equal privileges with
> England, Germany and other nations. I understand this is the first time
> that Ireland has secured the right of independent representation at an
> International Congress.[40]

In the emotional upheaval attendant upon executions, imprisonment, and bereavement, Bennett claimed the sacrifice made by the
leaders of the Rising was based upon a desire to achieve peace:

> I submit that Connolly never lost his faith in Internationalism, and in
> its importance for Irish politics and Irish labour. He gave his life to
> secure the case of Ireland as an International problem, relying, not upon
> the diplomatic intrigues of rulers or Government Ministers, but upon
> the honesty of the democracies of the world, in whose ultimate triumph
> he had faith.[41]

Despite this conversion, her preoccupation remained with the efforts being made to secure peace (now albeit with Ireland included in
the parameters of international concern) rather than with the ideals of
Irish republicanism.

At the same time, while in America in 1917, Hanna Sheehy-
Skeffington published a pamphlet entitled *British Militarism As I Have
Known It,* an account of her husband's murder and the attempts made
by the British to cover up what actually had happened in Portobello
Barracks. It was, essentially, the text of the lecture she delivered in
many states. Her audiences were left in no doubt that she fully supported the Rising, despite the fact that, indirectly, it had led to the
death of her husband:

> I knew the Irish Republican leaders and am proud to have known them
> and had their friendship. They fought a clean fight against terrible odds

—and terrible was the price they had to pay. They were filled with a high idealism. They had banks, factories, the GPO, the Four Courts, their enemies' strongholds, for days in their keeping, yet bankers, merchants and others testified as to the scrupulous way in which their stock was guarded. . . . It is the dreamers and the visionaries that keep hope alive and feed enthusiasm—not the statesmen and the politicans. . . . The lesson of the Irish Rising and its suppression is that our small nation, Ireland has a right also to its place in the sun. . . . At the end of the war we hope to see a 'United Europe' on the model of the United States, where each state is free and independent, yet all are part of a great federation. We want Ireland to belong to this united Europe, and not to be a vassal of Great Britain, a province of the British Empire, governed without consent.[42]

In 1921 Sheehy-Skeffington rejected the Treaty negotiated between Britain and Ireland that eventually concluded the War of Independence, writing to an American suffrage friend: "The Treaty is a bad compromise and I fear we are in for some decades of reaction under a temporary false prosperity, reinforced by our native militarism." She recognized that those who would vote for its acceptance were "the moderates, and the 'safe' people with stakes in the country, of the press, and the clerics." As many politically active women were against it (including the six women members of the Dail and the overwhelming majority of nationalist women in Cumann na mBan) she declared that there was "great bitterness against us all just now." An attempt to extend the franchise to women under thirty was defeated in the Dail, but it had been a campaign Sheehy-Skeffington had relished and one in which she had taken a prominent role: "The fight for this absorbed all my energies and it seemed like old suffragette times again."[43]

Political divisions over the Treaty led, inexorably, to full-scale civil war. During the interim period, when some hope remained that conflict could be averted, Bennett was candid about her previous lack of engagement in Irish affairs. She had come to a realization that, as a pacifist, she had an obligation to intervene:

When the Republicans were in the Four Courts I was reproached—I had often been reproached by Francis Sheehy-Skeffington—that although I was a Pacifist working for peace, I didn't do much for peace in Ireland. When the Four Courts were attacked I felt the moment had come for some definite action on our part.[44]

Ironically, Bennett and Sheehy-Skeffington were the leaders of the group chosen by the women's peace mission to go to the anti-Treaty headquarters in the Four Courts, then under attack by government forces. Bennett left the actual negotiations to Sheehy-Skeffington, who was much more sympathetic to the IRA position than her companion:

> I sat on a sack of flour or something. We couldn't see any of the Republicans, but eventually someone—a General-somebody or-other, but I could never remember since who he was—had a long talk with Mrs Sheehy-Skeffington. But they would not negotiate on any terms. They said they were into it now, and there was no way out but to fight it out.[45]

Despite having achieved some level of understanding as to why James Connolly had chosen the insurrectionary path, Bennett was never sympathetic to the republican struggle. While Sheehy-Skeffington became a prominent figure in the anti-Treaty Sinn Fein, Bennett ensured that the Irish Women Workers' Union, along with the Labour Party, remained neutral on the issue. It was, however, a neutrality which could be said to have favored the Free State authorities. In 1922, in protest against the presence of republican women within the Irish section of the Women's International League, Bennett resigned her position as secretary, warning about the danger of employing on the Committee women who took a prominent place in contemporary politics.[46] Bennett's argument was that Irish internal politics had nothing to do with the work of the Women's International League.

The difficulties experienced by the Irish section of the League were made worse in the 1922–23 period, when civil war fragmented Irish political life. The Free State government kept close watch on republican sympathizers. They arrested Bennett's successor, Rose Jacob, in January 1923 while Jacob was lending Hanna Sheehy-Skeffington's house to the fugitive republican publicity department. Sheehy-Skeffington was in America at the time, fund-raising for the republican cause. Daisy Swanton, a member of the Women's International League who sympathized with the Bennett view, wrote in her diary:

> Think her action was what Mrs S.S. would have agreed to, but considering Rose's position as secretary rather rash, as from our point of view

we are not benefitted in any way by having our secretary in prison. . . .
Very glad to have Mrs Dix as joint secretary—she is a sane and thor-
oughly pacifist person and does not stink in eyes of government like
Mrs Despard and Madame Gonne MacBride.[47]

It could be argued that, in periods of severe government repression,
outspoken people were precisely what were needed in a movement
dedicated to the achievement of peace. The government that objected
to the activities of women such as Charlotte Despard and Maud
Gonne MacBride was a government that had, in December 1922,
arbitrarily executed (among others) Liam Mellows, the man regarded
as the successor to Connolly, thus ensuring Hanna Sheehy-
Skeffington's complete rejection of the Free State regime. Thomas
Johnson, leader of the Irish Labour Party, had condemned the government for that murder, "most foul, bloody and unnatural."[48] There was
little point in believing one could have an impact upon the international stage while opting out of the home scene at a time when united
resistance to repression should have been a crucial element in the
pacifist agenda. In these circumstances, it is surprising that Bennett
reserved her harshest condemnation for the part played by republican
women:

> There was much that was admirable, much detestable, and much that
> was pitiful in the attitude of Republican women towards the recent civil
> strife in Ireland. They failed in sane, constructive thinking.[49]

The dilemma over whether or not Irish internal affairs could be
allowed to intrude into the international feminist arena continued,
reemerging in 1926 when the Congress of the Women's International
League was held in Dublin. This was an important occasion for
women; it was also of great significance for the Irish government
because it was one of the first international events to be staged since
the founding of the Free State. Delegates from America and Europe
gathered in Ireland, to participate in events attended by both William
Cosgrave, Irish head of government, and by Eamon de Valera, the
man considered by anti-Treaty republicans to be the rightful head of
state. The latter had been released from prison two years earlier. The
journalist R. M. Fox, who was also present, understood the political
use to which "pacifism" could be put. He wrote:

Pacifist women from Britain poured out a gospel of peaceful submission
to the Empire—a travesty of honest pacifism as understood by the
Skeffingtons. In their defence, it may be urged that many of them had
crossed to Dublin, without understanding in the least degree what Empire meant there.[50]

Louie Bennett, presiding over the opening ceremony, defused a potentially volatile scene by introducing Jane Addams, president of the
League, when the rival Irish groups expected either Cosgrave or de
Valera, both putative "presidents," to be named. Addams had met
Frank Skeffington while he was in America in 1915. (He had been
convicted in Ireland for anti-recruiting speeches, winning his release
from prison by undergoing a hunger and thirst strike. The subsequent
tour of America was a way of evading the authorities as he was liable
to re-arrest under the terms of the "Cat and Mouse" Act.) In the
course of her address Addams read a statement made by the man she
described as "a great Irish pacifist known to pacifists all the world
over":

> I advocate no mere servile lazy acquiesence in injustice. I am, and al-
> ways will be, a fighter. But I want to see the age-long fight against
> injustice clothe itself in new forms suited to a new age.[51]

His widow, Hanna, was called upon to speak on behalf of Irish
women. She endorsed her husband's message, but did more than that,
quoting the powerful words of Patrick Pearse, executed leader of the
Easter Rising, in a passionate plea for peace and freedom: "Ireland
unfree can never be at peace." Fox declared, "The audience rose to
her for she spoke as one inspired."[52] When recalling that scene twenty
years later he added, "One could sense the emotional pull between the
pacifists and the militant Republicans, who were still unreconciled to
peaceful methods."[53] Helena Swanwick, a British delegate who knew
the Irish situation well, testified to that tension, admitting that "Some
of our foreign delegations were much puzzled to choose between these
rebels and the members of the Irish section, who pursued the same
aims, but by other methods."[54] Swanwick claimed that Hanna Sheehy-
Skeffington, Charlotte Despard, and Maud Gonne MacBride were
among a group of women "some of whom had belonged or actually
did belong to the W.I.L., but who remained outside our Conference
because they had taken part in the civil war and were, even at that time,

involved in relations with revolutionary Republicans."[55] While it is true that nationalist women took the opportunity, as the "Republican Hostesses Committee," to brief delegates on the reasons for their alienation from the Free State, there is no evidence that Hanna Sheehy-Skeffington felt any reason to remain outside the normal proceedings of Congress. Swanwick's position was identical to Louie Bennett's, regretting that "there are sections of the Women's International League who believe that, for the sake of Peace and Freedom itself, they must be prepared to use force or, at any rate, to support those who do."[56] Hanna Sheehy-Skeffington, a member of feminist organizations for over twenty years and also, because of British opposition to Irish attempts to establish an independent republic, a leading member of Sinn Fein for the past eight years, saw no contradiction between those positions. On behalf of the Irish section of the League she presented a report to the Congress. It began with a strong condemnation of the continued influence of Britain upon Irish economic and political affairs:

> Ireland, is as you are doubtless aware, the worst example in the world today of a victim of imperialistic capitalism or of economic imperialism. Personally I find it, as other speakers have found it, very difficult to disentangle imperialism from militarism.[57]

When writing a report on the Congress for the *Irish World*, an Irish-American journal, she included Jane Addams's contribution while modestly omitting her own. However, she succeeded in inserting Pearse's message into a comment made by a French journalist, and she highlighted what she considered to be the main recommendations of Congress. One was a call for an international amnesty for political prisoners. The most significant, as far as Irish nationalists was concerned, was a proposition in a report which laid down, as she caustically observed,

> the self-evident axiom that uprisings by natives against foreign governments should not be classed as "rebellious," a proposition that Britain for one has never yet accepted in her relations with her oppressed nationalities.[58]

The desire for both peace and freedom was strongly felt by all. However, the conclusion appears to be that, at the 1926 Congress, an anxiety to achieve freedom dominated minds.

The parallel careers of Louie Bennett and Hanna Sheehy-Skeffington exemplify, in the most vivid words and images, the dilemmas confronting present-day feminists, as the question of Ireland's constitutional status continues to distort the body politic. The former, prominent in the nonmilitant suffrage movement and a pioneer of women's trade unionism, believed that Ireland's unresolved "national question" should be treated separately from all other political issues. The latter, while critical of nationalist reluctance to place women's concerns in the forefront of its agenda (with the exemplary exception of the Republican Proclamation of Easter Week) devoted much of her later political career to the task of developing a mutually enriching republican-feminism. Few others, however, followed her lead.

Salient examples from our feminist past make it plain that there can be no simplistic characterization or definition of what constitutes feminism. As an ideology it is modified by a host of other isms and, in turn, helps to shape the direction of movements receptive to the feminist voice. Modern-day feminism in Ireland has, in part, been shaped by the experiences of those who constituted the first wave of feminist campaigners. We still have different strands of feminism, operating in parallel, occasionally overlapping. We have those who prefer not to engage with the nationalist movement (of course we have nationalists who fail to see the relevance of feminism) and we also have a few who struggle to make feminism a force relevant to the different claims of today. In this respect, elements within Irish feminism in the north of Ireland deserve particular mention. Since the foundation of the state, Northern Irish political life has been almost exclusively male. There have been good reasons for women's reluctance to become involved. Times have changed. It is ludicrous to suppose there can be inclusive talks if the female half of the population continues to be excluded. But women, with the confidence of a supportive network of sisterhood, are now determined to make an effective challenge to this male monopoly. The Women's Coalition, through standing for election at the all-party talks intended to facilitate the peace process, has begun to confront the vested interests of predominantly male political parties from all political spectrums; Clar na mBan, a coalition of republican feminists, insists that women's voices must be listened to if any talks are to be meaningful; the Women's Support Network and the Women's Information Group are busily voicing the concerns of working class women.[59] Their differing responses to proposals for a resolution of "the troubles" echo in some respects the positions expressed by Louie Bennett and Hanna Sheehy-Skeffington. Can we hope that discussions initiated by our contemporary feminist movement will provide fresh thinking on the feminist-nationalist conundrum? If Irish women are prevented from engaging in creative dialogue with other political movements, the evidence of history—cease-fire or not—leads to the sombre conclusion that this latest attempt to resolve the Irish crisis will achieve little.

Notes

An earlier version of this paper was given to the "Irish Encounters" conference held in Bath College of Higher Education in July 1996. My thanks to participants for their comments. I would also like to thank Maryann Valiulis for her suggestions.

1. Karen Offen, "Defining Feminism: A Comparative Historical Approach," *Signs: Journal of Women in Culture and Society* 14, 1 (1988): 152.

2. Ibid., 151.

3. Ibid., 152.

4. See for example the interesting discussions contained in Mary Condren, "Work-in-Progress: Sacrifice and Political Legitimation: The Production of a Gendered Social Order," *Journal of Women's History* 6,4; 7,1 (1995): 160–89; Sarah Benton, "Women Disarmed: The Militarization of Politics in Ireland 1913–23," *Feminist Review* 50 (1995): 148–72.

5. The most documented debate has been from within the ranks of "nationalist feminism," between members of the Irish Women's Franchise League and Cumann na mBan on the priorities of campaigning for the vote versus campaigning for national independence. A number of studies have been concerned with this aspect of Irish women's history. See, for example, Dana Hearn, "The Irish Citizen, 1914–1916: Nationalism, Feminism and Militarism," *Canadian Journal of Irish Studies* 17, 1 (1992): 1–15; Beth McKillen, "Irish Feminism and National Separatism 1914–23," *Eire/Ireland* 18,3 (1982): 52–67; Cliona Murphy, "Suffragists and Nationalism in Early Twentieth-Century Ireland," *History of European Ideas* 16,4 (1993): 1009–15; Louise Ryan, "Traditions and Double Moral Standards: The Irish Suffragists' Critique of Nationalism," *Women's History Review* 4,4 (1995): 487–503; Margaret Ward, " 'Suffrage First Above All Else!': An Account of the Irish Suffrage Movement," *Feminist Review* 10 (1982): 22–36.

6. Murphy, "Suffragists and Nationalism," 1009.

7. For biographies of Hanna Sheehy-Skeffington, see R. M. Fox, *Rebel Irishwomen,* rev. ed. (Dublin: Progress House, 1967); Leah Levenson and Jerry Natterstad, *Hanna Sheehy-Skeffington: Irish Feminist* (Syracuse, N.Y.:

Syracuse University Press, 1986); Maria Luddy, *Hanna Sheehy-Skeffington* (Dundalk: Dundalgan Press, 1995); Margaret Ward, *Hanna Sheehy-Skeffington: A Life* (Dublin: Attic Press, forthcoming). Little has been written on Louie Bennett. See R. M. Fox, *Louie Bennett* (Dublin: Talbot Press, 1958); Ellen Hazlekorn, "The Social and Political Views of Louie Bennett, 1870–1965," *Saothar* 13 (1988): 32–44.

8. See Maryann Valiulis, "Power, Gender and Identity in the Irish Free State," *Journal of Women's History* 6,4; 7,1 (1995): 117–36. For useful documents concerning this period, see Margaret Ward, ed., *In Their Own Voice, Women and Irish Nationalism* (Dublin: Attic Press, 1995).

9. For an assessment of Louie Bennett's career as a trade unionist, see Mary Jones, *These Obstreperous Lassies, a History of the Irish Women Workers' Union* (Dublin: Gill and Macmillan, 1988).

10. Sharon Ouditt, *Fighting Forces, Writing Women: Identity and Ideology in the First World War* (London, Pandora, 1994), 146.

11. Hanna Sheehy-Skeffington, "The Women's Movement—Ireland," *Irish Review* (July 1912): 225–27.

12. Hazelkorn, "Social and Political Views," 34.

13. Dana Hearne, "The Irish Citizen," 9. See also Ouditt, *Fighting Forces,* 139–40.

14. Levenson and Natterstad, *Hanna Sheehy-Skeffington,* 143.

15. Luddy, *Hanna Sheehy-Skeffington,* 28.

16. Cliona Murphy, "The Tune of the Stars and Stripes: The American Influence on the Irish Suffrage Movement," in *Women Surviving: Studies in Irish Women's History in the nineteenth and twentieth centuries,* ed. Maria Luddy and Cliona Murphy (Dublin: Poolbeg, 1990), 180–205; Catherine Candy, "Relating Feminism, Nationalism and Imperialism. Ireland, India and Margaret Cousins' Sexual Politics," *Women's History Review* 3,4 (1994): 581–594.

17. Jo Vellacott, "A Place for Pacifism and Transnationalism in Feminist Theory," *Women's History Review* 2 (1993): 23–56.

18. *Jus Suffragii,* April 1915, quoted in Luddy, *Hanna Sheehy-Skeffington,* 26–27.

19. *Irish Citizen* (17 April 1915).

20. *Irish Citizen* (24 April 1915).

21. For more on the Hague Congress, see Anne Wiltsher, *Most Dangerous Women* (London: Pandora, 1985); Louise Ryan, *Irish Feminism and the Vote, An Anthology of the Irish Citizen Newspaper, 1912–1920* (Dublin: Folens, 1996), 108–9.

22. Sheehy-Skeffington Papers, Ms. 24,134 (National Library of Ireland).

23. Leah Levenson, *With Wooden Sword: A Portrait of Francis Sheehy-Skeffington, Militant Pacifist* (Dublin: Gill and Macmillan, 1983), 153.

24. Undated fragment, Sheehy-Skeffington Papers, Ms. 24,134 (National Library of Ireland).

25. *Irish Citizen* (23 May 1915).

26. *Irish Citizen* (22 May 1915).

27. Louie Bennett to Hanna Sheehy-Skeffington, 12 May 1915, Sheehy-Skeffington Papers, Ms. 22,675 (National Library of Ireland).

28. Undated fragment, Sheehy-Skeffington Papers, Ms. 24,134 (National Library of Ireland).

29. Conor Cruise O'Brien, *States of Ireland* (St. Albans, Herts: Panther, 1972), 103.

30. C. Desmond Greaves, *The Life and Times of James Connolly* (London: Lawrence and Wishart, 1972), 385.

31. Fox, *Louie Bennett*, 48–49.

32. Jacqueline Van Voris, *Constance de Markievicz and the Cause of Ireland* (Amherst: University of Massachusetts Press, 1967), 160.

33. Testimony of Dr. J. B. Skeffington to Royal Commission of Inquiry, *Sinn Fein Rebellion Handbook* (Dublin: Irish Times, 1917), 222.

34. Fox, *Rebel Irishwomen*, 76.

35. William O'Brien, *Forth the Banners Go* (Dublin: Sign of the Three Candles, 1979), 278.

36. Fox, *Louie Bennett*, 54.

37. Hanna Sheehy-Skeffington, "Memories of the Suffrage Campaign in Ireland," *The Vote* (30 August 1929): 277.

38. Eugene Sheehy, *May It Please the Court* (Dublin: C. J. Fallon, 1951), 123–24.

39. *Irish World* (3 May 1924).

40. Louie Bennett to editor, *New Ireland* (20 January 1917): 182. With thanks to Catherine Morris for drawing this to my attention.

41. Louie Bennett, *New Ireland* (16 June 1917): 92.

42. Hanna Sheehy-Skeffington, *British Militarism as I Have Known It* (New York: Donnelly Press, 1917), 18.

43. Hanna Sheehy-Skeffington to Alice Park (25 February 1922), Alice Park Collection, Hoover Institution on War, Revolution and Peace, Stanford, California.

44. Fox, *Louie Bennett*, 76.

45. Ibid., 78.

46. Daisy Lawrenson Swanton, *Emerging from the Shadow* (Dublin: Attic, 1994), 91.

47. Ibid., 92.

48. Arthur Mitchell and Padraig O Snodaigh, *Irish Political Documents 1916–1949* (Dublin: Irish Academic Press, 1985), 156.

49. Louie Bennett, "What the Workers Can Do in the New Day," in *The Voice of Ireland* ed. William Fitzgerald (Dublin and London: Virtue and Co., n.d.), 301.

50. Fox, *Rebel Irishwomen*, 81.

51. Francis Sheehy-Skeffington, "Open Letter to Thomas MacDonagh,"

reprinted in Owen Dudley-Edwards and Fergus Pyle, eds., *1916: The Easter Rising* (London: MacGibbon and Kee, 1968), 151.

52. Fox, *Rebel Irishwomen,* 81.

53. Fox, *Louie Bennett,* 89.

54. Helena Swanick, *I Have Been Young* (London: Victor Gollancz, 1935), 451.

55. Ibid., 450.

56. Ibid., 451.

57. Hanna Sheehy-Skeffington, transcript of speech to Congress of Women's International League (July 1926), Alice Park Collection, Hoover Institution on War, Revolution and Peace, Stanford, California.

58. *Irish World* (7 August 1926).

59. See Monica MacWilliams, "Struggling for Peace and Justice: Reflections on Women's Activism in Northern Ireland," *Journal of Women's History* 6,4; 7,1 (1995): 13–39; Eilish Rooney, "Women in Political Conflict," *Race and Class* 37, 1 (1995): 51–56; Margaret Ward "Finding a Place: Women and the Irish Peace Process," *Race and Class* 37, 1 (1995):41–50.

The Fionnuala Factor

Irish Sibling Emigration at the Turn of the Century

HISTORIANS STUDYING the cause of the postfamine Irish diaspora generally line up in two camps. One group supports Kerby Miller's persuasive argument that those who came to America were involuntary emigrants, exiles driven from Ireland because the British government's Irish policies restricted the economic development which could support the native population. Miller had described the characteristics of that exodus:

> In short, between 1856–1921, and particularly after 1880, the majority of Irish emigrants were Catholics from the three southern provinces, especially Munster and Connacht and from the poorest rural districts where peasant folkways and attenuated Gaelic culture survived. In terms of marketable skills, most were mere laborers and servants who carried little, if any, capital and whose emigration were financed by remittances from abroad. In addition, most were quite young, in their teens or early twenties; about half were females; few were married or travelling with parents.[1]

On the other hand, the pioneering work in Irish women's emigration by Hasia Diner, by Janet Nolan, and most recently by Donald Akenson have argued that emigration was not an exile but an opportunity, and that the choice to leave was a voluntary decision to opt for wider economic and social opportunities, particularly marriage opportunities, in North America.[2]

While scholars differ about the cause and character of postfamine emigration, they all have tended to regard the phenomenon as a single western journey across the Atlantic. While many emigrants left intending to return, Miller estimates that only about 10 percent actually returned, and that their return prompted more emigration.[3]

Among the returners were the self-dowered daughters who went to America to earn their own fortunes and who returned to Ireland intending to marry. Their plan to return to Ireland after a specific time, usually about six years, marks these women as *sojourners* rather than emigrants or exiles.[4] That these young women earned their own money gave them an independence in a countryside of arranged marriages. It also gave them the alternative of returning to a wider, freer marriage market in America. This essay will examine those who recrossed the Atlantic: those who returned intending to settle, those who returned for reasons of health or unemployment, and those who returned only to visit.

In his account of his ramble in the Congested Districts with Jack B. Yeats in 1905, John Millington Synge described a conversation with a local man about the self-dowered girls who had returned to the Mayo countryside near Swinford.

> "All the girls in this place," he said, "are going out to America when they are about seventeen years old. Then they work there for six years or more, till they grow weary of that fixed kind of life, with the early rising and the working late, and they do come home with a little stocking of fortune with them, and they do be tempting the boys with their chains and their rings, till they get a husband and settle down in this place. Such a lot of them is coming now there is hardly a marriage made in the place that the woman hasn't been in America."[5]

In his autobiography *Feamainn Bhealtaine,* the Aran poet Máirtín Ó Direáin described the pattern of girls working in America before marriage as he knew in his boyhood on the island:

> Ní raibh máthair clainne da bhaile nár caith seal éigin i Meiriceá. Chloisinn féin cuid mhaith cainte uatha ar Boston, ar Dorchester, ar Woburn agus áiteanna eile tráth a mbídís cruinnithe cois tine. Bhí an oiread eolais acu no cathracha céanna is bhí acu ar Ghaillimh. Déarfainn go raibh agus níos mór. Ní bheadh eolas ar bith ag a leithéidí ar Baile Atha Cliath ná ar aon chathair i Sasana an tráth úd.[6]

> (There wasn't a mother in the village who hadn't spent some time in America. We would hear a good bit of talk about Boston, Dorchester, and Woburn, and other places when we would be gathered around the fire. They knew as much about those cities as they knew about Galway. I would say, even more. They didn't have any idea about Dublin or the cities in England at that time.)

We find examples of the custom of the self-dowered returners in Ulster and Leinster as well as in the high emigration provinces of Munster and Connacht. A County Longford manuscript in the collection of the Department of Irish Folklore at University College, Dublin, recalls a local returner to the midlands:

> One of these Reillys, Maria, went to the States about seventy years ago and came home after a certain length of time and married a man named John Mollaghan, in the townland of Clonelly, parish of Dromard, in North Longford. She had made enough money to enable her to make a good match. She had literally made her fortune (in the sense of dowery) and then she came home to marry.[7]

That in some places the gent went to the highest bidder can be demonstrated by the story "A Westmeath Farmer's Wooing," which reported that a local man reneged on a made match to marry a woman whose fortune was thirty pounds greater.[8]

The tradition of self-dowering went on through the 1920s. Two women who came to America in 1926 reported that they emigrated to make their fortunes in order to return home to marry. Lily McLoughlin came from Westmeath at seventeen to earn her fortune of five hundred pounds, but decided, in the end, to marry an Irishman in New York. Mary O'Riordan came home with her fortune in 1936 after ten years in America. There was a certain interest in her, for Mary said, "[m]arrying a Yank was the goal of some of the local lads"; however, after having been taken to meet a local farmer, she opted to return to America.[9]

While local men were unequivocal about American-made fortunes, their attitude toward those women who returned was more complicated. When such women were regarded as successful, they could be enlisted to support local and national causes. Tomás O'Concannon, the *muinteoir taistil* or traveling organizer in County Clare for the Gaelic League, an organization that was generally opposed to emigration, cited the positive influence of two returners who joined one of O'Concannon's Irish classes:

> Two young girls just returned from America were amongst the pupils. Their presence helped greatly to encourage the others as they had come

back to their native place from a sojourn in the land of Stars and Stripes with an increased love for their country and their language.[10]

Part of the aura of success around the returner may have been her increased self-confidence and self-esteem. Even before the famine, the American traveler Asenath Nicholson noticed that time in America was a transforming experience for young Irish women.

> I had noticed throughout all Ireland when a servant girl returns from America that a great change is evident in dress, manner and language. She ceases to become a beast of burden, and the basket on her back, which she then throws off, she will never lift again. She confines her services more to the inside of the cabin and this undergoes a manifest change for the better.[11]

In her insightful essay "The Real Molly Macree," Margaret Mac-Curtain has analyzed the difference between the iconography of the Irish colleen and the reality of her life working as an unpaid servant or agricultural laborer in rural Ireland in the nineteenth century.[12] It appears the returners were able to mediate that difference and often were able to manage their lives so that they could use the skills they had acquired in America to improve the quality of their lives. Synge too noticed the difference between the girls at home and the girls who had been out to America. He described a young woman he had met on the train in West Kerry. They talked of politics and of art. In contrast, he observed, the sisters who saw her off were in bare feet with shawls over their heads.[13]

In rural communities that value hierarchial structure and the welfare of the group over that of the individual, the independence and autonomy of returners—with fortunes of their own and with experiences negotiating in a wider world—could be threatening. Their exploits were often memorable and the subject of local folklore. For example, there was the story told on the Blaskets of the woman who armed herself with an American fortune to protect the interests of her son.

Tomás Ó Crohan's sister Máire was widowed after one year of marriage. When one of her husband's brothers returned to live with her in-laws, Máire took her infant son and moved back with her own people. Her husband's people would give her nothing for the child's support. She left the boy with her parents and went off to America for three years. When she returned with her earnings, she took her in-laws to court and got her son's share.[14] When we think of stories like Frank O'Connor's "Peasants," "In the Train," and "The Majesty of the Law" that describe the social ostracism of one whose goes outside of traditional community methods of conflict resolution to take a grievance to the law, Máire Ní Crohan's actions are all the more remarkable.

The success and independence of women who returned from America certainly encouraged other spirited young women to think about spending their own share of time in America, but along with those self-made women returners were those who came back with their health broken or with little or no success in the American job market. The mother in Pádraig na Leine's (Pádraig O'Seaghdha) "Cailín Groidhe Gaedhealach" warns her daughter not to be taken in by the gold chains of returned Yanks. She suggests that they are really a kind of fool's gold, the slave's chains of a life of joyless drudgery.[15]

Illness and death developed as metaphors for the danger to girls of life in America. Charles Kickham's ballad "The Irish Peasant Girl" better known by its opening lines, "She lived beside the Anner / At the foot of Slievenamon" ends with death in America; however, it was the Irish girl returned home sick or dying who supplied the cautionary tale.

The heroine of J. M. Croft's ballad "Noreen Bawn" returns home to Donegal to die of consumption. Like Kickham's heroine, Noreen was an idealized colleen—pretty, gentle, and generous, popular in her own place—whose life was destroyed in America. Lorcan Ua Tuatháil's 1907 play *An Deoraidhe* (The Exile) with its subtitle *Dráma in aghaidh Imtheachda thar Sáile* (A Play against Emigration) describes a dying woman who returns to her own townland not only to warn of the poverty that awaits young people in America but also to give the young pair the money to stay in Ireland.[16] While she cannot save herself, she will save others, and her gesture is very much in keeping with the literary character of the self-sacrificing Irish servant girl.

Perhaps the most poignant description of the young woman who returned from America to die is Tomás Ó Crohan's recollection of the funeral of the daughter of Big Daly who had been mentioned as a match for Tomás himself before she went off to America. Her coffin was brought across the sea from Inishvickillaun accompanied by eighteen boats—the largest sea funeral he had ever seen. That image of the flotilla of black island canoes on the Blasket Sound is more than a moving tribute to Daly's daughter; it mourns the death of all Irish emigrant girls.[17]

In addition to the self-dowered young women who returned intending to marry and those who returned for the unhappy reasons of poor health or employment difficulties (especially during the American depression) the rest of the returners were visitors. Donald Cole gives some sense of how feasible it was to go home to Ireland for a visit in *Immigrant City,* his study of Lawrence, Massachusetts, a city with a large settlement of Irish. He writes that by 1912, one-sixth of all immigrant workers in Lawrence had made a trip home, and about one-third of those who had been in America ten years had made such a trip.[18]

While American letters and especially photographs from those who emigrated were intriguing to young people at home, nothing could match the excitement of the returner's visit. There were gifts like the gramophone, one of two for fifty miles, brought to Cloonfad, County Roscommon in 1927. (Readers familiar with Brian Friel's *Dancing at Lughnasa* will remember the significance of the wireless, which marked the year 1939 for the narrator.)

There were dances and gatherings and often some lavish spending by the Yanks, especially the male returner whose deep pockets were the measure of his success. Padraig Óg Ó Conaire's 1930 novel *Éan Cuideáin* describes a schoolboy's visit to a neighbor's house where a daughter home from America is holding court:

> Ag teacht abhaile dó bhuail sé isteach tí Mháire Nora, leis an bPuncán a fheiceáil . . . Bhí an chistineach lán roimhe, agus bhí roinnt eile ag teacht . . . í ag trácht ar chlaoine a bhí thall, agus acu sin ag strácádh leis an saol, cuid eile ag cur maoil a charráin airgid gan caint ar an éadáil a chuiridís abhaile a gcóir na siopadóirí fa Nollaig.[19]

> (Coming home he went to Máire Nora's house to see the Puncán . . . The kitchen was full and others were coming . . . she was talking about the family members who were in America, and those who were struggling with life and those who were making money not to speak of the riches they were sending home to the shopkeepers for Christmas.)

In the passage, the returner is called a Puncán, the Irish word for a Yankee.[20] Ó Conaire uses the word descriptively not pejoratively;

however as Philip O'Leary demonstrates in *The Prose Literature of the Gaelic Revival, 1891–1921,* the term carried with it certain criticism or ambivalence that suggested some of the complexity of the relationship between returned visitors and their family and friends at home.

A story called "An Puncán agus an Ghealach Mór" (The Yank and the Big Moon) describes a young woman who returns to Ireland to find fault with everything. Finally, when she is shown the moon, she dismisses it saying, "The moons you got here in Ireland, they ain't no good."[21] An essay by Séamus Ó Dubhghaill called "The Yankee" (1903) further ridicules the Puncánaí for their superior airs:

There's another group, people who think a great deal of themselves whom I don't have much respect for—the Puncáin—the Yankees. They speak through their noses and you would think with their hustle that they owned all of America and that the sun rose out of America.[22]

Ridicule, the usual form of social control, gives way to hostility in the *Weekly Freeman's* 1904 editorial, "I bhFochair na nGaedhal":

. . . pride and bad conduct send a big share of today's young people overseas. They're not there long until pretentiousness and vanity send them back, without a word in their mouths but Yankee English. The ignorant Gael who comes back after a couple of years in America is among the most dangerous enemies we have today. He is an enemy of our faith, an enemy of our heritage and our native land.[23]

In a 1932 letter from the Great Blasket, Éilís Ní Shuilleabháin wrote in praise of Pat Kearney's daughter saying she would not say the same about every returner.

There's a youth in Pat Kearney's now. His eldest daughter is home with the last two weeks. I don't know will you see her. The Yank would have plenty of English to give you this time anyway. She is a very nice girl. I like her although it is not every Yank I would like.[24]

There was ambivalence for the returner as well as about her. Consider for a moment what it would have been like for the young Irish woman to return from Brooklyn to rural Ireland in 1898 or 1908. First, there were the creature comforts: running water, gas light, and work indoors made easier by modern conveniences. While it may have been a tiny space in a stuffy attic, she had a roof of her own and it was dry.

If she lived in Brooklyn Heights, Carroll Gardens, or Park Slope, there were gardens and tree-lined streets and the expanse of Prospect Park a walk away. There were parish activities in the expanding Brooklyn diocese; there was a vibrant Irish community whose organizations sponsored picnics and dances where she could meet friends from home. She could stroll and shop. New York was across the river, and for a nickel, she could take the streetcar to Coney Island.

Most of all there was a measure of privacy, independence, and autonomy that was not possible in the poverty and patriarchy of rural Ireland. Paradoxically, nowhere did her independence and autonomy reveal themselves more than in her decision whether to settle in Ireland in a self-dowered match or to leave again for America. Whatever the dynamics of the decision to make her first voyage out, the decision to stay or go, when she returned, was hers.

For most returners, the decision to stay or go was not an easy one. Against the easier life, the financial independence, and the freedom that America offered were the compelling claims of family and community, the comfort of custom, and the intimacy of place. One informant who emigrated in 1936 and returned ten years later, spoke of standing silently with her mother each night in the doorway of their cottage overlooking Greatman's Bay. She knew her mind, that she would return to Boston and marry a Lettermore man she had met at a party on Beacon Hill, but the wrench of parting was so painful that she vowed, like other women I have interviewed, that she would never return to Ireland again.[25]

Whatever her decision, the young woman who returned home to settle or returned home to visit had to redefine herself in terms of her Irish home and family. If she stayed, she had to negotiate new work and social roles. If she returned to Ireland planning to stay and then decided to go back to America, she had to shift from the role of a sojourner to the role of a settler and take on, or take up again, the responsibilities of the American-based members of Irish kinship groups.

What do we know about the women who went back to the United States after having returned to visit or to resettle in Ireland? These are the women that the United States Immigration Service classified as non-immigrant aliens. There is data available in the passenger records about this group. In a sample of the 1,488 women aboard the Cunard and White Star liners that called at Queenstown in April 1898, 186 (12.5 percent) were non-immigrant aliens (table 1).

Table 1. Non-Immigrant Alien Women Returning to the United States from Queenstown, April 1898

Ship	Total Females	Returners	Percentage
Majestic	190	21	11
Campania	201	30	14.9
Umbria	122	17	13.9
Teutonic	407	46	11.3
Germanic	309	29	9.3
Lucania	259	43	16.6
Totals	1488	186	12.5

To take just one example, the Cunard liner *Campania* arrived at the port of New York on 16 April 1898, with 201 Irish women who boarded at Queenstown. Within that cohort were thirty women (14.9 percent) who were non-immigrant aliens. Twenty-eight of the thirty (93.33 percent) were unmarried, a figure slightly higher that the 91.54 percent figure for all of the Queenstown Irish women passengers.

The mean age of the non-immigrant aliens was twenty-five; they had spent an average of four years in America before returning to Ireland. A female sponsor in America was identified for 58.62 percent; 37.93 percent indicated they were going back to a sister in America.

The geographical distribution of non-immigrant aliens on the *Campania* replicates the geographical pattern established in other immigration studies, which locate the heaviest emigration from Connacht and Munster; however, the ships' records allow for an analysis of patterns within the region. The *Campania* data is interesting in showing that it is Roscommon, not Mayo, that leads the list of counties from which the non-immigrant aliens return.

In terms of human geography, the most sobering figure in the April 1898 records are the lists of the young women leaving in scores from towns and villages in east Mayo. If you were to draw a line from Ballina in the north east to Ballaghadereen (part of Mayo until the

Local Government Act of 1898 ceded the town to Roscommon), then south to Claremorris and west to Castlebar, the diamond-shaped area would enclose the towns of Foxford, Swinford, and Ballyhaunis, and smaller places like Kiltimagh and Balla. From this area in one month (April 1898), from one port (Queenstown), and on two companies of liners (White Star and Cunard), 342 young women left for America.

This small sample of 1,488 records is the beginning of a larger examination of passenger records in order to explore the conditions that contributed to the differences in regional numbers. What can be said for the moment is that there was more than usual deprivation and poverty in East Mayo in the spring of 1898. In December 1897, a priest told John Dillon who was M.P. for East Mayo that in the mountains beyond Kiltimagh, he did not remember such conditions since 1847 and that some five hundred of the eight hundred families in his parish would be desolate after Christmas.[26]

We know that in January 1898 the United Irish League was founded, with the intention of implementing local programs to move people to better land. We know that there were efforts made to improve the local economy by institutions like the Congested District Board, and by individuals like Mother Agnes Morrogh Bernard, who founded the Foxford Woolen Mill in May 1892. (A measure of its success is that Foxford had the lowest number of emigrants [2.63 percent] in the April 1898 cohort.) We know that land use was being shifted from tillage to grazing. Finally, we know that, with the landlord buyouts resulting from the Wyndham Act, longing for land was realized and would require cash from the only available source—from American remittances.

One might well ask whether the April 1898 profile of non-immigrant alien women holds over a longer term. Looking at comparable figures [table 2] from April 1908 (port of Queenstown, White Star and Cunard liners), the first thing to say is that the percentage of non-immigrant aliens nearly doubles from 12.5 to 23.91 percent in the sample of 983 Irish women.

Taking the first April sailing of the *Oceanic* as an example because it has the largest number of returners, we find that the mean age of the returners was 27.14, slightly higher than the 25.9 mean age of their 1898 non-immigrant alien counterparts. There were almost four times as many married women (23.81 percent) among the non-

Table 2. Non-Immigrant Alien Women Returning to the United States
from Queenstown, April 1908

Ship	Total Females	Returners	Percentage
Mauretania	69	20	28.98
Etruria	88	17	19.31
Baltic	142	43	30.28
Adriatic	92	21	27.83
Oceanic	51	21	41.00
Caronia	59	13	26.99
Lucania	61	15	21.31
Umbria	63	18	30.15
Cedric	64	12	35.55
Oceanic	179	25	13.96
Carminia	115	30	8.69
Totals	983	235	23.91

immigrant aliens in the 1908 *Oceanic* group as compared with the
1898 *Campania* group.

We see the very beginning of some diversity of occupation among
the non-immigrant aliens: a nurse and a couple of candy-makers;
however, what is more important is the differentiation between types
of domestic service. Housekeeper now appears as an occupation for
single non-immigrant aliens, where it had been used exclusively to
describe the occupation of married women. There is a listing for a
cook and for a waitress. These designations suggest a professionalization of domestic service, and they demonstrate that there was some
opportunity for mobility, however limited.

Geographically, Mayo continues to dominate the county lists of the
entire 1908 cohort, but there appears to be a shift from a concentration in East Mayo to areas in the western part of the county: the Erris
peninsula, Achill, and Malleranny.

The pattern of non-immigrant aliens continues to be remarkably
stable through the 1920s and 1930s. Looking at just one sample from
May 1938, 57 percent of the twenty women who sailed from Cobh
on the *Washington* were non-immigrant aliens. The mean age of the
entire cohort was 35.7. Mayo leads the county lists, as usual (21
percent), followed by Kerry and Sligo (14.4 percent each), but for the
first time Dublin appears in the top five counties, with 14.4 percent of

Table 3. Akenson Model with a Sample of 1898 and 1908 Women Passengers

Class/Percentage		1898 Data (N = 1796)	1908 Data (N = 1156)
Widow, children	1.5	0.67%	1.29%
Married, children	11.5	0.67%	1.38%
Married, no children	7.0	.9%	2.16%
Dependent females	15.21	2.5%	5.9%
Single females, 15–35	50.5	93.43%	84.1%
Single females, 35 +	.5	.5%	2.0%

the female passengers: new immigrants as well as non-immigrant aliens. The non-immigrant aliens with a mean age of thirty spent an average of eight years working in the United States. Among the women going to America for the first time, 75 percent had their passage paid by a sister and 100 percent were going to a sister.

While these samples are small, they do say much that is new. For example, using the classification system conceptualized by D. H. Akenson for Irish women's emigration in 1870, categories that he argues "represent the six most fundamental ways in which emigration fits into the life cycle of Irish women," and comparing it with the 1898 date (1,796 cases) and the 1908 data (1,156 cases), the results are predictable (table 3).[27]

An Irish female emigration pattern that is predominantly an emigration of single women 15–25 has been well established in the literature, so this classification system does not tell us much about the complexities of the single women group. The band is too narrow and is based on the usual male-centered interpretation of the immigration data.

When we look at the same numbers with the classification system that Deirdre Mageean developed in "Nineteenth-century Irish emigration: a case study using passenger lists," the numbers become more interesting.[28] Mageean developed a system of immigration patterns based on whether the immigrant traveled alone or as a member of one or another kind of group:

1. Individuals
2. Nuclear family: woman traveling with husband and children
3. Family: One adult (generally a woman) plus one or more children, generally women and children

4. Same name: Two people sharing a common surname without overt kinship or marital relationship
5. Married: Woman traveling with husband, no children
6. Extended: Group with kinship relationships extending beyond the nuclear family
7. Group: Individuals (often from the same area) traveling together but where there is no evident kinship relationship
8. Other: Groups that cannot be otherwise assigned

Applying Mageean's system to a small cohort of 105 returners who traveled on three ships in April 1898, the numbers open up (table 4). Mageean's analysis suggests that there are differences within the category of the 15–35-year-old single female. It further suggests that, as a social phenomenon, Irish female emigration was an emigration of siblings and cousins. (In terms of reciprocal responsibilities in the Irish countryside, cousins would be treated as siblings.)

Looking at the data of the non-immigrant alien women, we can see something of the dynamic that occurred between those returning and their emigrating siblings and cousins. Naturally, the non-immigrating aliens often acted as escorts and mentors for the emigrants. For many, the role was an extension of the nurturing role of the older sister who often assumed responsibility for younger siblings. That older females —sisters, cousins, aunts, and even older friends—would take responsibility for emigrants was consistent with the notion of *cóir,* or right (in the sense of obligation), and these duties—guiding, passage-paying, and initially supporting the new arrival—involved self-sacrifice.

Table 4. Mageean Model with a Sample of 1898 Women Passengers' Data

Category	Campania N = 30	Teutonic N = 46	Germanic N = 29
Individuals	15 (50.0%)	20 (43.5%)	10 (36.2%)
Nuclear family	1 (3%)	0 (0.0%)	2 (6.8%)
Family	0	3 (6.5%)	2 (6.8%)
Same name	7 (23.33%)	8 (17.4%)	3 (10.3%)
Married	0	0	1 (3.44%)
Extended	4 (13.3%)	4 (8.7%)	2 (6.8%)
Group	3 (10.0%)	11 (23.9%)	9 (31.0%)
Other	0	0	0

In addition to family and community mores, folklore and literature reinforced the values of sisters self-sacrificing for siblings, and warned that success did not come without pain. The folktale "The Girl Who Seeks Her Brother," a story collected widely in Mayo and Galway, describes the adventures of a sister, the youngest in the family, whose twelve brothers have been banished or transformed through circumstances associated with her birth.

The sister sets off to rescue her brothers. Her quest requires that she be courageous and clever. She must make twelve shirts out of bog cotton that she has gathered herself. Her charge also demands self-sacrifice and self-control. She must remain silent, for if she utters a word, her brothers are doomed. In most versions of the tale, she is courted by a prince, marries him, and has his children. The children either disappear or seem to be murdered; she is charged with the crime, but she refuses to speak in her defense and is sentenced to death.[29]

In the end, the sister finishes the last stitch on the last of the twelve shirts as the bonfire is lit for her execution. Shirts completed, the spell is broken and order restored. Máire Mac Neill has pointed out the popularity, in the Irish countryside, of folktales with themes involving restoration of the rightful kingdom; and this tale—especially the Patrick Kennedy version in *Fireside Stories of Ireland* (1870), reprinted by W. B. Yeats in *Fairy and Folk Tales of the Irish Peasantry* (1888)—was widely distributed.[30] There is no doubt that, at the turn of the century, a story about princes transformed into wild geese who are eventually returned to their own land and family carried a political message.

What is important about this story? Bruno Bettleheim, in *The Uses of Enchantment*, described stories involving ego control, stories demonstrating that self-sacrifice makes a return to order possible.[31] This story—of the girl in search of her brothers—reflects values of sibling loyalty and cooperation and, because the girl's brothers are enchanted and her prince/husband is unaware of the reality of her circumstances, of female empowerment.

The story argues that a young woman, on her own, can save the male members of her family. It does not differentiate between female and male ability to act independently and be successful in achieving a goal. This lack of gender difference is consistent with the findings of

Arensberg and Kimball that, in the west Clare rural society of the 1930s, sons and daughters were equally subordinate and no formal gender distinctions were made, particularly among non-inheriting/un-dowered siblings.[32]

This tale is an appropriate one in a culture expecting girls to sup-port—at considerable self-sacrifice—siblings of both genders. On this point it is important to consider the spiritual context of that sacrifice and to observe that immigration historians have generally neglected this dimension of immigrant lives—especially regarding women. Here, it is interesting to compare the differences in Kerby Miller's and Mar-garet MacCurtain's readings of the passage in Peig Sayers's autobiog-raphy explaining her refusal of a paid passage to America. While Miller mentions Peig's belief that she would be "more favored with grace" if she stayed to comfort her elderly mother, he suggests that her decision was largely a socially determined one: the greater claims of family. For MacCurtain, Peig's decision was imagined in the context of a distinct Irish spirituality.[33]

That older sisters shepherded and sheltered their siblings, cousins, and young neighbors across the Atlantic conjures the literary image of Fionnuala, the only daughter in "The Exile of the Children of Lir." Unlike the girl in search of her brothers, Fionnuala has the power of speech, and it is she who confronts her stepmother and negotiates the terms of the children's enchantment. She explains the predicament to their father, and it is her voice that articulates the desolation of their exile and that counsels her brothers to draw on faith to endure their suffering.

What I call the Fionnuala factor is Fionnuala's ability to not only protect her siblings, but, realizing the dissolution of her nuclear family, to reimagine a complete family unit in terms of her siblings. Separated during their term of exile in the Mull of Cantyre, she rejoices when first her brother Conn, and then Fiachra, appears. Warming Fiachra under her wings, she says, "[i]f only Aed would come, we would be without complaint."[34]

For the Irish immigrant woman, re-formation of the sibling unit, or a portion of it, was not an obligation, but *the* way to reimagine the family unit in America; settlement and socializing patterns of siblings and cousins demonstrate that these units were the core of Irish immi-grant women's lives in America. By reforming the family unit, it may have been possible to reframe one's life in terms of something other than exile.

Notes

1. Kerby A. Miller, *Emigrants and Exiles: Ireland and the Irish Exodus to America* (New York: Oxford University Press, 1985), 353.

2. See Hasia R. Diner, *Erin's Daughters in America* (Baltimore: Johns Hopkins University Press, 1983); Janet A. Nolan, *Ourselves Alone: Women's Emigration from Ireland, 1885–1920* (Lexington: University of Kentucky Press, 1989); and Donald Akenson, *The Irish Diaspora: A Primer* (Toronto: P.D. Meany, 1994).

3. Miller, *Emigrants and Exiles,* 426.

4. In her study of Irish immigration to the United States in the 1980s, Mary P. Corcoran makes the useful distinction between sojourner and settler. *Irish Illegals: Transients between Two Societies* (Westport: Greenwood Press, 1993), 35–36.

5. John Millington Synge, "The Inner Land of Mayo," *Collected Works II, Prose,* ed. Alan Price (London: Oxford University Press, 1966), 330.

6. Máirtín Ó Direáin, "Súil Thar Muir," *Feamainn Bhealtaine* (Baile Atha Cliath: An Clóchomhar, 1961): 27–28.

7. Manuscript 1430 (Department of Irish Folklore, University College, Dublin), 201.

8. *Longford Independent* (8 January 1912): 3.

9. Interview with Lily McLoughlin (Stuart, Fla., 10 November 1994). Interview with Mary O'Riordan Neary and Maureen Benzing, "The Greenhorn," *Irish Edition* (March 1983): 3.

10. Tomás O'Concannon, "The Organizer in Clare," *An Claidheamh Soluis* 1 (18 Samhain [Nov.] 1899): 565.

11. Asenath Nicholson, *Ireland's Welcome to the Stranger or, Excursions through Ireland in 1844 and 1845 for the Purposes of Investigating the Conditions of the Poor* (London: Gilpin, 1847), 318.

12. Margaret MacCurtain, "The Real Molly Macree," in *Visualizing Ireland. National Identity and the Pictorial Tradition,* ed. Adele Dalsimer (Boston: Faber and Faber, 1993), 9–21.

13. Synge, "The Inner Land of Mayo," 269.

14. Tomás Ó Crohan, *The Islandman* (London: Oxford University Press, 1951), 21.

15. Philip O'Leary, *The Prose Literature of the Gaelic Revival, 1881–1921: Ideology and Innovation* (University Park: Pennsylvania State University Press, 1994), 151, n.200.

16. Ibid., 149.

17. O'Crohan, *The Islandman,* 187–88.

18. Donald Cole, *Immigrant City, Lawrence, Massachusetts 1845–1921* (Chapel Hill: University of North Carolina Press, 1963), 100.

19. Micheál O Conghaile, *Conamara agus Arainn 1880–1980: Gnéithe den Stair Shoisialta.* (Béal an Daingin: Cló Iar-Chonnachta, 1988), 212.

20. The word Puncán is the name of a Massachusetts coastal tribe; however, in a note in *An Claidheamh Soluis agus Fáinne an Lae* 3 (20 November 1901): 293, the word is glossed as the Yankee name given to Indians in Massachusetts.

21. O'Leary, *Prose Literature,* 150.

22. Ibid., 152.

23. Ibid., 151.

24. Eibhlís Ní Shúilleabháin, *Letters from the Great Blasket* (Cork: Mercier, 1979), 46.

25. Interview with Cáit Ní Fhlathartiagh (Dorchester, Massachusetts, 18 November 1994).

26. F. S. L. Lyons, *John Dillon: A Biography* (Chicago: University of Chicago Press, 1968), 180.

27. Akenson, *The Irish Diaspora,* 172.

28. Deirdre M. Mageean, "Nineteenth-Century Irish Emigration: A Case Study Using Passenger Lists," in *Irish Studies 4. The Irish in America: Emigration, Assimilation and Impact,* ed. P. J. Drudy (London: Cambridge University Press, 1985), 52–53.

29. The requirement for silence is an interesting detail. Angela Bourke has pointed out how silence is used as a weapon by those who have been marginalized by society. Legends of women "taken" in childbirth often describe how those who returned were able to come back because they remained silent; others were silenced in various ways after the experience. See Lady Gregory, *Visions and Beliefs in the West of Ireland* (Gerrards Cross: Colin Smythe, 1970), 104–47. Finally, Nuala Ní Dhomhnaill's poem "Maighdean Mhara" (Mermaid) demonstrates the use of silence as the only weapon left to a mermaid caught above the highwater mark.

30. Máire Mac Neill, "Irish Folklore as a Source for Research," *Journal of the Folklore Institute* 2,3 (1965): 342.

31. Bruno Bettleheim, *The Uses of Enchantment* (New York: Vintage, 1977), 80.

32. Conrad Arensberg and Solon T. Kimball, *Family and Community in Ireland,* 2d ed. (Cambridge: Harvard University Press, 1968), 61.

33. Miller, *Emigrants and Exiles,* 475. Margaret MacCurtain, "Fullness of Life: Defining Irish Spirituality in Twentieth Century Ireland," in *Women Surviving: Studies in Irish Women's History in the 19th and 20th centuries,* ed. Maria Luddy and Clíona Murphy (Dublin: Poolbeg, 1989), 237–39.

34. Myles Dillon, "Oidheadh Clainne Lir," *Early Irish Literature* (Chicago: University of Chicago Press, 1948), 65.

MARY E. DALY

"Oh, Kathleen Ni Houlihan, Your Way's a Thorny Way!"

The Condition of Women in Twentieth-Century Ireland

THE GROWING interest in women's history in recent decades in Ireland, as elsewhere, is a direct outcome of the women's movement.[1] Olwen Hufton has remarked that "much has been written with a view to explaining the predicament of women in the twentieth century."[2] The writing of women's history has also been strongly influenced by women's studies, a discipline which Ailbhe Smyth has defined as "change-oriented, liberatory, enabling us to come to a more explicitly critical awareness of the material, social and cultural circumtances of our diversely lived lives."[3] Some volumes of essays, such as the 1995 special issue of the *Journal of Women's History,* contain contributions on women's history with papers that highlight the condition of women in contemporary Ireland,[4] as if to emphasize the continuity between past and present. However, this present-centered focus has led to an excessive preoccupation with matters that have concerned the feminist movement in recent decades: political representation, access to paid employment and equal pay, divorce, contraception, and abortion. These issues did not necessarily loom large in the lives of most Irish women in previous generations. In 1994, when a student at University College Dublin asked about the impact of the women's movement on the Irish Countrywomen's Association during the 1960s, one of the Association's members explained that access to running water was the primary concern of Irish rural women at that time. In particular, some of the historiography concerning Irish women has been unduly influenced by the fact that in the 1970s and 1980s, Irish women's access to divorce, contraception, and abortion lagged behind that of women in other developed countries. This has led to a tendency to project backwards a belief that the status afforded Irish women has, invariably, been markedly inferior to that of women elsewhere. Such analysis ignores the fact that during the 1930s the employment of married women in public service occupations was restricted in Britain, the United States, and Germany,[5] and that access to reliable contraception remained extremely limited until the 1960s, or 1970s, throughout much of Europe. Even the statistical data, which suggests that the proportion of Irish women engaged in the labor market was much lower than that of other European states, must be reconsidered.[6]

If the contemporary women's movement has given birth to Irish women's history, its practitioners have also been strongly influenced by the development of Irish history as an academic discipline. Modern Irish history, whether of the revisionist or anti-revisionist variety, has two conspicuous characteristics: a tendency to give primacy to political history, which has inevitably relegated women to a marginal role, and a strong belief in Irish exceptionalism.[7] Ronan Fanning, an acknowledged revisionist, has written:

> Nowhere else in the European, North American or antipodean democracies does the writing of twentieth-century history demand so constant a confrontation with mythologies designed to legitimise violence as a political weapon in a bid to overthrow the state.[8]

Meanwhile Brendan Bradshaw, the most vociferous academic critic of the revisionist position, refers to "the catastrophic dimension of Irish history."[9] Despite their widely differing views, both Fanning and Bradshaw paint a picture of Irish history as unique, atypical whether in the centrality of its violence, or of its catastrophic dimensions. Although Fanning would probably shudder at being bracketed with those who view modern Ireland as a postcolonial society,[10] he suggests that the nearest parallels to the issues that confront historians of twentieth-century Ireland lie in the Middle East. By definition, the history of every nation is unique; however, while being aware of this truism, it remains important not to lose sight of the extent to which developments in different societies follow similar paths. In their emphasis on Irish uniqueness, both Fanning and Bradshaw have fallen into the trap of seeing the Anglo-American experience as the norm, and of assuming that anything outside this is somehow exceptional.[11]

Irish women's history has suffered from a similar assumption—that the problems confronting Irish women have been somehow unique;

this reflects both the impact of Irish academic history, and the fact
that many of the first books and essays from the modern wave of
women's history to reach Ireland focused primarily on the attainment
of equal rights for women in politics, education, and economic life. In
particular, R. J. Evans's linking of feminism with liberal Protestant-
ism,[12] implicitly consigned a predominantly Catholic society, such as
Ireland, to the status of a feminist backwater. This viewpoint, of
course, was sympathetically received by many women who were involved in contemporary campaigns, where the demands of the wom-
en's movement for divorce or contraception came into direct conflict
with the teachings of the Catholic Church. It was also in keeping
with the prevailing gloomy view of post-independence Ireland as a
conservative, Catholic, and rural society, that had proved stifling both
to liberal intellectual thought,[13] and to women's rights. That political
independence was marked by a decline in the status of women has
almost become a truism. What is more interesting is the link posited
by some writers between partition and the declining status of women.
Jenny Beale emphasizes the baleful effect of partition on Irish women's
lives,[14] though the inference that the condition of women in Northern
Ireland was markedly superior to that in the Irish Free State seems, at
best, a dubious proposition, and one that fails to acknowledge the fact
that the views of many unionist politicians on matters such as divorce
or abortion, are virtually identical to those expressed by the Catholic
Church.[15] Margaret Ward noted that "[w]ith no organisation to give
priority to women's needs, post-partition Ireland was able to implement, with little resistance, highly reactionary policies in relation to
women, whose domestic role within the family became endowed with
almost sacramental qualities." Ward and many other writers link the
status of Irish women to "the confessional nature of the Irish state."[16]
Thus Catholicism, and the nature of Irish society—which is often
implicitly seen as uniquely conservative in comparison with other
western states—are presented as providing overarching explanations
for the plight of Irish women, whose condition is often implicitly
assumed to be markedly inferior to that of women elsewhere. This is
not to deny that Catholic social teaching viewed women primarily as
wives and mothers, and that it reiterated the message that women's
work should ideally take place either within the home or within its
immediate vicinity.[17] However, such views were not monopolized by

the Roman Catholic church: as James McMillan suggests in the case of nineteenth-century France, the belief that a woman's place lay in the home was widely held both by the Catholic Church and by those who were the church's most vocal opponents: anti-clerical republicans, anarchists, and leaders of the labor movement.[18] Betty Friedan has shown that such views were also common to large numbers of American college-educated women and men in the decade after World War II.[19]

This tendency to concentrate on campaigns for women's suffrage, or access to secondary and university education, and on the role and attitudes of an educated elite of laywomen, led to the neglect of some important aspects of the history of Irish women.[20] As a recent article by Margaret MacCurtain has shown, the achievements of many notable Irish women in the past were less "hidden from history" than we have perhaps recognized; rather, if they were hidden, they were often hidden in dusty books that lay unread on Irish library shelves. Most of the works in question recounted the lives and achievements of pioneering religious women, such as Mother Arsenius, the founder of the Foxford woollen mills, the lives of the Poor Clares nuns or the story of Nano Nagle, founder of the Presentation sisters.[21] Such women did not fit easily within the equal-rights feminist paradigm and hence were excluded from consideration.[22] The only essay to focus on the topic of women and religion in the pioneering book of essays on Irish women's history: *Women in Irish Society,* Joseph Lee's "Women and the Church since the Famine," concentrates on the role of the Church in reinforcing the post-famine demographic pattern of fewer and later marriages, rather than on the contribution made to post-famine Irish society by the growing number of female religious.[23]

Similarly the assumption of British Census takers that productive labor carried out by women within the factory or the office was worthy of being counted, whereas the contribution made by women within the family economy could safely be ignored—though the contribution of men working in a similar setting was invariably counted —means that Irish occupational data has seriously underestimated the contribution made by women who were engaged in the family economy.[24] To their credit the Irish Census Commissioners in 1871 not only counted the number of farmers' wives and shoemakers' wives who were engaged in the family business (something never done since); they also protested, though in vain, that the English method of recording occupational data, which they were forced to implement, was inappropriate.[25] After independence the Irish Registrar-General's Office, and its successor, the Central Statistics Office went some way to remedying this under-recording of women's work by including female relatives, other than wives, engaged in agriculture in the occupied labor force. The 1926 Census also created a nebulous category of women "engaged in home duties," though they were not included in the occupied labor force, and though only one woman, "engaged in home duties," was permitted in a household of six and under—regardless of the reality. If, however, the Irish Census of Population had followed the practice that applied in France, where farmers' wives were regularly counted as part of the occupied workforce, the proportion of Irish women in the labor force would have been very similar to the proportion in Britain.[26]

Thus, until recently, Irish women's history has usually been analyzed from a perspective that has led to an excessive emphasis on the uniqueness of the Irish experience,[27] and to an underestimation of the important contribution of Irish women.

Olwen Hufton has noted that "[m]uch of the writing in women's history emanating from the Anglo-Saxon tradition since the sixties has been focused on change, and, more specifically, on change for the worse. It is a saga of discontinuity or of 'descent from paradise'."[28] Irish history offers us a number of prelapsarian golden, or quasi-golden ages: Gaelic Ireland under the Brehon Laws where, according to Donncha Ó Corráin, "the position of a woman was made equal to a man in many respects";[29] prefamine Ireland, where women were engaged in a wide range of occupational activities, ranging from domestic spinning to weeding crops. Joseph Lee has asserted that "the Great Famine drastically weakened the position of women in Irish society. Before the Famine women's economic contribution was so essential to the family economy that they enjoyed considerable independence."[30] The Famine is widely regarded as ushering in a period of economic modernization and commercialization within Ireland. The idealization of women's roles in prefamine Ireland and the belief that the economic status of women declined in postfamine decades can be read as an Irish variant of the arguments advanced by English social historians, such as Alice Clark and Ivy Pinchbeck, concerning the impact of the industrial revolution on women's lives.[31] Ironically, the belief that the industrial revolution was detrimental to women's lives was apparently shared by Eamon de Valera. Catríona Clear claims that Eamon de Valera inserted article 41.2, of the 1937 constitution, the article recognizing the importance of women's roles within the home, "because he had been reading Ivy Pinchbeck's pioneering *Women Workers and the Industrial Revolution*, and feared that the appalling maternal ill health and infant mortality of early industrialisation might happen as a result of the industrialising drive of the 1930s."[32] Thus the article of the 1937 constitution to which feminists have repeatedly objected appears to have been prompted by the views expressed by a female historian writing about the lives of working women.

More immediately, as has been noted, the first two decades of the twentieth century are generally and justly regarded as a time when Ireland boasted an extremely active women's movement. After independence, however, the women's movement went into decline, due, allegedly, to the inhospitable climate found in the independent Irish state. Thus Frances Gardiner writes that "a budding feminist political consciousness was subsumed by nationalist hegemony" and is puzzled as to "why such a vibrant feminist political activism apparently atrophied after 1918."[33] Thus to the baleful effects of Catholicism and the famine, many writers have added the deadly embrace of Irish nationalism. In fact, we acknowledge that the Irish feminist movement was both precocious and successful, given that early twentieth-century Ireland was a predominantly agricultural and Catholic country. Indeed Irish political development as a whole can be regarded as being much more advanced than might be predicted from examining such socioeconomic indicators.[34] This is a reflection, both of Ireland's proximity to Britain—the British connection undoubtedly increased Irish political consciousness—and of the achievements of constitutional nationalists, such as Daniel O'Connell and Charles Stewart Parnell, in building strong political movements. The politicization of Irish men, via nationalist or indeed grassroots unionist movements[35] undoubtedly provided a valuable lesson for Irish women on the benefits of political organization, even if the Irish Parliamentary Party was unsympathetic to their cause. Equally, Irish women, both Catholic and Protestant, made significant gains in secondary and university education as a consequence of campaigns to provide better educational opportunities for Catholics.[36]

Although the Irish women's movement, as a political force, appears to have lost momentum after independence, this was equally true of the women's movement in the United States and in other European countries, particularly those where women obtained the franchise immediately after the end of World War I. This suggests that what happened to women in Ireland in the 1920s and 1930s is as much a reflection of international trends, as it is of the specific environment of the newly independent Irish state. The interwar years also saw the death or decline of many feminist organizations, particularly those that had concerned themselves with the suffrage question. In countries where women had won the vote, the focus shifted toward mainstream political parties. From 1916 onwards, many Irish feminists, most conspicuously Hanna Sheehy-Skeffington, became actively involved in Sinn Fein and in Cumann na mBan.[37] This can be regarded as tantamount to Irish women moving into the mainstream political movements of the period. They did so, both because an independent Ireland appeared to promise, and indeed delivered, formal political equality, and because, during this heady phase, Irish nationalism and unionism dwarfed all other political, social, and cultural movements. Tom Garvin argues that the uncompromising attitude shown by women within Sinn Fein to the Anglo-Irish Treaty gave rise to "the extreme male chauvinism exhibited by both male and female voters for a generation after the Civil War."[38] However, this statement presupposes that voters were presented with women candidates who were rejected in disproportionate numbers: there is no evidence to support this argument.

After 1922 women remained prominent within Sinn Fein. Cumann na mBan was the first organization to reject the Anglo-Irish Treaty; however, Sinn Fein's policy of abstaining from Dáil Éireann effectively condemned these women to a marginal political existence. Although Fianna Fáil attracted the more nationalist, and indeed, the more radical voices within Irish nationalism from 1926, most republican women remained with the declining Sinn Fein movement. Explanations for this phenomenon have tended to be couched in terms of women's irreconcilable views, and in their fidelity to the memory of dead heroes. Did a realization that the new party would be dominated by Eamon de Valera play a role in this decision? Constance Markievicz, a founding member of Fianna Fáil, was a notable exception, but she died in July 1927. Had she lived, would women have found a more prominent role within Fianna Fáil? This party offered much greater scope for political activism than any other, because of its extensive grassroots organization. Fianna Fáil's commitment to a program of government spending, which was designed to help the less well-off in Irish society, could conceivably have included measures designed to improve the welfare of women. By contrast, Cumann na nGaedheal had little to offer. The party was almost completely without a local organization, tending, rather, to rely on informal links with prosperous local business and professional men;[39] moreover it was committed to minimizing government expenditure on welfare. The Labour Party remained very much a minority party that tended to be dominated by the trade-union movement. Emmet O'Connor notes that "[t]he typical Labour TD *(Teachta Dála)* of the early intake was a union official, preoccupied with dwindling membership and wage rates."[40] Given the strong misogynistic tendencies that characterized organized labor, and the fact that, with the exception of the Irish Women Workers' Union, women played a very marginal role in the trade-union movement,[41] Labour offered few opportunities for women to engage in political life. However, we should beware of overemphasizing these points. Although the number of women deputies in the first three decades after independence may appear low, as Frances Gardiner has pointed out, in 1943 Ireland had a higher percentage of women in the lower house of parliament (the Dáil) than Iceland, Norway, or Denmark, though Scandinavian countries are often regarded as a reference point for pioneers of political equality. The proportion of women in Dáil Éireann in 1943 (2.2 percent) was greater than the proportion of women M.P.s elected to Westminster in 1935 (1.5 percent), the last election before the end of World War II.[42] Nor, as Maurice Manning has pointed out, was Ireland unique in having a disproportionate share of women TDs who were closely related to male politicians.[43]

The role of women in local government in the years before 1920 has received relatively little attention compared to that given the role of women in the nationalist movement or suffrage campaign.[44] Women appear to have been most active in the lesser bodies—Boards of Guardians, Urban and Rural District Councils, and on committees that included co-opted non-elected members, such as county tubercu-

losis committees. Public health and welfare, which were controlled by
Boards of Guardians and Rural District Councils (after 1898 membership of both bodies was, in practice, identical), were seen as appropriate
outlets for women's traditional roles as caregivers. Unfortunately, little
research has been carried out on Irish local government in general, so
we remain ignorant regarding the extent of the women's contribution.
That many of the first generation of women in local government—
such as Mrs. Dockrell, a member of Blackrock Urban District Council
—were unionists has probably contributed to this neglect. However,
there is sufficient evidence to suggest that they played an active role
and, moreover, that they continued to do so after the Sinn Fein take-
over of local government in 1920. Jenny Wyse-Power, a long-standing
member of Sinn Fein and Inghinidhe na hEireann, was appointed to
Dáil Éireann's Commission on Local Government in 1919. In January
1920 she was one of five women elected to serve on Dublin Corporation. In this capacity she subsequently served as chair of the Public
Health Committee, and as a member of the Technical Instruction
Committee and the management committee of the Richmond lunatic
asylum. When Dublin Corporation was suspended in 1924, she was
nominated by the Minister for Local Government and Public Health
as one of the three commissioners who were charged with running the
city.[45] Kathleen Clarke, the first woman to serve as lord mayor of
Dublin in 1939, is another example of a political activist, who spent
much of her career in local government, though Clarke was also a
member of both the Dáil and Seanad.[46] In County Offaly in 1920,
Mrs. Teresa Wyer, a Sinn Fein councillor was elected as chair of Tulla-
more Board of Guardians. Meanwhile Mrs. C. Fanning represented
Birr Board of Guardians in negotiations about the reorganization of
poor law services. Neither woman was in any sense a token figure;
indeed both were occasionally involved in acrimonious discussions
with fellow councillors and representatives of the Dáil Local Government Department.[47] The number of such case histories could be
multiplied through more local research. The abolition of Rural District Councils in 1924, and the reorganization of medical and welfare
services on a county basis resulted in a substantial reduction in the
number of elected local politicians, and undoubtedly reduced the
probability that women would chair local authorities. During the first
twenty years of the independent Irish state, many local authorities

were dissolved by both the Cumann na nGaedheal and the Fianna Fáil governments; local elections were postponed on many occasions; and power was increasingly transferred from elected representatives to professional managers, who were all male. These developments undoubtedly limited the political opportunities open to women within local government.[48]

Recent work on women in the interwar years has highlighted their involvement in " 'maternalist,' or 'relational,' 'welfare,' or 'social' feminism,' " though Gisela Bock and Pat Thane have warned of the dangers of assuming that there was "a clear political and chronological divide" between these movements and the feminist organizations that focused on equal rights, such as suffrage, or access to university education.[49] Research carried out by Catríona Clear indicates that organizations championing causes associated with second-wave feminism, or "social feminism" existed in Ireland. The National Council of Women, the Joint Committee of Women's Societies and Social Workers, the Catholic Federation of Women Secondary School Teachers, and the Irish County Women's Association were interested in the condition of "home-makers," and demanded support services such as baby-advice clubs, day nurseries, and some formal recognition of the contribution made by women who were engaged in voluntary work.[50]

Clear's article concentrates on the women's organizations that gave evidence to the Commission on Vocational Organisation, so her survey does not claim to be comprehensive. In 1919 there was a committee that lobbied for state pensions for necessitous mothers of orphans and other dependent children, though it appears to have had a largely male membership.[51] The Irish Housewives Association was founded in 1942 in response to wartime shortages; its campaigns, in favor of state provision of school meals for children, and for a range of consumer causes such as clean milk, suggest that it too should be classified with social feminist organizations.[52] Although other organizations probably remain to be rediscovered, the list appears slim in comparison with other countries, as does the contribution that they made toward shaping Irish social policy.

There is little evidence that women's organizations were influential in the introduction of Widows and Orphans Pensions in 1937. The debate on this measure in Dáil Éireann says little about the place of mothers in Irish society, except that widows with children were regarded as "deserving and helpless people."[53] The most sustained pressure for improvements in maternity and child health services, or for the provision of children's allowances, appears to have come from the medical profession, rather than from women's organizations. Article 41.2 of the 1937 Constitution, the article in which the State acknowledges the important role played by women within the home, does not appear to have been employed by any women's pressure group at the time to establish the case for mothers' pensions, or for any other social services.

And despite the upsurge of interest in social Catholicism during the interwar years, particularly following the publication, in 1931, of the papal encyclical *Quadragesimo Anno,* there was no Irish equivalent to the French social Catholic organizations, such as the *Union Feminine Civique et Sociale,* or the *Ligue de la Mère au Foyer.*[54] Current research by Maurice Curtis at University College Dublin suggests that Catholic action in Ireland tended to give a much higher priority to censorship of films and publications, than to efforts at reforming economic relations in support of the family. Campaigns in favor of censorship readily won government support; a campaign for a family wage, or for a generous system of childrens' allowances would have proved less welcome to Irish government ministers, particularly during the parsimonious 1920s.

As Ruth Barrington has shown, both Irish nationalist M.P.s and the Catholic Church were wary of expanding the scope of social insurance during the years 1910–14. Their reservations were prompted by fears that an Irish Home Rule parliament could not afford to provide a generous system of benefits and by the Catholic Church's suspicion of growing state intervention; moreover, both clergy and politicians convinced themselves that an extensive system of compulsory social insurance was not suited to the needs of a rural economy such as Ireland's.[55] Although French Catholics shared similar misgivings about the encroachment of the state, as Pederson shows, they ultimately became convinced of the need for a universal system of family allowances. Their change of heart was primarily due to the growing provision for family allowances in France through the establishment, often at the initiative of employers who were strong supporters of social Catholicism, of *caisses de compensation* (welfare funds). As it became apparent that such employer-led initiatives would bring children's allowances to only a minority of families, French Catholics accepted the need for a compulsory state scheme so that children's allowances could become available to all.[56]

Both social Catholicism, as it applied in the workplace, and industry-based insurance schemes appear to have been alien to Irish business life, which tended to draw its cultural values from a British tradition: hence the failure to develop any serious support for vocationalism, or corporatism.[57] (That Protestants continued to control a large share of Irish business would also have muted any such tendencies.) Patricia Harkin notes that "a striking feature of debates on social policy issues in Ireland in the 1930's, 40's and 50's is the constant preoccupation with protecting the family from 'excessive' or 'unwarranted' state intervention."[58]

The successful campaign for family allowances in France also drew heavily on that country's obsession with its falling birthrate. Although population decline was a recurring preoccupation in Ireland, the cause lay in emigration, not in a low birthrate, and conscious pronatalist measures were conspicuously absent. In 1936, economist George O'Brien noted that most Irish politicians were "generally interventionist and protectionist in outlook; [but] on the central problems of all, the numbers of the people, they are apparently apostles of almost complete laissez-faire."[59] In 1943, during the debate on the Children's Allowance Bill, Seán Lemass, Minister for Industry and Commerce emphasized that "it is not contemplated that the enactment of this measure and the establishment of children's allowances will influence either the birth rate or the marriage rate."[60] In contrast to France, therefore, measures to boost the Irish population concentrated on creating jobs, or on supplementing men's incomes in order to permit them to marry and support a family in Ireland. Reflecting the male breadwinner norm, the state's industrial development policy from 1932 expressed a preference for creating jobs for men, rather than for women, though the outcome proved somewhat different from the government's intent.[61] Similarly, Unemployment Assistance, which was provided as a means-tested benefit to non-insured workers, and paid an additional allowance for each dependent child, was primarily designed to supplement the incomes of small (male) farmers or casual (male) laborers. Although women were not formally excluded from the scheme,[62] in practice Unemployment Assistance was paid almost exclusively to men. Women constituted a significant proportion of those who lost their jobs during the Emergency, as a result of shortages of raw materials for processing in factories; nevertheless government relief work projects were exclusively concerned with providing work for men.[63]

At first glance pronatalism (the protection of the family) would appear to have offered Irish women the potential to develop a political voice wholly compatible with the prevailing cultural and religious values of Irish society; however, this did not happen—because of the persistence of high marital fertility. More intriguingly, given the high rate of Irish female mortality relative to men,[64] there is no evidence of any sustained campaign on the part of women for better maternity or child health services. Irish mothers appear to have remained silent during the debate over the Mother and Child Scheme, and, perhaps more significantly, during the earlier campaign, which led to increased awareness of the shortcomings of the existing system. The momentum for reform came largely from the medical profession,[65] and ironically, in light of the controversy over the Mother and Child Scheme, from the Catholic Church. In 1941 John Charles McQuaid, newly appointed archbishop of Dublin, established the Catholic Social Service Conference, a body which sought to improve the voluntary welfare services that were available, particularly in the Dublin area. McQuaid also advanced the campaign for a much-needed children's hospital in Dublin, where there was a chronic shortage of beds for sick children, by organizing the construction of the Our Lady's Hospital for Sick Children, in Crumlin. Both of these initiatives tackled matters of immediate concern to women; by 1943 the Social Service Conference was assisting up to nine hundred mothers in twenty-seven food and fourteen prenatal centers.[66]

The women who were most active in providing health and welfare services for mothers and children were members of religious orders rather than laywomen, and their actions were closely supervised by the Catholic hierarchy. Indeed it is significant that the male Catholic clergy (and indeed some politicians) went to considerable efforts to enhance the authority of religious sisters in hospital management—at the expense of lay nurses.[67] The large numbers of Catholic religious, and particularly of Catholic female religious—the numbers entering religion peaked in the decade after World War II—reduced the options that welfare services offered other women, either to establish careers, or to provide a basis for political action.

According to Joel Mokyr, "Irish history is population history" and historical demography offers one of the most important, and underexploited avenues for exploring the history of Irish women. Although there are numerous studies of Irish demographic history, its implications for the role and status of Irish women has hitherto been examined only to a limited extent, emigration being an exception.[68]

Table 1. Gross Birthrates per Thousand: Decennial Averages, 1900–79

	1900–09	1910–19	1920–29	1930–39	1940–49	1950–59	1960–69	1970–79
Belgium	28.6	18.0	19.7	16.2	15.4	16.8	16.4	13.1
Denmark	28.8	25.1	21.5	17.9	20.9	17.4	16.8	13.7
France	20.7	15.1	19.1	15.9	17.3	18.8	17.6	15.2
Germany	33.6	22.5	21.4	17.8	—	—	—	—
West Germany	—	—	—	—	—	16.1	17.3	10.6
Ireland	23.2	21.7	—	—	—	—	—	—
Irish Free State	—	—	20.6*	19.4	21.7	21.2	21.6	21.8
Northern Ireland	—	—	22.1*	20.0	21.8	21.1	22.6	18.4
Italy	32.7	27.4	28.7	23.9	20.9	18.0	18.3	14.8
Netherlands	30.9	29.8	24.8	21.0	23.9	21.7	20.0	14.3
Norway	27.9	24.7	21.0	15.4	19.2	16.6	17.5	14.6
Portugal	31.3	32.3	32.4	28.2	25.1	21.7	22.9	18.8
Spain	34.4	30.3	29.5	24.8	22.0	20.7	20.9	18.6
Sweden	26.0	22.2	18.4	14.5	18.3	15.0	14.8	12.8
Switzerland	27.3	21.3	18.9	16.0	18.6	17.4	18.3	13.1
England and Wales	24.7	21.8	19.3	15.1	16.8	15.7	17.6	13.4

* 1922–29

Source: Based on statistical data in B. R. Mitchell, *International Historical Statistics: Europe 1750–1988* (London: Stockton Press, 1992).

Ireland is unique in modern history in undergoing such a long period of sustained population decline, and in the duration and number of its emigrants, both male and female. During the 1980s, the Irish birthrate was, by far, the highest in western Europe; however, Irish birthrate and marital fertility have not always been so high when compared to other European countries. During the 1870s and 1880s Irish marital fertility rates were only marginally higher than those of the English.[69] Tony Wrigley has noted that "[i]n pre-industrial Europe the chief

means of social control over fertility was by prescribing the circumstances in which marriage was to be permitted."[70] The demography
of post-famine Ireland, which combined late marriages—and a significant proportion of adults remaining permanently unmarried—
with a very high level of marital fertility, shares many characteristics
with Wrigley's description of pre-industrial society.

As the table shows, in 1900–09 the Irish birthrate was below that
in every country listed, other than France. By 1960–69, however, the
crude birthrate in both parts of Ireland was greater than in any other
European country except Portugal. The Irish data appears even more
exceptional when we examine marital fertility (the number of children
born per one thousand married women, aged 15–44). By 1959 the
number of births per one thousand married women, aged 15–44, was
more than twice as high in the Irish Republic as in England and
Wales.[71] Walsh showed that during the 1960s "not only is Ireland's
marriage fertility higher than that of other European countries similar
in religion and level of economic development (Spain and Austria, for
example) but also that it is at least as high as that of the Latin American countries for which data are available."[72] What are the implications of this high marital fertility for the position of women in Irish
society? It is widely acknowledged that the peculiarities of marriage
patterns in post-famine Ireland are a reflection of the changed socioeconomic circumstances of that time. The shift from tillage to pasture
farming, the relationship between marriage and farm inheritance, and
the importance of dowries all served to postpone marriage and to
limit the numbers that married. At the same time the safety valve
of emigration, which permitted families to dispose of noninheriting
children, appears to have reduced the need to limit fertility within
marriage, a process which was underway in many other European
countries. The Catholic Church is seen as playing a pivotal role in
ensuring that marriages were delayed until they were economically
viable, and that premarital sexual relations did not jeopardize the
carefully constructed social system.[73] Similarly, the persistence of high
marital fertility into the second half of the twentieth century is often
ascribed to the influence of the Catholic Church, without much evidence being produced in support of this argument other than brief
references to the ban on contraceptives that was imposed in 1929 and
extended in 1935. However, the relationship between access to reliable

means of contraception and population decline is complex. As E. A. Wrigley and others have repeatedly emphasized, much of the decline in fertility and the transition to smaller families in other countries predated the availability of reliable forms of mechanical contraception.[74] Writing about Britain, Angus McLaren notes that "[t]he spread of new means of fertility regulation was more a result than a cause of the initial drop in family size." Neither did it depend greatly on access to family-planning clinics. Between 1921 and 1930, Britain's 156 birth-control clinics and two private consultants saw only twenty-one thousand patients.[75] Nevertheless, access to reliable methods of contraception and to information on family planning appears to have been more widespread in Britain than in many other parts of Europe. Legislation passed in France in 1920 prescribed heavy fines and prison terms for anyone who was convicted of spreading propaganda in favor of birth control, or facilitating the use of contraceptives. In 1923 stiff prison sentences were enacted for those who performed abortions, procured abortions, or actually had an abortion. This legislation was enacted, not because of the power of the Catholic Church in France, though it obviously supported the legislation, but in response to French concern with its declining population.[76] Contraception was not legalized in France until 1967, when the *loi Neuwirth* was enacted.[77] In 1923 the Belgian government prescribed prison terms for those who displayed, distributed, or advertized contraceptives, and for those who promoted information on the subject.[78] Between 1910 and 1938 legislation existed in Sweden prohibiting the dissemination of information about contraceptives, and their sale.[79] While legal prohibitions on contraception did not apply in Norway, Ida Blom claims that the (Lutheran) clergy of Norway did not accept contraception before 1940 and that senior obstetricians also proved unsympathetic.[80] There was often a considerable gap between the legal position vis-à-vis abortion and contraception, and the reality; the Belgian and French laws against the sale of contraceptives were widely breached,[81] and the extent to which such restrictions prevented the decline in fertility also proved limited. In both Italy and Spain, two Catholic countries that were subject to authoritarian regimes, the birthrate continued to fall, despite the imposition of much more thorough pronatalist measures than existed in Ireland.[82] As Robert Kennedy remarked, Irish couples in search of mechanical contraceptives could have crossed into Northern Ireland or brought them from Britain, as indeed happened during the 1960s and 1970s, when the legal restrictions on contraception came under attack.[83] Irish couples could also have had greater recourse to traditional methods such as coitus interruptus than appears to have been the case.

We are left therefore with the paradox: Why did marital fertility in Ireland remain at such a high level until the 1960s? The preceding evidence suggests that neither Catholicism nor the legal prohibitions on contraception offer a sufficient explanation, though both are contributing factors; indeed, Robert Kennedy notes that the marital fertility of non-Catholic Irish couples was also high by international standards.[84] There is some tentative evidence suggesting that some urban middle-class couples appear to have been consciously controlling family size by 1911. During the 1960s Walsh shows that fertility levels differed between socioeconomic groups, with the highest marital fertility and lowest marriage levels appearing among the rural and urban poor.[85] This pattern of differential fertility, with lower fertility emerging first among middle-class and professional couples, appears to be a common feature of the early stages of fertility decline in other societies.[86] The work of historical demographers such as Lesthaeghe and Wilson suggests that the decline in fertility took place as a result of a combination of economic and cultural factors. Fertility decline was slow in areas where the family economy remained dominant; however, moral and cultural attitudes, which were often influenced by religion, could either accelerate or delay this process.[87] In Ireland the dominance of family farming and small family businesses delayed the decline in fertility, as did emigration, which further reduced the cost of providing for children. The transition to a more urbanized and industrial economy did not become significant until the 1960s. During this decade the number of children remaining in school, an important factor in the cost of raising children, also rose sharply. However, the decline in completed family size was initially masked by an Irish birth and marriage boom, as couples took advantage of rising prosperity to marry earlier and in larger numbers.[88] In consequence, the first effect of increased economic growth on Irish women was a decline in the numbers at work and a withdrawal into domesticity.[89] Again, this process was not unique to Ireland, but should be seen as a belated variant of the postwar baby boom also experienced in other countries.

The history of women in twentieth-century Ireland is similar to that in other countries, yet different. Ireland's precocious politicization and attachment to the United Kingdom meant that Irish feminism was relatively advanced, perhaps artificially so, by the eve of World War I. The doldrums into which feminism fell after 1920 mirror developments in other countries where women gained the franchise; however, it also appears that Irish feminists found it difficult to replace the pre-war focus on equal rights with an ideology that might have been more in keeping with the culture of the independent Irish state. The continuing high level of marital fertility reduced the political dividends gained from pronatalism and probably meant that most Irish women lacked the leisure to engage in political or social activities outside the home. Arensberg and Kimball's account of the work of a farmer's wife in County Clare in the 1930s emphasized that the wife was the first to rise in the morning and the last to go to bed at night; in between she was continually busy with multiple household tasks.[90] Such a lifestyle was hardly conducive to joining political campaigns or social organizations. Caitríona Clear suggests that the women who joined the Irish Countrywomen's Association, the largest women's organization in Ireland, were those with some margin of leisure; the organization was weak in the poorer areas.[91] The slow rate of transition to a modern urban and industrial-cum-service economy delayed both the onset of fertility decline and the emergence of the demands associated with the modern women's movement. It can be argued that it was only when the fertility patterns desired by Irish couples began to conflict with state legislation, and when a critical mass of suburban housewives existed, that the modern women's movement could emerge in Ireland. We might also suggest that Ireland's ambiguous status as a rural Catholic country that had been governed and strongly influenced by a Protestant industrialized state, confuses the picture in many ways, not least perhaps in our expectations of Irish women and of Irish society historically.

Notes

1. In this article, unless otherwise stated, "Ireland" refers to the area comprising the Irish Free State or the Irish Republic. The chapter title is taken from Sean O'Casey, *The Shadow of a Gunman* in *Three Plays* (London: Macmillan, 1969), 88.

2. Olwen Hufton, *The Prospect before Her: A History of Women in Western Europe. Volume One 1500–1800* (London: Harper Collins, 1995), 1, 23.

3. Ailbhe Smyth, ed., *Irish Women's Studies Reader* (Dublin: Attic Press, 1993), i.

4. *Journal of Women's History* 6,4; 7,1 (1995).

5. Nancy Cott, *The Grounding of Modern Feminism* (New Haven, Conn.: Yale University Press, 1987), 180–211; Carol Dyhouse, *No Distinction of Sex? Women in British Universities 1870–1939* (London: University College London Press, 1995), 162; Jane Caplan, *Government without Consensus: The Administrative State and the Civil Service in Weimar and Nazi Germany* (Oxford: Oxford University Press, 1988), 98–99.

6. Mary E. Daly, *Women and Work in Ireland*, Studies in Irish Economic and Social History no. 7 (Dublin: Economic and Social History Society of Ireland, 1997).

7. On Irish exceptionalism see Liam Kennedy, "Out of History: Ireland 'That Most Distressful Country,'" in Liam Kennedy, *Colonialism, Religion and Nationalism in Ireland* (Belfast: Institute of Irish Studies, 1996), 182–223.

8. Ronan Fanning, "'The Great Enchantment': Uses and Abuses of Modern Irish History," in *Interpreting Irish History: The Debate on Historical Revisionism*, ed. Ciaran Brady (Dublin: Irish Academic Press, 1994), 156.

9. Brendan Bradshaw, "Nationalism and Historical scholarship," in ibid., 207–8.

10. Seamus Deane, General Introduction, *Field Day Anthology of Irish Writing*, Vol. 1 (Derry: Field Day, 1991), xxv–xxvi.

11. I discuss this topic at greater length in a forthcoming review article in the *Journal of Modern History*, "Recent Writings on Modern Irish History: The Interaction between Past and Present."

12. Richard J. Evans, *The Feminists* (London: Croom Helm, 1979), 17. I am aware that Evans was widely read and cited by many of the pioneering researchers in Irish women's history.

13. Terence Brown, *Ireland: A Social and Cultural History, 1922–79* (London: Fontana, 1981); F. S. L. Lyons, *Culture and Anarchy in Ireland, 1880–1939* (Oxford: Oxford University Press, 1980).

14. Jenny Beale, *Women in Ireland: Voices of Change* (Dublin: Gill and Macmillan, 1986), 5.

15. Monica McWilliams, "The Church, the State and the Women's Movement in Northern Ireland," in Smyth, *Irish Women's Studies Reader,* 79–99.

16. " 'Suffrage First—above all else!' An Account of the Irish Suffrage Movement," in ibid., 43. For a more nuanced and critical evaluation of this issue, see Liam O'Dowd, "State and Women: The Aftermath of Partition," in *Gender in Irish Society,* ed. Chris Curtin, Pauline Jackson, Barbara O'Connor (Galway: Galway University Press, 1987), 3–36.

17. E. J. Cahill, *The Framework of a Christian State* (Dublin: Gill, 1932).

18. James F. McMillan, *Housewife or Harlot: The Place of Women in French Society, 1870–1940* (New York: St. Martin's Press, 1981), 9–28.

19. Betty Friedan, *The Feminine Mystique* (London: Penguin, 1982).

20. Catríona Clear's *Nuns in Nineteenth Century Ireland* (Dublin: Gill and Macmillan, 1987) is an important exception; however, it tends to emphasize the constraints under which female religious operated, rather than their contribution to Irish society.

21. Margaret MacCurtain, "Late in the Field: Catholic Sisters in Twentieth-Century Ireland and the New Religious History," *Journal of Women's History* 6,4; 7,1 (1995): 49–63.

22. The neglect was not uniquely Irish. At a conference on women and religion that I attended at Harvard in June 1989, which was organized by Olwen Hufton, several American historians who were working in this field complained that they found it difficult to have their papers accepted at the more important conferences on women's history.

23. J. J. Lee, "Women and the Church since the Famine," in *Women in Irish Society: The Historical Dimension,* ed. Margaret MacCurtain and Donncha Ó Corráin (Dublin: Arlen House, 1978), 37–45.

24. Daly, *Women and Work in Ireland.*

25. *Census of Ireland for the Year 1871.* General Report, 65–67.

26. Paul Bairoch, *The Working Population and Its Structure* (Bruxelles: Université Libre de Bruxelles, Institut de Sociologie, Centre D' Économie Politique, 1968); Brendan Walsh, "Aspects of Labour Supply and Demand with Special Reference to the Employment of Women in Ireland," *Journal of the Statistical and Social Inquiry Society of Ireland* 22, 3 (1970–71). Walsh was writing about the year 1970; his point would be even more valid for earlier times when the number of farm households was greater.

27. One of the first works to break with this trend is Maryann Valiulis, "Neither Feminist nor Flapper: The Ecclesiastical Construction of the Ideal Irish Woman," in *Chattel, Servant or Citizen: Women's Status in Church, State and Society,* ed. Mary O' Dowd and Sabine Wichert (Belfast: Institute of Irish Studies, 1995), 168–78.

28. Hufton, *The Prospect before Her,* 22.

29. Donncha Ó Corráin, "Women in Early Irish Society," in MacCurtain and Ó Corráin, *Women in Irish Society,* 1. See also Donncha Ó Corráin,

"Women and the Law in Early Ireland," in O' Dowd and Wichert, *Chattel, Servant or Citizen*, 45–57.

30. Mary Cullen, "Breadwinners and Providers: Women in the Household Economy of Labouring Families, 1835–6," in *Women Surviving: Studies in Irish Women's History in the Nineteenth and Twentieth Centuries*, ed. Maria Luddy and Cliona Murphy (Dublin: Poolbeg Press, 1989), 85–116; Lee, "Women and the Church since the Famine," 37. For a more pessimistic viewpoint on women in pre-famine Ireland, see Daly, *Women and Work in Ireland*. Joanna Bourke [*From Husbandry to Housewifery: Women, Economic Change, and Housework in Ireland 1890–1914* (Oxford: Clarendon Press, 1993)] sees the decline in women's paid employment as a response to rising living standards.

31. Alice Clark, *Working Life of Women in the Seventeenth Century* (London: Routledge, 1919); Ivy Pinchbeck, *Women Workers and the Industrial Revolution*, rev. ed. (London: Virago, 1981); on Clark, see Hufton, *The Prospect before Her*, 23; on Clark and Pinchbeck, see Maxine Berg, "The First Women Economic Historians," *Economic History Review* 14, 2 (1992): 308–29. Pinchbeck noted that the Industrial Revolution reduced the opportunites for married women to engage in productive work within the home; however, she regarded this as beneficial because it meant that women were now in a position to devote their energies to homemaking and child care. For single women the industrial revolution meant a distinct gain in social and economic independence. *Women Workers*, 306–13.

32. Catríona Clear, " 'The Women Can Not be Blamed': The Commission on Vocational Organisation, Feminism and 'Home-Makers' in Independent Ireland in the 1930s and '40s," in O'Dowd and Wichert, *Chattel, Servant or Citizen*, 180.

33. Frances Gardiner, "Political Interest and Participation of Irish Women 1922–1992: The Unfinished Revolution," in Smyth, *Irish Women's Studies Reader*, 47–49.

34. For a discussion of this argument see Tom Garvin, *1922: The Birth of Irish Democracy* (Dublin: Gill and Macmillan, 1996), 191–99.

35. Margaret Ward, *Unmanageable Revolutionaries* (Tralee: Brandon, 1983); Diane Urquhart, "The Female of the Species is More Deadlier [*sic*] than the Male? The Ulster Women's Unionist Council, 191–40," in *Coming into the Light: The Work, Politics and Religion of Women in Ulster, 1840–1940*, ed. Janice Holmes and Diane Urquhart (Belfast: Institute of Irish Studies, 1994), 93–123.

36. Eibhlin Bhreathnach, "Charting New Waters: Women's Experience in Higher Education, 1879–1908," and Anne O'Connor, "The Revolution in Girls' Secondary Education in Ireland, 1860–1910," in *Girls Don't Do Honours: Irish Women in Education in the Nineteenth and Twentieth Centuries*, ed. Mary Cullen (Dublin: Women's Education Bureau, 1987), 31–54; 55–78.

37. For women and nationalism, see Ward, *Unmanageable Revolutionaries*.

38. Garvin, *1922*, 99.

39. Brian Maye, *Fine Gael 1923–87* (Dublin: Blackwater, 1993).

40. Emmet O'Connor, *A Labour History of Ireland 1824–1960* (Dublin: Gill and Macmillan, 1992), 120.

41. Mary E. Daly, *Industrial Development and Irish National Identity 1922–39* (Syracuse, N.Y.: Syracuse University Press, 1992), 123–24. Mary E. Daly, "Women and Trade Unions" in *Trade Union Century*, ed. Donal Nevin (Cork: Mercier, 1994), 106–16.

42. Gardiner, "Political Interest," 45. Martin Pugh, *Women and the Women's Movement in Britain 1914–1959* (London: Macmillan, 1992), 159.

43. Maurice Manning, "Women in National and Local Politics 1922–77," in MacCurtain and Ó Corráin, *Women in Irish Society*, 99–100.

44. Maria Luddy, *Women in Ireland, 1800–1918: A Documentary History* (Cork: Cork University Press, 1995), 242, 289–96, contains some contemporary documents on this subject; however Luddy's commentary on women in politics is rather dismissive of the whole subject of women in local government.

45. Marie O'Neill, *From Parnell to de Valera: A Biography of Jennie Wyse Power 1858–1941* (Dublin: Blackwater Press, 1991), 64, 114, 123, 151.

46. Helen Litton, ed., *Revolutionary Woman, Kathleen Clarke 1878–1972: An Autobiography* (Dublin: O'Brien Press, 1991).

47. Mary E. Daly, "From Kings' County to Offaly: Dáil Éireann and Local Government during the Years of Revolution," in *Offaly: A County History*, ed. Timothy P. O'Neill (Dublin: Geography Publications, forthcoming).

48. Mary E. Daly, *The Buffer State: The Historical Roots of the Department of the Environment* (Dublin: Institute of Public Administration, 1997), especially chapters 3 and 7.

49. Gisela Bock and Pat Thane, eds., *Maternity and Gender Policies: Women and the Rise of the European Welfare States, 1880s-1950s* (London: Routledge, 1991), 3; Theda Skocpol, *Protecting Soldiers and Mothers: The Political Origins of Social Policy in the United States* (Cambridge, Mass.: Belknap Press at Harvard University Press, 1992).

50. Clear, " 'The Women Can Not be Blamed,' " 183–84.

51. A. Alfred Dickie, "State Insurance and Mothers' Pensions," *Journal of the Statistical and Social Inquiry Society of Ireland* 13 (1919): 675.

52. Hilda Tweedy, *A Link in the Chain: The Story of the Irish Housewives Association 1942–1992* (Dublin: Attic Press, 1992), 16–18.

53. Sean T. O Kelly, Minister for Local Government and Public Health, *Published Debates Dáil Éireann* (4 June 1937), col. 2234.

54. Susan Pedersen, *Family, Dependence, and the Origins of the Welfare State: Britain and France 1914–1945* (Cambridge: Cambridge University Press, 1993), 393–95.

55. Ruth Barrington, *Health, Medicine and Politics in Ireland 1900–1940* (Dublin: Institute of Public Administration, 1987), 39–66.

56. Pedersen, *Family, Dependence, and the Origins of the Welfare State,* 75, 224–33.

57. Joseph Lee, "Aspects of Corporatist Thought in Ireland: The Commission on Vocational Organisation, 1939–43," in *Studies in Irish History,* ed. Art Cosgrove and Donal McCartney (Dublin: University College Dublin, 1979), 324–46.

58. Patricia Harkin, "La Famille, Fruit du Passé, Germe de l'Avenir: Family Policy in Ireland and Vichy France" (M.A. thesis, University College Dublin, 1992), 55.

59. George O'Brien, "The Coming Crisis of Population," *Studies* (December 1936): 580.

60. *Published Debates Dail Eireann* (28 November 1943), col. 28.

61. Daly, *Industrial Development and Irish National Identity,* 124–27; Daly, *Women and Work in Ireland, 1750–1990.*

62. Desmond Farley, *Social Insurance and Social Assistance in Ireland* (Dublin: Institute of Public Administration, 1964), 52.

63. National Archives, Department of the Taoiseach, S11916 A Unemployment in Dublin; Daly, *The Buffer State,* ch. 6.

64. Until the 1940s female age-specific death rates in the Irish Free State were higher than those for men in most age groups. Excess female mortality was most pronounced in rural areas. Kennedy sees this as evidence of the poor status of women in Irish rural society; however, this appears to be a topic in need of further research. Relative female mortality showed a sudden improvement between 1941 and 1950. Robert E. Kennedy Jr., *The Irish: Emigration, Marriage and Fertility* (Berkeley: University of California Press, 1973), 50–65.

65. James Deeney, *To Cure and to Care* (Dublin: Glendale Press, 1989); W. R. F. Collis, *The State of Medicine in Ireland* (Dublin, c. 1943/44); Charles Clancy-Gore, M.D., "Nutritional Standards of Some Working Class Families in Dublin," in *Journal of the Statistical and Social Inquiry Society of Ireland* 17 (1943–44): 241. Dr. Catherine O'Brien, "Irish Social Services," *Journal of the Statistical and Social Inquiry Society of Ireland* 17 (1942–43): 107; Gerard Fee, "The Effects of World War II on Dublin's Low Income Families" (Ph.D thesis, University College Dublin, 1996), ch. 6.

66. Barrington, *Health, Medicine and Politics,* 145–46.

67. Daly, *The Buffer State,* ch. 2; Noel Browne, *Against the Tide* (Dublin: Gill and Macmillan, 1986), 144–45; National Archives Department of the Taoiseach, S 15088 Regional Hospitals Staffing by Religious or by Lay Nurses. I shall explore some aspects of this topic at greater length in a forthcoming article: "Hospital Reform in the Irish Free State, 1922–39," in *Medicine, Health and Disease in Ireland 1750–1950,* ed. Elizabeth Malcolm and Greta Jones (Cork: Cork University Press, 1997).

68. Lynn Lees, *Exiles of Erin: Irish Migrants in Victorian London* (Manchester: Manchester University Press, 1979); Hasia Diner, *Erin's Daughters in America: Irish Immigrant Women* (Baltimore: Johns Hopkins University Press, 1983).

69. Robert Kennedy, *The Irish*, 177.

70. E. A. Wrigley, *Population and History* (London: Weidenfeld and Nicolson, 1969), 119.

71. Liam Kennedy, *People and Population Change* (Dublin and Belfast: Co-Operation North, 1994), 33.

72. Brendan Walsh, *Some Irish Population Problems Reconsidered*, Economic and Social Research Institute, paper no. 42 (November 1968), 5.

73. The literature on this subject is immense, but see K. H. Connell, "Catholicism and Marriage in Ireland in the Century after the Famine," in *Irish Peasant Society* (Oxford: Oxford University Press, 1968), 113–61. However, the subject would probably benefit from a reassessment which focused more closely on the position of women.

74. Wrigley, *Population and History*, 188–90.

75. Angus Mc Laren, "The Sexual Politics of Reproduction in Britain," in *The European Experience of Declining Fertility: A Quiet Revolution 1850–1970*, ed. John R. Gillis, Louise A. Tilly, and David Levine (Oxford: Blackwell, 1992), 98.

76. McMillan, *Housewife or Harlot*, 189.

77. Claire Laubier, *The Condition of Women in France, 1945 to the Present: A Documentary Anthology* (London: Routledge, 1990), 49–50.

78. D. V. Glass, *Population Policies and Movements in Europe* (Oxford: Oxford University Press, 1940), 159–60.

79. Ann-Sofie Ohlander, "The Invisible Child? The Struggle for a Social Democratic Family Policy in Sweden, 1900–1960s," in Bock and Thane, *Maternity and Gender Politics*, 63.

80. Ida Blom, "Voluntary Motherhood 1900–1930: Theories and Politics of a Norwegian Feminist in an International Perspective," in ibid., 33.

81. Glass, *Population Policies*, 160.

82. Mary Nash, "Pronatalism and Motherhood in Franco's Spain," in Bock and Thane, *Maternity and Gender Politics*, 160–75; Glass, *Population Policies*, 219–68.

83. Robert Kennedy, *The Irish*, 182.

84. Ibid., 184–87; See also Cormac Ó Gráda, "Did Ulster Catholics Always Have Larger Families," *Irish Economic and Social History*, 11 (1984): 89–98.

85. Cormac Ó Gráda, "Fertility Control in Ireland and Scotland, c. 1880–1930: Some New Findings," in *Conflict, Identity and Economic Development: Ireland and Scotland 1600–1939*, ed. Sean Connolly, R. A. Houston, and R. J. Morris (Carlisle: Carnegie Press, 1995); Walsh, *Some Irish Population Problems Reconsidered*, 8–9.

86. Michael R. Haines, "Occupation and Social Class during Fertility Decline: Historical Perspectives," in Gillis, Tilly, and Levine, *The European Experience,* 193–226.

87. Ron J. Lesthaeghe and Chris Wilson, "Modes of Production, Secularization, and the Pace of the Fertility Decline in Western Europe, 1870–1930," in *The Decline of Fertility in Europe,* ed. Ansley J. Coale and Susan Cotts Watkins (Princeton: Princeton University Press, 1986).

88. Finola Kennedy, "The Family in Transition," in *Ireland in Transition: Economic and Social Change since 1960,* ed. Kieran A. Kennedy (Cork: Mercier Press, 1986), 91–100.

89. Daly, *Women and Work.*

90. Conrad Arensberg and Solon T. Kimball, *Family and Community in Ireland* (Cambridge, Mass.: Harvard University Press, 1965).

91. Clear, " 'The Women Can Not be Blamed,' " 183.

LUCY MCDIARMID

The Posthumous Life of
Roger Casement

... that dear Norwegian girl helped me stow away all the old hairpins ...
Now, when I saw *Hibernia* on the caps of the men, I nearly kissed them ...
Roger Casement, 28 October 1914 letter

I see not the slightest objection to hanging Casement and afterwards giving as
much publicity to the contents of his diary as decency permits, so that at any
rate the public in America and elsewhere may know what sort of man they
are inclined to make a martyr of.
Sir Ernley Blackwell, legal advisor to the Foreign Office, summer 1916

> The Volkswagen parked in the gap,
> But gently ticking over.
> You wonder if it's lovers
> And not men hurrying back
> Across two fields and a river.
Paul Muldoon, "Ireland," 1980

I

THE INDETERMINACY of Roger Casement's posthumous life no doubt
began in the disguises of the living man, adopted to make his identity
indeterminate. Within a few short weeks, in October 1914, eluding
detection as he slipped into enemy territory—Germany—by way of
New York and Norway, Casement became, in quick succession, Mr.
R. Smythe of London (in New York); James E. Landy of New Jersey
(on shipboard); his own, nonexistent female American cousin (in a
letter); and Mr. Hammond of New York (in Berlin). A life between
accents, nationalities, allegiances, and genders, hybrid and subversive,
was given local habitation in these aliases. No wonder fellow travelers
assumed he was a spy. Casement had boarded the *Oskar II* as himself,

127

but as a disguised, effeminized Sir Roger, having shaved off the famous beard and washed his face in buttermilk to lighten his complexion. As the ship sailed out of New York harbor, he turned into James Landy —whose passport he carried—and openly joined Adler Christiansen, the Norwegian sailor he had picked up on Broadway and who accompanied him as his servant. When the ship was stopped by the British vessel *Hibernia*, Christiansen shaved Casement and discarded the razor blades ("all the old hairpins").[1]

In an unmailed letter addressed "Dear Sister," Casement described these events coyly, as if he and Christiansen were girls. The camp locutions ("that dear Norwegian girl," "the dear, kind captain, such a nice Dane with a beard just like cousin Roger's") sound like MacNeice's "Hetty to Nancy" in *Letters from Iceland,* the deliberately girlish utterances of a faux-homosexual voice. Patently comprehensible like all the codes Casement attempted, this one was intended to record his journey but deceive British agents, should they ever come across it. But at the same time as the letter hid treason, its style outed its author's sexual preference—or might have, to an alert reader. At the very least, the American, female persona allowed free expression to the writer's ambivalence about gender even as it obfuscated his political intentions.

The "official" British outing of Casement was every bit as equivocal and evasive as this simpering, camp epistle. When Sir Ernley Blackwell recommended that Casement's private diaries, with their record of homosexual assignations, be "given as much publicity as decency permits," he was outing Casement covertly. Neither the Foreign Office, nor the Home Office, nor the Attorney General wanted to be known publicly to be giving the diaries publicity: so the publicity had to be private publicity, *sub rosa* but not red-handed. Like dirty books in a primary school, typed transcripts and photographed copies of pages were surreptitiously shown by one man to another. The private publicity was sanctioned by officials of state: "Excellent," Asquith observed to the American ambassador at a dinner party the night before Casement's execution, learning that he had seen the diaries, "and you need not be particular about keeping it to yourself."[2] Once leaked, the forgotten private records became international smut. These quasi-outings were followed by quasi-definitive proofs that the diaries were forged and apparently definitive assertions that they were authentic. And judgments about authenticity, or the lack of it, have been inseparable from judgments about militant nationalism and about homosexual behavior—all issues which have not inspired unanimity of opinion at any moment during the past eighty years.

Nothing about Casement has ever been stable, definitive, determinate, "official," except the fact that he was hanged. Posthumous Casement, like living Casement, has endured in a blur of rumor, gossip, romance, and innuendo, public pronouncements and private uncertainty. "Be a good patriot, shut your mouth. Lie down," says the Cardinal to the dead hero in David Rudkin's play about Casement's funeral.[3] But by the time of de Valera's 1965 oration at the reinterment of the remains in Glasnevin, Casement had too long and complex a posthumous history to lie quiet. Even Parnell's posthumous life has been less volatile. Discourse about the problematic sexual lives of public figures—Parnell, Pearse, Eamon Casey—has become a distinct Irish speech genre, one that tends to fit Luke Gibbons's binaristic analysis of rumor as a corrective to "official" information in Irish public life, an "alternative line of communication" opposed to those of "political correspondents, public relations agencies and government information services."[4] Like the folk histories that oppose official histories, rumor, Jean-Noël Kapferer has argued, "constitutes a relation to authority . . . a counter-power." Rumors are "necessarily unofficial . . . they challenge official reality by proposing other realities."[5] Discourse about Casement is unique, however, because two governments are involved, and so there are two opposed "official" views, and a host of unofficial views, not necessarily consonant with or directly opposing their own nation's ideology. Even the dominant Irish view that he was a revolutionary hero has been contested by those who thought he was a minor player, or an ineffective one, on the national scene ("a side-bird to the main event," as a friend of mine called him); and that view has been countered by those who extol his international humanitarian contributions. There has always been a case to be made for every permutation of opinion. The leakage of the diaries was done unofficially, of course, and so could only be opposed unofficially, by those who thought they were forged or by those who thought they were genuine but irrelevant. And Irish and English opinions, over the years, have been complexly distributed: some Irish people have quietly assumed Casement was homosexual, and some English have protested against the "forgeries." When Yeats, speaking on his own behalf in 1937, uttered a passionate defense of Casement as a victim of English treachery, the Free State government, desperately in need of this kind of defense, immediately appropriated Yeats's ballad "Roger Casement."

A man who was busy most of his life with secret activities of various kinds, a man around whom other people's secret activities circulated, makes an attractive hero for a society that privileges the hidden. Eighty years-worth of rumors and ballads issued from a people with a deep, traditional distrust of the official; and with a corollary faith that the hidden is true, or if not true, at least valuable in its opposition to what is public. This value is not linked with any particular content, but with the condition of hiddenness, especially when some secret— piety or impiety, purity or contamination—is hidden from outsiders and unknowable to them. Like the parked Volkswagen in Paul Muldoon's poem "Ireland," posthumous Casement epitomized a secret, whatever it was, that was quintessentially national. Casement, too, was throbbing with hidden life, inspiring a pleasurable curiosity in the mind that savors the idea of illicit activity: "You wonder if it's lovers . . ." In addition, the conviction that national pride was involved made it a patriotic obligation to keep probing the secret places, Banna Strand, or Pentonville Prison, or the locked room in London where the diaries, or alleged diaries, were kept, or said to be kept.

"If ritual is suppressed in one form it crops up in others," Mary Douglas wrote in *Purity and Danger,* and in the absence of any definitive point of view or stabilizing ritual, Irish memory of Casement has taken the form of controversies—polyphonic, idiosyncratic, spontaneous, infinitely expressive and infinitely anxious.[6] Controversies tend to accumulate in interstitial areas, between laws, authorities, and institutions, areas where passions and angers may thrive forever without suppression. Controversies are not a means of resolution but a sign of its absence, a collective, "popular" genre that emerges as a conduit of strong feelings. Like athletic competition, they provide a culturally acceptable way of expressing antagonism, with just enough of the ludic or theatrical element to ensure that they are perceived as a "safe outlet" rather than a threat to society. Not all interstitial matter inspires controversy, but the "matter" of Casement, political and sexual, remains eternally "hot," and debate about him unrelenting. Casement could be said to be over-remembered. He has received more biographies than any other figure of 1916, and he can be found, in one form or another, in poems, plays, orations, memoirs, songs, legends, jokes, allusions, anecdotes, paintings, monuments, documentaries, film-scripts, and—by the thousands—letters-to-the-editor. The ubiquitous subject of an unendable argument or long national dream, Casement has proved disturbing, entertaining, irresistible. The sheer quantity of material about him defies measure. He makes cameo appearances in novels by Eimar O'Duffy, Joyce, Stevie Smith, Terence de Vere White, and in poems by Louis MacNeice, Paul Durcan, and Paul Muldoon. He is the entire subject of at least two ballads, and of poems by Alice Milligan, Eva Gore-Booth, Maeve Cavanagh, Liam O'Gogan, one "Baron von Huenefeld," Yeats, Richard Murphy, and Medbh McGuckian, and of the 1995 novel *The Flaming Heart* by Michael Carson. At least three (radio and television) documentaries and six plays have been written about him; three monuments in his memory are easily visitable, at Banna Strand, Ballyheigue, and Glasnevin, and a fourth, though well-hidden, is said to exist (at Murlough Bay). Although there appears to be a curse on films about Casement, there is always one under way: Thaddeus O'Sullivan is said to be making one now.[7]

In studying the way popular memory of Casement has spontaneously created its own rituals, this essay will divide as memory of Casement has divided, at the return of the remains, or "repatriation" of Casement, in 1965. The burial in Glasnevin marked a major turning point in Casement's posthumous life, and—quite apart from the State ritual—the rituals of popular memory changed dramatically once the remains had been reburied in Irish soil. Until that ceremony, Casement was the source of continuing, unambiguous national humiliation because the British government refused to return his body. His words on the subject were well known: when his cousin Gertrude Bannister visited him in Pentonville Prison just before his execution, Casement had said, "Go back to Ireland, and don't let me lie here in this dreadful place. Take my body back with you and let it lie in the old churchyard in Murlough Bay."[8] But Casement's body, like that of every criminal who had been executed at Pentonville, was put into quicklime in the prison grounds, and all requests for the remains were rejected until 1965. As Eva Gore-Booth wrote, "No cairn-shaped mound on a high windy hill / With Irish earth the hero's heart enfolds / But a burning grave at Pentonville / The broken heart of Ireland holds." [9] Casement had not been caoined, waked, or buried: he was one of the unquiet dead. At the twentieth anniversary of the Rising, its leaders were honored in a State ceremony with a salute fired over their mass grave at Arbour Hill and wreaths placed on it. Casement, at the same time, got a protest demonstration in London: thousands of people heard Hanna Sheehy-Skeffington and other speakers demand the return of the remains to Ireland. In the heat of a 1937 Casement controversy, a member of the government's Executive Council said that the Irish people "loved Roger Casement and await always, hoping for the bringing home of his remains, even of his dust." [10]

So long as this unfinished ritual business loomed, anxieties focused on a national father figure who could not quite be mourned and could not quite be venerated. Victim, hero, and martyr, evoked in the pious political discourse of 1930s Ireland, Casement appeared primarily as the subject of interminable letter controversies, whose participants attempted obsessively to stabilize and purify him. But in late February 1965, as soon as it was known that the remains were to be returned —even before the plane carrying what was said to be Casement's calcified remains touched down on Irish soil—an entirely new Casement made his entrance. Playful, irreverent, homosexual, camp, an odd mixture of bones and beard, a humorous dissident, a troublesome subversive—was this the man Ireland had waited forty-nine years for? The dug-up, reinterred, post-posthumous Casement was ready for the new Ireland of T. K. Whitaker and Sean Lemass, soon to become the Ireland of David Norris, Mary Robinson, Margaret MacCurtain, and Sinéad O'Connor.

2

The trial occurred at a time when the writings of Sigmund Freud had made psychopathy grotesquely fashionable. Everybody was expected to have a secret history unfit for publication.

Bernard Shaw, letter to the Irish Press, 11 February 1937

A polluting person is always in the wrong. He has developed some wrong
condition or simply crossed some line which should not have been crossed
and this displacement unleashes danger for someone.

Mary Douglas, Purity and Danger

To the mind of Alfred Noyes, at least in 1916, Roger Casement was a
"polluting person." The author of "The Highwayman" was working
in the News Department of the Foreign Office in the spring of 1916
when the librarian handed him typed transcripts of the notorious
diaries. Several months later, while Noyes was lecturing in America, a
Philadelphia newspaper asked him his opinion of what he had seen:
"I cannot print his own written confessions about himself," Noyes
said of Casement, "for they are filthy beyond all description. But I
have seen and read them and they touch the lowest depths that human
degradation has ever touched. Page after page of his diary would be
an insult to a pig's trough to let the foul record touch it." [11]

But Casement had his Antigone in the person of Nina Casement
Newman, desperate to save her brother's life and, after the execution,
just as desperate to defend his honor. In the autumn of 1916, as Noyes
stood to deliver a lecture in Philadelphia, Mrs. Newman—"a lady of
distinguished bearing," Noyes calls her in his memoir,

> rose in the audience and asked if she might say a few words. I at once
> made way for her, and, to my horror and that of the audience, she
> announced that she had come for the express purpose of exposing
> the speaker of the evening as a "blackguardly scoundrel." . . . "Your
> countrymen" she cried, "hanged my brother, Sir Roger Casement."
> Then, her tall spare figure quivering and her face white with anger, she
> poured out a torrent of invective against England . . . Overwrought and
> distraught as she was, there was a strange irrational nobility shining
> through all her wild charges and accusations. [12]

To Nina Newman's mind, Alfred Noyes was a "polluting person," and
her public denunciation of him performed the kind of ritual that
sprang up everywhere in the years between Casement's execution and
reinterment. What Mary Douglas calls "rites of reversing pollution,"
rites, that is, of "untying, washing, erasing, and fumigating," serve to
"expunge" a pollution that has threatened the life of a particular
culture by transgressing the "internal lines of its system." [13] The kinds
of pollution Douglas talks about include things like cooking food

improperly, or touching an untouchable person, or committing incest, cases in which social and moral issues are linked with a material form of pollution. Certainly Noyes's image of the "pig's trough" besmirched by the diaries' "foul record" conveys a vivid sense of the material; a material pollution is vestigially present in Newman's phrase, as Noyes quotes it, "blackguardly scoundrel," since blackguards originally were scullions who cleaned pots and pans. (The diaries came, of course, to be known as the "Black Diaries.") The feeling that, in Douglas's terms, "danger" had been "unleashed," and important cultural boundaries violated, explains much of the passion, intensity, and hysteria of the purifying rituals that sprang into being around Casement at odd moments and occasions, in poems, orations, letter controversies, and even christenings: the sculptor Herbert Ward, a friend of Casement's from Congo days, *un*named his third son Roger Casement Ward when he learned about the treason and the diaries. The young man—by petition of Parliament—became "Rodney," so he could keep his nickname Roddy, without the contamination of the original Roger.[14] However, de Valera named his next-born son Ruarí, after Casement, so the name was also considered to carry the sanctity of martyrdom.

These issues were aired in de Valera's Ireland in one of the most memorable appearances of the Casement controversy, a passionate correspondence in the *Irish Press* in February 1937. Its chief hero was Yeats, who seemed to speak as a Free State poet laureate, though the State's idea of pollution was hardly his. The "three monuments" he had just written about in 1925, the three dirty old men on their Dublin pedestals (Lord Nelson, O'Connell, and Parnell) laughed aloud at the notion that "purity built up the state, / And after kept it from decay."[15] Yeats *liked* the transgressive sexual activities of public figures and had been gathering expertise on the subject most of his life. In August 1936, just before this Casement commotion, he had been visited by the aging Parnellite Henry Harrison, who had written a book to restore Parnell's honor. Duly and passionately responding to this vindication, Yeats had created a *lieu de memoire* in "Come gather round me, Parnellites." In the lines "And Parnell loved his country, / And Parnell loved a lass," the syntactic parallel makes the two activities of equal value and deprives the hearty, ballad-like love for a "lass" of its adulterous pollution.[16]

Purity, however, had been legislated into existence with the 1925 bill prohibiting divorce legislation, the 1929 Censorship of Publications Act, the 1935 Public Dance Halls Act, and the prohibition of the sale of contraceptives in the same year (section 17 of the Criminal Law Amendment Act). In a sense this legislation also constituted a large scale "rite of reversing pollution," the social influence of English mores. The pollution of Casement's name had that same colonial origin, and there was individual and collective effort to reverse it. Parnell had Harrison as apologist, and Casement had (among others) William J. Maloney, a New York doctor, who had written a long and tiresome book. *The Forged Casement Diaries* (1936) argues that the British had interpolated into Casement's innocent, consular diaries those of one of the Peruvian criminals he had been investigating in 1910.[17] All the homosexual acts, then, were those of Armando Normand, a rubber agent of the Peruvian Amazon Company; and the true villains were the forgers in the War Office and their allies in the Home and Foreign Offices, Scotland Yard, and the British Embassy in Washington.

Maloney's research—published chapter by chapter in the *Irish Press* throughout the winter of 1936–37—reversed the pollution, but it was Yeats's poem, also published in the *Irish Press,* that provided the mnemonic device that made this idea stick in the popular mind; and stick it did, because it has been cited in every subsequent Casement controversy. Written in Yeats's faux-Catholic ballad stanza, it was eminently quotable:

> I say that Roger Casement
> Did what he had to do,
> He died upon the gallows
> But that is nothing new.[18]

The poem had instant, and sundry, ramifications. Yeats himself, excited by reading aloud his own poem, had to drink a glass of port to calm down.[19] On the day the poem appeared in the paper (February 2), Mrs. Yeats (not yet knowing of the publication) was surprised to find herself treated with unusual deference by shopkeepers all over Dublin; the people had been longing, it seems, for the restoration of this hero's purity.[20] And, acknowledging this national service, the government thanked Yeats. As he wrote to Dorothy Wellesley,

. . . I was publicly thanked by the vice-president of the Executive Coun-
sil, [sic] by De Valera's political secretary, by our chief antiquarian &
an old revolutionist, Count Plunket, who calls my poem "a ballad the
people much needed." De Valera's newspaper gave me a long leader
saying that for generations to come my poem will pour scorn on the
forgers & their backers.[21]

Inadvertently, Yeats had formulated the official state position. Outraged by forgery ("They turned a trick by forgery / And blackened his
good name"), he had seemed to speak out for purity; he appeared to
be doing the work of Free State hagiography. In fact his opinion of
Casement was not high; Casement was "not a very able man," Yeats
wrote Ethel Mannin, though he was "gallant and unselfish."[22] But
Yeats's hidden opinion, hidden from the Fianna Fáil press, was more
shocking: he *wanted* the diaries to be authentic. "Public opinion is
excited," he wrote Wellesley,

> & there is a demand for a production of the documents & their submis-
> sion to some impartial tribunal. It would be a great relief to me if they
> were so submitted & proved genuine. If Casement were a homo-sexual
> what matter! But if the British Government can with impunity forge
> evidence to prove him so no unpopular man with a cause will ever be
> safe.[23]

The man praised by patriots and thanked by the government for de-
fending Casement from the charge of homosexuality was in fact involved in an unconsummated affair with the lesbian Wellesley and
would have been quite happy, himself, with a homosexual martyr. The
chief pollution (for him) was forgery.

"You wonder if it's lovers . . ."—There may have been an even
more surprising, more hidden element in the controversy, the possibility that de Valera believed Casement to have been homosexual. On 17
February de Valera, whose newspaper had published Maloney, Yeats,
and all the ensuing correspondence, was questioned in the Dáil about
whether he would ask the British government to "submit the alleged
Casement Diary" to examination by that "impartial tribunal." He
must have surprised his supporters when he answered, "No Sir. Roger
Casement's reputation is safe in the affections of the Irish people, the
only people whose opinions mattered to him."[24] The situation at that
very moment—commotion over Maloney's "revelations," a Nobel-
Prize-winning poet supporting the purity of a martyred founding fa-

ther, general outrage at England's treatment of Casement—was absolutely perfect. Why ruin it by looking at the "alleged diary" and perhaps re-polluting Casement and purifying the British?

Both governments' refusals to have anything to do with this issue meant that it remained interstitial; the responsibility devolved on two poets to settle the thing, as if on behalf of their respective countries. Maloney's book had linked Noyes with the circulation of the diaries —the innocent thirty-six-year-old Alfred Noyes, quietly working in his News Department office and handed something "filthy beyond description." Yeats (who had praised Noyes's first volume of poetry) had named names and called on Noyes directly:

> Come Alfred Noyes and all the troup
> That cried it far and wide,
> Come from the forger and his desk,
> Desert the perjurer's side;
>
> Come speak your bit in public
> That some amends be made
> To this most gallant gentleman
> That is in quicklime laid.[25]

And the *Irish Press* had created a layout that dramatized national antagonisms visually: "Irish Poet's Striking Challenge" shouted their huge boldface headline, under which photographs of the poets, like two boxers, took up opposite sides of the page, Yeats on the left, Noyes on the right, each identified by a brief resumé.[26] To Yeats's surprise Noyes did speak his bit in public. The *Irish Press* had called Yeats's poem a "challenge to a brother poet," and in his letter to the paper Noyes responded fraternally, quoting "The Lake Isle of Innisfree," alluding to *Hamlet,* and even praising Casement's speech-from-the-dock.[27] Noyes called for an official re-examination of the diaries, and Yeats (in his letter responding to Noyes's letter responding to his poem) agreed. Pleased to be speaking as if from the lofty plane of Culture, to be sounding "noble" and magnanimous, yet uneasy about judging handwriting they had never seen, the poets happily deferred to some other, future, "impartial" judgment. Yeats also revised the poem, reversing the pollution of Noyes's name, and the newspaper printed it. After "writers by the score," it read "No matter what the names they wear."[28]

Appropriately ludic, as the best controversialists always are, Yeats
had many private opinions on Casement, not one of them matching
exactly his published opinion. Writing the Fenian Patrick McCartan,
who had just organized a testimonial gift to Yeats of one thousand
pounds, Yeats explained away his polite response to the Sasanach
Noyes: the revision was a "verse full of Christian Charity," he wrote
mockingly, "which was entirely the result of influenza."[29] Writing
Wellesley, who was lesbian and English, Yeats expressed the hope
that Casement had been gay and the English not forgers. Writing the
politically active Ethel Mannin, to whom Yeats had once refused his
signature on a petition, he insisted that his Casement poems had nothing to do with politics: "In them I defend a noble-natured man, I do
the old work of the poets but I will defend no cause."[30]

Simpler in all respects than Yeats, not the slightest bit intellectually
playful, Noyes was overwhelmed by the political issues involved in
the controversy. This new intrusion of Casement into his life changed
his entire notion of what, had he known the discourse, he might have
called the relation of culture to imperialism. Twenty-one years earlier,
as a young man, he had been happy to do the cultural work of his
government. He had, as requested, written an article on "the Irish
troubles" of 1916, an article issued through the government Press
Bureau to American newspapers. That autumn—as England waited
to see if America would enter the War—Noyes had been lecturing
all over America on "the case for English civilization." After Nina
Casement's interruption Noyes says he "made no reply or comment
on what she had said, but continued my address on the great English
poetry of the past"—as if under the circumstances that was not a
reply.[31] Not altogether innocently, Noyes was giving the cultural An-
glophiles a "soft-sell" approach to the War. But after two visitations
from the accusing ghost of Roger Casement, once as Nina C. and once
as W. B. Y., Noyes performed his own final rite-of-reversing-pollution
in his book *The Accusing Ghost or Justice for Roger Casement* (1957).
He demanded "that the body of this wronged man . . . be returned
to his native country" and condemned the "stupid and bull-headed
bureaucracy" of his own country.[32] By this time Noyes (a Catholic
convert) had learned that Casement died a Catholic death; and he had
discovered what a tall, good-looking family the Casements were. In
his letter to the *Irish Press* Noyes had written, "I had known nothing

of Casement personally, and the appearance of his sister was a tragic revelation to me of the distinguished race from which he sprang, and the blood that ran in his veins." [33] The oddity of a judgment of character based on stature is matched by a line in *The Accusing Ghost* about Casement on trial, a person "whose princely bearing more than confirmed his manhood." [34] This distinguished race had also been blessed in an earlier generation, because Casement's father had helped to save the Hungarian patriot Louis Kossuth, to whom tributes were "paid . . . by two great English poets, Landor and Swinburne." [35] Noyes took seriously the Yeatsian notion of "the old work of the poets," and in that "princely bearing" the "gallant gentleman" is visible. Had Casement been short, ugly, and stooped, his posthumous fate might have been that of Richard III.

The danger of *not* acknowledging that there was pollution to reverse became clear when Shaw joined the controversy. His letter explicitly denied all the articles of faith subscribed to by the readers of the *Irish Press*. Maloney's book, he said, was adding to the "bad blood" between England and Ireland—but of course it was! That was the point of it! He said that there was "no villainy" because F. E. Smith (who as Attorney General presided over Casement's trial) could not have known that the "documents" were "memoranda of Putomayan cases" and not Casement's own records. With typically Shavian provocation, he insisted that Smith was "irresistibly likeable" and acted with "good faith and good nature." Only Shaw could, at that time, in that paper, have treated the diaries nonchalantly. People in 1916, he opined, had a taste for such things: "Everybody was expected to have a secret history unfit for publication . . ." And of his own response, "we associated no general depravity with psychopathic eccentricities . . ." Having treated colonial rule and homosexuality with flippancy; having said in print the kind of thing Yeats only said in letters to his lovers; having violated the taboos of most *Irish Press* readers; Shaw finally acknowledged that "Casement's high reputation is still befouled by a slander" and suggested that the British government "clear up" the "misunderstanding." [36]

Naturally the response was hysteria. This was more pollution, a reversal of the reversal, and in a tone as offensive as the content. It had to be expunged. Yeats, of course, didn't take it too seriously; to Dorothy Wellesley he called it a "long, rambling, sexless, vegetarian letter."[37] But two days later the paper published a long, rambling sexless letter from Francis Stuart criticizing Shaw for being a "good-natured busybody" and *dissociating himself* from Shaw's position. Stuart wanted to reestablish the moral clarity of the *status quo,* in which there *were* villains. He concluded his letter,

> If any apology is needed for what I have written about a famous drama-
> tist who did me the honour to invite me to become a member of the
> Irish Academy of Letters, founded by himself and Mr. Yeats, let me say
> this: It is only because he has in the past been considered the spokesman
> of what I may call the Irish Intelligentsia that as a writer I repudiate any
> association with the views expressed in Mr. Shaw's letter. On the other
> hand, Mr. Yeats's poem, as a tribute from a great poet to "a gallant Irish
> gentleman," has set a fine precedent.[38]

Shaw had now taken the place of Alfred Noyes as the bearer of British pollution, and alliance with Yeats, against Shaw, on the part of a member of the younger generation, would serve to reaffirm Case-ment's, and Ireland's purity.

But then on 16 February the paper published a letter from Diar-muid Murphy *accusing Francis Stuart of not having a sense of humor.* The hysteria had now become intertextual. The headline over the letter says "THE CASEMENT DIARIES," but Casement's name doesn't occur anywhere in it, nor does any issue connected with him. Murphy wrote, "Let me quote but Mr. Stuart's quotation from Mr. Shaw." Mr. Murphy, too, wanted to keep the national identity pure, but his taboos were different. "Mr. George Bernard Shaw," he claimed, "has now every reason to excommunicate us from all kinship of the Irish nation, for we have, through the mouth of a 'novelist,' shown ourselves more lacking in humour than the dullest Saxon."[39] So Mr. Murphy, like Francis Stuart before him, was purifying the controversy of the previ-ous letter. Writing for that same purpose several days later, in order to reestablish the Maloney-Yeats point of view and to condemn Shaw, Maud Gonne complained about the "monumental impudence of such a man offering to write Casement's last speech for him."[40] She was wrong about that: Shaw had advised Casement not to waste money on lawyers, but to defend himself with a speech such as the one Shaw enclosed as a sample. So, to undo the pollution of Shaw's reputation, on 24 February the *Irish Press* reprinted a letter Shaw had written to an English newspaper in 1916, urging the British government not to execute Casement.[41] Adding to the intertextual hysteria the same day as Maud Gonne's letter (22 February), a letter from Hanna Sheehy-Skeffington alluded to the "recent controversy over Noyes, Yeats, Shaw, and Casement" and then went on to quote *her own 1918 pamphlet about British anti-Irish propaganda in America during the Great War.*[42]

There was so much anxiety and so little to go on. In the absence of that "impartial tribunal" Noyes and Yeats had called for, in the absence of any reliable truth, texts, all kinds of texts—poems, biographies, memoirs, government records, pamphlets, old newspapers, current newspapers, the "alleged diaries" themselves—had taken the role of official pronouncements. Textual analysis, interpretive, editorial, and even factual disputes about texts, gave a focus for all the anxieties stirred up by the indeterminate moral status of Casement. And the voices heard in these debates, nervous, witty, pompous, hysterical, posturing and performing to a small audience they knew and a larger audience they imagined, lacked the absolute power of the genuinely official. They could not soothe the uneasy, condemn or forgive the guilty, or redeem the wronged—or terminate the conflict. Hence the perpetual need for just one more letter, poem, or document, to provide the definitive, absolute ending. Newspapers and publishers provided arenas for the conflict, and the traditions of print controversies provided the rules of the game.

In the years before the reinterment, every review of every biography of Casement set off a new controversy, and letters-to-the-editor hastened to contradict the book, or the reviewer, or both, or some previous letter. A 1956 *Irish Times* controversy inspired by a review of the René MacColl biography shows a typical dynamic, generating spin-off controversies about who wrote what when and what it might mean. The MacColl book required instant and assured response, because it was unpleasant in tone (MacColl didn't like Casement) and because it claimed that the diaries were genuine. The *Irish Times* reviewer, Thomas Hogan, began the reversal of pollution by saying it was a pity the book perpetuated an injury to "this most gallant gentleman / That is in quicklime laid."[43] (The one stable point in Casement's posthumous life has always been Yeats's ballad.) MacColl had seen the diaries but according to the strictures of the Official Secrets Act he was not allowed to mention that fact, so his belief in their authenticity had no apparent foundation. MacColl's description of the diaries quickly became one of the disputed texts, as historians such as Owen Dudley Edwards wondered how he could characterize by number, size, and color documents whose existence no one could confirm. Two members of the Irish Bar focused on MacColl's interview with Serjeant A. M. Sullivan, who had defended Casement, and (forty years after the trial) had betrayed attorney-client confidentiality by revealing (if what he said could be trusted) what Casement had said to him about homosexuals, though the ideas quoted suggest that the subject had actually been nationalist revolutionaries.[44]

Because the MacColl book restored the sexual taint, some of the spin-off controversies had to confront the issue of sexuality, which they did with less evasion than the 1937 controversy had. The sexual taboo seemed to have lifted slightly, and there appeared, in print, a savoring of salacious details. But this commentary also remained focused on texts. In one of these, the sexual pollution was displaced onto Sir Basil Thomson, the Scotland Yard official who had found the diaries. The matter in question involved a 1925 episode in Hyde Park: had Sir Basil been found *in flagrante delicto* with a *man* or with a *woman?* Or, as the letter-writers put it, was Thomson a "pervert" engaged in a "form of bestiality" or was he enjoying himself with a female prostitute whose name, according to some records, was Thelma de Lava? And—did he or did he not say to the arresting policemen that if they would ignore the crime he would make them "independent for life"? And—did he die a *suicide* on the *Continent,* or of *natural causes* at home in *Teddington?*[45]

And in another spin-off controversy, one reader audaciously suggested that Ireland's homophobia, not Casement's sexuality, was at fault. Monk Gibbon (Yeats's second-cousin) found proof of homosexuality in Casement's *poem* "The Streets of Catania," which was duly sent in to the *Irish Times* by another reader. Catania is a city in Sicily, and, Gibbon wrote, "to those who know the reputation of Sicily in this respect" the author's sexuality was clear. "I suppose that I am starting another argument now which can be carried on till doomsday . . . A man is a great patriot; at all costs it must not transpire that he was also a homosexual! Ireland, presumably, would not still want his bones if he were?"[46] In suggesting, indirectly, that patriotism and homosexuality might be compatible, Gibbon was making an attempt to change the system whose "internal lines" had been "transgressed."

Less diplomatic than his cousin Yeats, and writing nineteen years later, Gibbon was impatient with the taboo attached to homosexuality and wanted to distinguish the moral qualities of patriotism from the mere "pollution" of one kind of sexuality.

Gibbon was thirty-seven years ahead of his time: homosexual acts between consenting adults over the age of seventeen were not decriminalized in Ireland until 1993. But his letter, as well as some of the less daring ones, shows that Casement controversies had become a site for Irish thinking about sexual behavior and, more generally, about the taboos that Free State social legislation linked with the State's definition of itself. The controversies encouraged speculation without ever offering certainty. Nor did the genre of the newspaper controversy require closure of any sort. Editors seemed willing to let the letters inspired by a single book review go on for months. In the adversarial but ludic mode of controversy, virtually anything could be said, and at odd moments new ideas—such as Monk Gibbon's—could be snuck in without attracting censure. Like the more-or-less spontaneous flow of the audience's ideas on a call-in show or the subscribers' on an unmoderated e-mail discussion list, the letters-to-the-editor in a controversy revealed what was on the national mind; and because Casement was the alleged subject, the most "forbidden" issues were on people's minds from the beginning.

3

This grave, like the graves of the other patriots who lie in this cemetery, like the graves in Arbour Hill . . . will become a place of pilgrimage . . . If there had been no 1916 and there had been no European war of 1914, the man whose bones lie here would deserve to be honoured and revered . . . for the noble part he played in exposing the atrocities in the Congo . . . [and in] Putamayo. It required courage to do what Casement did . . . we are glad to have him back amongst us.

Eamon de Valera, Glasnevin, 1 March 1965

> From gaol yard to the Liberator's tomb
> Pillared in frost, they carry the freed ash,
> Transmuted relic of a death-cell flame
> Which purged for martyrdom the diarist's flesh.

On the small screen I watch the packed cortège
Pace from High Mass. Rebels in silk hats now
Exploit the grave with an old comrade's speech:
White hair tossed, a black cape flecked with snow.

Richard Murphy, "Casement's Funeral"

During the forty-eight-and-a-half years in which he hadn't been properly buried, layers of identity had evolved in the Casement of Irish
memory, each subverting the selves above it. Whichever Casement you
liked, he was a man with many secrets, and he was bad at keeping
them: the charm of fiasco on the grand scale was not the least of his
charms. Beneath the knighted Protestant consul-traitor lay of course
the classic martyr, the Catholic Irish-speaking gun-running rebel; such
was the Casement of Yeats's poems, the hero of the 1937 *Irish Press*
controversy. But Casement Martyr was obviously as official, as much
a figment of state ideology, as Traitor Casement, and beneath the
perfect martyr another rebel Casement had been evolving, a rebel
against the dominant pieties of the high de Valeran period. So long as
the "state" involved was Great Britain, an Irish Casement was a folk
hero. But once the Irish state had him, another folk-Casement
emerged.

What reason was there for any more "popular memory" of Casement once the "suppressed ritual" had actually happened, and the
paradigmatic martyr been given a magnificent state funeral? Surely
when he had a visitable grave in Glasnevin, he was official? The folklore, the gossip, and the kinds of appearance Casement made in literature after 1965 suggest otherwise. Richard Murphy's poem observes
quietly that the quicklime "purged for martyrdom the diarist's flesh,"
implying that something in Casement needed purging before the diarist became the martyr.[47] David Rudkin's radio play *Cries from Casement as His Bones Are Brought to Dublin* showed a Casement
protesting his official status, taunting the cardinal at his funeral: "Am
I a property, then? . . . A relic of sacred bones? Oh, don't let your
young men in their worship come too near *me!* and my writings, will
they be a national treasure, too?"[48] Like Paul Muldoon's Volkswagen,
Roger Casement was still throbbing with the excitement of some forbidden activity. "You wonder if it's lovers": they certainly did wonder;

in fact they'd been wondering for almost half a century, and the reinterment gave people license to wonder out loud.

This dissident Casement tapped the secular energies suppressed but
never eradicated in the first decades of independence. There is little
print evidence for the non-official Casement of those years, though he
can be found in Yeats's letter to Dorothy Wellesley ("If Casement were
homosexual, what matter?") and in Monk Gibbon's daring suggestion, in 1956, that "The Streets of Catania" was about a homosexual
encounter. Here and there in exchanges unrecorded in the pages of *The
Bell* or the debates of the Dáil, a hidden, tolerant Ireland persisted. In
a 1973 *Irish Times* Casement controversy Mrs. Ita Kelly of Ballsbridge
wrote in to "concur" with a previous letter-writer, Mrs. Irving, who
had claimed that homosexuality was "just another kind of loving." To
this opinion Mrs. Kelly added an anecdote from her schooldays "many
moons ago" under the tutelage of Mother Scholastica. Reading "The
Ballad of Reading Gaol" to her students, Mother S. explained that
Wilde had been sent to gaol "just for loving another man." Mrs. Kelly
calls this a "splendid reply to a class of girls of seventeen years old,"
and wishes Mother Scholastica were alive to participate in the present
correspondence: "Her opinions certainly would be very valuable."[49]
The obscure but radical Mother Scholastica was, said her student, a
"brilliant intellectual" whose authority the girls never questioned. Ireland must have had many unrecorded Mother Scholasticas forming
the minds of people who wrote to the *Irish Times* in 1973 saying
things like "It does not matter a damn whether Roger Casement was
a homosexual or not" and "I am quite certain that the younger generation of Irish don't give one damn if the 'supposed diaries' were black,
red, pink, or blue."[50] Kieran Rose notes how difficult it is to find
evidence of lesbian and gay lives in Ireland except in legislation intended to control that behavior.[51] Although it might be even harder to
find evidence of toleration of homosexuality, the letters from self-
professed members of a generation past middle age in 1973 indicate
that it did exist in forms other than denial or embarrassment.

The return of the remains released the silent dissidents from the
need to maintain a sober patriotic attitude to Casement; or rather,
from the need to maintain it exclusively. It was possible to maintain
many concurrent ideas about Casement, and the newspaper contro-

versies continued (as they still do) in wearyingly familiar form. But
almost as soon as the plane carrying his remains touched down on
Irish soil, a new, "people's" Casement, a troublemaker, appeared on
the scene, interrupting the pious with the scatalogical. If jokes and
gossip tell anything at all about the collective national mind, they tell
us in this instance that Ireland, north and south, was obsessed with
what precisely of Casement was coming back. That mind was fixated
on the physical remains of the man, as well it might be, considering
that he had been buried in quicklime forty-eight-and-a-half years earlier. Eilish Pearce, who worked as senior assistant for broadcasting in
the Government Information Bureau, says it was "commonly accepted
that it was unlikely there were any bones" in the coffin.[52] The *Irish
Times* reported an "Ingenious Theory," cited in the *Evening Standard*,
explaining why the "Irish authorities" had no trouble in identifying
Casement's body. The body "is almost wholly preserved—teeth, hair
and flesh, even his beard . . . the quicklime—possibly because it had
an impure substance which mixed with the damp ground—formed a
kind of plaster cast around the body and preserved it extremely well."
In dry, formal tones, the *Irish Times* commented, "It is an ingenious
theory, but one understands it is incorrect."[53] Two days later the *Irish
Times* printed a less whimsical account of the exhumation, offering
official verification by the governor of the prison and clerical sanction
by an attendant priest. The prison records were consulted because
"Details, identifying each grave, were kept by the prison governor
and these were examined before the exhumation work began." And, as
"prison staff" started digging "while British and Irish officials looked
on," one Father Thomas Keane, "the Cork-born Catholic chaplain
of the prison," stood by the graveside. All the "principal members
of the skeleton were uncovered," and the "skeleton corresponded to
Casement's known physical measurements."[54] Comforting information, no doubt, but perhaps just more folklore. This was the moment,
this visiting of the tomb, around which stories clustered. David Rudkin's radio play *Cries from Casement as His Bones Are Brought to
Dublin* added its own version:

> *Lynch:* Officer Mahoney, how shall we be sure we dig up all the one
>   man?
> *Mahoney:* How do yous mean?
> *Lynch:* Not minus something, or plus parts of another?

Mahoney: You know the official line on that: impossible.

Lynch: But Officer Mahoney, I see what I can see. And what I see is, 'tis anybody's guess what's goin in this box.

Mahoney: It's the thought that counts. Here. These bones'll do. *(Brief formalized tearing of bones)* [55]

The rumor so ubiquitous it was almost official, that bits of the murderer Crippen got mixed in with bits of Casement, is elaborated in Rudkin's script, as—inside that coffin, so respectfully greeted by de Valera—Casement and Crippen have a cosy chat about national identity.

The same folk Casement appeared in the North. Roisin McAuley remembers that Eamon McCann published a letter "somewhere" suggesting that de Valera blow on the ashes and bring Casement back to life.[56] And according to a headline in the *Belfast Newsletter,* "CASEMENT GHOST SEEN IN BELFAST."

The tall, dark man pushed the door of the bar open and undid the buttons of his overcoat. Outside the heavy rain continued . . . The new arrival was bearded and boasted a head of dark, curly hair, thinning at the temples. His dark grey overcoat was perfectly dry, and his very narrow, rather old-fashioned trousers were creased. "I wonder if I could trouble you for a meat pie with all the trimmings," he inquired.[57]

The manager of the Golden Jubilee public house in Cromac Street was puzzled because "there was something peculiar about the man . . ." Then, twenty minutes later, the customer "walked to the oldest toilet in the pub—a toilet so situated that only long-standing customers knew its whereabouts . . ." More curious behavior followed: the customer never ate the meat pie, ordered a Guinness, but didn't drink that either. As he explained, "he had come a long way, he was tired, and . . . he didn't really drink." When Jo Gillespie, the pub manager, read the next day about the return of the remains of Sir Roger Casement, the mystery cleared up. "It's certainly very strange. I'll swear the man was Roger Casement. The whole thing is really quite unbelievable." [58]

The anxiety that the return be well-staged was inseparable from an impulse to think of unholy issues like the identity of the remains or the digestive systems of ghosts. The general feeling about Casement at the time of the reinterment, that he was "a Noble Character," especially because of his humanitarian work in Africa and South America, coexisted with jokes speculating about why de Valera did not walk closer to the coffin.[59] And the great concern with the reinterment as a public spectacle and media event arose, according to Eilish Pearce, because "it was generally recognized that this was a dress rehearsal for de Valera's funeral," an opportunity for Ireland on the international stage. Telefís Éireann was just four years old, and this was its chance to compete in the great age of televised state funerals such as Kennedy's and Churchill's.[60] The entire affair took place on a huge scale. Care was taken that every moment between the arrival of the remains at Baldonnel Airfield at 5 P.M. on Tuesday 23 February 1965 and the funeral on Monday 1 March and burial in Glasnevin be dignified, ritualized, and recorded for posterity. Casement's closest surviving relatives, the daughters of his brother Charles, were flown in from Australia by the Irish government; Casement cousins had special seats at the funeral; civil servants were given the day off; and most schools and businesses were closed. So many representatives of different religious faiths, Irish cities, and political parties were present as the coffin was wheeled to the graveside, that, said the *Irish Times,* "All Ireland was there."[61]

Not present was Richard Murphy, watching on "the small screen" and meditating on all the changes in Ireland since 1916. "Casement's Funeral" says everything that couldn't be said at the big ceremonial moments, acknowledging the ghoulish interest in the remains ("Now Casement's skeleton is flying home") and the hunch that the diaries were genuine ("the diarist's flesh"). But mixed with these mild impieties is an affectionate tolerance for official Ireland's appropriation of Casement: "Rebels in silk hats now / Exploit the grave with an old comrade's speech: / White hair tossed, a black cape flecked with snow." Ireland had its great black-and-white television moment, and Murphy manages delicately to affirm the friendship of old comrades, to praise the old, sick Dev for standing out in the cold so long, and to note how far Ireland has come: the rebels wear silk hats. David Rudkin's Casement, at that very moment, is more directly antagonistic to the "sacred relic" he has become. Outraged to find he's being buried in Glasnevin, not Murlough Bay, he insists *I will not lie here* but is silenced by the Captain attending the coffin: "Whisht Casement, the President is making a moving speech, your biographers have come, there's not a dry eye in the graveyard—" When he demands, "Why not in Antrim, to my specific dying wish?" the Cardinal says, "Balls to your specific dying wish, we've got you now" and then "Be a good hero, shut your mouth." [62] Thus to all dissidents.

As the reinterment quietly enabled the "forged" diaries to be considered authentic, it also redirected the impulse to blame England for Casement's fate: now possible Irish complicity could be confronted and examined. Murphy's poem sees the extravaganza of the funeral as atonement: "our new / Nation atones for her shawled motherland / Whose welcome gaoled him." In Rudkin's play all the Kerry witnesses subpoenaed to testify at Casement's trial in London visit the coffin as it lies in state and ask forgiveness. Each announces himself ("John MacCarthy, farmer" / "Mary Gorman, farmgirl" / "Martin Collins, with the pony and trap") and then says, "I'm sorry." [63] At the time of the lying-in-state an article in the *Irish Times* titled "Betrayal of Casement through Ignorance" said resonantly of these same Irish people, "They knew not what they did." [64] But the issue was more complicated than Murphy, Rudkin, and the *Irish Times* implied; the witnesses had nothing to apologize for. The next year, at the time of the fiftieth anniversary of the Rising, *The Kerryman* honored them with a large, boldface, page-one headline ("ARDFERT IS DEFENDED") and minutely detailed accounts of the traumas suffered by the Kerry people who, as the article said, "got innocently involved in this chain of misfortune that was forged in Banna's lonely Beach on that Good Friday morning 50 years ago." [65] But "all Ireland" did not read *The Kerryman,* and the popular belief persists that, as a priest once said to me, "the local people betrayed him." Nevertheless, the Tralee railroad station was named in his honor, and the Tralee office of Bord Fáilte is the only place in Ireland where a postcard of Casement (printed in Herefordshire) may be bought.

David Rudkin's hero, making smart-ass remarks from his coffin, lived on in all sorts of informal moments of interest only to the folklorist, irritating different people in different ways. When Casement's cousin, Professor A. J. Otway-Ruthven of Trinity, was asked by some Fianna Fáil TDs (in the 1960s) for her comments on Casement, she responded, "In our family we don't discuss the failures." [66] When the musical McPeake family was performing in Sligo in 1993, the patriarch of the family noted that the pipes on stage had been played at a feis in the presence of Roger Casement; he then leaned forward to the audience and said, as if intimately, "It's not true what they say about him." [67] Casement's aura was still powerful enough in 1988 for Oxford University Press to prevent Medbh McGuckian from using an epigraph by Casement for her volume *On Ballycastle Beach* and from mentioning him by name in a poem: "they were embarrassed by it," McGuckian says. [68]

Mischievous, impious Casement has been, *par excellence,* sexual Casement, but as the atmosphere around sex has changed in the 1990s, in Ireland and in the west generally, public discourse about sexuality has evolved a new kind of piety, and Casement has lost much of his naughty aura. According to some strains in contemporary thinking, it has become wrong *not* to talk about sex, wrong to suppress, hide, or lie about it: whatever you say, say everything. The private lives of Sinéad O'Connor and Bishop Eamon Casey, open to all in the pages of Irish newspapers, carry the moral weight of confession, as do the almost daily headlines about the secret families of Roman Catholic priests and the abuse inflicted on children years ago by members of the clergy. The unspeakable is now spoken on a regular basis. Casement has been repoliticized and claimed as a homosexual ancestor. In *Swoon,* an independent, low-budget cult film about the Leopold and Loeb murder case, the guests at a transvestite party leaf through a book of famous gay people as the camera zooms in on photographs and the voiceover says, "Oscar Wilde . . . Sir Roger Casement . . . Marcel Proust." [69] For lesbian and gay Irish, Casement is a precursor in a more particularized history, and Irish groups have claimed him often and audibly, in recent works such as Kieran Rose's *Diverse Communities* and Eibhear Walshe's "Oscar's Mirror." [70] When the members of ILGO (the Irish Lesbian and Gay Organization) march on St. Patrick's Day in New York, protesting their exclusion from the parade, they carry posters with pictures of Irish homosexuals—Frances Power Cobbe, Somerville and Ross, Wilde, Casement, Eva Gore-Booth—establishing a genealogy of people who never conceptualized such a genealogy themselves, at least not on paper. Paul Muldoon emphasized this ancestry in a poem printed on the editorial page of the *New York Times* in 1992, the first year that the Ancient Order of Hibernians refused to let ILGO march:

. . . As for the "Hibs" standing in the way
Of Irish Lesbians and Gays,
would they have stopped Casement when he tried to land
a boatload of guns on Banna Strand?[71]

Michael Carson's 1995 novel *The Knight of the Flaming Heart* imagines Casement's return to Banna Strand as a patron saint of homosexuals for contemporary Ireland.[72]

It was in the liberalizing atmosphere of spring 1993, after the decriminalizing in Ireland of homosexual acts between consenting adults over the age of seventeen, that Roisin McAuley and Nigel Acheson of the BBC decided to devote the 24 September weekly radio broadcast *Document* to the diaries.[73] For the first time the diaries were forensically examined and declared genuine. The permission thus granted to the BBC led the Home Office to make the diaries available to the general public the following year. The *Irish Times* printed excerpts from the diaries as soon as they were officially open, and the date was such that these passages—the most explicitly pornographic, of course —were published during Holy Week 1994 (Tuesday, March 29). Although the ensuing debate evolved along predictable lines, there emerged a totally outed Casement with almost nothing left to hide: folk Casement, the active homosexual hidden beneath the Republican martyr, was now a public persona. With details of his intercourse with "Millar" on 28 May 1910, in a hotel in Warrenpoint, printed unexpurgated on page 6 ("HOME NEWS"), he surely could no longer be linked with the hidden. The boldface headline inset in the excerpts printed this quotation from the diaries: "First time after so many years and so deep mutual longing."[74] The *Irish Times* editor wanted to emphasize the love, not the sin or the criminality. No longer naughty, no longer the all-purpose subversive, Casement became an object lesson in the many forms of patriotism for the new, revisionist Ireland. As Emer O'Kelly wrote in the *Sunday Independent*, ". . . the well-meaning custodians of Casement's political history and reputation are wrong when they suggest that his sexuality and sexual practices should now be put to rest . . . They must be kept alive, not because they show Casement in all his human unhappiness and loneliness (although they do), but because we have to learn to de-mythologize our history."[75] Entirely official, Casement was now an emblem of the United Ireland Yeats, Monk Gibbon, and maybe even Mother

Scholastica had envisioned, in which patriotic reverence and homosexual love were acknowledged to coexist.

4

What sense can it make to speak of Casement's "posthumous life"? The man must have been calcified over eighty years ago: he had no life after that. To talk about posthumous Casement is to talk about what Ireland has projected onto his name, and as Medbh McGuckian said in an interview, "He covers a lot of ground for a lot of people." [76] Republican, cultural nationalist, humanitarian, anti-imperialist, homosexual, native of Antrim, denizen of Glasnevin; maligned, hanged, canonized, reinterred, outed—he has offered a means of thinking about much of Irish life during this century. In Margaret MacCurtain's analysis, the moving statues of the Virgin in 1985 indicated that Irish society was "traumatised around women's issues," especially in the areas of "birth-control, illegitimacy, marriage and divorce," and "Some kind of fuse ignited the imagination around an object of popular devotion." [77] So in similar fashion, the sheer quantity of Casement memory—the poems, the books, the letters, the controversies—argues that Irish society has been traumatized around sexuality as it exists in a national field; as it is defined, organized, and controlled by national institutions—the State, the Church, the law.

Although the sexual lives of political figures like O'Connell or Parnell have long constituted topics of public debate, the issues surrounding Casement were unresolved, and much was at stake in their resolution. When national dignity was partially satisfied by the return of the remains, memory began to focus on all the other issues. The whole society, or so it sometimes seems, did its thinking about sex through Casement. He offered a way of thinking about difficult, long-buried matters without ever calling them by name; and without deliberately, systematically, consciously deciding to think about them. The 1937 controversy focused the new state's hysteria about all kinds of pollution; and later controversies offered opportunities to see what could be risked in sexual discourse. Casement's life fortunately made possible all sorts of safety nets: the speech from the dock could be adverted to when debate about the diaries grew too hot or too hopeless; Casement's generosity to the language movement could be invoked to counterbalance the failures of the Irish brigade and the gun-running; and when sex and nationalism both became too fraught, there was always the Congo. In the Congo and the Putomayo region Casement had achieved uncontestable success: he confronted atrocities that no one else had the courage and practical knowledge to discover or the persistence to record; his moral vision compelled him to follow through on this work, and only a passionate innocence could have made him think empires would behave in humanitarian ways. These labors deserve all the praise they have ever gotten, and more; yet it must be said that they also offered a recourse from the difficult subject of the rest of Casement's life. For much of this century, Ireland has lived vicariously through Roger Casement, using the manifold and extraordinary facts of his life to explore without risk topics otherwise unapproachable: for good or for ill, but certainly for sure, *ní bheidh a leithéid arís ann.*

Notes

1. The holograph copy of the 28 October 1914 Casement letter is in the National Library of Ireland, NLI 13082–4. I am grateful to Patricia Donlon for permission to quote it. Paul Muldoon's "Ireland" (*Why Brownlee Left* [Winston-Salem, N. C.: Wake Forest University Press, 1980], 19) is quoted with the permission of Wake Forest University Press and Faber and Faber. The sentences from Sir Ernley Blackwell's report are cited in virtually every biography of Casement: they may be found in B. L. Reid, *The Lives of Roger Casement* (New Haven and London: Yale University Press, 1976), 418; B. Inglis, *Roger Casement* (London: Hodder and Stoughton Ltd., 1973) 359–60; H. Montgomery Hyde, *Roger Casement* (Harmondsworth, Middlesex: Penguin, 1964), 139–40.

I am indebted to many people for sending me Casement trivia. Rather than thank them note by note throughout the essay, I shall say here how grateful I am especially to Maureen Murphy and the late Michael Durkan, who both gave me hundreds of Casement items; to Margaret MacCurtain and Helen O'Carroll for a tour of Banna Strand and much information about the Kerry witnesses; and also to Angela Bourke, Anne Colman, Roy Foster, Adrian Frazier, Tom Hachey, Michael Keohane, John Killen and the staff of the Linen Hall Library, Patricia King, Seth Koven, Derek Mahon, Mary McGrath, Deirdre McMahon, Medbh McGuckian, Rhoda Nathan, Philip O'Leary, Tom Rapp, Robert Rhodes, Emily Savin, Harris Savin, Daniel Scanlon, Patrick Sheeran, and Michael Steinman.

2. Roy Jenkins, *Asquith* (London: Collins, 1964), 403.

3. David Rudkin, *Cries from Casement as His Bones Are Brought to Dublin* (London: BBC,1974), 76.

4. Luke Gibbons, "The Camel in the Koran: Rumour in Irish Politics," *Irish Reporter* 5 (1992): 14.

5. Jean-Noël Kapferer, *Rumors: Uses, Interpretations, and Images* (New Brunswick and London: Transaction Publishers, 1990), 215, 263. This book is cited in Gibbons's essay mentioned above.

6. Mary Douglas, *Purity and Danger*, rev. ed. (London and New York: Routledge, 1991), 62.

7. Cameo appearances: novels that mention Casement include Eimar O'Duffy's *The Wasted Island* (1929), Joyce's *Ulysses* (1922), Stevie Smith's *Over the Frontier* (1938), Terence de Vere White's *Lucifer Falling* (1966); poems that mention Casement include Section 16 of Louis MacNeice's *Autumn Journal*, Paul Durcan's "The Martyrdom of Saint Sebastian" (from *Daddy, Daddy*), and Paul Muldoon's "A Clear Signal" (*New York Times* [17 March 1992]: A 25).

Two ballads include the anonymous "O lordly Roger Casement" (Inglis, *Roger Casement*, 392) and "Banna Strand" (arranged by A. J. Potter, 1965). The documentaries include a winter 1993 BBC television film called *Heart of Darkness* (mentioned by Brian Inglis, in the 1993 paperback edition of *Roger Casement* [Belfast: Blackstaff Press] 9) and a September 1993 BBC radio program, *Document*, devoted to the diaries.

The plays include *Traigh Bhanna*, a translation by Seamus Ó Dubhda from the English of John MacDonagh, presented at the Peacock Theatre, Dublin, as one of three plays commemorating the Rising [*Irish Times*, 15 April (1936): 8]; *The Challengers* (the third of its three plays is about Casement) by Padraic Colum, produced at the Lantern Theatre, Dublin, in February 1966; *Prisoner of the Crown* by Richard F. Stockton, produced at the Abbey in 1973 (sent to me courtesy of Teresa Kane); *Casement* by Alex Ferguson, produced by the Moving Theatre at Riverside Studios, London, May 1995; *Casement* by Charlie Dunne, produced by the Transatlantic Theatre Company, Ormond Multi Media Centre, Dublin, August 1995; a "five-act dramatisation" of Alfred Noyes's book *The Accusing Ghost, or Justice for Roger Casement* (1957), written with "Robert" McHugh (because the late Roger McHugh wrote a famous essay on Casement, I have taken the liberty of assuming that the name intended here is his; however, I have never been able to find a trace of this play, which is mentioned in the article on Alfred Noyes by Margaret B. McDowell in the *Dictionary of Literary Biography* [Vol. 20: *British Poets 1914–1915*, ed. Donald E. Sutherland (Detroit: Gale Researach Co., 1983), 255]); and (by far the best of the lot) David Rudkin's radio play cited in note 3 above. The Thaddeus O'Sullivan film was mentioned to me in conversation by Donald Taylor Black; the *Irish Times* of 25 May 1994 (weekend 2) quotes Mr. O'Sullivan about the film: "It's going to be a controversial project, I have no doubt . . . It will involve intimacy, romance, and humour mixed with adventure, politics, violence and horror in the hope of constructing a modern film which will reclaim Roger Casement as a man out of his time, as an entirely modern hero." The *Irish Press* (6 August 1956) printed an article about Shaw's comments on a planned 1934 film about Casement that had been "killed" by the "British Film Censorship authorities." The "Welsh film-maker" Kenneth Griffith was said to have made a film on Casement shown at the West Belfast Festival in August 1993 (*Irish Times*, 11 August 1993). In *On the Town* (*Irish Times*, 29 May 1993, weekend 2), Robert O'Byrne wrote of Sarah Lawson that "her interests now lie in other Irish-based projects and . . . she is actively seeking material over here, though not relating to Roger Casement. Seemingly, this is one affair which has exerted an irresistible, but none too beneficial, fascination on script writers." Casement's posthumous life in English popular culture may never be explored, but a good starting-point might be Agatha Christie's *N or M?*, in which Sheila Perenna identifies her father this way: "His name was Patrick Maguire. He—he was a follower of Casement in the last War. He was shot as a traitor! All for nothing! For an idea—he worked himself up with those other Irishmen. Why couldn't he just stay at home quietly and mind his own business? . . ." [rev. ed. (New York: Berkley Books, 1984), 59].

8. Reid, *The Lives of Roger Casement*, 434; Inglis, *Roger Casement*, 385. The "Casement" monument at Murlough Bay described in the 1992 Michelin guide to Ireland has several names on it, none of them Casement's.

9. Eva Gore-Booth, "Heroic Death, 1916," *Selected Poems of Eva Gore-Booth* (London: Longmans, Green and Co., 1933), 77.

10. For the mention of Hanna Sheehy-Skeffington, see the *Irish Times* (13 April 1936): 13. P. J. Little's remark may be found in the article "Vindication of Casement" in *Irish Press* (3 February 1937): 9.

11. Reid, *The Lives of Roger Casement*, 460–61.

12. Alfred Noyes, *Two Worlds for Memory* (Philadelphia and New York: J. B. Lippincott and Co., 1953), 124–25.

13. Douglas, *Purity and Danger*, 135.

14. Reid, *The Lives of Roger Casement*, 417.

15. W. B. Yeats, *The Variorum Edition of the Poems* (New York: Macmillan, 1957), 460–63.

16. Ibid., 586–87.

17. William J. Maloney, *The Forged Casement Diaries* (Dublin and Cork: The Talbot Press, 1936).

18. W. B. Yeats, "Roger Casement," *Irish Press*, (2 February 1937): 6.

19. Joseph Hone, *W. B. Yeats, 1865–1939* (New York: Macmillan, 1943), 481.

20. Dorothy Wellesley, ed., *Letters on Poetry from W. B. Yeats to Dorothy Wellesley* (London and Oxford: Oxford University Press, 1940), 126.

21. Ibid., 126.

22. *The Letters of W. B. Yeats,* ed. Allan Wade (London: Rupert Hart-Davis, 1954), 867.

23. Wellesley, *Letters on Poetry,* 128.

24. *Irish Press,* 18 February 1937: 9. For additional commentary on de Valera's probable belief in the authenticity of the diaries, see Deirdre Mc-Mahon, "Roger Casement: An Account from the Archives of His Reinterment in Ireland," *Journal of the Irish Society for Archives,* n.s., 3. 1 (Spring 1996): 4.

25. *Irish Press,* (2 February 1937): 6.

26. Ibid.

27. *Irish Press,* (12 February 1937): 8–9.

28. Ibid., (13 February 1937): 8.

29. *Yeats and Patrick McCartan, a Fenian Friendship: Letters with a Commentary by John Unterecker* (Dublin: The Dolmen Press, 1967), 393.

30. *Letters of W. B. Yeats,* 881–82.

31. Noyes, *Two Worlds,* 133.

32. Noyes, *The Accusing Ghost, or, Justice for Roger Casement* (London: Victor Golancz, 1957), 180.

33. *Irish Press,* (12 February 1937): 9.

34. Noyes, *The Accusing Ghost,* 152.

35. Ibid., 38–39.

36. *Irish Press,* (11 February 1937): 9.

37. Wellesley, *Letters on Poetry,* 128.

38. *Irish Press,* (13 February 1937): 8.

39. Ibid., (16 February 1937): 14.

40. Ibid., (22 February 1937): 2.

41. Ibid., (24 February 1937): 7.

42. Ibid., (22 February 1937): 2.

43. *Irish Times,* (7 April 1956): 9, 12.

Life is too short for even the most leisured centenarian to read every letter-to-the-editor in every Casement controversy. I have of necessity been selective in choosing controversies to study and letters to cite. The supply was overwhelming, and as recently as September 1996 letters about Casement (letters alas too late for me even to consider) were appearing in *An Phoblacht.* On the issue of plenitude, I shall quote letters from two Casement controversies: "The fascination of the voluminous correspondence on the moral character of Casement is only exceeded by its futility" [letter from Murroe FitzGerald, Co. Waterford, to the *Irish Times,* (17 May 1956): 7]. And from L. E. R. Peacocke, writing to the *Irish Times* on 5 June 1973, "I think the less written about the matter the better" (11).

44. *Irish Times,* (14 April 1956): 9; (16 April 1956): 5; (18 April 1956): 5; (19 April 1956).

45. Ibid., (17 April 1956): 7; (25 April 1956): 5; (30 April 1956): 5.

46. Ibid., (21 April 1956): 9.

47. Richard Murphy, "Casement's Funeral," *The Price of Stone and Earlier Poems* (Winston-Salem: Wake Forest University Press, 1985), 50.

48. Rudkin, *Cries from Casement,* 76.

49. Mrs. Irving's letter, *Irish Times,* (19 June 1973): 11; Mrs. Kelly's letter, (22 June 1973): 13.

50. Ibid., (5 June 1973): 11.

51. Kieran Rose, *Diverse Communities* (Cork: Cork University Press, 1994), 9.

52. Interview with Eilish Pearce, 9 July 1995.

53. *Irish Times,* (25 February 1965), 9.

54. Ibid., (27 February 1965): 11. Those few people as interested as this author in Casement's remains may want to know of another remains-related ritual that took place on 2 August 1953, when de Valera addressed a meeting called by the Casement Commemoration Committee at Murlough Bay (see *Irish News and Belfast Morning News* and *Belfast Telegraph* for predictably different accounts of the occasion). On this occasion a grave site was chosen, in anticipation of the return of the remains. In David Rudkin's play Casement complains when he realizes he is being buried in Glasnevin, not Murlough Bay.

55. Rudkin, *Cries from Casement,* 10. Now that Deirdre McMahon has published the definitive account, based on archival records, of the reinterment, it is possible to know the nonfolkloric truth about which bones survived the quicklime and where they were found (McMahon, "Roger Casement").

56. Conversation with Roisin McAuley, September 1993.

57. *Belfast Newsletter,* (3 March 1965): 1.

58. Ibid.

59. Interview with Eilish Pearce, 9 July 1995.

60. Ibid.

61. *Irish Times,* (2 March 1965): 1.

62. Rudkin, *Cries from Casement,* 74–75.

63. Ibid., 70.

64. *Irish Times,* (24 February 1965): 4.

65. *Kerryman,* (9 April 1966): 1, 5.

66. Anecdote told to me by Brian Walker, 1 October 1994.

67. Anecdote told to me by students at the Yeats International Summer School, Sligo, August 1993.

68. Interview with Medbh McGuckian, February 1994. I also thank Medbh McGuckian for letting me see her unpublished poems (including a sonnet sequence) about Roger Casement.

69. *Swoon* 1992, dir. Tom Kalin; prod. Christine Vachon; screen play, Tom Kalin and Hilton Als.

70. Rose, *Diverse Communities:* Eibhear Walshe, "Oscar's Mirror," in *Lesbian and Gay Visions of Ireland,* ed. Íde O'Carroll and Eoin Collins (London and New York: Cassell, 1995), 150.

71. *New York Times,* 17 March 1992: A25.

72. The Carson novel was published by Doubleday in 1995.

73. Conversation with Nigel Acheson, September 1996.

74. *Irish Times,* 29 March 1994, 6.

75. *Independent,* 3 April 1994.

76. Interview with Medbh McGuckian, February 1994.

77. Margaret MacCurtain, "Moving Statues and Irish Women," in *The Irish Women's Studies Reader,* ed. Ailbhe Smyth (Dublin: Attic Press, 1993), 206, 207.

Gender, Sexuality, and Englishness in Modern Irish Drama and Film

NINETEENTH-CENTURY representations of Irish characters by English dramatists took contradictory forms: unspoiled colleens and violent Paddies; quick-witted servants and loudmouthed soldiers; warm-hearted but impecunious noblemen and calculating fortune hunters. However mutable the stereotype, the charming Celt and the drunken savage had two things in common: they were theatrically effective because they differed from a norm called Englishness, and they sustained the culture of imperialism, which justified itself by establishing the inferiority of colonized peoples.

The stories of the Stage Irishman and the colleen have already been told;[1] the complementary story of the Stage Englishman has not. Although L. P. Curtis posits "the absence from the Irish scene of a stereotype of English character as rigid and elaborate as Paddy,"[2] he has been misled by the production of "Englishness" as an implicit norm accepted by both colonizer and colonized. Shaw argues that a secure national identity is invisible: "A healthy nation is as unconscious of its nationality as a healthy man of his bones."[3] Nineteenth-century British imperial power permitted the imaginative universalization of Englishness.

Irishness has been construed, negatively by imperialists and positively by the Irish themselves, as difference from English capitalist modernity. Cultural theorists such as Hyde, Yeats, and Pearse argued that Irishness was not equal to Englishness, but different and more desirable. The cultural production of Irish Otherness, however, placed it on the feminine end of the representational spectrum, which spelled disadvantage as well as distinctiveness. Although resisted by many Irish dramatists concerned to assert their manliness,[4] the connection between Irishness and femininity was reinforced by the native image of Ireland as a woman. Ancient sovereignty goddesses, eighteenth-century *aisling* poems in which a beautiful maiden lamented her rape

by the colonizer or the loss of her Irish prince, and post-Famine devotion to the Virgin, fed into an overdetermined tradition that, whether
it valorized or despised "feminine" qualities, regularly attributed them
to the "Celtic Race."[5]

In modern Irish drama, Englishness is almost completely identified
with maleness, though not always with masculinity. No Englishwomen like Forster's domineering memsahibs appear on the Irish
stage.[6] The colonial allegory either operates in heterosexual terms,
locating the colonizer in the superior male position and representing
the colony as the feminized object of desire and control, or, surprisingly, is inscribed on an all-male continuum ranging from the homosocial to the homoerotic. To create bonding where the audience expects
antipathy is clever dramaturgy, but more than technique is required to
explain why so many Irish dramatists construct Stage Englishmen
who fail to operate as villains of the anti-imperial piece, and whose
significant Other is Irish.

Friel's *Translations* (1980) suggests that the Irish can distinguish an
individual Englishman from his imperial mission:

> *Owen:* . . . Come on man,—speak in English.
> *Manus:* For the benefit of the colonist?
> *Owen:* He's a decent man.
> *Manus:* Aren't they all at some level?[7]

While Manus's irony suggests that to find the decent man inside the
colonist one has to dig deep, many twentieth-century Irish plays and
films depict Englishmen as good fellows at heart. (Neil Jordan's recent
Michael Collins is a striking exception to the rule.) To what should
we attribute the political tolerance of Irish dramatists? Though it is
tempting to see victims as more fair-minded than oppressors, historical
counterexamples abound. We would do better to look at the nineteenth-century melodramatic tradition and nineteenth-century formu-
lations of national character: at Dion Boucicault and Matthew
Arnold.

Boucicault, who needed to please English as well as Irish audiences
and to evade the Lord Chamberlain's political censorship, maintained
a critical attitude toward imperial policy but represented English characters sympathetically, and displaced the required generic villainy onto
Irishmen complicit with the colonial system. In *Arrah-na-Pogue*

(1864) the duty-bound British officer Major Coffin condemns the Irish hero Shaun to death, but is overruled by his merciful superior, the Secretary at Dublin Castle. Coffin's severity is also mitigated by his Stage Cockney sergeant, who keeps a sentimental vigil with the condemned man. In *The Shaughraun* (1874) Captain Molineux, "a good fellow, although he is an Englishman,"[8] falls in love with the nationalist Claire and connives at the escape of her brother Robert, a Fenian rebel; Robert graciously bestows Claire's hand on Molineux. In *Robert Emmet* (1884), the British officer Norman Claverhouse facilitates Sarah Curran's affair with Emmet, although he is in love with her himself. His behavior, while exquisite by the standards of sentimental melodrama, is, like Molineux's, treasonous. He is infatuated with Emmet: he falls weeping into the hero's arms and receives his last kisses before the executioners' volley rescues him from what threatens (or promises) to become a homoerotic embrace.[9]

Boucicault's Irish-loving Englishmen were the products of particular economic and theatrical exigencies, as well as of their author's conciliatory political temperament. Although they were utopian rather than realistic representations, they conveyed tactful conduct lessons from the colonized to the colonizer. When later dramatists like P. J. Bourke wrote historical melodramas for predominantly nationalist Irish audiences in the years before the Easter Rising, they placed the Englishman in the formulaic role of the heavy villain: as greedy, lustful, and cruel as the Irish hero was noble, patriotic, and unselfish. The Manichaean dualities characteristic of melodrama mapped neatly onto the colonial situation.[10] Perhaps because of their simplicity, however, these writers were less influential than Boucicault, who became the model for later dramatists and filmmakers.[11]

The Stage Irishman in the English theater was an outsider trying to ingratiate himself; the Stage Englishman in Boucicault's Ireland was an outsider trying to understand a puzzling subordinate race. Captain Molineux repeatedly comments on the bizarre customs of "you Irish"; he is particularly confounded by the "melancholy . . . entertainment" of a Sligo wake.[12] In *Arrah-na-Pogue* the Secretary voices the standard Stage English reaction to Irish impetuosity and generosity of spirit: "Shall I ever be able to understand this extraordinary people?"[13] This theatrical convention still persists: in *Translations* Friel's Lieutenant Yolland attempts in vain to decode the natives: "Even if I did speak

Irish I'd always be an outsider here, wouldn't I? I may learn the password but the language of the tribe will always elude me, won't it?"[14] The epistemological dynamic of the imperial encounter confronts the colonizing knower with the colonized object of knowledge, the seer with the object of vision. Boucicault and Friel reverse this dynamic, savoring the subversive potential (and theatrical effectiveness) of being indecipherable to the panoptic gaze of the English colonizer.

The Irish may be hard to decode, but the colonizer is not terribly perspicacious. While many Irish writers adopted Matthew Arnold's passionate, melancholy, feminine Celt, some also borrowed his phlegmatic, polite, and masculine Saxon. Introducing *Saint Oscar,* Terry Eagleton derides the moralism and *gravitas* of "the genetically empiricist English,"[15] who are repressed, joyless, and stupid by comparison with the quick-witted Irish: Arnold's nondescript Philistines to the life. This essentialist caricature escapes critique because it is ethically acceptable to stereotype the oppressor.

Boucicault's cross-national homosocial pairings of Ffolliet with Molineux and Emmet with Claverhouse are echoed and intensified by the intimate relationship between the Irishman Larry Doyle and the Englishman Tom Broadbent in Shaw's *John Bull's Other Island* (1904). Shaw seeks to explode national stereotypes, though ultimately he succeeds better with the bogus Stage Irishman Tim Haffigan than with his English counterpart.[16] Broadbent, who refers to himself as a "Saxon," buys into Arnold's notion of English character as cold, prosaic, and reserved: "I think you will accept the fact that I'm an Englishman as a guarantee that I am not a man to act hastily or romantically," he says to Nora.[17] But since he immediately proposes to a woman he has only just met, the audience knows better. Broadbent, in fact, is a hopeless romantic. Shaw acknowledges his debt to Boucicault, but fails to mention that, in his weepiness, his Hibernophilia, and his success with an Irish girl, Broadbent is the colonizer as decent chap: Molineux or Claverhouse redivivus. Shaw argues that, "[f]or stage purposes there are not many types of character available; and all the playwrights use them over and over again. Idiosyncrasies are useful on the stage only to give an air of infinite variety to the standard types."[18] Despite Shaw's claim to be dismantling fictions about the English, in many respects Broadbent replicates the "standard" English type. His sentimentality reverses Arnold's equation of Irishness with emotion, and Englishness with rationality; but his masculinity, efficiency, humorlessness, slow-wittedness, and ultimate victory confirm Arnold's analysis. When he thinks that Nora will reject him he weeps, even while insisting that he is "a plain unemotional Englishman"; but tears do not feminize him for long, and once he has won her he reverts to masculine chivalry and *"confident proprietorship."* The English found the play hilarious, but as Shaw points out in his preface, they could well afford to. Broadbent's foolishness is the ideological camouflage of a winner: like the caterpillar who "instinctively makes itself look exactly like a leaf," Broadbent plays the "plain" Englishman in order to be an effective predator.[19]

A Home Ruler who advocates limited independence for Ireland, Broadbent substitutes for overt imperialism a neocolonial capitalist tourist industry that will subjugate Ireland more thoroughly than the British military ever did. His possession of the land is allegorized by his conquest of Nora, Shaw's ironic version of Yeats and Gregory's Cathleen ni Houlihan.[20] The cynical Larry Doyle disparages the nationalist pretense that Ireland is "a little old woman," and deromanticizes Nora by attributing her charm to poor nutrition. For Larry, Nora is "an everyday woman fit only for the eighteenth century, helpless, useless, almost sexless, an invalid without the excuse of disease, an incarnation of everything in Ireland that drove him out of it." Through his overbearing stage directions Shaw ruthlessly deprives her, as he also deprives the "in no way remarkable" Aunt Judy and the spiritless Cornelius, of any claim to ethnic distinctiveness or charm.[21] For Broadbent, however, she is the essence of Ireland, an ethereal being with harps in her voice, encountered at twilight beside a round tower. Irishness is in the eye of the English beholder. In the end Broadbent appropriates both his romantic image and her material environment, on which he will build a hotel and a golf course.

Through Tom's "proprietorship" of Nora and the Roscullen estate Shaw satirizes the colonial trope that represents the Union between England and Ireland as a heterosexual marriage: John Bull proposes successfully to Cathleen ni Houlihan. The hierarchical difference between man and woman mirrors a colonial relationship that geographical proximity and similar pigmentation render unusually intimate: as long as Ireland occupies the female role, "she" can be viewed as close but comfortably subordinate. Melodrama requires a love-plot; melodramas that involve English males and Irish women use erotic interest to neutralize a hostile political situation. In such a heterosexual reconciliation scenario, familiar from Boucicault's *The Shaughraun*, gender assumes an allegorical significance.[22]

Shaw's mockery of the marriage trope, however, is subordinated to his representation of a serious relationship between men. Broadbent and Doyle are "bachelors and bosom friends" who work and live together in rooms "no woman would tolerate," and whose mutual fondness is constantly reiterated. Larry's preference for aggressive women who take the sexual initiative, "animated beefsteaks" who are "solid and bouncing and rather keen about him,"[23] suggests that he also plays the passive, feminine role in relation to Tom, who is something of an animated beefsteak himself. Their intimate interdependence easily survives the fact that Nora, who still loves Larry, nevertheless agrees to marry Tom. Although Nora was his first romantic interest, Larry has long since abandoned her: only on her engagement is the triangular circuit of desire reestablished and Larry's affection briefly rekindled: "I'm an Irishman and he's an Englishman. He wants you; and he grabs you. *I* want you; and I quarrel with you and have to go on wanting you." This is the first we have heard of Larry's wanting Nora, and he does not want her much; but he describes his relationship with Tom in matrimonial terms:

> *Larry:* We must be friends, you and I. I don't want his marriage to you to be his divorce from me.
> *Nora:* You care more for him than you ever did for me.
> *Larry: (with curt sincerity)* Yes of course I do: why should I tell you lies about it? Nora Reilly was a person of very little consequence to me or anyone else outside this miserable little hole. Mrs Tom Broadbent will be a person of very considerable consequence indeed.[24]

Larry's cold-blooded ceding of Nora to Tom, irrespective of her own desires, demonstrates his preference for homosocial over heterosexual bonds. Tom, who refuses to pursue Nora until he is sure that he is not "interfering with Larry,"[25] operates on the same scale of values. Eve Sedgwick argues that, although in contemporary Western society homosociality (men promoting the interests of men) is sharply differentiated from homoeroticism (men loving men), this differentiation is

designed to repress and deny "the potential unbrokenness of a continuum between homosocial and homosexual" desire.[26] Larry embodies
this continuum when he speaks as though he and Tom were erotic as
well as business partners: "I don't want his marriage to you to be his
divorce from me."

Shaw's political motivation for situating homosocial desire at the
heart of his play, and of Larry's character, is clear. A supporter of Irish
independence, he nevertheless respected the English and advocated a
close voluntary relationship between the two nations.[27] Although the
Nationalist and Separatist Cornelius is feminized by his colonial subject position, residence in England and Tom's friendship have "made
a man" of his son Larry.[28] Only the love between men can adequately
symbolize political equality: heterosexual love signifies asymmetries
of power between men and women. (According to Aristotle, men
and women could not even be friends, since friendship depends upon
equality.) Gayle Rubin argues that in many societies relationships between male kinship groups are cemented by "the traffic in women."[29]
Like Claire in *The Shaughraun*, Nora is a national token exchanged
between males to guarantee continued mutual support. An internationalist for whom flags and frontiers are a hindrance, Doyle substitutes the masculine energy of global capitalism, represented by his
partnership with Tom, for the wilted feminine symbol of Irish particularity. Nora's "consequence" to the Irishman depends on her relationship to the Englishman, in which "Nora Reilly" will be subsumed in
"Mrs. Tom Broadbent."[30]

Shaw is no more enamored of the coming exploitation of Roscullen
by the international leisure and heritage industries than he is of nationalist complaints: universalist Catholic socialism is the utopian antidote
proffered by the visionary Peter Keegan. Tom and Larry stand condemned as capitalists, but the play confusingly endorses their homosocial political alliance: even the censorious Keegan plans to vote for
Broadbent. Shaw's desire for cooperation between England and Ireland wars with his socialist presentiment about the exploitative form
that cooperation may take, and his approval of the bond between
Larry and Tom clashes with his bleak analysis of the tourist prospects
of Roscullen. In the absence of the socialist millennium a hotel is
inevitable, and the play ends with Larry and Tom setting out to choose
a site for the golf course.

Following in the tradition of Boucicault even as it revised him, *John Bull's Other Island* set a precedent for later Irish writers who stressed commonalities rather than differences between the English and the Irish. Both O'Casey and Behan, who were skeptical about the cultural particularity of the Irish Revival, admired the play. Through Broadbent's interest in antiquities and his plan to charge admission to the restored Round Tower, Shaw mockingly suggests that the real audience for the Irish-Ireland movement is the English cultural tourist. Broadbent anticipates Joyce's "ponderous Saxon" Haines, the Oxford-educated Gaelic-speaking collector of folklore who "thinks we ought to speak Irish in Ireland" and does so himself, much to the amazement of the anglophone natives, who cannot understand him.[31] In Behan's *The Hostage* (1958), Monsewer is another Englishman educated at Oxford (Arnold's alma mater) who wears a kilt, plays patriotic tunes on the bagpipes, and speaks Irish in Dublin even though this necessitates an interpreter.

Broadbent, Haines, and Monsewer are middle or upper class. The working-class Stage Englishman, whose genealogy may be traced to the valet Winterbottom and the kind-hearted Sergeant in Boucicault's *Arrah-na-Pogue*, plays a different and increasingly important part in twentieth-century Irish drama. While the British bourgeoisie benefits from imperialism, lower-class Englishmen are victims of internal oppression who ought to ally themselves with the Irish, but usually fail to do so. Matt Haffigan's laments about injustice and starvation cause Broadbent's valet Hodson to drop his "gentleman's gentleman" pose and emerge as a Stage Cockney with a red-hot class agenda:

> When Oi think of the things we Englishmen as to pat ap with, and eah you Awrish ahlin abaht your silly little grievances, and see the wy you mike it worse for haz by the rotten wiges youll cam over and tike and the rotten plices youll sleep in, I jast feel that I could tike the aowl bloomin British awland and mike you a present of it, jast to let you fawnd aht wot reel awdship's lawk.[32]

Hodson, it seems, has read Engels' racist description of the Irish in England. Because Irish laborers undercut them in the job market, the legitimate discontent of the English working classes was often channeled into xenophobia. In 1914 European workers rallied to the imagined communities of their different nations, rather than to the real interests of their class. O'Casey's *The Plough and the Stars* (1926) features an affable British Tommy who demonstrates the overriding pull of national loyalties:

> *The Covey:* . . . D'ye know, comrade, that more die o' consumption than are killed in th' wars? An' it's all because of th' system we're living undher?
>
> *Corporal Stoddart:* Ow, I know. I'm a Sowcialist moiself, but I 'as to do my dooty.
>
> *The Covey (ironically):* Dooty! Th' only dooty of a Socialist is th' emancipation of th' workers.
>
> *Corporal Stoddart:* Ow, a man's a man, an 'e 'as to foight for 'is country, 'asn't 'e?
>
> *Fluther (aggressively):* You're not fightin' for your counthry here, are you?[33]

Stoddart's clichéd equation of patriotism with virility is undermined by Fluther's reminder that his present task is the oppression of Ireland rather than the defense of England. O'Casey is not unsympathetic to his English Tommies, who end the play with cups of tea and a rendition of the famous World War I song, "Keep the Home Fires Burning." In an Irish context, however, the last line of the song, "Til the boys come 'owme," anticipates British military withdrawal from Irish soil.

The Treaty of 1921, which radically changed political relations between the two islands, did not immediately alter Irish representations of English males, although it conditioned their tone and questioned the equation of Englishness with success. Even *British* representations of Englishmen in Ireland borrowed from and replenished existing Irish tradition. After the War and the Troubles, the increased popularity of cinema and the lack of an indigenous film industry meant that Irish audiences, who transferred their allegiance from melodrama to its cinematic successor, became dependent on American and British representations of Ireland. In *Ryan's Daughter* (1970), set in the South just after the Easter Rising, English director David Lean and scriptwriter Robert Bolt recreate the cross-national erotic triangle popularized by Boucicault and Shaw: the British officer Major Doryan replaces the local schoolteacher in the affections of the Irish heroine Rosie.

Although Lean chose the Irish setting simply because it was remote and picturesque, Bolt uses it to represent the end of Empire and the decay of the landed gentry. The Major, whose snapshots reveal that his family owns a castle, is a formulaic repressed Stage Englishman. But the reserve of the "crippled bloody hero" results from shell shock, and the stiff upper lip hides a shattered psyche. The facade of English imperturbability has been cracked by the First World War and the Easter Rising; unlike Broadbent, this English outsider in Ireland maintains a fragile equilibrium within a history that is no longer unequivocally on his side. Although his passion for Rosie fails to loosen his tongue, it liberates other parts: unusually for an Englishman, he seems to be good in bed—or rather, on the turf, since all the sex, improbably enough in Ireland, takes place out of doors. Despite the overblown poeticism of Lean's thrashing leaves and drifting dandelion seeds, however, sex between political enemies cannot closet itself within an idyllic "natural" space. Rosie's affair, revealed by the mute idiot Michael, is resented by the villagers as a national as well as an erotic betrayal: to them she is a "British soldier's whore," and they strip her and cut off her hair. With impeccably English good manners Major Doryan removes himself from an awkward situation by blowing himself up, and Rosie returns to her Irish husband.

Although it is motivated not by politics but by Rosie's ending of their affair, Major Doryan's climactic withdrawal from the plot prefigures the British retreat from Ireland.[34] His last moments, like his last cigarettes, are shared with Michael, whose twisted body and grotesque features recall the simian Paddy of post-Fenian, post-Darwinian Victorian cartoons.[35] A shot in which the jerky, prognathous Caliban walks behind the crippled Major reveals identical limps. Identified in silhouette with the handsome Screen Englishman, his dark double the mute Screen Irishman shows his gratitude for the cigarettes by leading Major Doryan to a box of dynamite washed ashore during a German arms shipment to the rebels. Misunderstanding the Major's warning demonstration that the fuses are live, he runs away, pursued by Doryan's last words, "I thought we were friends." A similar appeal from the colonizer to the colonized at the end of Forster's *Passage to India*, "Why can't we be friends now?" is definitively answered: "No, not yet."[36] Waiting until the sun sets (possibly upon the British Empire), Major Doryan kills himself by detonating the dynamite procured for him by the film's most extreme caricature of Irishness.[37]

Although its dwarfing of politics by landscape irritated Irish critics,

Ryan's Daughter ran for a year in Dublin.[38] Whether or not Brian Friel saw it, *Translations* (1980) displays a similar debt to Boucicault and depicts an identical erotic triangle: the British officer Yolland displaces the Irish schoolmaster Manus in the heart of the "colleen" Maire, and the community, personified by the Donnelly twins and the mute Sarah (who plays the same role in Friel's plot as the mute Michael does in Bolt's), exposes and punishes their exogamous love. At the end the Englishman dies, the Irishman is on the run, and the colleen will soon emigrate. Although the play is set in 1833, it can be read through the lens of the Northern Troubles.[39] In 1980 Boucicault's optimistic vision of a decent English officer marrying an Irish woman is no longer viable.

Descended from Shaw's Broadbent, Yolland is a "bloody romantic" who once saw Wordsworth plain, a sentimentalist, and "a committed Hibernophile."[40] Although he loves Maire, his most sustained relationship is with the Irishman Owen, who—in his cleverness, cynicism, preference for English employers, and lack of heterosexual interest—resembles Larry Doyle. Pine describes their drunken collaboration on the new map as a "symbolic . . . embrace";[41] Kearney calls it "an exchange of identity."[42] Yolland's relation to Ireland is less exploitative than Broadbent's, and he voices ethical doubts about the politics of translation. But although he falls in love with the countryside and wants to stay there "always," he fails to appreciate the narrowness and poverty that drive Maire toward the emigrant ship and the English language. The famous scene in which they communicate their love through the recitation of Irish place names ends in misunderstanding: Yolland insists that he will never leave, while Maire begs him to "take me away."[43] Like Larry Doyle, she sees no romance in the parochial Irish life that to Yolland appears Edenic: to her the names of English villages—Winfarthing, Barton Bendish, Saxingham Nethergate—represent the exotic Other. Even after Yolland's death she persists in her desire to speak English, though in Brooklyn rather than Barton Bendish.

While he would never have built a hotel, Yolland might well have bought a quaint Irish cottage and painted the door emerald green, like John Wayne in *The Quiet Man*. Broadbent, whose guidebook contains more about Irish antiquities than the locals will ever know, nevertheless looks toward the golfing tourist of the future; but Yolland, the cultural tourist with a passion for Ireland's past, wants to learn the soon-to-be-moribund Irish language. He calls the anglicizing of Irish place-names "an eviction of sorts" and insists that the Irish tradition of *dinnseanchas* be respected by retaining the name "Tobair Vree" in order to "keep piety with a man long dead."[44] The romantic Englishman who falls in love with a mythical Irish past may be relatively attractive, like Broadbent and Yolland, or sinister, like Haines and Monsewer, but he is usually a comic and always a suspect figure. Arnold recommends cultural surveillance as a political tool: "What we want is to *know* the Celt and his genius."[45] Margot Harkin's film *Hush-a-Bye Baby* (1989) represents mastery of the Irish language as a weapon of the colonizer. The IRA sympathizer Ciaran, a beginning student of Irish, tries to impress his girlfriend Goretti by taunting an impassive British soldier with a meaningless recitation of the names of state-supported enterprises: *Bord Fáilte, Aer Lingus, Bord naMona.* When he concludes with the Republican slogan *tiocfaidh ár lá* (our day will come), the soldier replies in fluent Irish, "Tell me what impact the Troubles have had on Irish social, political, and economic life?" Placed in an inferior position by this unexpected linguistic competence, Ciaran is reduced to patronizing Goretti: "You wouldn't understand what we were saying." Harkin's Irish-speaking squaddie probably owes more to literary tradition than to the streets of Derry.[46]

The doomed romantic Yolland never progresses linguistically beyond the pronunciation of the Irish place names he has come to change. His abduction replicates the 1977 disappearance of the SAS undercover operative Captain Robert Nairac. Nairac was a real Stage Englishman: an English Catholic with a history degree from Oxford, described by his teachers as "a romantic."[47] After he went missing in South Armagh his sister told reporters, "Since he has always loved Ireland and the Irish, it is ironic that he may have died while trying as a volunteer to contribute to peace in Ireland."[48] The contribution of the SAS to peace in Ireland is apparent only to the British, whose press portrayed Nairac as a gallant idealist murdered by the IRA.

Friel's Lieutenant Yolland resembles the Nairac of English newspaper propaganda: a soldier-romantic and Hibernophile murdered by unseen terrorists. Joe Conran, the double-agent in Anne Devlin's *Ourselves Alone* (1986) who claims Anglo-Irish descent but whose education, army training, and English mother mark him as more Anglo than Irish, is modeled on the historical Nairac.[49] Like Nairac, Conran attended Ampleforth, the English Catholic public school that was a breeding ground for SAS men. Nairac went to Oxford, Conran to Cambridge: both were enrolled at Sandhurst, the upper-class officer training academy; and both posed as engineers. While Yolland is a genuine romantic, "a soldier by accident"[50] who dislikes the army, Conran insinuates himself into the IRA by pretending to be someone like Yolland, someone who derives from the stage tradition of the English Hibernophile. From the same upper-middle-class background as Yolland, he is married to an urban colleen, "a wee hussy from the Bogside,"[51] and becomes the lover of Josie, a working-class IRA volunteer from West Belfast. To complete the cross-national triangle, Conran's seduction of Josie rekindles the passion of her Irish lover, IRA chief Cathal O'Donnell; but as usual, the Englishman initially triumphs in the erotic contest. The woman, however, is secondary to the relation between the two men: Conran's interest is not in Josie but in his male victim and psychic double O'Donnell, whom he has come to Belfast to capture. Sedgwick defines desire as the "glue, even when its manifestation is hostility or hatred . . . that shapes an important relationship":[52] Conran's homosocial desire is for the man whose place in Josie's bed he has usurped. O'Donnell in some measure recip-rocates this desire: he is the last to accept that his erotic rival is also a traitor. O'Donnell is deluded from the start: instead of suspecting Conran's social background and Army contacts, and eliminating him at once, he makes a fatal literary-critical misjudgment. Taken in by the Stage English credentials of this unlikely IRA recruit, he declares confidently: "It's really very simple. He's a romantic."[53]

No more a romantic than Nairac, Conran is a spy who impregnates and then abandons Josie, and betrays an IRA arms shipment to the Irish security police. As the pre-Rising years produced the English villains of Bourke, so the post-Hunger Strike phase of the Troubles and the British shoot-to-kill policy prompted Devlin's duplicitous Anglo-Irishman.[54] The historical Nairac, trained in Kitson's school of Counter Insurgency Operations, may have directed loyalist death squads. He frequented the bars in the borderlands of South Armagh, affecting a Belfast accent, and proclaiming his allegiance to the Official IRA. He was nicknamed "Danny Boy" because he sang Irish ballads and rebel songs at the pub microphone. The Stage Englishman, the

Oxford Hibernophile, put on a bizarre performance as the Stage Irish-man. His act ran for thirty months.

Broadbent, Doryan, Yolland, and Conran represent the power dis-parity between the English male and the Irish female through class as well as gender. Nora, Rosie, Maire, and Josie are lower in social status than their middle-or upper-middle-class English lovers. In both the Irish and English versions of Behan's *An Giall/The Hostage* (1958), however, class differences are erased. The love of the doomed hostage Leslie for the Irish girl Teresa replicates the pattern of the English male and the colleen; but both soldier and servant girl are displaced and impoverished orphans who are symbolically outside history,[55] about which they are refreshingly ignorant. To Teresa's suggestion that En-gland has been "doing something to Ireland," Leslie replies, "That was donkey's years ago. Everybody was doing something to someone in those days."[56] Behan finds similarities between ostensible opponents, comparing Cockneys with Dubliners, Monsewer with Leslie's old Brit-ish Colonel, and Leslie with his fellow-victim, the IRA "boy in Belfast jail" whose hanging will precipitate the hostage's death.[57] His Irish characters understand the dramatic genre to which Leslie belongs:

> *Volunteer:* He's a decent boy, for all he's a British soldier.
> *Meg:* Ah, there's many a good heart beats under a khaki tunic.[58]

Although the prudishness of the IRA and the Gaelic League was a prime target in *An Giall*, the bisexual Behan nevertheless knew his Irish-speaking audience well enough to keep overtly gay characters out of the Dublin theater. In *The Hostage*, staged in London by Joan Littlewood, he introduced the male prostitute Rio Rita ("a homosex-ual navvy") and his "coloured boyfriend" Princess Grace, who carries a placard inscribed "Keep Ireland Black."[59] This pair, who contribute little to the plot, nevertheless raise previously closeted issues of race and sexual orientation simply by being on stage. As they sing:

> We're here because we're queer
> Because we're queer because we're here.[60]

Behan's "whores and queers" may be "the outcasts of the world," but they manage to "corrupt the morals" of the secret policeman Mul-leady, and nearly succeed in seducing Leslie, who admits that he would like to try their kind of life.[61] In leading an abortive attempt to rescue the British soldier, the three queers Mulleady, Rio Rita, and Princess Grace symbolically affirm the power of homoerotic desire to breach national boundaries, and oppose the patriotism and sexual puritanism of the Officer of the IRA, a "thin-faced fanatic" who, like Pearse, is a schoolmaster.[62]

A contemporary reviewer of the straight play *An Giall* complained that Behan exploited the audience's natural attraction to the young lovers in order to blacken Leslie's IRA captors, who cause his death. Behan juxtaposes the cause of Irish freedom with "the cruelest and most unanswerable of media [*sic*]—love between boy and girl. No ideology or idealism has yet found an answer to such a challenge."[63] Hostage drama frequently uses the clash between erotic attraction and national identification as its motivating conflict. In *The Crying Game* (1992) Neil Jordan turns Teresa into a man without changing the function of her role. The relation between Jody, the working-class British soldier, and Fergus, the working-class IRA volunteer, blackens Jody's other IRA captors by contrasting their fanaticism with the love between boy and boy.[64]

Behan and Jordan increase audience sympathy for their British characters by downplaying their responsibility for events in Ireland. In *An Giall* Leslie is a regular soldier, but he has joined up early to anticipate the inevitable draft. In *The Hostage* he is a National Service conscript. When asked, "Ah you murdering bastard. Why don't you go home to your own country?" he replies with perfect justification, "You can take me out of it as soon as you like. I never bloody-well asked to be brought here."[65] Jordan's non-conscripted Jody also blames his job:

> *Jody:* I'm saying what the fuck am I doing here anyway.
> *Fergus:* What the fuck were you doing here?
> *Jody:* I got sent.
> *Fergus:* You could have said no.
> *Jody:* Can't. Once I signed up.
> *Fergus:* Why did you sign up?
> *Jody:* It was a job.[66]

While Fergus's skeptical grunt reveals that Jordan sees through this argument, he nevertheless empathizes with Jody. In *Carthaginians* (1986), however, Frank McGuinness skewers the "job" scenario as part of the Stage English repertoire. In his play-within-a-play *The Burning Balaclava*, McGuinness's gay hero Dido impersonates "a British soldier, nameless, faceless, in enemy uniform, in deep torment because he is a working-class cockney sent here to oppress the working class." His camp exaggeration exposes the shallowness of an argument that uses class as an excuse for violence: " 'Oh, the agony of being a working-class boy sent here to oppress the working class. Why did I do it? Why do I do it?' 'The money?' " [67] Jordan does, however, complicate the significance of the Stage Cockney by crossing class with race. Jody, whose family comes from Antigua, is not only a working-class lad sent to oppress the working classes, but a victim of British colonialism sent to police his fellow-victims. Fergus's final address to the dead Jody's picture, "You should have stayed at home," [68] suggests both Jordan's critique of the economic argument and his interrogation of geographical and racial identity: would Jody's "home" be Tottenham or Antigua?

The Crying Game begins by gesturing toward the traditional gendered formula as Jody crudely attempts to seduce the Irishwoman Jude, girlfriend of the IRA volunteer Fergus. Like Shaw's Nora, however, Jude is marginalized by the relation between the two men, whom she cannot tell apart erotically:

> *Jude:* . . . One of you made me want it . . .
> *Fergus:* Which one?
> (She doesn't answer. They embrace.) [69]

Claiming that "there's always homoerotic feeling between men in conflict," [70] Jordan develops the relationship between the British hostage and his Irish captor at the expense of Jude, whose brutal attacks on Jody express her frustration at being sexually displaced. The erotic initiator is Jody, who flatters and seduces Fergus into increasingly intimate bodily contact. Three separate "love" scenes in which Fergus feeds Jody, tells him his name, and takes his penis out of his trousers to help him urinate, end with the IRA man saying, "My pleasure," "My pleasure, Jody," and "The pleasure was all mine." [71] The direction *"Fergus begins to laugh, without knowing why"* indicates his ignorance of his own desires, [72] although his cryptic allusion to St. Paul provides a clue to his feelings: "when I was a child . . . I thought as a child. But when I became a man I put away childish things."[73] These lines from 1 Corinthians, which are also spoken by the dying IRA man Johnny in Carol Reed's *Odd Man Out,* can only be understood in their context, St. Paul's famous celebration of love, which claims that it transcends even martyrdom: "though I give my body to be burned, and have not charity, it profiteth me nothing."[74]

Evoking and revaluing the nineteenth-century racist discourse that linked the Irish with Negroes rather than with "white" Caucasians,[75] and echoing Princess Grace's defiant placard "Keep Ireland Black," Jordan stresses the resemblances rather than the national or racial differences between his two "simple" soldiers: Jody's blackness ought to align him politically with Fergus rather than with the British state that has colonized them both.[76] As their brief, sexually charged relationship draws to its close, Jody gives his "female" lover Dil to his Irish "brother." Jordan writes: "A hostage, a captor, and an absent lover. The lover became the focus for the erotic subtext, loved by both men in a way they couldn't love each other."[77] Because the British transvestite Dil is also black, the pattern of racial, national, and erotic boundary-crossing is sustained. Although Fergus vomits when he sees Dil's penis, denying his homoerotic desires, Dil knows better: "even when you were throwing up, I could tell you cared." Fergus's "charity" toward Dil contrasts with the racism of Jude, who contemptuously gestures toward the golliwog on a pot of Robertson's jam to characterize "the wee black chick."[78]

By substituting Dil for the violent and dehumanized Jude, Jordan alters the convention in which the woman in the cross-national triangle is Irish, and even the convention that "she" is a woman; but his manipulations of the formula underscore its previous hegemony, and emphasize the continuum between homoerotic desire and the homosocial bonds that subtend conventional erotic triangles. The relationship between Fergus and Dil is constantly mediated by the apparition of Jody in his cricket gear. Cricket, the film's most complex visual metaphor, is at once the emblem of English fair play ("that's not cricket") and the means by which Caribbean nations have struck back at their former masters. Jody the "shit-hot bowler"[79] has appropriated both the game and its white uniform. When, in a scene of displaced eroticism, Fergus dresses Dil in Jody's "whites," the circuit of desire

between the Irishman and the dead soldier is reestablished. Acknowledging the influence of Behan, Jordan claims historical sanction for
queering the colonial allegory:

> The attraction of such a theme for Irish writers, the friendship that
> develops between two protagonists in a conflict, that grows paradoxi-
> cally deeper than any of their other allegiances, lies in the broader
> history of Anglo-Irish relationships: two cultures in need of each other,
> yet at war with each other.

The irrelevance of women in Jordan's formulation of "an erotic possibility, a sense of mutual need and identification" between Fergus and
Jody, is highlighted when he writes that Behan "dealt with simple
friendship between two men." [80] Behan dealt with nothing of the sort:
Jordan has forgotten that Teresa is a woman.

Whatever the degree of Jordan's misogyny, or of the unconscious
racism implied by his exoticization of Dil,[81] his representation of the
love between Jody and Fergus as a nexus of nationality and desire is
justified in terms of Irish theater history. Boucicault established the
decent military Stage Englishman as less villain than love object, but
the gradual shift in power between colonizer and colonized since Independence has adversely affected his ultimate theatrical fate. Whether
he is upper-class like Major Doryan and Lieutenant Yolland or lower-
class like Leslie and Jody, the Stage Englishman is doomed as well as
beloved. Blown up on the beach, "disappeared" in the borderlands,
suffocated in a cupboard, or squashed by a Saracen, the British soldier
in Ireland no longer heads for a happy ending.

Like *The Crying Game,* Frank McGuinness's hostage drama *Someone Who'll Watch Over Me* appeared in 1992. The emergence of overt
representations of gay men coincides historically with the reform of
Irish anti-homosexual legislation that was initiated by Senator David
Norris's 1988 victory in the European Court of Human Rights, and
completed in 1993.[82] Jordan and McGuinness inherit the same matrix
of Irish literary, popular, and legislative culture.[83] Although McGuinness moves his characters out of Ireland and into a Lebanese cell, he
took up the topical subject of the Beirut hostages "because of the
nationalities involved. If you put an Englishman and an Irishman in
a room together there will be war—ancestral voices predict it." [84]
Recognizing that the sun has set on the Empire, both Jordan and

McGuinness compromise the "imperial" masculinity of their English characters by representing them as gay; but Jordan's Jody, who plays the protective "gentleman" in his relationship with the "feminine" Dil, has no camp mannerisms. He is homosexual without being effeminate. McGuinness, however, turns his Stage Englishman into a queer by camping up his Englishness. The Irishman Edward categorizes him instantly:

> *Michael:* I'm terribly sorry, but where am I?
> *Edward:* So it's yourself, is it?
> *Michael:* Pardon?
> *Edward:* Do you not recognize me? We were at school together.
> *Michael:* I don't think so.
> *Edward:* Eton, wasn't it? Or Harrow?
> *Michael:* No, I don't—where am I?
> *Edward:* In the officer's mess, Brit Boy.[85]

Edward's references to the public school and the officer's mess locate Michael within the representational tradition of the military Stage Englishman, although he is a lecturer in English literature. Michael is absurdly polite: he apologizes for everything, agrees for agreement's sake, abhors swearing, and suggests that "we could at least maintain the semblance of civility." Writing an imaginary letter to his mother, he says, "I share accommodation with an American and an Irishman and so I am often flooded by a torrent of emotions, which I rise above." Michael's quintessentially English attempts to rise above his emotions are frequently sabotaged by Edward, who is initially unable to see the man for the mannerisms he cruelly mimics: "How dreadfully unfair. Not cricket." "Come on, give us a dose of the stiff upper lip. Raise our morale, old boy." [86]

Edward also treats the Englishman's ambiguous sexual orientation as a stereotypical joke. When Michael mentions the pear flan he was making when he was kidnapped, Edward calls him "sweetheart," suggesting none too subtly that real men don't cook, especially not dessert. The pear flan becomes a running gag, which, combined with Michael's constant worry about his mother in Peterborough, offers plenty of ammunition to the homophobic Edward. Michael comes to anticipate his innuendoes: "Oh go ahead, Edward . . . Attack me for writing to my mother. Pansy little Englishman. I don't mind. I've had it before. I can tell you, there were people who were surprised I got married."[87] If the Englishman is a "pansy," the symbolic association of British power with masculinity has vanished. By locating the victim of homophobia within the stereotype of the oppressor, McGuinness defies conventional ideas about nation and sexuality.

The decay of Empire and the loss of international influence is figured in Michael's academic redundancy and economic impotence: "They're not teaching much Old and Middle English these days. A dying concern." Deploying a trope from recent Irish cultural criticism, Edward represents the language Michael teaches as a battlefield on which the Irish have triumphed over their oppressors:

> Listen, times have changed, you English mouth, and I mean mouth. One time when you and your brood opened that same mouth, you ruled the roost, you ruled the world, because it was your language. Not any more. We've taken it from you. We've made it our own. And now we've bettered you at it . . . We took you and your language on, and we won.[88]

Jody might have said the same about cricket. But there is something strained about Edward's triumphalism, which is sexual as well as linguistic. In captivity, he obsesses: "Have they, or have they not, made me less of a man, by reason of what they've done to me?" His constant aggression against Michael is fueled not only by Irish grievances (he holds the Englishman "personally responsible" for the Famine), but by fear of diminished manliness if he ruptures the barrier between homosocial bonding (his unspoken love for Adam, the black American) and homoerotic experience. After Adam's death, he gives rein to an outburst of homophobia: "There are times when the sight and sound of you disgust me. I can feel a smell off you. Sickening." Michael's rejoinder, "Did you sleep with Adam?"[89] is only superficially a non sequitur.

Jordan and McGuinness associate repression with the Irish, not the English, character. Jody has no problem with his sexuality, but Fergus's homophobia has to be eroded by Dil's persistence. Edward denies his desire for Adam, canceling the possibility of erotic attraction between men in order to keep intact the sex/gender categories that subtend the patriarchy: "I need to be a father to my children." But Michael refuses to endorse the conventional connection between weakness and femininity. When Edward goes on hunger strike to protest Adam's murder, Michael teaches him first to accept Adam's death, and then to celebrate him: "Bury him . . . Remember him." [90] Edward's inarticulacy, "I believe it goes without saying, love, so I never said," is revised by Michael's recitation of George Herbert's poem "Love," a testament to the therapeutic powers of the English poetic canon:

> *Michael:* . . . You must sit down, sayes Love, and taste my meat:
>   So I did sit and eat.
> *Edward:* I'm hungry.
> *Michael:* Then eat.
> *Edward:* Dear friend.
> (EDWARD *eats.*)
> He's dead.
> *Michael:* We're not.[91]

In stopping Edward's politically resonant hunger strike, Michael asserts that strength resides not in self-destruction, but in love and endurance.

Michael's campiest moment comes in the brilliant scene where he re-enacts Virginia Wade's triumph in the 1977 Wimbledon Ladies Final, which was attended by Queen Elizabeth. The national and sexual valences of this performance are complex. To impersonate Virginia Wade is to impersonate a woman who, like Billie Jean King, is more noted for strength than femininity. Nevertheless, her victory for Great Britain interrupted a long history of defeat: no British woman has won Wimbledon subsequently, and Britain's waning dominance in sports mirrors her waning influence in the world. Edward, for whom sport is politics by other means, starts off rooting for Virginia's opponent, "poor wee Betty Stove," [92] but his knee-jerk Irish sympathy for the six-foot, twelve-stone underdog is modified by a discussion of the limits of England's historical responsibility for Ireland's problems. (This topic was raised earlier in connection with the Famine, which for the Englishman happened "a hundred and fifty fucking years ago," for the Irishman "yesterday.") [93] Michael's insistence that the outcome of Virginia's match is predetermined prompts Edward to remark, "That's unfair"; Michael replies flatly, "That's history." But when the conversation moves to the situation in Derry, he asks a serious question: "Is it really our fault for your troubles at home? Is it the English people's fault?" to which Edward replies, "Ridiculous." By the end of the scene, the men's verdicts on the tennis match are closer, more generous, and less chauvinistic. Edward now celebrates Virginia Wade, while Michael sympathizes with Betty Stove:

> *Michael:* And have we faith?
> *Edward:* Do you want proof?
> *Michael:* Yes. Give it to me.
> *Edward:* Who won the 1977 Wimbledon Women's Final?
> *Michael:* An Englishwoman won it.
> *Edward:* I rest my case that there is a God.
> *Michael:* Well done, Virginia.
> *Edward:* Well done, Virginia.
> *Michael:* Poor wee Betty Stove.
> *Edward:* There always has to be a loser. In every game, a loser.
> *Michael:* Yes, that's history.
> (EDWARD *sings*)
> *Edward:* For she's a jolly good fellow . . .[94]

This mutual understanding, generated by two men impersonating powerful women (Edward plays the Queen), ends with the Irishman singing a gender-bending version of an English song.

McGuinness equates the maintenance of conventional gender categories and sexual orientations with a politics of national difference and historical grievance. But Michael's heterosexual devotion to his dead wife is as intense as his "queer" obsession with his living mother and his literary identification with his dead father. Despite his parodic Stage Englishness, Michael's capacity for love, his fluid sexual identity, and his refusal to identify femaleness with the exaggerated femininity travestied by Dil make him the unexpected sexual hero of McGuinness's play. His defense of the stiff upper lip, the controlling of pain and fear, derives, as might be expected, from his father, but it is not "masculine":

> You have been raised by a strong woman. The bravest men sometimes behave like women. Before the Spartans went into battle they combed each other's hair. The enemy laughed at them for being effeminate. But the Spartans won the battle.[95]

Spartan stoicism is also the message of the Old English elegy *The Wanderer,* from which Michael derives his paternity and his national identity: "I heard my father . . . in that ancient poem, speaking with the voice of England, talking to itself, for the first time. Our beginning, our end, England's." *The Wanderer,* a lament over loss, loneliness, and defeat, allows Michael to express a legitimate national pride predicated not upon conquest, but upon courage in the face of adversity and admiration for the creative act: "I love my country because I love its literature very much." McGuinness's use of a gay character to recuperate the father, the English literary canon, and the idea of Englishness, is a brave and generous imaginative act. Edward, whose release leaves Michael, like the speaker of *The Wanderer,* alone at the end, acknowledges the superior strength of the "pansy little Englishman" and overcomes his homophobic fear of effeminacy: in an expressively "Spartan" gesture he combs Michael's hair, and allows Michael to comb his. "I need you," the Irishman says to the Englishman.[96]

In contrast with McGuinness's emphasis on reconciliation between the Irish and the British, Neil Jordan's most recent film subverts the dramatic tradition that I have just analyzed. *Michael Collins* (1996), which resembles the Manichaean melodrama of P. J. Bourke rather than the reconciliatory project of Boucicault, abandons the idea of love between national enemies to concentrate on the love between Irishmen who chose different sides in the Civil War. Jordan replaces the cross-national male triangle of *The Crying Game* with a local sexual and political configuration, symbolically representing Eamon De Valera as a whore in drag who interrupts the passionate friendship between Collins and Harry Boland.[97] Their English adversaries, led by the suavely vicious, well-groomed, and efficient Soames, embody only the negative aspects of the Stage English stereotype; consequently the audience is unmoved when they meet violent deaths. Conversely, the tradition that I have traced emphasizes encounters between male opponents that modify the severe and exclusionary outlines of national stereotypes. Although utopian in impulse, however, it is neither universal nor uniformly progressive. Narratives of homosocial or homoerotic bonding between English and Irish males may function to obliterate women except as objects of exchange between men, or they may appropriate "feminine" qualities while demonizing real females; frequently they challenge Republican nationalism. Strategies of resistance do not necessarily inhabit the same counter-hegemonic space, and the interests of men who love men do not always coincide with those of women or nationalists. Yet neither is it axiomatic that they should conflict. While acknowledging difference, the tradition that leads from Boucicault to *The Crying Game* and *Someone Who'll Watch Over Me* simultaneously accredits sameness, attempts to level real or symbolic inequalities of power, and makes a case for peace based on mutual need. This not a radical political agenda, but it seems currently beyond reach.

Notes

1. Among the numerous studies see George Duggan, *The Stage Irishman* (New York: Benjamin Blom, 1937), and Richard Cave, "Staging the Irishman," in *Acts of Supremacy*, ed. J. S. Bratton et al. (Manchester: Manchester University Press, 1991).

2. L. P. Curtis, *Anglo-Saxons and Celts* (Bridgeport, Conn.: University of Bridgeport, 1968), 110.

3. George Bernard Shaw, *John Bull's Other Island* in *The Works*, 30 vols. (London: Constable, 1930), 11: 41.

4. See David Cairns and Shaun Richards, *Writing Ireland* (Manchester: Manchester University Press, 1988), 49–50; on gender and colonialism see Ashis Nandy, *The Intimate Enemy* (Oxford: Oxford University Press, 1983), 7–10.

5. See Proinsias MacCana, "Women in Irish Mythology," *Crane Bag* 4. 1 (1980); Richard Kearney, "Myth and Motherland," in *Ireland's Field Day* (Notre Dame: University of Notre Dame Press, 1986); Belinda Loftus, *Mirrors: William III & Mother Ireland* (Dundrum: Picture Press, 1990); *Mother Ireland,* dir. Anne Crilly, Derry Film and Video, 1988; David Cairns and Shaun Richards, "Tropes and Traps: Aspects of 'Woman' and Nationality in Twentieth-Century Irish Drama," in *Gender in Irish Writing,* ed. David Cairns and Toni O'Brien Johnson (Milton Keynes: Open University Press, 1991); Joseph Th. Leerson, *Mere Irish & Fíor-Ghael* (Amsterdam: Benjamins, 1986), 246–50; Elizabeth Butler Cullingford, *Gender and History in Yeats's Love Poetry* (Cambridge: Cambridge University Press, 1993), 55–72.

6. Few Englishwomen appear at all: Mabel Bagenal in Friel's *Making History* is one of the exceptions.

7. Brian Friel, *Translations* (London: Faber, 1981), 46.

8. Dion Boucicault, *Selected Plays,* ed. Andrew Parkin (Gerrards Cross: Colin Smythe, 1987), 262.

9. For an extended study of this issue, see my essay, "The Stage Englishman of Boucicault's Irish Drama," forthcoming in *Theatre Journal* (Fall 1997). On Boucicault see Stephen Watt, *Joyce, O'Casey, and the Irish Popular Theater* (Syracuse: Syracuse University Press, 1991), 48–88.

10. See Cheryl Herr, ed., *For the Land They Loved: Irish Political Melo-dramas 1890–1925* (Syracuse: Syracuse University Press, 1991).

11. Luke Gibbons, "Romanticism, Realism and Irish Cinema," in *Cinema and Ireland,* ed. Kevin Rockett, Luke Gibbons, and John Hill (London: Routledge, 1988), 219–21.

12. Boucicault, *Plays,* 311, 317.

13. Dion Boucicault, *Arrah-na-Pogue,* ed. David Krause (Dublin: Dolmen Press, 1964), 157.

14. Friel, *Translations,* 40.

15. Terry Eagleton, *Saint Oscar* (Derry: Field Day, 1989), xi.

16. On Shaw and national stereotypes see Declan Kiberd, *Inventing Ireland* (London: Cape, 1995), 51–63. Though I differ with him occasionally, this essay is deeply indebted to Kiberd's work.

17. Shaw, *John Bull's Other Island,* 115.

18. Quoted in Martin Meisel, *Shaw and the Nineteenth-Century Theater* (Princeton: Princeton University Press, 1963), 18.

19. Shaw, *John Bull's Other Island,* 165–66, 92.

20. Kiberd, *Inventing Ireland,* 57.

21. Shaw, *John Bull's Other Island,* 87, 101, 107.

22. For "reconciliation" see Watt, *Joyce, O'Casey, . . .,* 64–76.

23. Shaw, *John Bull's Other Island,* 73, 166.

24. Ibid., 170.

25. Ibid., 152.

26. Eve Kosofsky Sedgwick, *Between Men: English Literature and Male Homosocial Desire* (New York: Columbia University Press, 1985), 1.

27. Kiberd, *Inventing Ireland,* 63.

28. Shaw, *John Bull's Other Island,* 89.

29. Gayle Rubin, "The Traffic in Women," in *Women, Class, and the Feminist Imagination,* ed. Karen V. Hansen and Ilene J. Philipson (Philadelphia: Temple University Press, 1990), 74–94.

30. See Sedgwick, *Between Men,* 21.

31. James Joyce, *Ulysses,* ed. Hans Walter Gabler (New York: Vintage, 1986), 79, 12.

32. Shaw, *John Bull's Other Island,* 173.

33. Sean O'Casey, *Three Plays* (London: Macmillan, 1966), 208–9.

34. Gibbons's critique of Lean's pastoralism (*Cinema and Ireland,* 196–200, 228–31) does not mention Major Doryan.

35. L. P. Curtis, *Apes and Angels* (Washington, D.C.: Smithsonian Institution Press, 1971), 42–43.

36. E. M. Forster, *A Passage to India* (New York: Harcourt Brace, 1952), 322.

37. *Ryan's Daughter,* dir. David Lean, MGM, 1970.

38. Kevin Rockett, "An Irish Film Studio," in *Cinema and Ireland,* 113.

39. J. H. Andrews calls *Translations* "a play about late twentieth-century

Ireland" in *"Translations* and *A Paper Landscape," Crane Bag* 7.2 (1983): 120. Edna Longley concurs in "Poetry and Politics in Northern Ireland," *Crane Bag* 9.1 (1985): 28–29. See also Marilynn Richtarik, *Acting between the Lines* (Oxford: Clarendon Press, 1994), 28–64.

40. Friel, *Translations*, 38, 32. The connection between Yolland and Broadbent has been noted by Anthony Roche, *Contemporary Irish Drama* (New York: St. Martin's Press, 1995), 249.

41. Richard Pine, *Brian Friel and Ireland's Drama* (London: Routledge, 1990), 176.

42. Richard Kearney, *Transitions* (Dublin: Wolfhound, 1988), 137.

43. Friel, *Translations*, 52.

44. Ibid., 43–44.

45. Matthew Arnold, *On the Study of Celtic Literature* (New York: Macmillan, 1909), 54.

46. *Hush-a-Bye Baby,* dir. Margo Harkin, Derry Film and Video, 1988.

47. Martin Dillon, *The Dirty War* (London: Arrow, 1991), 162.

48. Anthony Bradley, *Requiem for a Spy* (Cork: Mercier, 1993), 47.

49. The connection between Nairac, Friel, and Devlin can be made because Nairac's bizarre story was prominently featured in the media. In *The Romans in Britain* (London: Methuen, 1980), English playwright Howard Brenton figures Nairac as Captain Thomas Chichester, an SAS assassin who passes himself off as Irish by singing "a few rebel songs in the pub," and is killed by the IRA.

50. Friel, *Translations*, 30.

51. Anne Devlin, *Ourselves Alone* (London: Faber, 1986), 51.

52. Sedgwick, *Between Men*, 2.

53. Devlin, *Ourselves Alone*, 71.

54. For the shoot-to-kill policy (1982), see J. Bowyer Bell, *The Irish Troubles* (New York: St. Martins Press, 1993), 652–56.

55. Kiberd, *Inventing Ireland*, 526.

56. Brendan Behan, *An Giall/The Hostage*, trans. and ed. Richard Wall (Washington, D.C.: Catholic University of America Press, 1987), 126.

57. Ibid., 57, 129, 70.

58. Ibid., 138.

59. Ibid., 80, 141.

60. Ibid., 159.

61. Ibid., 160.

62. Ibid., 104.

63. Quoted in ibid., 8.

64. *The Crying Game,* dir. Neil Jordan, Miramax, 1992. Ronan Bennett attacks Jordan's film for its stereotyped representations of "terrorists" in "The Bomber Next Door," *Guardian*, 23 November 1992; David Lloyd catalogs its historical improbabilities in a paper delivered at the University of Texas at Austin (1994). The central act of hostage-taking, which Lloyd censures as

anachronistic, derives from literary tradition rather than contemporary events.

65. Behan, *An Giall/The Hostage,* 122.

66. Neil Jordan, *The Crying Game* (London: Vintage, 1993), 12.

67. Frank McGuinness, *Carthaginians* and *Baglady* (London: Faber, 1988), 36, 38.

68. Jordan, *Crying Game,* 68.

69. Ibid., 7.

70. Jordan, "Interview," *Film Ireland* 32 (April/May 1993): 20.

71. Jordan, *Crying Game,* 8, 13, 14.

72. Lance Pettitt ["Pigs, Provos and Prostitutes: Gay Representation in Recent Irish Film," in *Sex, Nation and Dissent,* ed. Eibhlear Walshe (Cork: Cork University Press, 1997)] argues that despite attacks on the film's representations of transsexuals, women, and blacks, it "retains positive aspects for gay viewers."

73. Jordan, *Crying Game,* 20.

74. 1 Corinthians 13.3.

75. See Theodore W. Allen, *The Invention of the White Race,* Vol. 1 (London: Verso, 1994), 27–51.

76. bell hooks attacks the film's representation of race without acknowledging the Irish experience of colonization: for her, Fergus is "the white colonizer" or simply "white folks," in *Outlaw Culture* (New York: Routledge, 1994), 59, 62.

77. Jordan, *Crying Game,* viii.

78. Ibid., 45, 49.

79. Ibid., 12.

80. Ibid., viii.

81. For a feminist critique of *The Crying Game,* see Sarah Edge, "Women Are Trouble, Did You Know That, Fergus?" *Feminist Review* 50 (1995): 173–86; on Dil and race see bell hooks, *Outlaw Culture* (New York: Routledge, 1994), 55–57.

82. See Kieran Rose, *Diverse Communities* (Cork: Cork University Press, 1994), 34–59.

83. Both feature an Irishman who bonds with a black man, and both contrive to have the black man murdered halfway through the action.

84. Frank McGuinness, "A Dramatist Deep-Rooted in Ireland: Interview with Sue Summers," *Daily Telegraph,* July 7, 1992, 14. McGuinness insists that his characters are not based on the actual hostages, Irishman Brian Keenan and Englishman John McCarthy.

85. Frank McGuinness, *Someone Who'll Watch Over Me* (London: Faber, 1992), 9.

86. Ibid., 31, 24, 10, 16.

87. Ibid., 10, 24–25.

88. Ibid., 13, 30.

89. Ibid., 28, 30, 48–49.
90. Ibid., 49, 40.
91. Ibid., 41–42.
92. Ibid., 43.
93. Ibid., 30.
94. Ibid., 46–47.
95. Ibid., 50.
96. Ibid., 50–51, 58.
97. Neil Jordan, *Michael Collins* (New York: Plume, 1966), 136–39.

"Our Bodies' Eyes and Writing Hands"

Secrecy and Sensuality in Ní Chuilleanáin's Baroque Art

IN HER AUTOBIOGRAPHICAL treatise, "The Life of the Woman and the Poet in Our Time," Eavan Boland remarks that "Irish women poets had gone from being the objects of the Irish poem to being its authors in a relatively short space of time."[1] That final spatializing locution offers a clue as to why the most respected women poets in Ireland represent this shift they have undergone—from aesthetic object to poetic subject—in terms of painting. Boland herself, Medbh McGuckian, Paula Meehan, and Eiléan Ní Chuilleanáin vocalize the once-mute objects of male artists, raise questions about fixed perspective and aesthetic distance, and undertake complex questions about the erotic in ekphrastic poems, poems that "read" well-known paintings or invent what John Hollander calls "notional" paintings.[2] Although Meehan's "The Statue of the Virgin at Granard Speaks" and "Zugswang" offer witty forums for two otherwise silent objects of art, ekphrastic poems are not a central part of her work. While McGuckian refers directly to Vermeer and evokes other painters, she employs color so pervasively that she becomes more nearly a painter than a mirrorer of painting.[3] Boland, on the other hand, must receive further attention in this paper because her difference from Ní Chuilleanáin can help us situate Ní Chuilleanáin's rich, complex, and relatively neglected poetry.

Perspective and the Gaze: Boland and Ní Chuilleanáin

Boland's and Ní Chuilleanáin's approaches to perspective in poetry, which have received some critical attention, could hardly be more different. Boland favors not only the authoritative point of view, which she calls "the difficult 'I' of perception,"[4] but also the visual over the tactile or the auditory. In contrast to this conventional viewpoint, in art and poetry, Ní Chuilleanáin renders the angle of vision, the integrity of the viewer, and even the viewer's gender problematic and shifting, often with direct reference to painting. For example, in a poem with a painterly title "River, with Boats,"[5] we enjoy two stanzas of tactile, auditory, and visual imagery from the secure perspective of a room looking out on a river. In the final stanza, the tidal river raises a boat to the level of the room's window, and the perspective reverses —"The window is blocked / By the one framed eye / Of a tethered coaster / . . . / And the faces of the mariners / Crowd at the glass . . ." —and then flips again: ". . . like fishes," the viewer becoming the viewed becoming the viewer.

In several cases, Ní Chuilleanáin's poems form a commentary, whether intentional or accidental, on Boland's, whereby Ní Chuilleanáin clarifies certain of her ideas concerning perspective, the artist's relation to—and distance from—the world she portrays, and the relation between the iconic and the sacred. For example, Boland's objection to "the sexual perspective of the poet" distancing and controlling "the erotic object, as an image"[6] applies to painting the popular feminist extension of Freud's concept of *the gaze*.[7] Boland herself makes this extension in "Degas's Laundresses,"[8] where, as the possessive title suggests, we are concerned less with the projection of the painter's desire than with the appropriation of the woman as object.

The poem addresses two women who appear in a series of drawings and paintings, the most finished of which depicts one laundress bearing down stiff-armed on an iron while the other, holding a bottle of water for sprinkling the cloth, stretches and yawns. The poem is composed of six stanzas of six lines each, the final thirty-sixth line standing alone. In its complex formal qualities, the poem complements Degas's art. The stanzas cohere less by terminal rhyme, for which occasional consonantal, assonantal, or alliterative chimings serve as proxies, than by extensive internal—often to words as well as lines —rhyme: *pit . . . stitches / . . . fitted; seam dreams; chat's sabbatical; pleasure . . . leisured; neat heaps; ease / . . . easel; sharpening charcoal; blind designs.* Less restricted than end rhyme, internal rhyme matches verbs to their appropriate objects by sound as well as syntax and otherwise interweaves aspects of work by sound. More unusual, what might be the names for their mistresses' decorative possessions—*dawn, silk, seam, basket*—designate for these women working verbs or participles: "you *dawn*," "*silking* the fitted sheets," and so on. Strangely but appropriately, the laundresses' employers—*"leisured* women"—are characterized by a participle that has no active infinitive.

The first three stanzas, addressed to the laundresses in second person, describe the women's work, with frequent references to class distinctions. In the fourth stanza, the poem erupts into alarmed imperatives: "Wait. There. Behind you. / A man. There behind you. / Whatever you do don't turn. / Why is he watching you? / Whatever you do don't turn. / Whatever you do don't turn." The appearance of the painter himself occasions this anxiety, but for the actual cause we must look elsewhere. From Degas's "ease" with his "easel" we might infer some sort of class condescension, but the poet has already offered parole to the "leisured" mistresses of the workers. Because the second-person address erases questions of the painter's perspective as the basis for exploitation, to comprehend why the painter's mind might be, as the last line says, the laundresses' "winding sheet," we have to assume some unspoken argument about the necessity of exploitation or appropriation between male artist and female subject.

In this same relationship between male artist and female subject, Ní Chuilleanáin seems to accept both a separation between artist and subject and need and desire as the motivation for art. In *The Brazen Serpent* we arrive at the sinister-sounding "Man Watching a Woman"[9] with some trepidation after the sexual violence of "Passing Over in Silence" and "Vierge Ouvrante." With no initial clue to the man's identity, we are told: "A sense of being nowhere at all, / Set him on his way . . .," as we follow him through dark yards to arrive under "windows / Lit softly above the privet hedge. / He stops and watches. He needs to see this." The man's voyeuristic need and the violation of the woman's privacy, "above the privet hedge," only heighten our suspicion. In the second stanza, we see what he "needs to see . . .":

> A woman working late in the refectory,
> Sewing a curtain, the lines of her face
> Dropping into fatigue, severity, age,
> The hair falling out of its clasp at her poll.
> The hands are raised to thread the needle,
> The tongue moves behind her lips.
> He cannot see the feet or shoes, they are trapped
> In toils of cloth. He is comforted.

The seamstress remains inaudible to this man, but he observes sympathetically her rhythms of labor and decline—*working, sewing, dropping, falling*. Although she is "trapped / In toils of cloth," a pun on *toile,* the appropriately French word for cloth or linen or even a painter's canvas, he brings her no winding sheet. We are told that "he is comforted" although by tomorrow night, her finished curtains may deprive him of comfort.[10] For this night, however, "He can move on" to "the wide cafés," not for the "Trombone music over polished tables" but to observe the barmaids' labor and fatigue with a sympathy and sense of rhythm tuned at the refectory window: "He will watch the faces behind the bar, tired girls, / Their muscles bracing under breakers of music / And the weight of their balancing trays, drinks, ice and change." Because of her second-person address in "Degas's Laundresses," Boland relinquishes some of her position as a fixed and foregrounded observer. Consequently, in this one case her observer approaches Ní Chuilleanáin's watcher in fulfilling Norman Bryson's prescription for a more humane relation between artist and subject:

> To dissolve the Gaze . . . we must willingly enter into . . . the Glance . . . [,] dispense with the conception of form as con-sideration, as Arrest, and try to conceive of form instead in dynamic terms, as matter in process, . . . in the mobility and vibrancy of its somatic rhythms; the body of labour, of material practice.[11]

However, as if these two poems were set in dialogue with each other, Boland's poem extends this humanizing perspective to her speaker but not to Degas, whereas Ní Chuilleanáin's watcher exercises enough sympathy to conceive of Edouard Manet's *Bar at the Folies Bergère* (1881–82) or, for that matter, Degas's laundresses, painted in the same year as Manet's famous painting.

Boland's poetry and prose address more directly political and social aspects of feminism whereas Ní Chuilleanáin's poetry taps deeply into philosophical aspects such as the body or, as she says elsewhere, "our bodies' eyes,"[12] the relation of the sexual to the sacred, and the sacred to the secret. These concerns grow out of, and relate to, two traditions with which Boland is not concerned: the Counter Reformation and the Gaelic language. Ní Chuilleanáin recalls an early encounter with proto-Baroque art, that reaction against classical art which will become an expression of the Counter Reformation. In her twentieth year, she was viewing the paintings in Berlin's Dahlem Gemäldegalerie when she stepped through a door out of the darkness of Lowlands art into the dazzle of Correggio's *Leda*, "full of blue and white, narrative space, and perversity."[13] Even reproductions convey the charm of Correggio's painting, perhaps surprising for any viewer who associates the subject with the "sudden blow" and subsequent violence of Yeats's treatment.[14] In a discussion of *Leda* and three other paintings that depict the *Loves of Jupiter,* a Correggio scholar accounts for their charm in this manner: "The fact that all four remain great art and not pornography is partly due to the extreme skill and delicacy of the painter, and partly also to the fact that none of them includes the form of a man. . . ."[15] As a consequence of this omission, the painter can focus on Leda's body, on her curiosity and pleasure in the initial stages of coition, while still representing the difference between herself and the diminutive lover. Ní Chuilleanáin sharpens the contrast between what she calls "Brownish Rembrandts" from the Calvinist Netherlands and this Mediterranean nude:

> Here was the body at the centre of a story, female and pleased in all its dimensions. I was suddenly back in a world before the upheaval of the Reformation, before the Protestant war on icons of the body, rituals, and material ceremonies.

So that we not mistakenly assume that Ní Chuilleanáin is indulging an atavism and merely raising those ancient tribal issues that are alleged to divide Ireland, we can recall Ted Hughes's broader and more radical generalization that

> the fundamental guiding ideas of our Western Civilization . . . are . . . that the earth is a heap of raw materials given to man by God for his exclusive profit and use . . . The subtly apotheosized misogyny of Reformed Christianity is proportionate to the fanatic rejection of Nature, and the result has been to exile man from Mother Nature—from both inner and outer nature.[16]

Ní Chuilleanáin and Baroque Art and Architecture

Correggio's painting helped Ní Chuilleanáin discover the importance of what she calls "the life of the body," not only to history but also to "the way we apprehend language or visible beauty." It also must have drawn her, soon after, to Correggio's great ceiling mural in the Duomo of Parma, which becomes the subject of "Fireman's Lift," the opening poem in *The Brazen Serpent* (1995). Recently, Ní Chuilleanáin said of this poem, "When I found myself compelled to write about Correggio's *Assumption of the Virgin*, . . . I could only concentrate on one aspect, the way it shows bodily effort and the body's weight." [17]

In this massive mural on the cupola of the Duomo in Parma, which Cecil Gould praises as "perhaps the greatest *tour de force* in Italian art," [18] saints and angels are depicted merging into a vortex of torsos and faces, legs and arms, lifting the Virgin toward heaven and a waiting Christ. In the mass of her body, the angels' efforts, and the colposcopic view of the cervical cupola, the painting could be said to reflect and celebrate the feminine body. Of course at the height of the camera/cervix, Christ waits, as if he were Irigaray's *kore*—a diminished man or the gynecological philosopher's reflected pupil—preoccupying Mary's space. [19] On the other hand, the figure of Christ, diminished, slightly off-center, and embryonic, seems more swaddler than savior, an about-to-be-reborn Christ, still a resident of his mother's assumed body.

In "Fireman's Lift," [20] the dome added to a Romanesque church in Parma participates gymnastically in the Assumption of the Virgin. The spiraling, ascending interaction of art and architecture, characteristic of baroque buildings, was first suggested by the work of Michelangelo, according to art critics Bearden and Holty:

> In the passionate and often unfinished volumes of his last sculptures, in the restless and flamelike action of his frescoes (especially such works as *The Brazen Serpent* . . .) were born the mannerisms of the baroque style. [21]

By widespread consensus, however, the true protobaroque painter was Correggio: "the most precocious of the great masters of the High Renaissance, who seems to us today to have been in reality a Baroque painter born a hundred years too soon . . .; . . . More than any other painter, Correggio prefigures the Baroque." [22] Ní Chuilleanáin's enjambed lines, alliterative pauses, and internal rhyme or assonantal chimes project the sound incrementally and thereby imitate this energetic collective heaving up of Mary's carnality, which becomes a "fireman's lift" of "teams of angelic arms," a baroque collusion of paint, plaster, parapet and squinch, arch and architrave:

> The back making itself a roof
> The legs a bridge, the hands
> A crane and a cradle.
>
> Their heads bowed over to reflect on her
> Fair face and hair so like their own
> As she passed through their hands. We saw them
> Lifting her, the pillars of their arms
>
> (Her face a capital leaning into an arch)
> As the muscles clung and shifted
> For a final purchase together
> Under her weight as she came to the edge of the cloud.

When we recognize that this depiction of a joyful boosterism by which Mary reaches heaven complements as it contrasts with contemporary paintings of the rescue-squad deposition of Christ's body, then we see how the poem elevates the feminine side of Catholicism as well as woman's body. This recognition becomes enforced by the point of view. As has been noted, frequently Ní Chuilleanáin's poems maintain their secrets of plot by dispersing point of view. In this poem, the poet follows Correggio: "The whole of the zone of the Duomo cupola containing the angels is tilted in the direction of the spectator advancing east from the nave, and this introduces a new and dynamic principle. . . . The idea of forceful communion between the spectator and the figures in the painting . . . is now applied to murals."[23] Similarly, Ní Chuilleanáin invites the reader immediately into the poem: "I was standing beside you looking up / Through the big tree of the cupola." Later, when "we stepped / Back, as the painter longed to / . . . / We saw the work entire . . . ," the point of view shifts out of an authorial perspective fixed in space and time. We enter, in fact, the perspective of memory ("This is what love sees, that angle") as the dates—1962, when the student poet visited Parma with her mother, and 1994, when her mother died and she wrote this poem to her— indicate to us. Now we can recognize that the opening *you* must be primarily her mother for whom, amid an uncertainty that the title and joking tone suggest, the poet hopes, desires, and composes an equally loving assumption. In the words *purchase* and *weight,* in the adhesive *u* syllables—*usc, ung, urch, und, oud*—and in the drawn-out closing hectasyllabic, the closing lines emphasize that body goes with soul in this final hoist toward the terminal bourn: "As the muscles clung and shifted / For a final purchase together / Under her weight as she came to the edge of the cloud."

In a manner analogous to Correggio's, and later Bernini's, "conflation of painting and stucco with real and simulated architecture" where "the eye was meant to be deceived and to accept the illusionist convention that the architecture merged into the painted or half-painted heaven of the ceiling,"[24] Ní Chuilleanáin's poetry resists containment, within the literal or physical or domestic, as she wanders beyond borders and margins and walls of structures. She often represents such traversing of thresholds and boundaries in relation to architecture. In "The Architectural Metaphor,"[25] we tour a convent which was founded "Here, a good mile on the safe side of the border / Before the border was changed." This feminine space contains secret recesses that deliver not births so much as qualified rebirths. Speaking of such spaces, Ní Chuilleanáin has described her "dreams about houses . . . in which you particularly find there's an extra room. . . . I was interested in those before I ever read Freud on the interpretation of dreams . . . the house and the body both come into that."[26] In this region of shifting boundaries, we follow a sort of psychopomp, a Mercurial "guide in the flashing cap" who leads us through the convent into the still-functioning but secularized laundry:

> Now light scatters, a door opens, laughter breaks in,
> A young girl barefoot, a man pushing her
> Backwards against the hatch—

And here we recognize that the architectural metaphor is actually a pun, enriched by "nested" and the foraging hatchling in subsequent lines.

> It flies up suddenly—
> There lies the foundress, pale
> In her funeral sheets, her face turned west

Representing the Virgin, the opaque rose-window is meant to nurture meditation:

Searching for the rose-window. It shows her
What she never saw from any angle but this:
Weeds nested in the churchyard, catching the late sun,

Herself at fourteen stumbling downhill
And landing, and crouching to watch
The sly limbering of the bantam hen

Foraging between gravestones—

Help is at hand
Though out of reach:

The world not dead after all.

In these last four lines the antistrophic structure and wry qualifications may owe something to Kinsella, as in *Out of Ireland,* but this deft reversal is distinctly Ní Chuilleanáin's own.

Buildings such as this convent and the Duomo are also "brazen serpents" after all, both iconic and functional, aesthetic and practical. In Ní Chuilleanáin's poetry, structures receive and sustain us, often appropriately as feminine spaces, institutions that have paid tribute to women, such as the Duomo of Parma, or even offered women a degree of independence or autonomy. "I'm interested . . . in non-biological families, like religious communities . . . ," Ní Chuilleanáin said recently.[27]

In acknowledging that architecture offers Ní Chuilleanáin more than themes, Eamon Grennan guides us toward an understanding of her use of such structures in her poetry:

> In some sense the narrative voice, narration itself, is not unlike architecture, in that it can be a means of establishing the secure *ground* of the experience which is the poem's subject. It can also create difficulty, however, since it may not be given a visible or comprehensible context: it may simply be there—a story or a picture existing (for us, though presumably not for the speaker) in its own terms only. . . . Confronted by such conditions of ignorance, a reader simply has to hang on to what's given and enter (with a small act of faith) the moment of mystery and exhilaration.[28]

In "simply being there," architecture represents the traditions we are born into, structures we enter and inhabit long before any understanding arrives. Architecture even participates in these births: in "The

Architectural Metaphor," the hatch colludes in a rebirth of the world if not finally of the foundress; in "Home Town," alleyways get "ready to arch and push" as the speaker approaches her house of birth; in "Daniel Grose" "The breach widens at every push," although preparing for ruin this time; and in "Fireman's Lift" the cupola and the Church both assume the mother and Mary and participate in their rebirths while the poet is both midwife and source. "All for You"[29] begins with a trochaic foot just stepping into a domain with enough allusions to Advent to be Christ's first home: "Once beyond the gate of the strange stableyard, we dismount. / The donkey walks on, straight in at a wide door / And sticks his head in a manger." With plenty of room in this inn, however, the manor actively, even corporally, receives the speaker's company, a *we* who soon defers to *you*, the reader and inheritor: "The great staircase of the hall slouches back, / Sprawling between warm wings. It is for you. / As the steps wind and warp / . . . the breath of ovens / Flows out . . ." The poem concludes with details of a thoroughly provident household economy that *we* can only accept as we do bodies and lives into which we are born:

> It is for you, the dry fragrance of tea-chests
> The tins shining in ranks, the ten-pound jars
> Rich with shrivelled fruit. Where better to lie down
> And sleep, along the labelled shelves,
> With the key still in your pocket?

The Counter Reformation and Baroque Art

Like the brass serpent approved by God in the twenty-first chapter of Numbers, which serves as Ní Chuilleanáin's epigraph, the works of man's hand" icons, art, architecture—can recall one to God or serve as prophylactics against the misery God sends. More generously, one might infer that God allows us to use icons, constructions, or fictions in an intercessory role. The later Old Testament chapter of 2 Kings 18 "reforms" this concession, however, interdicting such icons—or any visual representation—because they had been confused with "the real thing." One might see much of the adversity of the Reformation and the Counter Reformation springing from these two contradictory passages. This struggle, central to Ireland today as it was in the seventeenth century, lies behind much of *The Brazen Serpent* and, less deliberately, of Ní Chuilleanáin's earlier volumes. Insofar as baroque art emerged from and represented the Counter Reformation, the baroque tradition may help define, at least metaphorically, Ní Chuilleanáin's poetry. In the succinct summary of one art historian:

> The Baroque represents Catholic supremacy at its height—after the shattering doubts resulting from the Protestant Reformation . . . but before the scepticism of the Age of Reason. It is between these polarities that Baroque art lies, growing out of the Mannerism of the sixteenth century and merging, perhaps less perceptibly, into the Rococo of the eighteenth.[30]

The sack of Rome and scattering of painters to new centers in 1527, just after Correggio's completion of his Duomo mural, ended the High Renaissance. The Council of Trent from 1545 to 1563—initiating reform within the Catholic Church and a counterattack on the Reformation—was a precondition for baroque art, which did not flourish, however, until the seventeenth century. As part of this renewal, Loyola's *Spiritual Exercise* inculcated an important dimension of the baroque aesthetic, the practice of re-imagining Christian abstraction in terms of the body and its suffering.[31] Martin Jay's terse characterization of philosophical manifestations of the baroque may be usefully related to Ní Chuilleanáin's shifting perspectives and her sudden, strange exposures of the sacred:

> In philosophical terms, although no one system can be seen as its correlate, Leibniz's pluralism of monadic viewpoints, Pascal's meditations on paradox, and the Counter Reformation mystics' submission to vertiginous experiences of rapture might all be seen as related to baroque vision. Moreover, the philosophy it favored self-consciously eschewed the model of intellectual clarity expressed in a literal language purified of ambiguity. Instead, it recognized the inextricability of rhetoric and vision, which meant that images were signs and that concepts always contained an irreducibly imagistic component.

Citing the contemporary French writer Christine Buci-Glucksman, Jay further argues that "the baroque self-consciously revels in the contradictions between surface and depth, disparaging as a result any attempt to reduce the multiplicity of visual spaces into any one coherent essence" and thereby opposes "the absolute ocularcentrism of its Cartesian perspectivalist rival."[32]

Jay cites Buci-Glucksman because he supports her argument that baroque perspective and classical Albertian perspectives continue to the present as antithetical aesthetics: "It is precisely the explosive power of baroque vision that is seen as the most significant alternative to the hegemonic visual style we have called Cartesian perspectivalism."[33]

Boland's Cartesian Perspectivalism and "The Real Thing"

To the extent that these perspectives persist as alternatives, we might clarify Ní Chuilleanáin's baroque perspective by contrasting it with the fixed and foregrounded first-person of Eavan Boland's poetry. Boland's insistence on speaking in the first person and on filtering all experience through an autobiograpical speaker corresponds, at least analogically, to the classic perspective as first defined in Alberti's *De Pictura* (1435). According to Bryson, Alberti intended that

> the eye of the viewer is to take up a position in relation to the scene that is identical to the position originally occupied by the painter, as though both painter and viewer looked through the same viewfinder on to a world unified spatially around the centric ray, the line running from viewpoint to vanishing point (it is probable that Alberti had in mind the model of the *camera obscura*); unified spatially, but also informationally, since all the data presented by the image are to cohere around a core narrative structure.[34]

Boland's preference in painters signals her differences from Ní Chuilleanáin's baroque perspective and point of view. In her autobiographical treatise on poetry, *Object Lessons*, Boland tells of searching for a model for celebrating women's ordinary life but one free of feminist anger in response to that life's restrictions:

> In the genre painters of the French eighteenth century—in Jean Baptiste Chardin in particular—I saw what I was looking for. Chardin's paintings were ordinary in the accepted sense of the word. They were unglamorous, workaday, authentic. Yet in his work these objects were not merely described; they were revealed.[35]

A Chardin scholar praises this reactionary against French academic painting for his "single-minded, uncompromising and passionate commitment to the thing seen."[36] Although Chardin's interiors limit spacious prospects, he conforms to a conventional Renaissance or Albertian perspective which situates our point of view securely with the artist's. As an analogue to the perspectivist tradition in which Chardin participated where the paired orthogonal lines fade to an intersection, Boland's poems conventionally employ an imperial first-person speaker, and frequently open with the pronoun "I," identified with the poet. The superb "Oral Tradition" [37] with its fixed first-person and its Chardinesque palette begins, "I was standing there," *there* being with her more than with the occasion, which is "a reading / or a workshop or whatever." From this position she overhears two women in muted conversation, scraps of one's story about her great-grandmother's birth of her grandfather in an open field. Conveyed by women's memory down several generations to lodge in a present moment, this story's summer setting contrasts sharply with the setting of its retelling: a bitter winter's night and this temporary refuge: "a firelit room / in which the color scheme / crouched well down—/ golds, a sort of dun / a distressed ocher—/ and the sole richness was / in the suggestion of a texture / like the low flax gleam / that comes off polished leather." A little later, the settling firelog inserts a flickering parenthesis in the woman's story: "(Wood . . . / . . . / broke apart in sparks, / a windfall of light / in the room's darkness)," an interruption that emphasizes the fragile momentariness of the woman's retelling. The seasonally enforced contrast between the original event and this retelling extends into a contrast between the pellucid language and the textured objects it describes and between the story's relative sparseness of detail—"and she had on a skirt / of cross-woven linen"—and its resonance of elaborated details in the poet's mind: "the bruised summer light, / the musical subtext /

of mauve eaves on lilac
and the laburnum past
and shadows where the lime
tree dropped its bracts
in frills of contrast

where she lay down
in vetch and linen
and lifted up her son
to the archive
they would shelter in:

This sheltering "archive" ("a public office" from the Greek root "to command," not to be confused with the plural, meaning "a body of records") becomes ostensibly "the oral song," but in its poetic elaboration—the apparently happenstance but actually highly opportunistic rhyme, the short pulsing lines—the woman's story enters the archive of the poem, through the strict governance of the poet. Although we receive directly scraps of talk, we perceive through the poet who begins by standing, then journeying, then reaching her epode, "a sense / suddenly of truth, / its resonance." This last phrase could characterize a typical Boland poem which conveys quotidian accident through the channel of the poet toward, if not truth, a sense of truth, poetically delineated and elaborated through images presumed to be from a shared world.[38]

We might presume that Ní Chuilleanáin's poem entitled "The Real Thing"[39] underwrites such Bolandesque assumptions by seeming to nominate "Sister Custos," (L. guard or custodian), as the passive butt of irony. In this convent bricked off from modern life, she "Exposes her major relic, the longest / Known fragment of the Brazen Serpent." On the basis of this irony, we might suppose that the poem supports Eavan Boland's appeal to poets in "The Journey" to turn from mythic artifice to subjects such as antibiotics or "the protein treasures of the sea bed": "Depend upon it, somewhere a poet is wasting / his sweet uncluttered meters on the obvious / emblem instead of the real thing."[40]

Another reading of the last stanza of Ní Chuilleanáin's poem, however, can support a different interpretation, one more consistent with other poems in the volume.

> Her history is a blank sheet,
> Her vows a folded paper locked like a well.
> The torn end of the serpent
> Tilts the lace edge of the veil.
> The real thing, the one free foot kicking
> Under the white sheet of history.

Here, the force of displaced or latent action—choices of faith *folded* and *locked;* rejected icons *torn* and *kicking*—and the image of blankness suggest that the acting out and writing of history depend on such emblems of faith or such "unreasonable" fictions freely chosen, which therefore are "the real thing," as Sister Custos says.

Ní Chuilleanáin's poem "Daniel Grose"[41] addresses more directly the relation of geometric, scientifically endorsed perspectives to the history they repress, reminding us that, as W. J. T. Mitchell writes, "Perspective is a figure for what we would call ideology—a historical, cultural formation that masquerades as a universal, natural code."[42] Early in the poem, the poet steps aside from the artist's line of sight, which is aimed like a weapon: "Now the military draughtsman / Is training his eye / On the upright of the tower, / Noting the doors that open on treetops." The draughtsman, Daniel Grose, assumed the authorship of *Antiquities of Ireland* (1792) at the death of his more famous uncle the Englishman Francis Grose, and provided most of the etchings of picturesque ruins that filled this book.[43] His actual drawings, which include such famous ruins as Kells Church and Tower, Mellifont Abbey, and Boyle Abbey, are parodied here in the "Abbey of the Five Wounds," his vanishing point. Nowhere explicit in Grose's text, Christ's woundings echo in the words—*shatter, falls, pierced, spasm, the first wounding*—associated with the destruction of these buildings and their societies, which began during the Reformation's confiscation of church properties: "Then silence for three centuries / While a taste for ruins develops." In this picturesque panorama, history is omitted: "No crowds engaged in rape or killing, / No marshalling of boy soldiers, / No cutting the hair of novices."[44]

Responding to one of the strongest eckphrastic attractions, the poet then temporalizes space, opening this picturesque effect to its historical causes:

> Where is the human figure
> He needs to show the scale
> And all the time that's passed
> And how different things are now?

The response is startling, even uncanny:

> The old woman by the oak tree
> Can be pressed into service
> To occupy the foreground.
> Her feet are warmed by drifting leaves.

This final line recalls the association of autumnal life and a repressed past in Shakespeare's indirect reference—"bare ruined choirs"—to ruins of the "Old Church" (Sonnet 73). The aged woman, standing druidically beside the oak, is the *cailleach,* that mysterious abandoned figure of Irish society and legend, a persona assumed sometimes by Eithne Strong and Nuala Ní Dhomhnaill in their poetries and by Ní Chuilleanáin herself in a recent essay subtitled "The *Cailleach* Writes about the Renaissance." She also suggests the *spéirbhean,* the sky-woman appearing here in her third emanation as the hag,[45] and therefore a figure of colonial repression, employed to enforce the Anglo-Irish draughtsman's perspective but otherwise ignored:

> He stands too far away
> To hear what she is saying,
> How she routinely measures
> The verse called the midwife's curse
> On all that catches her eye, naming
> The scholar's index finger, the piper's hunch,
> The squint, the rub, the itch of every trade.

The *cailleach* represents the poet herself as the return of the repressed, a baroque *extravagance,* who, literally, "takes us beyond" the framed or bound space of the engraving, aside from the geometric perspective, beyond spatial into poetic measure and, thereby, into unrepresentable time.

Baroque Art and the Irish Language Tradition

Our use of *baroque* must be heavily qualified before it can become a valuable way of characterizing Ní Chuilleanáin's poetry. An epochally, culturally, and generically specific term must be translated from the seventeenth century to the edge of the twenty-first, from a counter-reformational Italy to the Irish nation whose major religion was repressed, and from painting to poetry. In fact, it is tempting to do as art historians have done, according to Jay, ever since the late-Victorian publication of Heinrich Wölfflin's *Renaissance and Baroque:*

> postulate a perennial oscillation between two styles in both painting and architecture. In opposition to the lucid, linear, solid, fixed, plimetric, closed form of the Renaissance, or as Wölfflin later called it, the classical style, the baroque was painterly, recessional, soft-focused, multiple, and open.[46]

We might free the term altogether from its seventeenth-century base as Jay and Buci-Glucksman do when they declare *baroque* "the scopic regime that has finally come into its own in our time."[47] One could suspect that their claim merely refashions standard binaries such as romantic and classic, Arnold's celtic and saxon, or even Catholic and Protestant. Yet, even if we see such binaries as fictions of a dialectical view of history, we have to concede also some oppositional, and thereby binary, element in all literature. Certainly, Ireland's colonial position has forced many of its writers—particularly but not exclusively Catholic ones—to recover their own traditions within an adversarial situation. Without extending the term in this essay, we might entertain the possibility that the word *baroque* could helpfully distinguish certain Irish writers from other British or Irish writers.

Although other Irish writers, such as Joyce, Synge, the Yeats of "Vacillation" and the Crazy Jane poems, Devlin, Flann O'Brien, Clarke, Kinsella, Montague, Muldoon, McGuckian, and Ní Dhomhnaill, to name only a few, may reveal baroque characteristics, the term seems paricularly appropriate for the poetry of Ní Chuilleanáin. In those qualities we have named—a return of the feminine, shifting or indeterminate points of view, an emphasis on the body and desire, a disjunction between different levels of reality, mobile or disappearing borders or frames, startling metamorphoses, sudden or fleeting references to the sacred, and the housing in architecture of her own art—Ní Chuilleanáin translates the Baroque aesthetic into her own distinctive poetic art. Because her subject, and that of the writers named above, is the return of the repressed—religion, the Irish language, the feminine—her poetry necessarily conveys glimpses, incomplete or unrecovered narratives, and sudden eruptions.

Representing this gap between an emotional response to some event and an account of that event, or between what can be told and what must remain secret or unsaid, preoccupies much of Ní Chuilleanáin's poetry. As one reviewer states succinctly, "Usually her poems encapsulate a telling scene from a larger untold narrative . . ."[48] Furthermore, this very absence or suppression of the context for poems or stories or songs has its own tradition in Irish culture. We find this gap represented in enigmatic and secret poems not only by Ní Chuilleanáin but also by some of the other poets most deeply rooted in Irish tradition, such as Kinsella, Carson, Muldoon, and

McGuckian. Of these poets, Ní Chuilleanáin may—perhaps with Carson—observe most closely the traditional practices of narrative secrecy.

According to Hugh Shields, "Uncertain or ambiguous action is so common a feature of Gaelic song—lyrical, non-narrative song but song which hints at a story it does not tell. . . ."[49] Song celebrated an occasion or expressed an emotional response to events, the narration of which was told in prose and, often then for various reasons, separated or lost to the song. Consequently, according to Shields, "Many lyric songs in Irish in this way conceal some objective reality, referring to it by allusion, without coherence, in a suggestive manner. . . ." Shields then gives us a helpful term for this authenticating context: "Too often the body of fact which would have validated a song rendition—the *údar*—is missing from past record." The Irish audience for such songs, or for Ní Chuilleanáin's poems perhaps, may distinguish itself from those unfamiliar with the tradition not because it understands the missing context but because it knows that one exists: "The confirmatory '*údar*,' whether told or not told, exists or else may be invented. Those who listen to songs know that certain things occurred which were the occasion of the songs, even if they do not know what things they were."[50]

In "A Voice,"[51] Ní Chuilleanáin achieves the displaced or dream-like effect that the suppression of the *údar* gives to traditional songs. The poem begins:

> Having come this far, in response
> To a woman's voice, a distant wailing,
> Now he thinks he can distinguish words:
> *You may come in—*
> *You are already in.*

The singer, he finds, is a skeleton, but he reasserts his reason and "takes account" of stones and walls to disperse this voice. Nevertheless, with the woman now lying "in the bed of the stream," the voice returns, singing from her "Gravegoods of horsehair and an ebony peg." The poem concludes:

> What sort of ornament is this?
> What sort of mutilation? Where's
> The muscle that called up the sound

The tug of hair and the turned cheek?'
The sign persists, in the ridged fingerbone.
And he hears her voice, a wail of strings.

The context that gave rise to this poem is sufficiently removed that we
can only guess at it; the distance our speculation travels becomes, in a
sense, the point of the poem. We can speculate that it alludes to a
ballad—"Two Sisters"—in which one jealous sister drowns another
to marry the widower and then makes of her sister's "little finger
bones" a fiddle-peg and of her hair the fiddle strings that can only play
a song that reveals her murder to the husband.[52] Consequently, the
body of fact that would have validated a song rendition—the *údar*—
must here itself be a traditional song—Child Ballad 10, long ago
adapted into Donegal Irish—rather than any account of the original
murder.

In *The Brazen Serpent,* Ní Chuilleanáin adapts the complex poem
"Following" from "She Moved through the Fair," a thorough revision
by Padraic Colum of a traditional song "Our Wedding Day." In Colum's song, the woman's love-pledge and then her jilting of her lover
achieve a mystery that is heightened by her return in a dream—"So
softly she entered, her feet made no din." Two poems after "Following
her coffin in a dream . . .," "Following" echoes some of Colum's second stanza—"She stepped away from me and she moved through the
fair, / And fondly I watched her go here and go there"—but in this
case the *aisling* is her father whom the woman tracks through a mas-
culinized landscape:

> So she follows the trail of her father's coat through the fair
> Shouldering past beasts packed solid as books,
> And the dealing men nearly as slow to give way—
> A block of a belly, a back like a mountain,
> A shifting elbow like a plumber's bend—

She traces her father's "light footsteps" through a bog into an other-
world so haunted by its past—"gesturing trunks," "Hands of women"
shroud-sewers—that, when she overtakes her father, patriarchal in his
fine clothes and amid his orderly library, we are prepared for the
return of the repressed, in which something like her own nature, incorporated into these books and this setting, breaks out, through progres-
sively energetic enjambments, from its confinement:

The smooth foxed leaf has been hidden
In a forest of fine shufflings,
The square of white linen
That held three drops
Of her heart's blood is shelved
Between the gatherings
That go to make a book—
The crushed flowers among the pages crack
The spine open, push the bindings apart.[53]

The last two lines echo the awakening of Galatea in "Pygmalion's Image," the important opening poem of *The Magdalene Sermon* and itself a revision of Patrick Kavanagh's "Pygmalion." In transforming Colum's slow air, Ní Chuilleanáin reassigns gender roles and gains a haunting, unconventional third-person voice, but she also suggests, paradoxically, that when she, like Galatea, sprouts "her green leaf of language," she gestures toward the "Real," toward something of bestial and human nature beyond the margins of the father's books and order.

In the dark heart of *The Brazen Serpent*, Ní Chuilleanáin, probably writing out of that de-shelled fragility that follows deaths of loved ones, touches on another margin of language and *the Real*: the relation of language to the inexpressibly atrocious, traumatic, or unspeakable events that are encountered or glimpsed but never assimilated into consciousness. "Passing Over in Silence,"[54] first entitled *Praeteritio* (a rhetorical term meaning I will not speak of something about which I cannot remain silent), opens with the line "She never told what she saw in the wood." The first stanza, which goes on to suggest, in particularly disturbing glimpses, murder and rape, concludes, "She held her peace about the man who waited / Beside the lettered slab. He sang." We are not permitted to read the lettered slab, but we hear the man's song, a disturbing, because apparently trivializingly digressive, account of a barmaid who wept silently for "the pierced head, / The tears our Saviour shed." The reader's first response to these lines—that real atrocities are not like our sentimentalized representations of the crucifixion—soon gives way to the disquieting thought that neither was the actual crucifixion—"pierced *head?*"—and that such representations indicate the limits of the linguistic garrison that fences out the unspeakable.

More extensively, "Vierge Ouvrante"[55] undertakes a similar indirect commentary on man's inhumanity to man and, especially, to woman. Here, we enter another architectural structure, perhaps an enlargement of a reliquary, representing the Virgin's body and meant to harbor bones of martyrs or saints. Instead, we glimpse photographs of violated corpses, as we move through increasingly darker rooms to view the body of the Virgin herself, or her violated successors, restrained by ropes or routines from even writing. She can only "commit / To the long band of memory" until she unwinds withershins as she discharges this memory of violation and fills this space "full of the stuff, sticky / White as a blue-bleached sheet in the sun." This shining, seminal "blank chronicle of thread" overexposes and blots out any clear representations of this dark history: women's suffering which must remain secreted within the body represented by the Virgin's icon.

The Sacred and the Body

In a 1992 interview, Ní Chuilleanáin commented on two distortions of history: the filtering out of "injustice, deprivation, victimization" and the misrepresentation of the sacred as something that had passed out of our lives, when in fact our beliefs remain vital.[56] In "Passing Over in Silence" and the "Vierge Ouvrant," Ní Chuilleanáin associates unspeakable suffering with sacred icons—the Crucifixion and the Virgin—and thereby recalls their original, powerful function: to represent the incarnation on its most credible level, the level of the body and its suffering. Recently, she wrote,

> In the last decade or so, I find that it is that other icon that draws me, of the body turned inside out, the heart exposed and bleeding, the man's flesh feminised—the Sacred Heart, which was so common on the walls of Irish houses when I was a child.[57]

She then associates this icon with "its August equivalent," Bernini's high baroque sculpture of the *Ecstasy of Saint Teresa* "where the saint in a hurricane of cloth is being pierced by a smiling angel."

In "God and the *Jouissance* of the Woman," Jacques Lacan suggests that "mystical ejaculations" of saints and expressions of *jouissance* are directed outside of language toward what he calls *the Real*. He then characterizes Bernini's sculpture more explicitly than does Ní Chuilleanáin: "You only have to go and look at Bernini's statue in

Rome to understand immediately that she's coming, there is no doubt about it."[58] He goes on to ask, "And what is her *jouissance*, her *coming* from? It is clear that the essential testimony of the mystics is that they are experiencing it but know nothing about it."

According to Lacan, *jouissance* does not enter into our sexual economy but remains part of the unconscious and of the undifferentiated ground of the body, which our culture can only associate with the feminine because it can accommodate neither *mater* nor *matter*. Lacan asks of *jouissance*, "Might not this *jouissance* which one experiences and knows nothing of, be that which puts us on the path of ex-istence? And why not interpret one face of the Other, the God face, as supported by feminine *jouissance*?"[59]

Although Ní Chuilleanáin reassures us and herself that "the sculptor is following the saint herself in her account of her wounding," she acknowledges that baroque sensuality here turns blatantly sexual: "The sexual metaphor was never so clearly exposed as merely metaphor, and yet nonetheless it remains sexualised."[60] Some commentators on the baroque, such as Buci-Glucksman, make such desire crucial to the baroque:

> It was closer to what a long tradition of aesthetics called the sublime, in contrast to the beautiful, because of its yearning for a presence that can never be fulfilled. Indeed, desire, in its erotic as well as metaphysical forms, courses through the baroque scopic regime. The body returns to dethrone the disinterested gaze of the disincarnated Cartesian spectator.[61]

Ní Chuilleanáin understands that the point about the baroque aesthetic is not "the tension generated by the compresence of sensualism and spirituality . . .,"[62] but that we know the spiritual only through the body and that in the lives we must live the sacred and the sensual are inextricable. As she says in concluding her comments on Bernini: "We reach out of our bodies with our bodies' eyes and writing hands."[63]

Notes

1. Eavan Boland, *Object Lessons: The Life of the Woman and the Poet in Our Time* (New York: W.W. Norton, 1995), 236.

2. John Hollander, *The Gazer's Spirit: Poems Speaking to Silent Works of Art* (Chicago: University of Chicago Press, 1995), 7.

3. Paula Meehan, *The Man Who Was Marked by Winter* (Oldcastle: The Gallery Press, 1991; Cheney: Eastern Washington University Press, 1994). Medbh McGuckian, *The Flower Master and Other Poems* (Oldcastle: The Gallery Press, 1993). In an "Afterword" to *Irish Poetry after Joyce*, 2d. ed. (Syracuse: Syracuse University Press, 1997), I discuss the poetry of Boland, McGuckian, Meehan, and Ní Chuilleanáin in relation to painting. Some of my readings of Boland's and Ní Chuilleanáin's poems appear there in a preliminary form.

4. Boland, *Object Lessons*, 178.

5. Eiléan Ní Chuilleanáin, *The Magdalene Sermon and Earlier Poems* (Oldcastle: The Gallery Press, 1989; Winston-Salem, N.C.: Wake Forest University Press, 1991), 23.

6. Boland, *Object Lessons*, 212.

7. In "The uncanny" (*Standard Edition*, 17: 219–52), Freud associates the *gaze* with the anal desire for mastery. In Toril Moi's phrasing, "The *gaze* enacts the voyeur's desire for sadistic power, in which the object of the gaze is cast as its passive, masochistic, feminine victim" [*Sexual Textual Politics* (London: Routledge, 1985), 180].

8. Eavan Boland, *Outside History: Selected Poems, 1980–1990* (New York: W.W. Norton; Manchester: Caranat, 1990), 119–20.

9. Ní Chuilleanáin, *The Brazen Serpent* (Oldcastle: The Gallery Press, 1994; Winston-Salem, N.C.: Wake Forest University Press, 1995), 38.

10. Leigh Bartholdson, a student in English 368 at Wake Forest University (Spring, 1996), pointed this out to me. In our discussion of "The Tale of Me," Annie Leist recognized "broad Leaves" as a transliteration of "bread loaves." Generally, I am indebted also to Carey Morton and other members of this class for their discussion of Ní Chuilleanáin's poetry.

11. Norman Bryson, *Vision and Painting: The Logic of the Gaze* (New Haven: Yale University Press, 1983), 131.

12. Eiléan Ní Chuilleanáin, "Acts and Monuments of an Unelected Nation: The *Cailleach* Writes about the Renaissance," *Southern Review* 31.3 (July 1995): 570–80, 577.

13. Ibid., 576.

14. In mislabeling the sixteenth-century "Leda" as "Leda and the Swan," Ní Chuilleanáin extends the antitheses of Counter-Reformational and Reformational art to Correggio's freely assenting woman and Yeats's "staggering girl."

15. Cecil Gould, *The Paintings of Correggio* (Ithaca: Cornell University Press, 1976), 132. The painting also represents, in the background, either two other stages of the seduction with other Ledas and attendants or two other maidens also courted by swans, all accompanied by cupid playing his harp. In her happy litheness, Correggio's Leda contrasts sharply with the near contem-

porary drawing by Michelangelo of a Leda who is interchangeable with his figure of Night.

16. Ted Hughes, *Winter Pollen: Occasional Prose*, ed. William Scrammel (New York: Picador, 1995), 129.

17. Ní Chuilleanáin, "Acts . . . ," 575, 578.

18. Gould, *The Paintings of Corregio*, 114.

19. Luce Irigaray, *Speculum of the Other Woman*, trans. Gillian C. Gill (Ithaca: Cornell University Press, 1985).

20. Ní Chuilleanáin, *The Brazen Serpent*, 10–11.

21. Romare Bearden and Carl Holty, *The Painter's Mind: A Study of the Relation of Structure and Space in Painting* (New York: Crown Publishing, 1969), 129.

22. Ellis Waterhouse, *Italian Baroque Painting* (London: Phaidon Press, 1962), 105; Charles McCorquodale, *The Baroque Painters of Italy* (Oxford: Phaidon, 1979), 12.

23. Gould, *The Paintings of Corregio*, 109.

24. Waterhouse, *Italian Baroque Painters*, 69.

25. Ní Chuilleanáin, *The Brazen Serpent*, 14–15.

26. Kevin Ray, "Interview with Eiléan Ní Chuilleanáin." *Eire-Ireland* 31, 1 & 2 (Spring/Summer, 1996): 62–73.

27. Ibid.

28. Eamon Grennan, "Real Things," *Poetry Ireland Review* 46 (Summer 1995): 44–52, 47.

29. Ní Chuilleanáin, *The Brazen Serpent*, 19.

30. McCorquodale, *The Baroque Painters of Italy*, 7.

31. Ibid., 7–9.

32. Martin Jay, "Scopic Regimes of Modernity," in *Vision and Visuality*, ed. Hal Foster (Seattle: Bay Press, 1988), 3–23, 17.

33. Ibid., 16.

34. Bryson, *Vision and Painting*, 104.

35. Boland, *Object Lessons*, 252–53.

36. Philip Conisbee, *Chardin*. (Lewisburg: Bucknell University Press), 1986.

37. Boland, *Outside History*, 75–77.

38. If Boland's subtle but clear depiction in muted colors of the ordinary and, otherwise lost subject verbalizes Chardin, Medbh McGuckian branches from Vermeer, as I have argued in the Afterword to *Irish Poetry after Joyce* (1997). Martin Jay admits northern painting, as it is influenced by Vermeer, as a third term between the baroque and the classic, of which it is a modification.

39. Ní Chuilleanáin, *The Brazen Serpent*, 16.

40. Boland, *Outside History*, 93.

41. Ní Chuilleanáin, *The Brazen Serpent*, 34–35.

42. W. J. T. Mitchell, *Picture Theory: Essays on Verbal and Visual Representation* (Chicago: University of Chicago Press, 1994), 31.

43. Walter George Strickland, *A Dictionary of Irish Artists,* 2 vols. (Shannon: Irish University Press, 1969), 1: 415–20.

44. In eighteenth-century Britain and Ireland this taste for scenic ruins, and the divorce of these ruins from their historical causes, may have been influenced by a similar practice—which validated the grand tour of Catholic countries—of making Roman ruins, rather than Romish art, the ostensible focus of an aesthetic tourism. Certainly the place of Latin and the classics in the university curriculum would have also attracted British tourists to Roman ruins.

45. In her informative study *Women Creating Women* (Syracuse: Syracuse University Press, 1996), Patricia Haberstroh quotes from Padraic Colum's introduction to Strong's *Songs of Living* (1961) where he says this ancient figure of the sphere-woman appears in Strong's poetry in her three guises "bringing 'her knowledgeableness out in measured sayings' " (31).

46. Jay, "Scopic Regimes," 16.

47. Ibid., 19.

48. Jonathan Allison, "Poetry from the Irish," *Irish Literary Supplement,* Spring 1991; 14.

49. Hugh Shields, *Narrative Singing in Ireland: Lays, Ballads, Come-All-Yes and Other Songs* (Blackrock: Irish Academic Press, 1993), 5.

50. Ibid., 5, 79.

51. Ní Chuilleanáin, *The Magdalene Sermon* 27.

52. Shields, *Narrative Singing,* 68.

53. Ní Chuilleanáin, *The Brazen Serpent,* 32.

54. Ibid., 23.

55. Ibid., 36–37.

56. Deborah McWilliams Consalvo, "An Interview with Eiléan Ní Chuilleanáin," *Irish Literary Supplement* Spring 1993, 15–17.

57. Ní Chuilleanáin, "Acts . . .," 577.

58. Jacques Lacan, "God and the *Jouissance* of the Woman," in *Feminine Sexuality: Jacques Lacan and the "école freudienne,"* trans. Jacqueline Rose, ed. Juliet Mitchell and Jacqueline Rose (New York: W.W. Norton, 1985), 147.

59. Mitchell, *Picture Theory,* 147.

60. Ní Chuilleanáin, "Acts . . .," 577.

61. Jay, "Scopic Regimes," 17–18.

62. Lowry Nelson Jr., *Baroque Lyric Poetry* (New Haven: Yale University Press, 1961), 9.

63. Ní Chuilleanáin, "Acts . . .," 577.

"The More with Which We Are Connected"

The Muse of the Minus in the Poetry of McGuckian and Kinsella

When we make nature over again,
The experience not bright, the thought not red,
The soul being a substance cannot explain
Just that red as felt in the room or bed:

Or how the rest of the merely understandable
World, whose art of persistence is to be dead,
Enters like twilight perched in her disrobing
The more with which we are connected.

Medbh McGuckian, "Vibratory Description"

The sterile: it is a whole matter in itself.

Fantastic millions of
fragile

in every single

Thomas Kinsella, "All Is Emptiness, and I Must Spin"

MEDBH MCGUCKIAN and Thomas Kinsella might seem (depending on one's disposition) either to represent the healthy diversity of poetic productivity in Ireland or the perversities of its feminine and masculine extremes. McGuckian, in "Vibratory Description," builds from "not" to "not" to "cannot" to a "more" that connects at the very moment when "red"—having rhymed with "bed" and "dead"—finds a feminine ending, and a compelling surplus, in "connected." [1] Kinsella's unstated, and implicitly unconnected, single drop of semen in "All Is Emptiness . . ." nevertheless delineates, negatively, a "wholeness" that awaits it at the locus of potential life where it may fail to arrive. [2]

Writing poems that challenge current critical approaches to poetry, gender, and reproductivity, these poets blur the distinctions between the hormonal home place and demiurgic workshop, returning—in surprisingly similar ways—poetry to its sources in an embodied or even sexualized imagination.

They have both written about "home" as though it is transient, permeable, incompletable, and, surprisingly, replete with procreative processes. In Kinsella's "His Father's Hands," the stump into which so many cobbler's grandchildren drove practice nails comes alive with spermatozoal life.[3] Family—its past and its future—seethes even as it mulches in that deconstructing memorial, regardless of the "dispersals or migrations" that preceded it or that will ensue. Indeed, the uprootings that characterize his family's (and in this sense his country's) history offer to this poet certainty only that the body's code moves from one still-unknown, self-destructive place to the next. McGuckian, in an essay entitled "Home," similarly connects familial migration with the driven nail. Opening with a description of her unfinished house in Ballycastle, McGuckian calls this dwelling "A grave into the ground." Its funereal attributes are soon subsumed by more fetal (but not more familiarly domestic) properties: "The house grew; its brain began; its grey matter formed meaning. It took something and gave something back, added and subtracted." But subtraction, like the unknown, is substantive, she concludes, as she recalls her family's persistence in twice rebuilding a home (which once belonged to Protestants) that her Catholic family had first to take apart in order to inhabit:

> There was a deep unspoken sense of intrusion into a foreign place, advertised not in *The Irish News* but *The Belfast Telegraph,* a tense and furtive awareness that the building we were dismantling plank by single plank in the chill of the late fifties had belonged to a non-Catholic family in an area unknown and unvisited by day. . . . after the two farm summers it flew across the glen to where it stands now, or continues to fall.[4]

McGuckian and Kinsella understand that a muse of the minus presides over unfinished life both in its beginnings and in its endings, and they both evoke and imitate the spaces and processes of this matrix who can so often seem to be also, to use Kinsella's term, a predatrix. It is a genuinely uncanny space of nothingness (or less) but also of surplus, haunted by both the foreign and the familial. Yet the minus in the poetry of McGuckian and Kinsella may be characterized as "feminine" and "maternal" only at the risk of underrepresenting the importance of fathers, and particularly of a father's hands, to two poets who so often enact, in poems, the process of putting hand to pen, fingers upon keys, and words onto paper.[5]

In the interlocking absences of "The Time before You,"[6] which McGuckian has said she wrote as "a funeral rite for Paul [Muldoon] leaving Belfast,"[7] the speaker links the "littering" of "a new poetry" with the process of simultaneously fingering the keys of an accordion and expanding or contracting an enclosed space, opening and shutting "both doors." "Litter," a noun that designates both detritus and surplus birth, is in Kinsella's "Worker in Mirror, at His Bench" inseparable from the secret of creation; "emptiness" is in fact the "peace of fullness."[8] A "guardian structure" whose authority is "elaborate, and wasteful," the "mirror effect" both nurtures ("peace nursed out of wreckage") and "lacerates" (for mirrors, of course, also break into shards) as it "arouses" a "structure" that is, I will argue, feminine.[9]

2

Kinsella's lifework typically has been judged to be an act of "structuring" that separates the poet from the psychic shattering that might have ensued had he remained within the matriarchal imaginary. Yet one might argue that the Jungian psychoanalysis that has been so often invoked to explain this poet has more often illuminated the scholarly drive for order than the poet's urge to re-order.[10] In part this is because Jung's work can be accommodated—as Kristeva, the later Lacan, and even Freud (after Laplanche and Pontalis) cannot be— to humanist critical models that defend the value of poetry through reference to its capacity to help poet and reader engage in acts of "individuation" that lead to a "whole" or "complete" self. Poetry, according to this view, in promoting self-development, enables the conscious mind to actively assimilate and thereby to master the collective and unconscious materials that are feminine, archaic, or "immature" versions of the "self." In presuming that Kinsella's objective as a poet is to unify the self by exposing and then disempowering whatever matriarchal forces lie hidden from public view, Kinsella's best scholars have followed the gendered biases of established cultural hierarchies. Keenly attending to Kinsella's interest in the public sphere, they under-represent the ways in which the public and the historical not only overlap but also interpenetrate the private, the familial, and, indeed, the feminine.[11]

Yet in his negotiation of the spaces of nation, art, and self, Kinsella insists on the significance, not of assimilation, unification, develop-ment, or achievement, but rather of an ongoing, "polyglot" resource-fulness in which process, waste, and (arguably) regression (what Freud called the repetition compulsions of the death drive) figure largely. The "mother-pit" or "predatrix" whose place is both the "All" and the "emptiness" that the male poet/spider imitates in "All Is Emptiness," is not a mirroring and incommensurable other but rather the containing structure, or matrix, that is simultaneously form *and* matter, whole and hole. Insofar as this orificial structure may be sexualized, it would seem to be female: its form—zero—is what it is, and what (until invested with semen) it contains.[12] The Worker, far from banishing and thereby surpassing the feminine or (to use a Freudian term) "working through" his regressive attachment to her lost, if spacious, matriarchal presence,[13] imitates her "random/persistent coherences," her "Emptiness, / is that not peace?" The face into which the Worker stares as a final "mirror effect" returns in later poems as the *shila na gig* whom neither priest nor philosopher can banish from sacred space in "Out of Ireland," and as the feminine other[14] who creates, destroys, and judges in Kinsella's latest "Invocation":[15]

> Sweet mother, sweet muscle,
> predatrix,
>
> always in the midst
> yet walking to one side
>
> silent, reticent, rarely seen
> yet persistent,
>
> we implore—the subsequent
> bustling in the previous:
>
> Judge not.
> But judge.

Turning, through a single negative, a command into a countermanding order, Kinsella then reverses both effects with a conjunction that reverts—or regresses—to the original, maternal authority. The effect is both to deploy the resources of linguistic predication that found the symbolic order (what Lacan calls the Name or Law of the Father) and to negate them.[16] In such lines Kinsella delineates the negative contours of a maternal space whose "vertical smile," "dwelling" like the Worker in Mirror "upon itself for ever,"[17] structures spatially and temporally a poetry of process in which the "stony" will of the Worker at last melts "to ineffable zero"[18] in the face of the persistent minus and its instructive intelligence.

Kinsella's "motherpit" may seem remote from the McGuckian mother-poet whom her advocates, in relentlessly promoting the "feminine" attributes of her poetry, have constructed. Modulating the "Deathly nameless angel" of her "Teraphim"[19] into a secular, middle-class, and eminently ordinary household goddess, McGuckian's readers have, for the most part, underrepresented the fact that McGuckian describes the motivations, processes, and ends of her art in terms of her self-avowed kinship with Blake and Yeats.[20] Her scholarly readers, seeking in poems written by an English-speaking woman a mirror for something recognizable, or even familiar, as they lay claim to a feminist poetics of identity, have, not surprisingly, found there—or, one might even say, *misrecognized* there—the familiar details of a Western, middle-class, and heterosexual woman's domestic life.[21] While McGuckian herself, in interviews, typically endorses rather than refutes such reassuringly representational readings of her poetry, she has, nevertheless, also made it fairly clear that she believes her authority, indeed her gift, as a poet originates not in her capacity to create life as we know it within the body's space, or even to sustain life there, but rather in the restructuring of imagination. That process began for her in the morbidity (indeed, the nearly infantalizing helplessness) of postpartum depression.[22] In the aftermath of that psychic collapse, her descriptions of pregnancy and birth are anything but conventional in their deployment of terms from the gothic or from science fiction. Describing pregnancy as "This ravenous thing. . . . At the very moment when she has life within her she's marked for death," as a mother, she concludes, "You are being eaten." The fetus, which a more ordinary mind might characterize as enclosed and protected within the mother's earthbound body, McGuckian sends "Orbiting, like it was a space world." Yet if pregnancy, in McGuckian's terms, is perilous for both maternal-host and child-hostage, the delivery of a baby is "not just a physical death, it's a mental death" for the mother and, perhaps she is saying, for the child as well.[23]

Remembering that psychic crisis,[24] McGuckian claims that she discovered, in a visionary experience that confirmed her kinship with Blake, Yeats, Hopkins, and Eliot, resources not only for her emotional recovery (which allowed her to resume responsibilities as a mother) but also for her writing. In seeming contradiction, she has also described her poetry as impossible for the male reader (and, implicitly, for the male poet) to understand; she calls her writing "all moody and menstrual," locating her "brain" in her "womb."[25] Yet McGuckian, on these occasions, seems less interested in ratifying a sexual poetics of separatism than in expressing gratitude and encouragement to those of her readers who supplement their scholarship with Luce Irigaray's critique of masculinist philosophy, Cixous's seductive essentialism, and Kristeva's dialectical, sexualized (and poetically productive) linguistics. In this sense the McGuckian scholar who seeks paradigms for her readings of the poetry in poststructuralist psychoanalysis (and I do not hesitate to include myself in this group) would seem to share motives (if not paradigms) with the Kinsella scholar who has sought reassurance for his or her readings in Jung's paradigmatic humanism. In McGuckian's case as in Kinsella's, however, the context one chooses may not only overdetermine the way the poetry is read but also lead to a diminution of the poetry's original and, indeed, disturbing negation of familiar and consoling symbolic constructions.

Death—gendered as female, rendered as archaic, violent, and matriarchal—is often present in poems by McGuckian and Kinsella. It appears at the very moment when either life or words are "delivered" in such poems as McGuckian's "She Which Is Not, He Which Is": "Carry me who am death / Like a bowl of water / Filled to the brim / From one place to another."[26] Death is there as the "more" that connects the hand that mourns the dead in Kinsella's "The Messenger" through an autoerotic act that "conceives" in its various senses. In the decay of the father's body ("A dead egg . . . pearl in muck"), death guides the speaker to "conceive" "an impossible Possible / and exhausts in mid-reach. / What could be more natural?"[27] It leads to a poetry that regresses even as it progresses until at last the "eggseed Goodness" moves, at the funeral, from the waste-matter of the dead to "Our scattered tribe": "grandchildren, colourful and silent." Perhaps it is not possible to distinguish death from the "All" that is itself (in Kinsella's predication) an "emptiness" of pure potential, or to understand the morbidity that haunts the significant silence that he calls, in "Minstrel," "an enormous black beat." In sending forth messages to that outer space, we await, from inner space, a reply that can only be a "missed" or "black beat" of dark "matter" that evokes also *mater*.[28]

In similar fashion, both poets describe poetry as a paradoxical effort to represent the matrix or "shape" of reality that requires of the poet a "falling apart," as in the following poem by McGuckian:

> It seems as though
> To explain the shape of the world
> We must fall apart,
> Throw ourselves upon the world,
> Slip away from ourselves
> Through the world's inner road,
> Whose atoms make us weary.[29]

Kinsella in "Hen Woman"[30] encounters "the vast indifferent spaces / with which I am empty," and through which, he says, a smashed "egg of being" will fall "until I die." The poet who negotiates such spaces must be simultaneously a driver of the carriage horse of language and an imitative inhabitant of its empty geographical *and* linguistic "address." "I drive words abreast / Into the interior of words," McGuckian writes in "Sky in Narrow Streets,"[31] "knife-rest or a spoon-rest / For your winter's love, the hollow bitten / Into the midday dream of your address." Writing poems adequate to a postempirical (and postimperial) Nature, McGuckian and Kinsella find in the negative realm that Kinsella has called the "zero" of the "land of the dead" and that McGuckian has designated by such negative addresses as "Minus 18 Street" or "No Streets, No Numbers" an unapprehensible "matter" that is bodily, and in Lacan's sense "Real," insofar as it is absent.[32]

"Absence" in contemporary theory leads, of course, to the term "desire," yet because desire in its various guises is made so explicitly an object of investigation in the poetry of McGuckian and Kinsella (and because difference and deferral figure so largely, and so self-evidently, in their poems), the critic accustomed to delivering *"différ-ence"* (with a short lecture on the futility of finding origins) as her closing speech will find that the poetry has made such roles redundant. Similarly, the now-familiar terms of the Oedipus complex relinquishes, in these frank and troubling poems, its cathectic grip (or critical point). In poems about the sexuality of parents (and grandparents) or about a child's sadistic curiosity, Kinsella and McGuckian deliberately and productively confuse the poetic speaker with his or her origins or offspring.[33] In so doing, the speaker in such poems may seem to identify with the dead or with the unborn, whether it is the dead father's "root" which the poet's hand seeks in his own lap, or, in McGuckian's "Breaking the Blue," a "deluged" yet "womb-encased" child's "un-speaking likeness," "leaf to my / Emptying shell," "the spaces between words in the act of reading." [34]

3

Kinsella, having twice faced with his wife the possibility of her death (and the risk she accepted in bringing three children into the world), has said in interviews that his first genuine poems were those inspired by what we can only, through the poetry, imagine to have been an uneasy rapprochement of desire, sympathy, fear, anger, and awe before Eleanor Walsh's masterful reading of the body. She would have known intimately that the body may yield life even when ravaged by disease. Death and the processes that lead to the creation of poetry have been, Kinsella says, preeminent concerns throughout his career. His interest in "primal creation" derives, Kinsella suggests, from what he perceives as both a thematic and formal problem for contemporary writers. Given the difficulty of communicating to a presumed audience in an age when what "we share is a general sense of unease and distress, betrayal and disappointment," Kinsella claims he learned from Low-ell's *Life Studies* to "rely [on] the few things we actually share: the fact that we are human beings, have mothers, fathers, uncles—families in general . . . taking a single consciousness and moving it step by step out among the grades of shared being." In *Notes from the Land of the Dead,* Kinsella continues, he sought "to start almost before consciousness and let the dawning of individuation control what is happening."[35] While this statement may seem to ratify a humanist interpretation of Kinsella's project, the poet in fact concludes with a far from optimistic understanding of the difficulties of universal claims to truth and/or beauty. Poetic communication can never be less than difficult because the genesis (the "dawning of individuation") of the poem begins,[36] and the poem itself is resolved, before the reader enters the memorial to a poet's (now past) experience. The published poem that washes up on the beachhead of the reader's imagination is in fact a shell that the hermit-poet has long since evacuated. Citing "Worker in Mirror, at His Bench," Kinsella suggests that a poem comes into being for the poet as what we might call an imaginary object.[37] Into that object the artist projects or invests his experience; insofar as the poem itself has life, it is always a haunting, long after the fact of its purpose to the self-reflective artist of mirrors. What the Worker calls "waste," Kinsella, in this interview, calls a "by-product": the poem, "evidence that a further stage" in the poet's understanding of the "self" has occurred and that the poem (by implication) is no longer necessary to the poet for that purpose. When the reader, in Kinsella's words, enters the shell-poem, he or she " 'puts on' the poem, so to speak, puts on this poetic sensitivity, engaged at this given time, with all its contexts, and extends his self . . . so as, in his turn, to ingest and understand." The "imaginary object," in other words, is ingested as well as inhabited.

The relationship between ingestion, or incorporation, and language is, throughout Kinsella's oeuvre, psychoanalytically complex, and apt.[38] *Notes from the Land of the Dead* opens with an explicit connection between reading, writing, thinking—what he will call in *Songs of the Psyche* a "burrowing" into the domicile of knowledge—and eating, an association that further links the poet/creator both with "mother liquid," whose nutriment is "welling up from God knows what hole," and with alchemical mystery—being created and creating out of a "ceasing" to "exist." Like the hen (or the grandmother) the speaker broods, redundantly, not only *on* but also *in* what he calls "my shell of solitude": a shell that is not unlike one that has been cracked for cooking, for while preparing to create he eats "forkfuls / of scrambled egg."[39]

In this introductory poem to the volume, Kinsella explicitly associates the number "zero"—the egg-shaped numeral designating the original invasion of Ireland (before the second invasion, itself numbered "one")—with an unspecified source of surplus: "—what shall we not begin to have, on the count of . . ." The word "zero" in the text is, at this point, supplanted by an over-sized illustration of an egg, zero, or uroboros (images of closure that are also empty), anticipating (in this volume) such poems as "All Is Emptiness," which uses aposeopesis[40] to imply presence through absence (in this case, the missing referents are "semen" and "drop") and "Hen Woman,"[41] where loss is "all the one."

In the latter poem, dropping and falling are the moments just beyond zero when (as in the poem that opens "an egg of being") the egg emerges from the maternal sphincter while, simultaneously, a *cailleach* figure emerges from the dark door of a sunlit house. The creation upon which she (like the narrator, as boy and as adult) "broods"—"a tender blank brain / under torsion, a clean new world"—begins its "drop to the shore" only to "smash," wasted. At that moment of failure, meanwhile, a dungbeetle pushes its own piece of waste matter, which promises, larvally, the life that has gone from the egg. "It's all the one. / There's plenty more where that came from!" exclaims the old woman, suggesting that in waste lies plenty. The poet, in mirroring identity with her and with the egg/brain/wasted life upon which he also feeds, understands that the time before the fall—the minus of zero, of mother-liquid—possesses seemingly infinite plenitude or, alternatively, an incompletable narrative:[42]

> I feed upon it still, as you see;
> there is no end to that which,
> not understood, may yet be noted
> and hoarded in the imagination,
> in the yolk of one's being, so to speak,
> there to undergo its (quite animal) growth,
> dividing blindly,
> twitching, packed with will,
> searching in its own tissue
> for the structure
> in which it may wake.

"Hen Woman" echoes two earlier poems that are indispensable for understanding the relationship in Kinsella's poetry between incompletion, or even waste—the fecundity of "the vast indifferent spaces /

with which" the narrator is (like the brooding hen or grandmother) empty—and acts of incorporation into, or invasion of, that space. "Ballydavid Pier"[43] recently has been characterized in Thomas Jackson's thorough study of Kinsella as "No mere emblem . . . of the outrageous rot Time relentlessly throws up"; given the authority of Jackson's readerly repugnance, he might well speculate "There is something beyond stoicism here":[44]

> Noon. The luminous tide
> Climbs through the heat, covering
> Grey shingle. A film of scum
> Searches first among litter,
> Cloudy with (I remember)
> Life; then crystal-clear shallows
> Cool on the stones, silent
> With shells and claws, white fish bones;
> Farther out a bag of flesh,
> Foetus of goat or sheep,
> Wavers below the surface.

"Allegory forms of itself," begins the next stanza, until "the more foul / Monsters of life digest." Dillon Johnston, in a reading of this poem's references to "allegory," concludes that it is allegory, "this unborn idea, rather than the bag of flesh whose features are submerged, that is 'lost in self-search' and which remains embryonic. The thought of this creature defines itself only ironically."[45] That reading is very much to the point of Kinsella's project in several poems: the abrupt interruption or cessation of the delivery of meaning (which halts the "replacing" of "one world with another"), the delay of symbolic movement from object to word as from creator to created object to reader. Yet it does not fully evoke the abhorrent authority of that object which refuses to be digested by language, or by understanding: a "misbirth," an aborted or miscarried product of an uncannily visible maternal space. The poet asks "Does that structure satisfy?" and this space is, indeed, a structure, an enclosed absence which is supposed to create an object and, like language, to deliver it. Like the egg upon which the poet feeds in *Notes* both literally and imaginatively, the "bag of flesh" that "Wavers below the surface" can almost (but not quite) be buried for it is indispensable to the Worker's art. A mirror, it "glistens like quicksilver," "Lost in its self-search /—A swollen blind brow" that is before (and like) the poet who himself returns endlessly to his own "ghost tissue," a time "unshaken / By the spasms of birth and death." Simultaneously nothing and too much, this womb mirrors not only the thinking (reflective) poet but also, premonitorily, the harbor that, when "empty," betrays its burials (memories, memorials). "The vacant harbour / Is filling; it will empty," repeating ceaselessly life's sources and depletions.[46] The indigestible and unallegorical materiality of the maternal will surface repeatedly as its failure, which is itself, paradoxically, a kind of fecundity.

The fetal sea becomes nearly endlessly replenishing in the volume's subsequent poem "Phoenix Park," yet it remains in the realm both of the maternal and of death:

> *The dream*
> Look into the cup: the tissues of order
> Form under your stare. The living surfaces
> Mirror each other, gather everything
> Into their crystalline world. Figure echoes
>   Figure faintly in the saturated depths; . . .[47]

In this unconventional variation on Wagnerian eroticism and metaphysical love poetry, an ordinary pint of Guinness becomes an ordeal cup in which life breeds beneath the brooding mothers who hover above its cauldron. Offering this strange brew to his beloved not, the speaker tells us, as a song,[48] he describes it, rather, as a mirror in which "tissues of order / Form." "Your body," he says to his lover, "would know that it is positive /—Everything you know you know bodily." "Law" and "structure"—attributes associated so often for readers of Kinsella with a patriarchal persona—are here attributed by the poet to his wife, Eleanor; the hands, that so often in Kinsella's poems, pick, prod, or engage in acts of knife, fork, or pen, become at this moment attributes of a woman whose intelligence is indistinguishable from her body's wisdom and its generosity. "Life is hunger, hunger is for order," the poem continues. "And hunger satisfied brings on new hunger." If the waste of life that obtrudes in the reflecting surfaces of water in "Ballydavid Pier" is not altogether assimilated into the dream of "Phoenix Park" 's teeming cup, it is at least echoed in the death of childhood (a death the poem has already prepared us for in the subsection *The preparation*," in which a child, "devouring mushrooms straight out of the ground" receives "the taste of death").[49]

This cup-held vision of birth and mortality, out of which emerges the urge, through bodily union, to give form to the not-yet-living who are also the once-alive, returns to Kinsella's poetry almost three decades later. "Morning Coffee" appears, appropriately, at an intimate and underground site in *From Centre City* (1994).[50] The fetus-belly from "Ballydavid Pier," the "Phoenix Park" cauldron, and the zeroes, invasions, and settlements of *Notes from the Land of the Dead* all return in the deft and startling opening lines that were added after the poem first appeared in the Peppercanister volume *Madonna and Other Poems* (1991):

> We thought at first it was a body
> rolling up with a blank belly onto the beach
> the year our first-born babies died.
>
> A big white earthenware vessel
> settled staring up
> open mouthed at us.
>
> The first few who reached it
> said they thought they caught
> the smell of blood and milk.
>
> Soon we were making up stories
> about the First People
> and telling them to our second born.

The original opening of "Morning Coffee" follows an asterisk, with a description of a boy with wings and an "empty quiver," "vanished, but remembered." Recalling Kinsella's description of the soul's entry into the maternal egg in "The Messenger" (a winged "gossamer ghost" whose "tail-tip winces and quivers"), this subsection is followed by the closing of section I, in which the speaker gazes into his reflection in a well ("a thirsty thing to mine, / I think I know you well"); in section II he sits "late in the morning dark, . . . the cup hot in my hands," suggesting the forming, yet once more, of life, as the poet's hands imitate the porcelain matrix before he abandons "my cup for the woman waiting."[51] Once again the ordeal cup, in the poet's hands, suggests renewed generative powers.[52]

4

Let us turn now to a poem by McGuckian that also concerns the loss of a child and a morning "cup." "No Streets, No Numbers" differs from McGuckian's "Minus 18 Street" in tone and (although it can be perilous to make such claims in reading this poet) in relation to a topic the two McGuckian poems share: prenatal existence. The "minus" of the latter poem pairs two absences: the dreaming sexual partner's "gate of time" where he kneels before an image of fertility that "quarters," and the speaker's speechlessness ("The breeze and I breakfasted / With the pure desire of speech").[53] Across the chasm of difference and deferral that conjoins these different spaces blow "The wedding-boots of the wind." Replacing the gentle and silent breeze, the wind's heavy, metric breaths "Blow footsteps behind me, / I count each season for the sign / Of wasted children."[54] But if one partner's "sleep" *wastes* the possibility of fertilization, it also leads to an increase: it is not the "more" of desire (associated here, as in Lacan, with absence) or the "more" of the life that germinates through desire's expression. Rather, it is the "more" of a homelier connection: "love," expressed as an extra syllable in the line that follows "more": "I never loved you more / Than when I let you sleep another hour." A near-rhyme of "more," the word "hour" literalizes extra time and, poetically, extra measure.

The breeze's speechless desire discovers an object only to abuse it in "No Streets, No Numbers." In the opening line the "blo*w*" of the wind, the force of spirit or annunciation, takes place in an absent rhyme and at an absent object, where "wind" would have become its site of passage: wind*ow*. This negative space becomes, as the poem progresses, the displaced site where fetal life appears to have been delivered prematurely.[55] Various poems in *On Ballycastle Beach* and *Marconi's Cottage* imply or allude to an interrupted or not-yet-completed delivery or "post": the sunrise of a canceled stamp ("A Conversation Set to Flowers");[56] "A letter breaking / The bounds of letters" ("The Book Room");[57] a card that arrives and is "folded" to be read later ("Through the Round Window").[58] Windows and doors elsewhere in these poems are open to insemination or closed in rejection or in pregnancy.[59] In various poems "blue" (or *blew*) is drunk by and absorbed into a house, into a speaker who resides there, and even into a not-yet-delivered (or undeliverable) new life, a ghostly daughter grown into a boyish, self-destructive, underage muse. As the speaker tells us in another unlikely "address" poem—"Four O'Clock, Summer Street"[60]—"I knew she was drinking blue and it had dried / In her; she carried it wide awake in herself / Ever after, and its music blew that other look / To bits." In bringing together such resonances, "No Streets, No Numbers" uses its non-address, in the most general sense, to remind McGuckian's readers that, in part, her poetry's opacity derives from simultaneous and overlapping absences: a poem may lack a clearly defined subject who speaks, a clearly defined referent, and a verifiable addressee ("reader") to whom the words are delivered.[61] More helpfully, and more specifically, this poem transforms the failure of delivery into a material loss: miscarriage, where carriage is troped as "Two men back to back carrying furniture" across a street from one "room" to another.[62] The image materializes the root meaning of the word "metaphor" (to bear away or carry across), which suggests birth but also pallbearing; indeed, the object dies only to be reincarnated as word, in the passage we call language. Annunciation leads to enunciation, an overripeness "like an unsold fruit or a child who writes / Its first word." But this is a poem about the failure of both, the "Double knock of the stains of birth and death."

The blows of the bootstepping wind bruise and stripe the curtains' skin *"like"* soon-perished fruit, "like" a child who has been dealt a blow, and "like" writing (whose markings end, in a sense, childhood), but only several lines later does the speaker allude to "a *woman*'s very deep / Violation as a woman." "Later, later" becomes the erosion, rather than the fact, of difference and deferral—"the wall / Pulled down" of a womb that, in delivering prematurely, drowns its occupant long before it can become a child who will no longer remain a child when it "writes its first word." The "blue stripes" succeed to a belated rain; indeed, the stripes may also signify the residue of a previous drenching no less than the wind's bruising and drying. Probing or exacerbating rather than relieving the persistence of an inner, "sand-ribbed" desert-like space of desertion, "missed rain" becomes itself a kind of weather, personified as a girl whose too-old eyes are empty, a wound that signifies a now-missing knife. A failure of condensation, "missed rain" seems to require in this stanza compensatory feminine rhyme endings that rhyme or slant-rhyme "rain" and "stain": "desolation," "vegetation," "violation"; "rain," "rain," "stains." Around something missing, "a life crystallizes."

From that crystal forming in a violated space, the second stanza moves to a diamond lizard "brooch" that holds together a "breech." The space of desolation itself—an enclosure that has been broken open—becomes an inner place, still furnished but inappropriately so, into which the speaker may peer:

> But I'm afraid of the morning most,
> Which stands like a chance of life
> On a shelf, or a ruby velvet dress,
> Cut to the middle of the back,
> That can be held on the shoulder by a diamond lizard.

Brooches in McGuckian's poems suggest both the infertile, unnurturing crevices of an older, death-bearing muse and various objects that make "breeches" tolerable: in "Echo-Poem" the "cleavage" of "Death" "feeds / Some foam-born / Germ in me";[63] the "large china brooch / Of fivefold crimson" implies renewed fertility in that same poem; a "brooch in the shape of an anchor" appears in "Through the Round Window";[64] and a ring inside a pocket (emptiness within emptiness) becomes, in "Shaferi," a "book-shaped / Brooch."[65] Seduction, in these images, crossed with "attachment," seems appropriate for evening; if the morning does not arrive with a message, delivered by semen or by "post," then the "chance of life" remains, immoveable, on its "shelf." It is "post," after the fact.

From the stone of the lizard-jewel that holds together a severed dress, "No Streets, No Numbers" shifts to a severed life. Inside that negative address a small body, as impenetrable as stone, is nevertheless vulnerable beyond the "curtain" (still striped) of "ribs." It will drown within a blue, "sea-coloured dress" that will too soon turn tidal:

> A stone is nearly a perfect secret, always
> By itself, though it touches so much, shielding
> Its heart beyond its strong curtain of ribs
> With its arm. Not that I want you
> To tell me what you have not told anyone:
> How your narrow house propped up window
> After window, while the light sank and sank.
> Why your edges, though they shine,
> No longer grip precisely like other people.

> How sometimes the house won, and sometimes
> The sea-coloured, sea-clear dress,
> Made new from one over a hundred years old,
> That foamed away the true break
> In the year, leaving the house
> Masterless and flagless.

"Stone" in the later (and eponymous) poem "Marconi's Cottage" [66] describes the safekeeping of that house's "castle-thick walls" (stone which the speaker will "open" her "arms" to embrace). In "Brothers and Uncles" [67] "stone" characterizes a room associated with adapting bodily interiors ("The stone of a room will digest the half-bared / Moonlight"). But in "No Streets, No Numbers" the secretive stone is nearly existentially alone ("always / By itself") and self-defensive: "shielding / Its heart beyond its strong curtain of ribs / With its arms." When its defenses fail, the "break" engendered becomes displaced, by the speaker, to the minus-time of a not-yet-new year:

> . . . That dream
> Of a too early body undamaged
> And beautiful, head smashed to pulp,
> Still grows in my breakfast cup;
> It used up the sore red of the applebox,
> It nibbled at the fortnight of our violent
> Christmas like a centenarian fir tree.

Even the lunar promise of the recurrence (and subsidence) of an egg's fertility in the menstrual or postpartum "sore red" is "used up" by a dream that (like the fetus it recalls) "nibbles" at the end of the year when "nativity" is usually celebrated.

The breaking does not end with the smashed egg of the cup vision, for the next lines evoke a broken "roof" of shelves and then a "clicking-to" of porcelain: "dawn-blue plates." Here the "hands" are "refusing to let go" even as the inevitable breakage happens. At last the speaker asks:

> And how am I to break into
> This other life, this small eyebrow,
> Six inches off mine, which has been
> Blown from my life like the most aerial
> Of birds? . . .

The "blue" of the jay has from the beginning suggested the violence of annunciation, whether dove or swan. If this most "aerial / Of birds" has like an egg been "smashed," McGuckian nevertheless concludes, as Kinsella does in "Hen Woman," with a more optimistic avian allusion. In an inversion of the uningestible contents of the morning cup, the speaker will later drink from other cups at a different address where a bird, if not its egg, survives: "On the pavement of Bird Street," whose "warmth" and "patch of vegetation" may have inspired this poem-long reverie, she may drink the blue that will bring forth "the voice reserved for children."

There are several poems in *On Ballycastle Beach* and *Marconi's Cottage* that concern the breakage of porcelain, perhaps uterine, vessels. As in "No Streets, No Numbers," these already fragile structures can metamorphose disconcertingly into clothing or other forms and, from there, into irretrievable (and perhaps un-addressable) loss. "To the Oak-Leaf Camps" seems a nearly direct statement concerning not only the writing of poetry as impregnation but also the loss that may follow or even abort a poem's gestation. Like "papa's," the hands of a poet may, at a critical moment in labor, be rendered useless. In the *filidh*-like process that the speaker describes ("Both of us lie in the dark to compose"), the gestation of a poem leads to thoughts of "a child you know will be born dead / At three minutes to ten." The "sore-red" of the applebox becomes "Blood in the mouth, red of red" but also "read": "As a book read robs you of the fever / You had when you were writing it." The poet, in a final stage, puts on the "garment" of (in various senses) creation: "Your sky is as close to me / As some particular garment." Yet only after the appearance of yet another avian image: "To know that must be to crush / A small bird to death every morning." [68] In "First Letters from a Steamer" the speaker describes sunlight as "A red coat I'm still a little afraid of" as she paints "A broken vase I loved," remembering "Fruit that won't go into your jars." [69] "Blue Vase," the poem that follows, begins with a description of "My overblouse," "a roving ache," then shifts to a description of the rhyming "My house," "a small blue vase," mishandled "by my own / Determined touch"; as a result, the poem leaves us to conclude, a ship "dims . . . Early in the voyage." [70] What might seem metaphors that are easily associable with the life-giving (or life-shattering) womb, McGuckian transforms—with dizzying rapidity—into a shawl, dress, or other garment that the speaker herself inhabits, or perhaps sheds. Such a garment may be the life she carries within her either to term or (perhaps) to premature or even failed delivery, or it may be a death that recalls the beginnings of life in that intimate space, where it once put on (as in "No Streets, No Numbers") a "sea-coloured dress." In "The Rosary Dress" the speaker describes "A white armless dress, a cloak of roses / A coat of morning as August grows. / I must install myself inside that seed."[71] In "Four O'Clock, Summer Street" the speaker "would shine in the window" of her absent child's "blood like wine, / Or perfume, or till nothing was left of me but listening."[72]

Into garments, in McGuckian's poems, are often sewn distended or secret pockets that serve as alternative spaces to the metaphor-like crossings of what she calls, in "On Ballycastle Beach," "the homeless flow of life / From room to homesick room." One of McGuckian's most powerful poems, "On Ballycastle Beach" opens with an address to a lost child discovered near a sea that was "born" of "France." In rapid succession both the child and the words used to reach the child are transformed into a ship that at first seems not to "dim" or sink—failing in or refusing its delivery—but, instead, reaches its destination.[73]

If "words" flow, like children growing inevitably beyond the speechlessness of innocence, or (one might add) like the dying de-parting into a realm beyond words, then the reverse might also be true: to acquire words is, in a real sense, to leave home in an inevitable journey that can only end in the "homesick room" of the grave. In-deed, words are casually yet magically translated, in the stanzas that follow, into the sheltered and sleeping objects of the speaker's love; yet they remain (like true orphans) "just beyond my reach." At last words, like the lost child, drown in a "mid-August misstep" where the "toys and treasures of a late summer house," a maternal home in a womb-sea by the sea, are forsaken for the "snow" that lies beyond McGuckian's revision of MacNeice's "bay" window. Yet while a "breakdown" of the Atlantic—literally a breaking of the blue—has begun, an older language nevertheless is both recovered and re-covered in its Atlantis-like sinking: "a city that has vanished to regain / Its language." The "words" that seemed first in this poem to serve as objects of comfort and consolation even if they were distant ("The words and you would fall asleep, / Sheltering just beyond my reach /

In a city . . .") metamorphose from "children," into "traps," into the contents of a book packed with DNA code that lies buried inside the lost city/child: "My forbidden squares and your small circles / Were a book that formed within you / In some pocket, so permanently distended / That what does not face north, faces east." From daybreak or the sea's edge words are heard as the "faithless" voice of the "water" that "escapes" (breaks from?) home until, at last, the voice of a once-again lost child is delivered. It is "the longest I heard in my mind," this "water's speech, faithless to the end." With or without words, that voice remains in the speaker's "mind," even if the "breakdown" is perhaps locatable there as well.[74]

If we return at this point to the seashore of Kinsella's "Ballydavid Pier" and "Morning Coffee," where miscarried life similarly refuses to submerge into the allegorical (and therefore consolatory) waters of "words," we might recognize that McGuckian's poem—no less than Kinsella's several poems on seacoasts that lead to the delivery of life or the invasions of insular peoples—concerns "delivery" at the level of political, as well as familial, bodily, and linguistic, meaning. Neither level is subsumed into (or, one might say, drowned by) the other. At this point, some information concerning the publication of *On Ballycastle Beach* is illuminating. McGuckian planned to include in the volume an epigraph concerning the writings of Roger Casement, whose family came from the poet's original (and now second) home on the Antrim coast. In the epigraph, Casement recalls the exhilaration of landing on Banna Strand, even though he foresaw the fate that awaited him. Oxford University Press chose not to publish the epigraph. Were Casement associated with the various opened and closed "casements" in the volume, or his unsuccessful effort to deliver arms by sea on Banna Strand linked to other miscarriages implied in the poems, then we might well conclude that the linguistic proximity of "On Ballycastle Beach" to *On Baile's Strand* encouraged McGuckian to consider (as did Yeats) how a parent's destruction of his child at the margin of land and sea may be likened to an empire's miscarriage of justice in its relations with a colony that is seeking to be reborn as a nation.[75] In this, the waste, failure, and surplus that are thematized in McGuckian's poems may be likened to Kinsella's own poetry of seminal and national migration, invasion, and re-creation.

5

That the archaic muse who both inspires and is the locus of such invasions, evictions, and plantations carries associations of the grave as well as the womb, or that the *aisling* who calls young men to arms is also a *cailleach, morrigen,* or crone, might seem simply a given of Irish, as of western European, literature. Robert Graves drew heavily from Celtic mythology for his portrayal of a "triple muse," an archetypal goddess of birth, fertility, and death. Yet in Kinsella's portrayals of a maternal muse who may turn murderous or be murdered, and in McGuckian's "Clotho," "Brothers and Uncles," and "Teraphim," we glimpse the contours not of a perennial virgin/hag but rather of a creative maternity that has been banished to the perimeters of ordinary language. She is neither "body" to the masculine poet's "mind," nor bearer (like Eve, Persephone, or even Psyche) of the seeds of mortal death, nor wielder of the scissors that slit the thin-spun life. Rather it is we, these poets tell us, who murder *her.*[76]

In Kinsella's "Ely Place" a boy in a fit of unspecified rage takes his "pen-knife" to a woman's throat, ghosting her "spirit" in the "spirting gullet." "Vanishing," she "disappears, buried / in heaven, faint, far off," her body food for "brief tongues of movement / ravenous, burrowing and feeding, / invisible in blind savagery."[77] "Feeding" and "burrowing," incorporating and being incorporated *into* a maternal source of nutriment and habitation, these infantile and original connections to a maternal body remain, in Kinsella's poetry, acts of reading and thinking that revive in the adult poet an abiding maternal aspect of the masculine (no less than the feminine) imagination. Without access to her presence, then to "cower close / on innermost knowledge," to "burrow with special care," may seem inevitably to lead to plunder: "they have eaten / and must eat."[78] The intellectual act that forswears the feminine may conversely evoke a plundering predatrix that has been evoked by masculine acts of violence: the pens and knives that, in pursuit of truth, dissect the body and that, in pursuit of nurture, feed on flesh, in *A Technical Supplement,* transform a "*serious* read" into an encounter with the maternal "more" that lives within, and beyond, the text—not as a "nutrient smile" but, instead, as a black-hearted *morrigen.*[79]

If at last we are to learn to connect this dark wing-beat with the affirmative "black beat" of "returning matter" that hearkens to the poetic impulse in "Minstrel," Kinsella in "Out of Ireland" suggests that we must first connect the "distinct" pens of the toiling, burrowing scholar ("long library bodies, their pens / distinct against the sinking sun") with the indistinctness of a sexual union that he describes not as phallic presence but as feminine absence: "ineffable zero." [80] Such the speaker learns from the wife who once taught him, in "Phoenix Park" that the "Fragility echoing fragilities / From whom I have had every distinctness" may "Accommodate me still, where—folded in peace" the poet is "undergoing with ghostly gaiety / Inner immolation, shallowly breathing." [81] Extending the lessons he once learned as a boy in the minus domain of decimals ("I am going to know everything," the speaker exclaims in "Model School Inchicore"),[82] "Out of Ireland" represents the schoolmaster's negative knowledge as neither beyond nor better than the wife/muse's instruction—once again—in what he called in "Phoenix Park" *her* "Laws of order." As she restores to him what Kinsella called in "Good Night" the "psyche in its sweet wet," [83] the speaker in turn kisses with dry lips her "rain-wet hair." Refusing to erect distinctions between structure and flux, between a "resurrection" that is a "returning into God's light" from the bodily fire and generation of his union with his wife/muse, he also resists separating the truth this muse of shape and form has imparted to him from what he has learned in this day visit to the stone ruins of Eriugena (who died, literally, by the pen).

Kinsella's association of the muse with "music" leads him, in such poems, back not only to his wife/muse but also to Sean O'Riada, metamorphosed into a masculine and Mahler-rapt *morrigen*. Such an association also occurs in McGuckian's "Clotho," which begins "Music is my heroine." This muse, however, soon becomes a soundless, broken idol with whom the sympathetic speaker can communicate only without words: "not even a broken stalk / Of lilac-veined sound behind her broken eyes"; "I dropped three-quarters / Of my words for I did not need them." The muse is associated in this McGuckian poem both with a "satellite" which "is never / anything but feminine" and a "Radioactive moon" that is "Past childbearing." [84] The now-sterile satellite, the speaker writes, has "a horror of touch," yet this poem about the muse of the distaff, the moon, and music makes of "hands" a condensation of the horrors, the widescale *waste,*

of modern mass extermination. "The most expensive white," the
speaker observes, "Of all those pairs of hands" are "born," yet they
are brought forth only "for a few sealed railway trains." Clotho, the
speaker concludes, is "My house god, my all-powerful / Mistress of
tone" yet she is in this poem abused as a servant. The speaker causes
her muse to "moan" and, at last, to speak "as if translating."

In "Teraphim," however, the poet restores the authority of the feminine god of domestic interiors. Encountering her not in enclosure but
rather in a lost paradise of mist, garden, and breath whose "openness"
the poet claims to imitate, the speaker says to her teraphim "only you
can take me back / Beyond yourself" to an absent "earlierness / Now
forever forsaken," "a natural radiance, / Or a story we were not born
into."[85] From this apostrophe to a "Deathly nameless angel" the poem
moves to an "unborn" story and then to a space "in the garden we
have felt before / That makes itself, where even the ground speaks."
In this sense "Teraphim" bears comparison with "Open Rose." In that
poem the speaker declares "I have grown inside words / Into a state
of unbornness," having discovered through her muse the words and
stories of a poetry that is as open as her matrix of life and death. Its
"folds" of petals bear, pudenda-like, "the lost / Strangeness of our
namelessness."[86]

In the umbilical, underwater language of Marconi, which relies of
course on touch (the tapping of keys with the hands, in a manner
closer to typewriting than to speech), the poet has found in *Marconi's
Cottage* an apt model for an art that confounds distinctions between
absence and presence. For the successful, if until then unlikely, delivery
of messages that Marconi invented bears close resemblance to the
speaker's description in a "A Dream in Three Colours," from the earlier
volume *On Ballycastle Beach,* of her broken, yet miraculously deliver-
able, messages:

> Every hour the voices of nouns
> Wind me up from their scattered rooms,
> Where they sit for years, unable to meet,
> Like pearls that have lost their clasp,
>
> Or boards snapped by sea-water
> That slither towards a shore.[87]

Marconi's Cottage concludes with a poem in which a successfully delivered child recalls a kind of wholeness from which she has, in her words, "fallen apart." In this poem titled "On Her Second Birthday" an infant daughter implores her adult reader to remember the wisdom of an innocence that survives the perilous passage of nonbeing into a prenatal life where an embryonic Eve-like spirit is guided by a maternal Nature (the watery matrix whom Eve, according to Milton, mistook for her own). In McGuckian's revision of Milton's mirroring matrix, the maternal looking glass is inseparable from the voice of divine spirit "between the trees" that Milton's Adam heard as his masculine God. The infant speaker was, like the Word, "In the beginning." Yet she was also, in this paradoxical opening line, "no more," already a ghostly apparition:

> In the beginning I was no more
> Than a rising and falling mist
> You could see through without seeing.
> . . . .
>
> Suddenly ever more lost
> Between the trees
> I saw the edge of the forest
> Which had no end,
> Which I came dangerously close
> To accepting for my life,
>
> And followed with my eye a shadow
> Floating from horizon to horizon
> Which I mistook for my own.
> It grew greater while I grew less,
> Gliding like a world, a tapestry
> One looks at from the back.
>
> The more it changed
> The more it changed me into itself,
> Till I regarded it as more real
> Than all else, more ardent
> Than love. Higher than the air
> Of a dream,
> A field in which I ripened
> From an unmoving, continually nascent
>   Light into pure light.[88]

From that union with the shadowy and maternal figure who ghosts both child and living mother even as she is the "field" in which the not-yet-life germinates, the embryo acquires sufficient strength not to break but to be born. The contours of that maternal "more" ("The more it changed / The more it changed me into itself / Till I regarded it as more real / Than all else") persists even beyond birth, even though the infant's union with "it" has become imperfect. In this relationship of process—"flow," "flower" [89]—in which the "Deathly, nameless angel" can be (but is not) named, maternal shadow and living daughter echo each other's absences as a promise of, one day, "more":

> But I flow outwards till I am something
> Belonging to it and flower again
> More perfectly everywhere present in it.
> It believes in me,
> It cannot do without me,
> I know its name:
>   One day it will pass my mind into its body.

In the ungendered "it" of the lines with which I am concluding, let us leave literally open, as do the poems of McGuckian and Kinsella, the negative space of an embodied creativity. Available regardless of the genders that our bodies acquire, such creativity cannot "do without" the "me"-ness of incarnation, however quickly the "something" may end, as it began, in nothing.

Notes

1. Medbh McGuckian, "Vibratory Description," *Marconi's Cottage* (Oldcastle: Gallery Press, 1991; Winston-Salem: Wake Forest University Press, 1992), 95.

2. Thomas Kinsella, "All Is Emptiness and I Must Spin," *Poems, 1956–1973* (Winston-Salem, N.C.: Wake Forest University Press, 1979), 54–55.

3. Thomas Kinsella, "His Father's Hands," *Peppercanister Poems, 1972–1978* (Winston-Salem, N.C.: Wake Forest University Press, 1979), 67.

4. Sophia Hillan King and Sean McMahon, eds., *Hope and History: Eyewitness Accounts of Life in Twentieth-Century Ulster* (Belfast: Friar's Bush Press, 1996), 210–11.

5. See especially McGuckian's "Lighthouse with Dead Leaves" (*On Ballycastle Beach* [Winston-Salem, N.C.: Wake Forest University Press, 1988; Oldcastle: Gallery Press, 1995]) and "The Unplayed Rosalind" *(Marconi's Cottage)* and Kinsella's "Soft Toy" *(Poems, 1956–1973)* and "The Little Chil-

dren" (*Blood and Family* [Oxford and New York: Oxford University Press, 1988]).

6. McGuckian, "The Time Before You," *On Ballycastle Beach*, 43.

7. Interview with Kathleen McCracken, *Irish Literary Supplement* 9.2 (Fall 1990).

8. Kinsella, "Worker in Mirror at His Bench," *Poems 1956–1973*, 178.

9. This process is quite close to Kinsella's description, in interviews with Daniel O'Hara and John F. Deane, of his own processes. See Daniel O'Hara, "An Interview with Thomas Kinsella" [*Contemporary Poetry: A Journal of Criticism* 4.1 (1981): 1–18] and John F. Deane, "A Conversation with Thomas Kinsella" [*Tracks: Thomas Kinsella Issue* 7 (1987): 86–91]. As David Kellogg suggested in a paper delivered to the Southern American Conference for Irish Studies ("The Spaces of Kinsella's Childhood," February 1996), a consideration of Kinsella's poetry in relation to Lacan's delineation of the mirror stage would constitute a full study in itself.

10. Carolyn Rosenberg, in her dissertation, "Let Our Gaze Blaze: The Recent Poetry of Thomas Kinsella" (Kent State University, 1980), reports that Kinsella began reading Jung in the early seventies when his American students told him of parallels between Jung's studies of unconscious materials and the poet's exploration of the mythic origins of an insular people (Rosenberg, 48). Interestingly, in response to readers who ask Kinsella to discuss the influence of Jung on his work, he focuses less on the process of individuation than on "process," period:

> I can't pretend to have been in any sense soundly influenced by Jung, because I simply haven't read that much of him. I've taken 'cuttings' out of him, especially things having to do with artistic creation and the imagination. I can feel him being right about the processes of poetry. (O'Hara, "An Interview," 8)

11. Such disparate readers of Kinsella as Thomas Jackson (in his apprecia-tive *The Whole Matter: The Poetic Evolution of Thomas Kinsella* [Syracuse: Syracuse University Press, 1995]); David Kellogg (in "Kinsella, Geography, and History," *South Atlantic Quarterly* 95.1 [Winter 1996]: 145–170); and Bill McCormack (in "Politics or Community?" *Tracks: Thomas Kinsella Issue* 7 [1987]: 61–77) are united in their underrepresentation of the body as they explore the interconnectedness of intimate and public spaces in Kinsella's poetry. The "place" that "receives our life's heat," even at the moment when, as Kellogg suggests, Kinsella is making a straightforward observation about addiction problems in a local neighborhood, proves also to be the cutaneous (and subcutaneous) orifice opened by a poet who is injecting *his* scribal pen-point into the tender flesh. See the opening poem of the sequence "St. Cather-ine's Clock" in *Blood and Family*, 69. One may appreciate Kellogg's argument in "The Spaces of Kinsella's Childhood," that Kinsella's concern, in his por-trayals of older relatives as versions of the *cailleach* or *morrigen*, is to expose the cultural forces in Ireland that misshape such lives. Yet we might leave

open the possibility that Kinsella understands that such cultural forces also depend on the ideological shaping of a "consciousness" that defines itself in relation to an abjected "other," a consciousness that excludes such lives in order to believe in its own "health."

12. It might also, arguably, be homosexual; "All Is Emptiness . . ." derives from Whitman, after all. To the degree that our culture automatically assigns the feminine gender to absence denotes not only a devaluation of the female but also, of course, a corresponding demotion, or even denial, of the orifices associated with male homoeroticism.

13. The Worker's goal, according to Rosenberg ("Let Our Gaze Blaze") and Jackson *(The Whole Matter)*, is not only the assimilation of these allegedly "feminine" unconscious materials but also a "mature" surpassing of both *mater* and the *material*.

14. In this sense Kinsella recognizes the persistence of the feminine other as what Lacan, in crossing through that designation, describes as her/its connection with the "Real": that which cannot be represented or signified in language.

15. Kinsella, "Invocation," *Blood and Family,* 23.

16. Julia Kristeva in *Revolution in Poetic Language* calls the linguistic deployment of the death drive "semiotic," a key aspect of the dialectical struggle between the negative forces of the bodily drives and the ideological authority of the Symbolic Order. She calls this dialectical engagement "poetic language." See the translation by Margaret Waller (New York: Columbia University Press, 1984).

17. Kinsella also refers to "her two nutrient smiles" ("Her Vertical Smile," *Blood and Family,* 55).

18. "Out of Ireland," ibid., 62.

19. McGuckian, "Teraphim," *Marconi's Cottage,* 104–5.

20. An investigation of McGuckian's references to "rose" and to versions of the lapis stone in relation to mystical traditions might lead to interesting conclusions.

21. In this sense, despite their own disparate—and otherwise defensible—critical dispositions (from Patricia Haberstroh's politics of identity to Clair Wills's postmodern and postcolonial perspective), these readers share a presumption that McGuckian writes poetry primarily in order to express what makes women's experience "different." To recognize that this presumption limits McGuckian's poetic aims and accomplishments is not, however, to disparage the scholarly achievement, and sheer usefulness, of work undertaken by these scholars who have been consistently sympathetic to a poet who has too often been attacked on spurious grounds vaguely associated with her gender. Neither is it to diminish the importance of what Ann Beer, Arthur McGuinness, and Wills define as McGuckian's political commitments to (respectively) "peace" and the de-colonization of the female, or what Wills, Susan Porter, Thomas Docherty, and Eileen Cahill have described as a commitment

to a deconstructive and postmodern poetics (one also inflected for these critics with postcolonialism). My point is that to overrepresent a "feminine" poetics and politics, whether it allegedly promotes "nurture" and/or allegedly expresses a nonunitary self and sexuality, may misrepresent a poet whose deconstructiveness also disrupts the spaces of maternal sustenance. It further diminishes McGuckian's willingness to figuratively explode the structures through which late capitalist economies enclose the imaginations of both genders by promulgating images of bourgeois domesticity that inspire private, homebound consumption. "You can't even step in the door but you've been barraged with false images of satisfaction," McGuckian notes in an interview with Susan Shaw Sailer [*Michigan Quarterly Review* 32 (Winter 1993): 111–27, citation 118], and "[t]he words: the words then are a battle, always a battle against these forces." See essays by Ann Beer ["Medbh McGuckian's Poetry: Maternal Thinking and a Politics of Peace," *Canadian Journal of Irish Studies* 18 (July 1992): 192–203]; Eileen Cahill's sophisticated use of Irigaray and Derrida [" 'Because I Never Garden': Medbh McGuckian's Solitary Way," *Irish University Review* 24 (Autumn/Winter 1994): 264–71]; Thomas Docherty ["Initiations, Tempers, Seductions: Postmodern McGuckian," in *The Chosen Ground: Essays on Contemporary Poetry of Northern Ireland,* ed. Neil Corcoran (Chester Springs, Pa.: Dufour Editions, 1992), 191–212]; Patricia Haberstroh [*Women Creating Women: Contemporary Irish Women Poets* (Syracuse: Syracuse University Press, 1996)]; Arthur McGuinness ["Hearth and History: Poetry by Contemporary Women," in *Cultural Contexts and Literary Idioms in Contemporary Irish Literature,* ed. Michael Kenneally (Gerrards Cross: Colin Smythe, 1988), 197–220]; Susan Porter ["The 'Imaginative Space' of Medbh McGuckian," *Canadian Journal of Irish Studies* 15 (December 1989): 93–104]; and, in the richest study of McGuckian to date, Clair Wills [*Improprieties: Politics and Sexuality in Northern Irish Poetry* (Oxford: Oxford University Press, 1993)].

22. An unlikely nurturer at this moment in her maternity, she was (she tells us) spoon fed by her husband. See *"Comhrá,"* a conversation between Medbh McGuckian and Nuala Ní Dhomhnaill, facilitated by Laura O'Connor, *Southern Review* 31 (Summer 1995): 581–614, citation 595.

23. Ibid., 601.

24. McGuckian reached a climactic resolution of postpartum crisis in a moment that, as she describes it, involved composition, sleep, the movement of hands, and an opening up—themes that haunt her recent poetry:

I was just so distressed. I decided I would try to compose myself for a sleep, and maybe I would sleep and get away from this awful thing. Suddenly my whole body . . . suddenly without wanting it the hands went like this . . . went into this attitude of prayer. And yet at the same time, my whole body seemed to open up in orgasm. At one point I relived the whole twelve-hour birth process, the breathing and the baby coming out. And at this moment I felt an absolute conviction that birth, death, and orgasm were all exactly the same sensation. I felt that . . . other people have explained this. Poetry is full of this. . . . because of this praying and Virgin Mary thing I went to Mass, and the experience was exactly like it had been with my grandmother a long time ago. The preconceptual. . . . That was when I began to realize what poetry could be. I realised I had some kind of message to hand on and that I was in some degree a priest, from having been through this awful sacrificial thing. (*Southern Review,* 595–96)

Characterizing her relationship to poetry as "mystical," McGuckian defines that relationship as "Embracing everything that has been, or will be":

It ties in with the notion of the Muse. I certainly feel when I'm writing at the peak of my capacity that I'm not writing it at all, that it's being written through me. There is a flow happening beyond my control. . . . It gives me a feeling that the poetic power you call up is timeless. It can see ahead. It can see back. It can see forwards. It is totally underestimated. It's reduced. It's made into a description of your experience or it's made into some kind of exercise. You play around with words, and something comes out that is external to you. (*Southern Review,* 597)

Readers might have been prepared for these revelations; in another interview, she puts herself on the "Tree of Poetry on the same limb as Blake and Yeats," but, in a metaphor that is McGuckianesque in the palpable presence of its absent referent ("trunk"), says she's "many phone calls below them." "I've been called religious and it is Blake who says God is the true subject of all art. I think it is fair to say I feel part of that heritage, closest to Hopkins and Eliot, with a sense and sensuousness clashing with sensibility. . . . I hope I don't preach or moralize, but if I'm erotic, maybe *agape* has a lot to do with it" (Interview with McCracken).

25. These citations are from, respectively, the McCracken and the Sailer interviews.

26. McGuckian, "She Which Is, He Which Is Not," *Marconi's Cottage,* 93. In compelling ways, this poem is a rewriting of Keats's "To Autumn": "My words will be without words / . . . . / This face, these clothes, will be a field in autumn / And the following autumn, will be two sounds, / The second of which is deeper."

27. Kinsella, "The Messenger," *Peppercanister Poems 1972–1978* (Winston-Salem, N.C.: Wake Forest University Press, 1979), 119.

28. "Minstrel," in ibid., 66.

29. McGuckian, "On Her Second Birthday," *Marconi's Cottage,* 107.

30. Kinsella, *Poems, 1956–1973,* 136.

31. McGuckian, "Sky in Narrow Streets," *Marconi's Cottage,* 100.

32. For a full and fascinating discussion of the rise of reason and of idealist

philosophy at the expense of a "materialism" replaced by such "paterialism," see Jean-Joseph Goux, *Symbolic Economies: After Marx and Freud,* trans. Jennifer Curtiss Gage (Ithaca: Cornell University Press, 1990).

33. I find astonishing Docherty's progression in his analysis of McGuckian's poetry from what he claims to be her masturbatory "hands," to a masculinist delineation of the (probably female) speaker's "oedipus complex," to a humanist reading of what he alleges to be her resignation to "the Fall," to a conclusion that her intention is to demystify ideology in the manner of "Kant" or "Deleuze": "she has discovered the reversal which makes movement itself subordinate to time, secularism. . . . there will be no movement over the border so long as time remains on its hinges—so long, that is, as a particular relation to secularity is maintained whereby the secular is but a pale shadow of the eternal or the sacred. . . . The poetry is a call to critical historicism" ("Initiations, Tempers, Seductions," 204).

34. McGuckian, "Breaking the Blue," *Marconi's Cottage,* 84.

35. O'Hara, "An Interview," 4, 7.

36. This raises a question as to what *does* constitute the "community" to which McCormack ("Politics or Community?") presumes that Kinsella gestures.

37. See note 9. I also mean by this—and I think Kinsella himself implies this meaning—the psychoanalytic sense of "imaginary" as the mirror stage that begins with an infant's search for origins and self-completion and that continues in the adult's work of the imagination that, if self-knowing, recognizes it can never be complete. The relationship between Kinsella's lifelong investigations of the mirror and the artistic act—what else, finally, is the "established personal place" that can both "receive our lives' heat" and "give it back // to the darkness of our understanding"—would require us to consider its associations with the "regressive" behaviors of the death drive and of melancholia that we need not follow Freud in condemning.

38. See especially the similarities between Kinsella's various representations of incorporation and the maternal body and Julia Kristeva's discussion of "abjection" in *Powers of Horror: Essays in Abjection,* trans. Leon S. Roudiez (New York: Columbia University Press, 1984).

39. Kinsella, "hesitate, cease to exist, glitter again," from *Notes from the Land of the Dead,* in *Poems, 1956–1973,* 129.

40. Dillon Johnston makes this observation in *Irish Poetry after Joyce,* 2d ed. (Syracuse: Syracuse University Press, 1997), 114.

41. Kinsella, "Hen Woman," *Poems, 1956–1973,* 134.

42. The cave, and the sense of a narrative that might survive history by retreating, periodically, to such maternal (and funereal) enclosures, returns in the poem "Survivor" *(Poems, 1956–1973):* "The cavern is a perfect shell of force; / the torsions that brought this place forth / maintain it. It is spoken of, always, / in terms of mystery—our first home . . ." (155). Kinsella's use of the cave in this poem bears comparison with Irigaray's inversion of Plato in *The*

Speculum of the Other Woman, trans. Gillian C. Gill (Ithaca: Cornell University Press, 1985).

43. Kinsella, *Poems, 1956–1973,* 80.

44. Jackson, *The Whole Matter,* 39.

45. *Irish Poetry after Joyce,* 107.

46. Kinsella, *Poems, 1956–1973,* 80–81.

47. Ibid., 117.

48. The association of song, throat, and nursing breast remains an important theme, from "A Hand of Solo" to "Out of Ireland," a poem to which I will turn at the end of this essay.

49. Kinsella, *Poems, 1956–1973,* 120, 120, 118.

50. Thomas Kinsella, *From Centre City* (Oxford and New York: Oxford University Press, 1994), 50. See also Kinsella, *Madonna and Other Poems* (Dublin: Peppercanister Books [The Dedalus Press], 1991), 14.

51. Indeed, in a poem that follows "Morning Coffee," the poet as Hephaestus-figure presents a finely wrought cup to his mother (Kinsella, "At the Head Table," *From Centre City,* 54).

52. Kinsella described that cup in an interview as an "emblem" in which the poet "contains" "matters" that are "processes . . . enabling processes," the end of which, he concludes (acknowledging his departure from Jung on this matter) need not be "life after death" (need not be, he continues, the necessity not to "waste" the perfecting of the life and art) but, rather, an "end" to that "process" (O'Hara, 10–11).

53. McGuckian, "Minus 18 Street," *On Ballycastle Beach,* 19.

54. "The wind," the speaker says in another poem that uses this traditional trope for poetic inspiration and vocalization, "is at its cruellest at breakfast." See McGuckian, "To Call Paula Paul," *Marconi's Cottage,* 16.

55. That McGuckian's rebus-like poems employ displacement, condensation, and other elements of Freud's dreamwork has become a commonplace of her scholars, but a detailed study, with several close readings of poems, remains to be done.

56. McGuckian, "A Conversation Set to Flowers," *On Ballycastle Beach,* 16.

57. McGuckian, "The Book Room," *Marconi's Cottage,* 46.

58. McGuckian, "Through the Round Window," *On Ballycastle Beach,* 52.

59. See Wills's different interpretation of the troping of such closures in "Medbh McGuckian: The Intimate Sphere," *Improprieties,* 158–93.

60. McGuckian, "Four O'Clock, Summer Street," *On Ballycastle Beach,* 31.

61. As McGuckian has said in interviews, a friend's circumstances may appear in a McGuckian poem but remain unrecognizable even to that friend.

62. McGuckian, "No Streets, No Numbers," *Marconi's Cottage,* 39.

63. "Echo Poem," ibid., 67.

64. McGuckian, "Through the Round Window," *On Ballycastle Beach*, 52.

65. McGuckian, "Shaferi," *Marconi's Cottage*, 29.

66. "Marconi's Cottage," ibid., 103.

67. "Brothers and Uncles," ibid., 27.

68. McGuckian, "To the Oak-Leaf Camps," *On Ballycastle Beach*, 47.

69. "First Letters from a Steamer," ibid., 28.

70. "Blue Vase," ibid., 29.

71. McGuckian, "The Rosary Dress," *Marconi's Cottage*, 55.

72. McGuckian, "Four O'Clock, Summer Street," *On Ballycastle Beach*, 31.

73. "On Ballycastle Beach," ibid., 59.

74. Perhaps in response to Yeats's "blood-dimmed tide," McGuckian offers several intriguing tropes of mind, sea, and madness. In "Apple Flesh" (*On Ballycastle Beach*, 13) birds "died in the brainwashed sea"; "the sea went out of its mind."

75. Wills suggests that there are echoes of *On Baile's Strand* but she presumes that McGuckian differs from Yeats in her poetic relationship, as a "mother," to a son lost in sea battle. I am suggesting that, in fact, McGuckian —through her interest in Casement—takes a more overtly political interest in this lost son.

76. This bears comparison with the process that Julia Kristeva describes in *Black Sun* as "matricide," the process by which the child separates from the mother, in an act of death-driven aggression that he or she in turn projects upon the figure of the mother. See *Black Sun: Depression and Melancholia*, trans. Leon S. Roudiez (New York: Columbia University Press, 1989).

77. Kinsella, "Ely Place," *Poems, 1956–1973*, 166–67.

78. "Songs of the Psyche, IV," *Blood and Family*, 25.

79. Note the proximity of this description of Kinsella's discussion of poetic audience in the interview with O'Hara cited earlier. The "encounter" (as in "Ballydavid Pier" and "Morning Coffee") of a "life not of our kind" is also uncannily, of course, *of* our "kind." At the moment of reading, the maternal muse as *aisling* (a projection, he supposes of "my own nervous nakedness"), becomes a black-hearted *cailleach*.

80. Kinsella, "Out of Ireland," *Blood and Family*, 59.

81. Kinsella, "Phoenix Park," *Poems 1956–1973*, 123.

82. Kinsella, "Model School Inchicore," *Blood and Family*, 19.

83. Kinsella, "Good Night," *Poems, 1956–1973*, 171.

84. McGuckian, "Clotho," *Marconi's Cottage*, 50–51. McGuckian's various uses of lunar imagery bears comparison with Kinsella's "Nightwalker" (*Poems 1956–1973*, 101): "There it hangs, / A mask of grey dismay sagging open / In the depths of torture, moron voiceless moon" (102).

85. McGuckian, "Teraphim," *Marconi's Cottage*, 104.

86. "Open Rose," ibid., 80.

87. McGuckian, "A Dream in Three Colors," *On Ballycastle Beach*, 44.

88. McGuckian, "On Her Second Birthday," *Marconi's Cottage*, 107.

89. In this variation on the themes of Blake's illustrated "Infant Joy" ("I happy am / Joy is my name.—/ Sweet joy befall thee!"), a poem of innocence that anticipates an imminent fall by employing the oxymoron of an infant who names, mother, child, and winged spirit are enclosed in a flower. See William Blake, *Songs of Innocence and of Experience* [The Illuminated Books, vol. 2 (Princeton: Princeton University Press, 1991), plate 25].

Godly Burden

Catholic Sisterhoods in 20th-Century Ireland

Into Thy vineyard I come in haste
Eleven sounds from its ancient tower;
So many years have gone to waste
What can I do in a single hour?

from an Irish nun's journal, c.1923

BY 1900 THERE were just over eight thousand nuns and thirty-five female religious orders in Ireland. There were 368 convents. More than half of the high-walled stone buildings that became a feature of twentieth-century towns and cities were Mercy and Presentation foundations that had stemmed from the modest beginnings of Catherine McAuley's vision and Nano Nagle's aspirations to teach poor children—even before Catholic Emancipation had been won in 1829. The second half of the nineteenth century witnessed a dramatic growth in the number of women who entered convents—from 1,552 in the 1851 Census to 8,031 in 1901.[1] Invitations had come steadily from Catholic bishops to superiors of religious orders to establish convents in their dioceses and to offer educational facilities to girls of all ages.

The terms "sister" and "nun" have distinct meanings in canon law but there is a wide practice of employing them interchangeably. The sisterhoods in this essay signify what canon law recognized as "active orders" in the present century, becoming "apostolic orders" in 1967 with the Decree on Religious Life issued by the Second Vatican Council. The problem of jurisdiction, that is, whether the religious orders were governed directly from the Vatican or by the local bishop, had been resolved by the beginning of the twentieth century in favor of the local bishop. Enclosure within the convent precincts and supervision of the convent *horarium,* as well as visitation, were potential areas of tension between bishops and the sisterhoods prior to the Second Vatican Council.

The distribution of convents in twentieth-century Ireland still lacks geographical analysis. Caitríona Clear in her study, *Nuns in Nineteenth-Century Ireland*, examined the distribution of convents after the Great Famine (1846–47) with reference to Limerick and Galway, and Dr. Tony Fahey commented on the regional unevenness in the growth of congregations throughout the island, citing the 1911 Census for his statement that there were more than twice as many nuns recorded in Leinster as in Connaught: 33.8 per ten thousand women in Leinster, 17.8 per ten thousand in Connaught.[2] For Ulster there is Marie O'Connell's work, published in essay form, "The Genesis of Convent Foundations and Their Institution in Ulster, 1840–1920." Her appendices, where she lists, by diocese, the institutes managed and the work carried out by convents in Ulster between 1840 and 1920, are useful for their itemization of ministries. In 1840 the Poor Clare convent in Newry was the only convent in Ulster. By 1920 there were sixty-two convents: Mercy foundations numbered twenty-eight; St. Louis, five; Poor Clare, four; and Presentation, only two.[3] Research is only beginning on the subject of the sisterhoods in twentieth-century Ireland, though yearly studies of foundresses and the history of particular religious congregations exist.[4]

The centralization of the Catholic Church became concrete with the Dogma of Papal Infallibility in 1870 at the First Vatican Council. As well as increasing church bureaucracy, it strengthened the control of the bishop and parish priest. "The Church," wrote Pope Pius X, "is essentially an unequal society, comprising two categories of persons, the Pastors and the flock." Such was the climate into which the sisterhoods settled uneasily in 1900, desperately needed as auxiliaries by bishops, possessing an ill-defined status as sisterhoods with simple vows, yet bearing the burden of enclosure and, in some orders with medieval origins, the uncertainty of not knowing whether the sisters were in simple or solemn vows. The encroachment of the bishop's jurisdiction over the movements of sisters was further augmented by the Code of Canon Law promulgated in 1917.

Vocations continued to pour into Irish convents. Suellen Hoy has analyzed the successive waves of vocations in her seminal essay, "The Journey Out: The Recruitment and Emigration of Irish Religious

Women to the United States, 1812–1914," and she suggests that Catholic Emancipation and the pastoral demands in the United States made the first wave a reality after 1834. The foundations that were established in that period were generally made in the lifetime of the foundress, who exercised a fair measure of autonomy in her choice of place for the new project. Hoy situates the second wave between 1860 and 1917, when recruitment to religious orders was by way of invitation from nuns who had built the convents in regions chosen by the foundress or one of her companions. In that later recruitment, schools played a decisive role and the Sodality of the Blessed Virgin Mary (the "Blue Ribbon," the Jesuit-inspired *Enfant de Marie*) was central to the recruiting process. Hoy demonstrates that the Sodality was not a middle-class phenomenon associated with boarding schools; it was equally effective when established in the milieu of the factory worker's club or when a domestic servant was introduced to it by the mistress of the house or by a priest confessor. Hoy further suggests that changes in immigration laws in the United States affected the flow of vocations from Ireland to convents in that country.[5]

There was no decrease in the number of entrants to Irish convents in the following decades. They continued to multiply and to find outlets for ministry throughout the world. The explanation lies partially in the missionary enterprise that marks church activity in the first half of the twentieth century. In that unprecedented growth Belgium and Ireland were at the fore. In an examination of the Irish missionary movement, Edmund Hogan describes the aftermath of the Easter Rising as a time of intense idealism in which the founding of the Maynooth Mission to China and that of the Columban Sisters to the "Far East" took place.[6] It was a period when young people searched for outlets for a heroic life because they were disillusioned by the misplaced ardor of war. The missionary movement, as it expressed itself in Irish Catholic life, provided young people with an opportunity in the decades after the civil war of 1922–23 to turn away from the troubling dilemma of legitimized physical force. It was an age when devotional Catholicism peaked. The popes, Pius XI and Pius XII, vigorously advocated a style of religious observance and practice that combined expressions of piety in the context of church-based devotions. The establishment of new religious feasts—in particular the cult of Mary—and the encouragement of pilgrimages to her shrines received papal approval. Novenas such as the Miraculous Medal, the Nine First Fridays, and sodalities were assiduously promoted at parish level. The culmination of this highly charged, emotional Catholicism was the promulgation in 1950 of the dogma of Mary's assumption into heaven, followed in 1954 (the year decreed by Pius XII as "the Marian year") by an epidemic of shrine-building all over Ireland. The 1950s were the high point of female religious vocations in twentieth-century Ireland. The 1941 census revealed that one out of every four hundred women was entering a convent and admissions increased in the following decade. So great was the prestige of the sisterhoods in Ireland by the midcentury that in 1949 a lecturer from England at the annual Conference of Convent Secondary Schools in Ireland declared to the assembly: "It is wonderful to see the power you have in education. In fact the Nuns have all the power to guide and control education policy. You have the Department of Education in the hollow of your hand."[7]

Behind the success and triumphalism of the mid-century lay the larger issue of what constituted work and/or ministry for the sisterhoods. In the previous century the convent was subsidized by dowries. The rural middle classes, daughters of substantial farmers and shopkeepers, brought to religious communities sizeable dowries; the Mercy Sisters' Account Book in Baggot Street convent in Dublin records sums between three and six hundred pounds. That sum remained constant well into the next century, and heiresses always brought large sums of money with them. By the end of the nineteenth century the dowry as asset had been augmented by the boarding school. Religious communities established fee-paying boarding schools to provide room and board for students who lived far away and whose parents sincerely desired a formative Catholic environment for the education of their daughters. The decision by the government to hand over the Poor Law Union hospitals, the so-called Workhouse Hospitals, to the care of the Sisters of Mercy from the 1860s onward was decisive and significant in involving sisters in the work of the state.

The emergence of the secondary school was a major development in what constituted the ministry of the convent. The Intermediate Act (1878) was a milestone in girls' schooling, allowing girls a state qualification to enter civil service appointments and prepare for matriculation into the universities. Single sex or separate schools for boys and girls along denominational lines set the pattern for twentieth-century state schooling in Ireland. By 1922 all churches, and the Jewish community, had well-established claims on the state. A mutually beneficial relationship was hammered out between the British Ministry of Education and the Stormont government of Northern Ireland, and between the Free State and the church schools. For the Free State with its largely Catholic population the gain was financial and ideological. A considerable number of day-to-day expenses were borne by religious orders. Because the system of education had inherited the single sex structure from the previous era, girls' education was largely in the hands of the nuns for the next decades. Moreover, the Catholic school developed qualities the state desired in its citizens: orderliness, discipline, obedience, self-control. The involvement of the sisterhoods, and the larger church investment in education, added to the political legitimacy of the educational system as it evolved in the Dublin civil service over the next decades.

The background of this alliance between the convents and the state enables scrutiny of the policy-makers in the convents. The first university degrees were awarded in the 1890s, and, ironically, Ireland had little acceptable work for these graduates. Quite a number of them entered religious life, and the flow continued steadily and in increasing numbers until the 1940s when the rule of enclosure was relaxed to allow sisters to attend university classes and take examinations. Remarkable women, born in the 1870s, became a pioneering graduate elite—tutored in womens' colleges funded by religious orders such as the Loretos, Ursulines, and Dominicans. If they planned a career in teaching, their role models were their tutors, nuns skilled in the languages of western Europe and at home in the world of the classics. They were drawn to community life and to the positive aspects of celibacy and dedication to learning.[8] They became nuns at a later age than those who did so in the 1930s, and frequently they came bearing their masterships in arts or in science. They knew they were a pioneering generation as the new century precipitated them into the franchise debate and the subsequent agitation for the vote.

A substantial number joined religious orders after the Civil War and claimed membership in Cumann na mBan while at university. Catherine Dixon cycled across Dublin during curfew and delivered Eamon de Valera's American passport to him in the tense aftermath of Easter Week 1916. She subsequently joined the Dominican nuns in Sion Hill convent in Blackrock outside Dublin. Marie Martin, the foundress of the Medical Missionaries of Mary had served as a Volunteer Aid Detachment nurse in World War I. How did that idealistic and high-spirited generation deal with the growing authoritarianism of the political and church climate in the 1930s, '40s, and '50s? Did they assume leadership at a sensitive time? What solutions did they offer to problems like the growing inequalities in the society they ministered to?

One situation in convent life that was not addressed until the mid-century was the status of the lay sister. Lay sisters are present in records from the abbeys and monasteries of the Middle Ages when it was customary for wealthy women who entered the cloister to bring their serving women with them, or, if they were very young, their nurses. There is no evidence that there was such a division in the small groups of Irish nuns who came together in dwelling houses during the eighteenth century when convents and Catholic schools were forbidden to function by state law. With the resurgence of religious life for women in nineteenth-century Ireland the lay sisters became a visible structure within the convent. They entered without dowry, coming from small farming families or artisan backgrounds. They were responsible for support tasks in the convent: cooking, laundering, working in the farm, cleaning the school and dormitories. They led a hidden life. They possessed no vote in community affairs and they did not elect to the leadership of the community; nor were they eligible for election as superior.

Yet the lay sisters were not perceived as domestic servants in an age when Dublin had fifty servants for every thousand women. They had a freedom to converse with men on the farm, to supervise the entrance door as portresses, and to attend the sick. The ideology of the time held that the home and work done therein were suitable for girls or women, so domestic service appealed to parents as a safe occupation for daughters despite the isolation of the work and poor marriage prospects.[9] Convent life with its rhythm, its security, and its sense of space was a desirable option for girls without dowry. What is perplexing is that the two-tiered system remained in existence in Ireland long after it was abolished in the new world of America and Australia. The anomaly of the Irish twentieth-century lay sister contributed to the stratification of Irish society for many decades. Hierarchy within the convent reflected public life in twentieth-century Ireland.

From the mid-nineteenth century, Protestant missionaries had taken the lead in sending thousands of missionaries to Asia: doctors, catechists, leaders of mission stations in far-off places like outer Mongolia or deepest Africa. Early in 1912 the Maryknoll Missionary Sisters were founded in the United States by an Irish-American woman, Mollie Rogers. A decade later the Columban Missionary Sisterhood was founded by Frances Moloney, a widow. In 1924 Mary Ryan founded the Holy Rosary Sisters of Killeshandra for mission in Africa. In 1902, previous to these endeavours, Teresa Keaney had gone to equatorial Africa, and gradually it became clear to her that the resources of Catholic church missions in issues of disease and health care were inadequate. Thereafter, she crusaded tirelessly for hospital training, including midwifery certification. Finally she established her own sisterhood, the Franciscan Missionaries to Africa, and opened a midwifery training school in Uganda.[10] The quest for the acquisition of professional qualification in surgery and obstetrics, Rome's "forbidden skills," is the subject of a section of Hogan's study of the Irish missionary experience in the twentieth century. At the heart of the struggle lay the embargo, enshrined in the 1917 Code of Canon Law, forbidding Sisters to take studies in midwifery, obstetrics, and all branches of medicine, including surgery and gynecology. The struggle to win recognition from the great medical schools was complicated by the necessity to lobby the papacy, and the Roman curia. Pope Benedict XV remained impervious and the capitulation to a clamant demand on the part of missionary bishops and heads of religious orders occurred in 1936 when Pius XI issued Canon 489: Maternity Training for Missionary Sisters.

The Medical Missionaries of Mary, founded by Marie Martin in 1936, were, possibly, the most innovative of the Irish missionary orders of women in twentieth-century Ireland. Her institute was devoted to health care and her Sisters studied all branches of medicine and qualified as surgeons. Their example was quickly followed by other missionary groups. An examination of the politics of the religious women's campaign for medical training reveals the adventurous dimension of the religious calling in decades that were perceived as dehumanizing to sisters working in Irish orphanages and boarding

schools. These were the same decades in which Austin Clarke chided
nuns for choosing a "tidy bed, / Full board and launderette," thereby
robbing themselves of spontaneity. And somewhat later Edna O'Brien
arrested a moment of icy institutional coldness in her description of
her convent boarding school.[11]

There were two areas in the daily lives of sisters where the burden
of religion sat heavily on their shoulders. The first was the Code of
Canon Law as it applied to women religious. By 1900 apostolic activity as a legitimate exercise of a convent's mission had been acknowledged both by Rome and by local bishops. There was recognition that
travel, dress, and the strict laws of enclosure needed modernization.
The 1917 Code of Canon Law set, for decades to come, the limits of
autonomy for women religious: weekly confession, daily Eucharist,
set hours for prayer including meditation. Laws of fast and abstinence
were strictly enforced in convents during Lent and Advent and each
Friday of the year. The practice of religious life became a process of
fulfilling a series of obligations. Catholicism, until the Second Vatican
Council, was a religion of authority concealed by the beauty of the
liturgical revolution, which revitalized Gregorian chant and brought
ritual into the lives of ordinary church-goers. It was an age of pag-
eantry and ritual; the liturgical plainchant of the choir office became
an art form in convent culture and drew an appreciative audience to
the solemn liturgies of Holy Week, Easter, and Christmas. It took its
toll on the health of the sisters already overburdened in classroom and
hospital ward. The shock of recognition and the identification with
the central character in *The Nun's Story* (played by actress Audrey
Hepburn) was a prelude to acknowledging a reality that would later
cause women who had spent a number of years in religious life to
leave the convent.[12]

The image of the nun in midcentury Ireland (and elsewhere) was
that of a docile and submissive figure clad in a black or white or blue
sweep of garment with a medieval headdress who rarely raised her
voice or eyes. Yet these same women were major players in church-
state relations below the official level of the Catholic hierarchy. Own-
ers and matrons of the main hospital system in the country, they
were entrusted by the state with the state's industrial schools and
orphanages and with the reponsibility of implementing the state's fragile and largely underdeveloped welfare policy.[13] Though set in wartime

France, Eiléan Ní Chuilleanáin's elegy for her aunt Anna encapsulates the contradictions and perplexities of the nun's role in that period.

> When young in the Franciscan house at Calais
> She complained to the dentist, *I have a pain in our teeth*
>
> . . . Stripping the hospital, loading the sick on lorries,
> While Reverend Mother walked the wards and nourished them
> With jugs of wine to hold their strength.[14]

One canon of the 1917 Code is frequently overlooked: Catholics were forbidden to attend schools open to non-Catholics. That stricture was brought to bear in the negotiations between the Catholic hierarchy and the Free State Department of Education in 1924, formally recognizing Catholic schools as state schools. Salary scales were implemented, capitation and building grants were agreed upon. Examining convent accounts,[15] it is evident that, initially, the relief was great: the burden of teaching extracurricular subjects, such as music, singing, voice projection—for necessary revenue—was lifted. Then, in 1929, came Pope Pius XI's encyclical, *The Christian Education of Youth,* which put a seal of approval on the ministry for educating the young at school and college level. Thus, far from discouraging sisters from acquiring professional qualifications, Pius XI urged the heads of religious orders to qualify sisters for the schools and colleges he advocated. It should have been the beginning of the modernization of the Irish sister. She now attended university or hospital as a student (wherever possible one with a Catholic ethos). If unable to study by day because of other work, she studied by night and during weekends. Summer schools were not offered in the Ireland of that period. It was in truth an age of "eternal verities." The sisterhoods represented an eternity on earth: clothes, ways of thinking, rules were changeless. The imposition of cloister and the frequent canonical and episcopal strictures on its enforcement placed women religious in Ireland in a culturally rigid role. Impossible burdens of work and unrealistic asceticisms dried up human affectivity in the increasingly younger aspirant to religious life who moved from the institutionalized boarding school into the structured novitiate.

In 1950 Pope Pius XII, concerned with evidence that the level of professional excellence among many of the sisters was far below that of their lay counterparts, summoned an international congress of superior generals to Rome and exhorted them to educate their subjects on a par with their lay colleagues. Inspired by his mandate, the 1950s was a decade of summer schools in theology, scriptural studies, and the updating of subjects taught at school level. Sisters began to take higher degrees and lectureships at third level. On the eve of the Second Vatican Council, the sisterhoods had organized themselves into confederations and were talking among themselves, comparing experiences and inviting sisters from other religious orders to address them. The isolation was breaking down. One of the lightning conductors was the development of the theology and spirituality of religious life. The Pontifical Institute of Regina Mundi was set up in Rome by directive of Pius XII in 1954 to offer three-year religious courses for women, both lay and religious, and those who enrolled returned to positions of responsibility within novitiates.[16]

They brought back a new concept of the mission of religious orders, one that placed emphasis on vowed poverty as a way of witnessing and serving the needy in society. Celibacy was valued in its ability to give greater freedom of time and energies to those in need. Obedience was interpreted as listening to the Gospel values and to the overall mission of the Church. Thus it can be argued that the renewal of religious life anticipated the mandates of Vatican Two. The change that seemed so gradual in the first sixty years of the twentieth century was unthreatening to Rome and to convent structures. Popes had encouraged it. In the earlier part of the century the Irish state and the Stormont government in Northern Ireland had facilitated church-state relationships in granting recognition to the apostolic ministries of teaching and social welfare, as well as bestowing positions of responsibility on sisters, without examining their professional qualifications. The Vatican had, in turn, granted dispensations, for the professionalization of the sisters, that seemed harmless enough, such as permission to travel singly, to discard the religious garb if studying medicine, to absent oneself from the common table and even common prayer. Too late it was perceived that removal of the Canon concerning cloister was a structural change of such magnitude that it would affect all elements of religious life in the convent in twentieth-century Ireland.

There were other factors certainly; change was in the air in the early sixties, but the demands of professional work standards and the obligations of conventual living set in a nineteenth-century mold were to prove incompatible. In Ursula Le Guin's *Earthsea Trilogy,* the second adventure—*The Tombs of Atuan*—tells the story of the priestess, Tenar.[17] She is given a choice: either to stay and be afraid of the dark and make her peace with those she serves in the Temple or to leave the Tombs of Atuan and begin another story and another life. By stopping on the threshold of the post-Vatican Two era there is a completion to the narrative. What happened next belongs to a new Ireland and a questioning Catholicism.

Notes

1. Tony Fahey, "Nuns in the Catholic Church in Ireland in the Nineteenth Century," in *Girls Don't Do Honours: Irish Women in Education in the Nineteenth and Twentieth Centuries,* ed. Mary Cullen (Dublin: Webb, 1987), 7. Data for years 1851 and 1901, "Tables of Occupation," Census of Population of Ireland.

2. For an analysis of nineteenth-century distribution of convents, Caitríona Clear, *Nuns in Nineteenth-Century Ireland* (Washington, D.C.: Catholic University of America Press, 1987), 36–68; Tony Fahey, "Female Asceticism in the Catholic Church: A Case Study of Nuns in Nineteenth-Century Ireland" (Ph.D. thesis, University of Illinois, 1981), 66–74.

3. Marie O'Connell, "The Genesis of Convent Foundations and Their Institutions in Ulster, 1840–1920," in *Coming into the Light: The Work, Politics and Religion of Women in Ulster 1840–1940,* ed. Janice Holmes and Diane Urquhart (Belfast: Institute of Irish Studies, 1994), 179–201.

4. Margaret MacCurtain, "Late in the Field: Catholic Sisters in Twentieth-Century Ireland and the New Religious History," in *Chattel, Servant or Citizen: Women's Status in Church, State and Society,* ed. Mary O'Dowd and Sabine Wichert (Belfast: Institute of Irish Studies, 1995), 34–44.

5. Suellen Hoy, "The Journey Out: The Recruitment and Emigration of Irish Religious Women to the United States, 1812–1914," in *Journal of Women's History* 6,7 (1995): 64–98.

6. Edmund Hogan, *The Irish Missionary Movement: A Historical Survey, 1830–1980* (Dublin: Gill and Macmillan, 1992), 95–97.

7. Report of Conference of Secondary Schools in Ireland 1949 (52 in Archives Education Secretariat, Conference of Religious of Ireland, Milltown Park, Dublin).

8. Research in progress by author. See M. MacCurtain, "Women of Eccles Street" in *The Lanthorn* (Dublin: Dominican Publications, 1982), 54–60.

9. Suellen Hoy and Margaret MacCurtain, *From Dublin to New Orleans: The Journey of Nora and Alice* (Dublin: Attic Press, 1994), 30–31.

10. Hogan, *The Irish Missionary Movement,* 114–16.

11. Austin Clarke, "Living on Sin," in *Collected Poems* (Dublin: Dol-

men Press, 1974), 271; Edna O'Brien, *The Country Girls* (London: Penguin Books, 1960).

12. The exodus from Irish convents of sisters who had spent a substantial part of their lives in religious vows became noticeable in the 1970s and continued as a significant trend for well over a decade.

13. Sheila Lunney, "Institutional Solutions to a Social Problem: Childcare in Ireland 1869–1950," (M.A. thesis, University College Dublin, 1995), publication forthcoming.

14. Eiléan Ní Chuilleanáin, "J'ai mal à nos dents," in *The Magdalene Sermon* (Dublin: The Gallery Press, 1989), 29.

15. The Conference of Religious of Ireland was founded in 1961 as the Conference of Major Superiors. For some years it was a loosely knit group meeting periodically. From the beginning, one of its main tasks was to bring the managerial and ownership structures of the complex school systems of the Catholic religious orders under its jurisdiction.

16. Patricia Wittberg, *The Rise and Decline of Catholic Religious Orders* (Albany: State University of New York Press, 1994), 211.

17. Ursula K. Le Guin, *The Tombs of Atuan* (London: Victor Gollancz, 1972).

CATHERINE B. SHANNON

The Changing Face
of Cathleen ni Houlihan

Women and Politics in Ireland,
1960–1996

RECENT DESCRIPTIONS of Ireland as the "in country" in the European Union underscore the dramatic transformation of the Republic of Ireland's image as Europe's "old hag" in the 1950s and early 1960s into something of a "young queen" in the mid-1990s.[1] The inward-looking, isolated, impoverished, rural, conservative, and culturally repressive atmosphere of mid-century has given way to one characterized by growing national confidence, economic optimism, and cultural sophistication. This new mood springs from the most profound and rapid economic and social change since 1850. During the past three decades the cumulative effects of industrialization, urbanization, and secularization have seriously eroded the Catholic, parochial, socially and economically conservative values and structures that were shaped by post-famine economic readjustment, the Catholic Devotional Revolution, the rise of democratic nationalism, and the winning of truncated independence for the twenty-six counties. This zeitgeist had reached its apogee between 1932 and 1958 when the Irish political stage was dominated by Eamon de Valera as Fianna Fáil leader and Taoiseach. His success in subverting the limitations of dominion status and infusing the Catholic and Gaelic values of the majority into the political and social structures, and especially into the Irish constitution of 1937, nurtured the long electoral hegemony of Fianna Fáil.[2]

However, the deficiencies of de Valera's stewardship in meeting the aspirations of small farmers, rural youth, and the urban poor have long been acknowledged by historians in their explanations of the headlong rush toward industrialization initiated by de Valera's successor Seán Lemass in the 1960s and continued by successive Irish governments down to the present. What the de Valera years and the transformations wrought by industrialization, urbanization, and secularization have meant specifically for Irish women is only recently entering into the mainstream of Irish historiography.[3]

The intention of this essay is to describe and explain the changes in the political and public profile of Irish women from the early 1960s to the present. The analysis is a synthesis of recent research supplemented by the author's personal observations of the conditions governing Irish women's lives in the early 1960s and of how these conditions have been subsequently altered. At the beginning of this era Eamon de Valera's vision of Cathleen ni Houlihan still cast a dark shadow over the lives of Irish women. The acknowledgment of women in his 1937 constitution as the guardians of public morals and sound family life, and his utopian vision of comely maidens dancing at the crossroads preparatory to their destiny as devoted mothers living in frugal comfort in cozy rural homesteads brought little practical benefit to the majority of Irish women. In reality, women were nearly invisible in the formal and public structures of Irish life. Their political, social, and economic powerlessness was one of the features of Irish life that struck me forcefully when living in Dublin, as a graduate student at University College, in the early 1960s. At that time, and indeed since the 1920s, to be female in Ireland held virtually no opportunities to participate actively in politics or in the higher levels of education, the civil service, journalism, or indeed business. Women's absence from the corridors of power was rooted in their limited educational and employment opportunities and four decades of social conditioning that relegated them to the private sphere. This will be apparent from the following description of the conditions that shaped the lives of Irish women at various class levels during the 1960s and effectively excluded them from political and public life.[4]

The impact of social conditioning was clearly apparent at University College, Dublin, where female undergraduates were only 28 percent of the student body. Most were from upper middle-class backgrounds, had "diamond fever," and spent more time worrying about getting a man than in using a very unique and privileged opportunity to obtain a university degree in preparation for a career. On the other hand, the women religious attending the university proved to be highly dedicated and accomplished students whose academic qualifications were directly linked to prospective careers in the educational, medical, and social service sectors. Indeed, the power, influence, and status that Irish nuns held as teachers, doctors, nurses, and administrators in Ireland and in missions throughout the world, contrasted sharply with that available to their lay sisters and undoubtedly compensated for some of the restrictions and limitations otherwise imposed by religious life. The attractions of convent life for those who did not want to emigrate or were unlikely to marry remained strong through the 1960s, before declining dramatically after 1972; this latter development was related as much to falling emigration and rising marriage rates as to increasing secularization in Irish life.[5]

Young women in the business sector appeared to view their jobs as purely temporary positions prior to marriage, and they showed little desire to advance. Their ambitions for further training and promotion appeared nonexistent, and promotions were often never suggested or contemplated because, according to the male-dominated management, women had shown no desire to advance. The relatively unambitious attitude of Irish working women at this stage derived partly from the "marriage bar" which required most women to resign their positions upon marriage. Although legislated initially for the teaching profession in 1933, "marriage bars" were subsequently implemented by the civil service, local authorities, health boards, and most businesses. The provisions contained in the 1935 Conditions of Employment Act allowed government to regulate working conditions, to ban women from employment in certain industries, and to impose gender quotas in others. Since these powers were rarely used, there was little improvement in working conditions and wage rates within the textile and footwear industries, where women dominated the workforce, until the demise of these industries in the face of postwar foreign competition. Moreover, the higher paid jobs that emerged in the new industries established in the 1960s remained predominantly male preserves.[6] The small increase in the overall labor participation rates of Irish women from approximately 26 percent to 29 percent between 1926 and 1960, combined with a married women's participation rate of only 5 percent in 1960 and educational and religious conditioning of young girls to "wife-mother roles," was hardly conducive to nurturing female career ambitions or providing the financial and networking supports essential to launching a political career.

The prospects for young women in the large urban working-class were particularly bleak in the early 1960s. In the absence of state funding for secondary education, the majority left school at age fourteen, and a large proportion of these without obtaining even a primary certificate. Additionally the pressure within poorer working-class families for children to secure a job as quickly as possible consigned young women to low-skilled, poorly paid factory or service jobs. Gender-differentiated occupations and wage scales meant that average female earnings were only 53 percent of male earnings in 1961.[7] Thus few working-class women were able to accrue substantial savings prior to marriage. A family would start soon after, which—given the lack of legal access to any birth control except the rhythm method—left these women, by their mid-thirties, to raise four or five children on their husband's slim pay packet, often in drab and cramped council housing. Patrick Lynch's Organisation for Economic Co-operation and Development (OECD) Report of 1966, *Investment in Education,* and Father Liam Ryan's *Christus Rex* article of 1967 highlighted the educational and social deprivation experienced by urban working-class children and their families through the mid-1960s.[8]

The position of rural women and especially of those in the west of Ireland was not enviable either. Marriage to a farmer whose income was barely above subsistence brought a life of endless work and chores, not only in household management, but also in additional farming tasks such as milking, tending chickens, raising vegetables, and, more often than not, caring for elderly parents or in-laws as well as a number of children. Few farm wives received any cash remuneration for their labor and the opportunities to earn cash as paid agricultural workers or by marketing poultry and eggs were diminishing considerably owing to increasing mechanization, commercialization, and specialization.[9] The modern conveniences American women took for granted in the 1960s, such as refrigerators, washers, and dryers were unheard of in most rural Irish areas. In some areas of Connacht even running water was absent, which made the work of women in those districts doubly onerous.

The marriage profile of most rural couples featured a large age gap between husband and wife, ten to fifteen years was not unusual, and a fairly late age at marriage, thereby increasing the potential for male dominance and authoritarianism in the marriage. The tradition of patrilineal land inheritance in conjunction with a century of strong male bonding through pub life and sports events did little to foster intimate marital relationships based on love and mutual intellectual interests or hobbies.[10] In both rural and urban areas the authority of the Roman Catholic Church was more or less unquestioned, a situation that came from the high per capita number of priests and nuns in the Irish population whose pastoral and educational work tended to inculcate passive attitudes among Irish women.[11] Clerical authoritarianism was reinforced by the survival within Irish law of Victorian influences that denied women individual legal rights and viewed them as their husband's property. For instance, a woman could not open a bank account, contract a loan or hire-purchase agreement, or buy insurance without her husband's signature. Women had no legal claim to their spouse's income and the child-benefit allowance from the state was paid to the father.[12] Moreover, there was little legal protection or even social support for women in abusive marriages or for wives and children who were victims of male desertion.

These conditions fueled a virtual flight from the countryside by more independent-minded young rural women who headed for Dublin, London, Birmingham, and even America in search of positions as domestics, factory operatives, and some as nurses—to secure better and more satisfying lives than their mothers experienced.[13] Although the hemorrhage of female emigration was predominantly rural, even urban women with good educational qualifications found that to acquire positions equal to their training and talents, they had to go abroad, either permanently or temporarily.[14] About the best a well-educated young Irish woman could expect in the early 1960s was employment with Aer Lingus as a stewardess or ticket agent, or teaching in a secondary school.

The most telling sign of the continued challenge to de Valera's vision and these unpalatable conditions for Irish women lies in the contrast between the Irish president of 1963 and the Irish President of 1996. Eamon de Valera—who had conferred, in article 41 of the 1937 Irish constitution, a de jure recognition to the privatized "wife-mother" role that had been evolving gradually since the post-famine era—was President when I left Ireland in 1963. Today the Irish President is Mary Robinson, a woman who first gained public recognition by her unstinting efforts, as a lawyer and Irish senator, to amend those provisions of de Valera's constitution and Irish statutory law that discriminated against women and effectively denied them full citizenship. The significance of Mrs. Robinson's Presidency and the high acclaim and respect she enjoys, not only in Ireland but also on the international stage, is best illustrated by examining Irish women's political status in the post-independence era.

Despite the prominent roles women played in Irish political and cultural revivals between 1880 and 1921, a dominant feature of the post-independence era was the almost total absence of women on the Irish political stage.[15] The bitter civil war over the Anglo-Irish Treaty of 1921 and Sinn Féin's abstentionist policy towards the Irish Free State effectively ended the political careers of five of the six republican women elected to the revolutionary Dáil in 1919. Meanwhile, the controversies over the exclusion of Ulster, culminating in the 1920 partition, destroyed any possibility of a strong island-wide suffragist movement. Similar to other European states in the post-war era, the new Cumann na nGaedheal government adopted conservative economic and social policies which emphasized women's traditional roles. The reintegration of the anti-Treaty republicans into constitutional politics in 1926 made no significant difference since Eamon de Valera and the Fianna Fáil party did not share the commitment to women's rights that James Connolly, the executed leader of the Irish Citizen Army, had insisted be included in the 1916 republican proclamation. Upon achieving power in 1932 Fianna Fáil did nothing to alter the restrictions on women's rights imposed by earlier Cumann na nGaedheal legislation which effectively censored information on birth control, banned divorce, and virtually excluded women from jury service in criminal and civil cases. Subsequent Fianna Fáil policy geared to restricting female employment and, most especially, the provisions of de Valera's 1937 constitution declaring the family as the basic social unit and woman's primary role that of "wife and mother," were formidable disincentives to women's political participation.

Thus, despite the right to vote and hold office conferred on women over age twenty-one by the Irish constitution of 1922, there were only twenty-four women among the 650 Dáil deputies elected between 1922 and 1977. The majority were elected by virtue of being the widows, daughters, or sisters of fallen national heroes. Between 1927 and 1977 women never represented more than 3 percent of candidates in Dáil elections and fifteen out of twenty-six counties never elected a woman deputy. In 1961 there were only three women deputies and it was 1969 before the number of women candidates in Dáil elections numbered more than ten.

The antipathy of the male political establishment to women's participation in Irish political life was reflected also in the low profile of women in the Senate. Only very rarely have women been nominated as party candidates for the highly coveted forty-three Senate seats. It was only in 1969 that Trinity College alumni elected Mary Robinson as their first woman senator. Even more revealing was the failure of successive Taoisigh to use their eleven Senate appointments to advance women's involvement in politics and decision-making at the national level. Eamon de Valera made only three female appointments out of fifty-five nominations, John Costello made one out of twenty-two, Seán Lemass three out of twenty-two.[16]

Starting in the early 1970s the confluence of five notable factors rejuvenated a long dormant Irish women's movement enabling it to accomplish some major gains for Irish women during the past two decades. First, exposure to the international feminist ferment, through television and the print media, provided an analytical and comparative context that enabled Irish women to express anger over the second class status to which church and state policy had consigned them.[17] Numerous women's groups, representing a broad spectrum of feminist philosophies ranging from radical and socialist to reformist equity feminism, formed in the late sixties and early seventies, especially in the Dublin area. Through hard campaigning and effective use of their close links to the Dublin-dominated media, they forced the question of Irish women's status into public discussion.[18]

For instance, in early 1971 the small but radical feminist Irish Women's Liberation Movement (IWLM), in their pamphlet *Chains or Change? The Civil Wrongs of Irish Women* and in a subsequent appearance on the Late Late Show, provided a succinct account of the numerous inequities that Irish women faced. IWLM's demands for equal pay, employment, and educational opportunities for women, and for adequate social welfare support for widows, deserted wives, and single mothers resonated with large numbers of Irish women. On the other hand, IWLM demands for legalized contraception and expanded housing raised religious and class tensions which ultimately divided the radical feminists from the liberal reformist or equity feminists.

Nonetheless, the IWLM-led Condom Train event in May 1971, during which condoms purchased in Belfast were openly flaunted before Gardai officers too embarrassed to seize the contraband, gave public expression to a silent but nonetheless rising concern, especially among educated middle-class women, over lack of legal access to birth control. This mood was reflected more subtly in the marked escalation since 1962 of prescriptions for birth control pills. Despite the 1968 papal prohibition, in *Humanae Vitae,* of their use for anything but medically necessary cycle regulation, an estimated thirty-eight thousand Irish women were on the pill by 1973.[19] No legislative initiatives were taken at this time to legalize the sale of contraceptives, owing to church opposition and the reluctance of the majority of women to take up the issue publicly. However, a series of legal challenges on the issue—initially filed by Mary Robinson in 1973 in the *Magee vs. the Attorney General* case—were presented to the European Court and, eventually, the Irish Supreme Court, and they ultimately resulted in the Health and Family Planning Act of 1979. Married couples could now procure contraceptives provided they had a doctor's prescription. Further legislation in 1985 and 1993 virtually has eliminated all restrictions on the sale and distribution of condoms to anyone aged eighteen or over. Regional health boards are required now to make family planning services available to their clients and to low income clients qualifying for a medical card. The availability of contraception explains the dramatic fall in Irish women's average fertility rate from 3.07 in 1981 to 1.89 in 1991.[20] The lengthy litigation on the contraceptive issue eventually showed Irish women that skillful use of the judicial system could overturn discriminatory laws and policies; this political lesson was eventually and successfully applied to other areas of grievance, such as jury service, family law, social benefits, and employment conditions.

Second, the publication in December 1972 of the report of the first Commission on the Status of Women proved crucial in mobilizing an even broader spectrum of women to demand fundamental change. Established by a Fianna Fáil government in 1970 at the request of an ad hoc committee representing larger and more traditional women's organizations and chaired by the most senior woman civil servant, Dr.

Thelka Beere, the commission gathered comprehensive and irrefutable evidence of the discrimination women faced in employment, education, legal status, and in the area of state benefits and social policy. When, during the 1973 Dáil elections, the commission's forty-nine recommendations for legislative, judicial, and political reform were pressed upon candidates, without much effect, the Council on the Status of Women was formed specifically to lobby for, and monitor progress towards, full equality of citizenship and legal status for Irish women. The fledgling Women's Political Association, convinced that changes in the status quo depended on women's active involvement in politics, worked diligently, throughout the decade, to promote women candidates for the national legislature and local councils.

Third, increased travel to America and the Continent, and most especially Ireland's entrance into the European Union in 1973, highlighted the severity of the structural inequalities and discrimination that Irish women faced compared to their American and European sisters. Indeed, pressure from Europe to conform to community legal standards regarding women's rights proved to be an important factor in forcing a reluctant Irish male political elite to address many of the economic and social policy issues raised by the IWLM and the Beere report. Moreover, the right of appeal to the European Courts of Justice and Human Rights on matters governed by European law has been used in a number of instances to alter existing Irish law on contraception, homosexuality, and, more recently, on the rights of Irish women, as European citizens, to information and travel pertaining to the abortion provision.

Fourth, the rapid pace of industrialization, urbanization, and suburbanization in the 1970s created an additional dynamic that inevitably subverted the traditional "wife/mother" role. The expanding needs of industry and business for additional workers—especially in the service areas—as well as the government's need to boost its own revenues, required that women's employment levels be expanded and able to continue after marriage. Spiraling housing costs in major urban areas and the increasingly consumer-oriented life style of young couples underscored the need to remove marriage bars and the other impediments that contributed to Ireland's having the lowest female employment levels of any European country.[21] Concern over these economic issues precipitated increasing activism by women in the mid-

1970s. This was exemplified in 1977 by the successful petition campaign that forced trade union and government leaders to implement, without delay, European directives calling for more comprehensive equal pay legislation.[22]

Last, gradually expanding educational opportunities have been crucial to the heightened political consciousness of Irish women. The introduction of free post-primary education in 1967 followed by a significant rise of female students at third level institutions in the late 1970s expanded the personal and career aspirations of a large portion of young Irish women. No longer content with the role of passive political bystanders, more women began involving themselves in party politics and in the voluntary and trade union sectors as essential steps toward securing full equality of status and citizenship for all Irish women. With females comprising approximately half of today's university graduates, the pool of potential political activists and candidates is growing steadily.

The first clear signs of women's rising political consciousness and of the male establishment's dawning appreciation of women's potential political power appeared in the national elections of 1977. Twenty-five women ran as Dáil candidates whereas only eleven had run in 1960, and six won seats in this election, doubling the number of women in the Dáil. Moreover, the Fianna Fáil leader Jack Lynch personally intervened to add six women to his party's candidate list for this election, and subsequently he appointed three women senators when the Fianna Fáil victory secured his second term as Taoiseach. In the same year, the new Fine Gael leader Garret FitzGerald, anxious to expand his party's membership, recommended the establishment of a Fine Gael women's section, a suggestion that the women members turned down temporarily.[23] In the same year, Gemma Hussey was the first woman elected to a National University Senate seat after a campaign focusing primarily on women's rights. In 1977 Máire Geoghegan-Quinn became the first woman since Countess Markievicz to hold a cabinet position when she was appointed Minister for the Gaeltacht in the Fianna Fáil government. In 1982 Mary Harney, Mary Flaherty, and Alice Glenn made notable Dáil debuts having won their seats on their own merits rather than because of links to established political families.

Although women's political interest and activity were obviously increasing, the actual gains in women's political representation in the Dáil and in local government were fairly minimal through the 1980s when the women's percentage of both Dáil and local council seats ranged between 6 and 8.4. The male ethos surrounding the criteria and processes of candidate selection, party governance, and the scheduling of party meetings, as well as the strength at the grass roots level of traditional views regarding women's family duties, continued to be formidable obstacles to women's political participation and to giving women's concerns a high priority on the legislative agenda.[24] Indeed, the campaigns surrounding the referenda of 1983 and 1986, which, respectively, imposed a constitutional ban on abortion and upheld the existing one on divorce, were salient reminders of the persistence of these attitudes.

Nonetheless, the present decade has witnessed a marked upsurge in women's political interest, participation, and success rates. The sense of validation, empowerment, and pride that Mary Robinson's 1990 election as president conferred on Irish women may have been a factor in the modest gain—from 8 percent to 11.7 percent—of women elected to local councils in 1991. Commenting on Robinson's election and the mushrooming of women's groups all over the country, Carmel Foley, Director of the Employment Equality Agency, observed in March 1992, ". . . women are walking 10 ft tall since she (Robinson) was elected. They see her on top of the pyramid of power and think, 'If she can do that, I can do it in my own life.' "[25] The next national elections in late 1992 witnessed a 58 percent increase over 1987 in the number of women candidates that stood for the Dáil. With eighty-nine women running and constituting 18 percent of candidates, this election had the highest female participation rate since the founding of the state. A record twenty women were elected, giving women 12.4 percent of the Dáil seats as compared to previous highs of 8.4 percent in the mid-1980s. Seven women were elected to the Senate while one woman was appointed, giving women 13 percent of Senate seats and a total of twenty-eight or 12.4 percent of seats in the Oireachtas, making it sixth among the European parliaments in the number of women members. Other notable features were the election of nine women deputies with no links to political families and the fact that six were elected from the smaller parties, five from Labour and one from Democratic Left. The smaller parties have better records in promoting women candidates and, unlike Fianna Fáil and Fine Gael, now have established quotas to insure women's representation on their executive committees. These are 20 percent for Labour, 40 percent Democratic Left, 25 percent for Sinn Féin, and 50 percent for the small Green Party.[26]

The impact of the 1992 X abortion case that convulsed the country from February to June may also have been a factor both in encouraging more women to stand in the November 1992 elections and in their subsequent victories at the polls. The shock and dismay expressed over the High Court's order that initially prevented a pregnant fourteen-year-old rape victim from securing an abortion in England sparked some of the largest public demonstrations in Dublin since the Hunger Strikes of 1981.[27] Despite the Supreme Court's reversal of the High Court order and its subsequent March ruling that abortion is legal if there is a substantial threat to the life of a pregnant woman, the case exposed that the Irish government, in preparing for the Maastricht treaty, had secured a secret protocol which gave primacy to the Republic's constitutional ban on abortion over European law. The protocol called into question the rights of women to travel and to secure information on abortion services outside of Ireland, and it blatantly highlighted the magnitude of the state's patriarchal control over Irish women's bodies. Faced with widespread outrage from women, and indeed many men, as well as fears that this controversy might dissuade Irish voters from ratifying the Maastricht agreement in a June referendum, the government was forced to seek an amendment to the protocol and to schedule further referenda that would guarantee the rights of Irish women, as European citizens, to travel and to information. Memories of the aggressive campaigning by arch-conservative Catholic lay organizations (such as The Society for the Protection of the Unborn Child, Opus Dei, and Family Solidarity) and the political bungling and opportunism of Fine Gael and Fianna Fáil (which produced the constitutional ban on abortion in 1983 and preserved the existing ban on divorce in 1986) were revived by the X case and probably gave further impetus to a growing trend towards women's political involvement.[28] Indeed, some women deputies from the Joint Oireachtas Committee on Women's Rights addressed this issue on a bipartisan basis when they pressed the government to schedule referenda on travel and information.[29] The Council on the Status of Women, then representing approximately eighty-nine women's groups, heavily lobbied the government to resolve this issue; it also pressed for the introduction of legislation implementing the Supreme Court decision.

Other signs, besides their Dáil presence, indicate an improving profile for women on the Irish political stage. The present Fine Gael-Labour coalition cabinet has two women ministers. Nora Owen is both Fine Gael Deputy Leader and Minister of Justice, while Niamh Bhreathnach of the Labour party is Minister of Education. The four women serving as ministers of State are Joan Burton and Eithne Fitzgerald of Labour, Avril Doyle of Fine Gael, and Liz McManus of Democratic Left. Mary Banotti, Nuala Ahern, Patricia McKenna, and Bernice Malone hold four of the fifteen Irish seats in the European Parliament. Mary Harney became Leader of the small Progressive Democratic Party in 1993 and Mary O'Rourke currently serves as Deputy leader of Fianna Fáil. Notwithstanding the gains in Dáil representation and the presence of a few women at ministerial level, the experience of other European countries suggests that dramatic and substantial changes to the party system and to the political agenda reflecting women's concerns will not take place until women constitute about a third of the legislature.[30]

Yet the possibility of reaching that goal is improving steadily given that Irish feminism has grown stronger, more socially pervasive, and more determined than ever to secure change. Women in community groups and organizations are enthusiastically networking and affiliating with the National Women's Council of Ireland (NWCI) which provides a crucial collective voice for 124 women's organizations with a combined membership of approximately three hundred thousand women. Formerly known as the Council on the Status of Women, the NWCI, through its national and international networking, research, publications, educational conferences and advising activities, ensures that women's views and interests on matters of public interest, policy, and law are clearly presented to government, business, and the general public. These activities in conjunction with their various public campaigns—such as one in 1996 directed at encouraging more women to sign on to the Live Register (which determines access to social welfare benefits and job training schemes)—demonstrate at the local level the importance of women's political involvement and activism.[31] Reinforced by European community policies calling for gender balance and social inclusion, the National Women's Council is insisting on the need for active promotion of women's participation in policy and decision-making in all areas: public budgeting and economic development, the development of the political agenda (to include issues of importance to women), and the provision of affordable and high quality child-care.[32]

Another development that may promote more political involvement of women has been the dynamic growth in the major universities of Women's Studies programs at both the graduate and undergraduate level. Through their feminist analysis, research, and expanding outreach activities beyond academia, these programs nurture political awareness and provide an important antidote to the persistence of traditional views that tend to discourage women from active involvement in party politics.

Another encouraging sign of women's increasing presence in public life lies in recent judicial appointments. The Supreme Court has one woman, the Honorable Justice Susan Deneham, and three women serve on the High Court. The most recent appointee was Judge Catherine McGuinness who was a masterful and diplomatic chair of the Forum for Peace and Reconciliation established in the wake of the Provisional Irish Republican Army cease-fire of 1994. In April 1993 Maureen Gaffney, a noted clinical psychologist and broadcaster, was appointed chair of the newly formed National Economic and Social Forum, which was charged with developing a national consensus on major issues of economic and social policy as well as new initiatives to address unemployment.[33] These appointments, so crucial to the resolution of the northern conflict and the shaping of government economic and social initiatives, would have been unimaginable even ten years ago, let alone in 1960.

Despite the gains herein described, the struggle of Irish women for full equality in political, economic, and social life is far from over. Women involved in politics and active in women's lobbying groups face major challenges in ensuring that the various recommendations of the second Commission on the Status of Women be implemented. Its 1993 report noted that despite the legislative reforms of the late 1970s—providing for improved social benefits and employment conditions for women—and in the absence of a comprehensive antidiscrimination law, there remain many areas where Irish women are still denied full equality as adult individuals. For instance, the economic contribution of farm wives remains unacknowledged in relation to pension rights, maternity benefits, social insurance, and property rights. Far too many women in urban areas and poor rural districts are still burdened by poverty, unemployment, inadequate education, and scarce social amenities. Other problem areas are women's lack of access to credit, training programs, and various social institutions such as golf and tennis clubs. Although the commission's recommendation for a Cabinet-level Minister and a Department of Women's Affairs has not materialized, in 1993 the Fianna Fáil Labour Coalition gave full cabinet status to a Minister for Equality and Law Reform and committed itself to the principle of equality. With the removal of the ban on divorce secured by referendum in November 1995, Mr. Mervyn Taylor, Labour TD and the Minister for Equity and Law Reform, is facing increasing pressure from the NWCI and the Joint Oireachtas Committee on Women's Rights to introduce comprehensive Equal Employment and Equal Status Bills.[34] Indeed, Mr. Taylor has been a sympathetic ally, as illustrated by his comments on International Women's Day in 1995: "I look to an Ireland based on parity of representation and esteem of women and men: an Ireland where the limits, the ceilings and barriers to the full flourishing of every Irish woman are removed forever, to an Ireland where every woman can celebrate, belong to, and participate fully in an equal and democratic society in all of its vital and energetic diversity."[35]

The public recognition now accorded Irish women writers and artists has echoed and amplified the demands for fundamental political, social, and economic change made by women in political and public life. The poetry, prose, drama, and painting produced by creative artists such as Eavan Boland, Nuala ní Dhomhnaill, Mary Leland, Marina Carr, Garry Hynes, Pauline Cummins, and Rita Duffy, to name but a few, reflect the growing solidarity of Irish women and their courage in confronting the difficult questions of morality and economic and social justice that Irish society faces. In articulating the tolerant, compassionate, and human values that President Robinson has identified as the core of true feminism, they, too, are liberating Irish women from the patriarchal constraints of the past, while simultaneously preserving the best of Irish communal values.[36] Out of the interaction of these political, social, and cultural developments is emerging a new, more complex and authentic image of Cathleen ní Houlihan, an image being shaped and defined this time by Irish women themselves and one which promises to secure respect and dignity for all the citizens of the nation. Thus the prospects look brighter for Irish women today than at any other time in the twentieth century.

Notes

1. *Europe: the Magazine of the European Union*, no. 358 (July/August 1996): 8–23.

2. Tim Pat Coogan, *Eamon de Valera: The Man Who Was Ireland* (New York: Harper Collins, 1995); Richard Dunphy, *The Making of Fianna Fáil Power in Ireland, 1923–1948* (Oxford: Clarendon Press, 1995).

3. Margaret Ward, *The Missing Sex: Putting Women into Irish History* (Dublin: Attic Press, 1991); Margaret MacCurtain, Mary O'Dowd, Maria Luddy, "An Agenda for Women's History in Ireland, 1500–1900," *Irish Historical Studies* 38, 109 (May 1992): 1–37.

4. For analysis of the economic, political, and cultural factors that shaped Irish women's roles prior to 1960, see Liam O'Dowd, "Church, State and Women: The Aftermath of Partition," in *Gender in Irish Society*, ed. Chris Curtin, Pauline Jackson, Barbara O'Connor (Galway: Galway University Press, 1987), 3–36; Maryann Valiulis, "Neither Feminist nor Flapper: the Ecclesiastical Construction of the Ideal Irish Woman," in *Chattel, Servant or Citizen: Women's Status in Church, State and Society*, ed. Mary O'Dowd and Sabine Wichert (Belfast: The Institute of Irish Studies, 1995), 168–78.

5. Margaret MacCurtain, "Late in the Field: Catholic Sisters in Twentieth Century Ireland and the New Religious History," in O'Dowd and Wichert, *Chattel*, 49–63; Tom Inglis, *Moral Monopoly: The Catholic Church and Modern Irish Society* (Dublin: Gill and MacMillan, 1987), 33–62.

6. Mary Daly, "Women in the Irish Free State, 1922–39: The Interaction between Economics and Ideology," *Irish Women's Voices: Past and Present*, ed. Joan Hoff and Maureen Coulter, special issue of *Journal of Women's History*, 6,4; 7,1 (1995): 110.

7. Mary Daly, "Women, Work and Trade Unionism," *Women in Irish Society: The Historical Dimension*, ed. Margaret MacCurtain and Donncha Ó Corráin (Dublin: Arlen House, 1978), 79.

8. Dermot Keogh, *Twentieth Century Ireland* (Dublin: Gill and MacMillan, 1994), 272–73.

9. Carmel Duggan, "Farming Women or Farmers' Wives?" in Curtin, Jackson, O'Connor, *Gender in Irish Society*, 54–69.

10. Margaret MacCurtain, summary of lecture to the Parnell Summer School, August 1994, *History Ireland* 2. 3 (Autumn 1994): 5. See also Jenny Beale, *Women in Ireland: Voices of Change* (Dublin: Gill and Macmillan, 1986), 63–84.

11. Joseph Lee calculated that, by 1960, the ratio of clergy to people was one priest to every six hundred and one nun to every four hundred persons. "Women and the Church since the Famine," in MacCurtain and Ó Corráin, *Women in Irish Society,* 30–40; on Irish female deference to priests, see Inglis, *Moral Monopoly,* 198–214.

12. Evelyn Mahon, "Women's Rights and Catholicism in Ireland," *New Left Review,* no. 166 (Nov./Dec. 1987): 18–19.

13. The 1961 census revealed that in County Leitrim female flight from the land left two bachelors to every single woman between the ages of fifteen and forty-five. For the links between limited educational and marriage opportunities and female emigration from Connacht, see Patricia O'Hara, "What Became of Them?: Women in the West of Ireland Labour Force," in Curtin, Jackson, O'Connor, *Gender in Irish Society,* 79–82; also Beale, *Women in Ireland,* 20–40.

14. For a useful discussion on the persistence of Irish female emigration, see Pauric Travers, "Emigration and Gender: The Case of Ireland 1922–60," in O'Dowd and Wichert, *Chattel,* 187–99.

15. For details of women's involvement in the national struggle, see Margaret Ward, *Unmanageable Revolutionaries* (Dingle: Brandon Books, 1983); Ruth Tallion, *The Women of 1916* (Belfast: Beyond the Pale Publications, 1996).

16. Maurice Manning, "Women in Irish National and Local Politics, 1922–77," in MacCurtain and O'Corráin, *Women in Irish Society,* 92–102.

17. Inglis, *Moral Monopoly,* 94; Noreen Byrne's Keynote Address, in *Women's Power . . . for a Change: A Report on a Conference of Women's Networks in Ireland,* ed. Cris Malvey April 24–25, 1995 (Dublin: Aontas, 1995), 11–14.

18. Mary Maher of the *Irish Times* and Mary Kenny of the *Irish Press* were crucial in providing these links. For further details on these developments see Mahon, "Women's Rights," 53–77, and Ailbhe Smyth, "The Women's Movement in the Republic of Ireland 1970–1990," in *Irish Women's Studies Reader,* ed. Ailbhe Smyth (Dublin: Attic Press, 1993), 245–269.

19. Ann Rossiter, "Between the Devil and the Deep Blue Sea: Irish Women, Catholicism and Colonialism," in *Refusing Holy Orders: Women and Fundamentalism in Great Britain,* ed. Gita Sahgal and Nira Yuval-Davis (London: Virago, 1992).

20. *Eurostat Demographic Statistics,* publication data (1995), 222.

21. Beale, *Women in Ireland,* 139–63; summary by Margret Fine-Davis, of her *Women and Work in Ireland: A Sociological Perspective* (Dublin: Council on the Status of Women, 1983), 18–23.

22. Sylvia Meehan, interview with author, July 1988.

23. Garrett FitzGerald, *All in a Life* (Dublin: Gill and MacMillan, 1991), 329.

24. Yvonne Galligan, "Women in Irish Politics," in *Politics in Irish Life,* 2d. ed., ed. John Coakley and Michael Gallagher (Limerick: Political Science Association of Ireland Press, 1993), 214–18.

25. *Time* (16 March 1992), 61; see also Ailbhe Smyth, "A Great Day for the Women of Ireland: The Meaning of Mary Robinson's Presidency for Irish Women," Canadian Journal of Irish Studies, 18.1 (1992): 61–75.

26. F. Gardiner, "Political Interest and Participation of Irish Women 1922–1992: The Unfinished Revolution," in Smyth, *Irish Women's Studies Reader,* 45–78; Joanna McMinn, ed., *Beijing and Beyond: An Independent Report to the 4th UN World Conference on Women* (Dublin: National Women's Council of Ireland, 1995), 25.

27. The author was in Dublin at this time and personally witnessed these demonstrations. See also Ailbhe Smyth, ed., *The Abortion Papers: Ireland* (Dublin: Attic Press, 1992).

28. For analysis of these groups see Emily O'Reilly, *Masterminds of the Right* (Dublin: Attic Press, 1991).

29. Catherine B. Shannon, "The Balance Tilts," *Fortnight* (July/August 1992): 21–22.

30. Gardiner, "Political Interest," 75.

31. *In Focus,* quarterly newsletter of the National Women's Council nos. 1–4 (1995–96).

32. *Beijing and Beyond,* 24; "Women in Contemporary Ireland," 1992 speech by Frances Fitzgerald; typescript of speech sent to author.

33. *Irish Times* (29 April 1993).

34. *In Focus,* no. 2 (March/April 1996).

35. Mary Cummins, *Irish Times* (9 March 1995).

36. Mary Robinson, *Striking the Balance,* Alan Lane Lecture, Trinity College (February 1992); Shannon, "The Balance Tilts," 22. Fintan O'Toole has also paid tribute to the crucial role Irish feminism has played in challenging the moral absolutism and political exclusiveness that characterized Ireland until recent times [*Irish Times* (19 May 1995)]. For an additional perspective on the erosion of traditional attitudes, see Colm Tóibín, "Dublin's Epiphany," *The New Yorker* (3 April 1995): 45–53.

"Hello Divorce, Goodbye Daddy"
Women, Gender and the
Divorce Debate

THE ATMOSPHERE was very tense as the votes were counted in Ireland's second divorce referendum on 25 November 1995, and especially in Dublin's Royal Dublin Society hall, where the Dublin votes were being counted and where the size of the Dublin majority would decide whether the vote would be won or lost. It was a knife-edge balance all day, but by evening the result had become clear—the proponents of the constitutional amendment to end the sixty-year-old ban on divorce would win, albeit by the narrowest of margins. One anti-divorce campaigner, Una Bean nic Mhathuna, could not contain her fury and angrily denounced her opponents with the words: "Go away, ye wife-swapping sodomites."[1] To which a passing pro-divorce campaigner, Peter Ward, remarked over his shoulder "If only we had that much fun during the campaign."[2]

Picked up by the cameras, and repeated gleefully by the other media, this outburst quickly became an emblem for the campaign, suggesting a preoccupation with sex and its repression on the part of those opposing divorce. The two individuals involved in the exchange also seemed, for some, to symbolize the two sides in the campaign: Una Bean nic Mhathuna was a middle-aged married woman and mother—with a long history of campaigning on issues close to the heart of the Catholic right; Peter Ward was an up-and-coming young single barrister, whose very profession, it was suggested at some anti-divorce public meetings, was riddled with libertines.

The issues involved, however, were much more complex, and concerned not only questions of sexuality and gender, but a general unease at the direction in which Western society was going, and uncertainty as to whether Irish society should follow it. The electorate felt there was much more at stake than increasing people's legally sanctioned opportunities for sex. Central to its preoccupations was a concern for the family as an institution, and a general, if vague, attachment to an "Irish way of life," one that included close family attachments, and that united both sides of the debate. Issues concerning the changing roles of women and men in society, the right of the state to regulate people's behavior in their personal lives, and the tension between individual rights and social obligations were themes that existed, but remained undeveloped throughout the debate.

It has become axiomatic to state that Irish society has changed a lot in the past twenty-five years. The shift in economic policy in the 1960s to rely more and more heavily on foreign capital, with the consequent mushrooming of foreign-owned enterprises in the computer and chemical sectors; the changes in agricultural policy arising from European Community (EC) membership, which has led to an intensification of agriculture and an increase in the size and productivity of holdings; the accompanying collapse of indigenous industry and the flight from the land, along with a growth in unemployment; the massive expansion of the educational system to draw in the majority of young people until the age of about twenty; the sharp increase in the number of married women, and those with children, in the workforce—have all combined to create a society that is much more urbanized, much more sophisticated, much more educated, and much more economically and socially polarized, than it was in 1970.

This has gone hand-in-hand with a drop in religious observance (though it is still very high by international standards),[3] a much more critical attitude toward the Catholic Church among its remaining faithful, and a general secularization of society. The teachings of the Church are ignored in many areas. This is reflected in the explosion of the number of births outside marriage—they now number more than one in five;[4] a collapse in the birth rate—it now approaches the European average of 1.86;[5] widespread premarital sexual activity among the young; and the departure abroad every year of approximately five thousand young Irish women seeking abortions. Over the past ten or so years the abuse of children in their own homes, as well as by those who are responsible for them—notably Catholic religious —has emerged as a dark undercurrent that has existed in Irish society for many decades, and has galvanized society to take the rights of children more seriously.[6]

Less noted is the flouting of Catholic teachings in other areas—

personal enrichment is widely seen as a more important goal than social responsibility; tax evasion and fraud are not uncommon; and more obvious crimes, like robbery, murder, and drug abuse, have increased, though not to the extent often suggested by the more hysterical media commentators. So Irish society has already stepped onto the path marked out by many Western societies—notably our neighbours on both sides of the Atlantic, Britain and the United States.

Yet Ireland remains a more humane and less fragmented society than either of these. Family bonds are still close, and the extended family still a source of strength to most people. If the family is looked at more critically in light of the revelations of child abuse, it is done within the context of a widespread attachment to the family. The mishandling of child sex abuse allegations against a Catholic priest, Father Brendan Smyth, brought down a government in November 1994. An organization which campaigns for children's rights in Britain found this so extraordinary that it invited a speaker from Ireland (this author) to a conference to discuss the event. It was reported to that conference that a certain British newspaper columnist had dismissed the issue of child sex abuse on the grounds that if it was as widespread as suggested it clearly did not do much harm. Such a remark by the press would be impossible in the mainstream Irish media.

Not surprisingly, social change has also led to an increase in marital breakdown. In the Ireland of the 1930s, 1940s, and 1950s, marriage was still the only lifestyle choice, apart from the convent, open to women. In rural Ireland marriages were contracted more for the preservation of property and the assurance of inheritance than for love and companionship. Opportunities for young people to get to know each other in an unsupervised environment were rare and unapproved of. If they occurred, the very rarity of the opportunity meant they were more likely to result in physical than emotional intimacy. So people usually entered marriage not knowing each other well, with little expectation of emotional intimacy, and with a sense that marriage was more a social obligation than an opportunity for personal fulfillment. This done, society's attitude was, "You made your bed, now you lie in it."

The 1960s and 1970s brought more educational opportunites for everyone, and more job opportunities for women. Later, in the 1980s, the growth of jobs in the computer field and in the service sector brought more women into the workforce. The 1960s also brought a greater emphasis on individual happiness and an atmosphere in which young people met and socialized more freely. Coeducational schools became more common, and the growth in third-level colleges, almost all coeducational, enabled young people to get to know each other. The urbanization of society and the collapse in the number of small family firms made family alliances through marriage less imperative for the middle class. Personal intimacy and fulfillment became important in marriage, the corollary being that, if intimacy and fulfillment did not materialize, or disappeared, the marriage itself was questioned. Some marriages in Ireland had always failed; this was usually disguised by the husband going to England, ostensibly to work, even if the wife sometimes never heard from him again. But by the 1970s marital breakdown was publicly acknowledged, and in 1979 the census included, for the first time, a category for separated people.

The number of people thus describing themselves rose steeply in successive censuses, so that by the 1991 census 33,793 women and 21,350 men featured as separated.[7] The discrepancy in the numbers is probably accounted for by the fact that some separated men had probably left the state, while others may still have described themselves as married because they were claiming tax allowances as married men. But the figure for women shows that this number of marriages had ended in separation, each, of course, affecting two people. The 1993 Labour Force survey put the number of separated women at 38,600.[8] Therefore the government was able to claim, in advocating the ending of the ban on divorce, that 80,000 men and women were affected by marriage breakdown. This was to be the main, and for a long time the only, plank in its platform.

However, the debate did not occur in an ideological vacuum. For over twenty-five years, there has been a heterogeneous feminist movement in Ireland, ranging from government-sponsored organizations—to promote equality in the workplace and society at large (including the recently formed Department of Equality and Law Reform, which sponsored the constitutional amendment)—to groups supporting the rights of lesbians, and including departments of women's studies in the major universities. As a result, the main national media and successive governments have declared themselves committed to equal opportunities for women, and to removing sexual discrimination from Irish society. They have been pushed in this direction by a succession of directives from the European Community, now the European Union, of which Ireland is an enthusiastic member. Two government-appointed Commissions on the Status of Women (CSW) have produced major reports, one in 1972, the second in 1993, intended to provide the framework for legislative reform. The report of the Second Commission supported the then government's commitment to amend the Constitution to remove the ban on divorce.[9] But while the proposal to end the ban on divorce was part of the general trend toward equality, its proponents did not, in the course of the campaign, link it specifically with women's rights. The absence of any argument in favor of the right to divorce, other than the statistics on marriage break-down, was a marked feature of the government campaign. Its failure to link this right with the growing independence of Irish women, and their need to be able to make a new life for themselves and their children if their marriages broke down, undoubtedly contributed to the decline in support, among young women, for the government proposals. In fact, the people who invoked the rights and welfare of women during the debate were those on the anti-divorce side.

There has been little publicly organized opposition to the growing influence of feminism in Ireland over the past twenty-five years, and the form such opposition has taken has tended to be concentrated on single issues, like abortion or divorce. However, a number of groups exist which claim to support "family values" in opposition to the "feminist agenda." They exist alongside, and often are sponsored by or share membership with, long-standing lay Catholic organizations like the Knights of Columbanus or Opus Dei. In recent years organizations espousing "family values" have come onto the political scene with, for example, the Solidarity movement, led by Nora Bennis, campaigning for a seat in the European Parliament in 1993 and winning a respectable seventeen thousand first-preference votes in the Munster constituency.[10]

One such group is the Responsible Society, founded and run by John O'Reilly, an engineer in local government, and a main architect of the Anti-Divorce Campaign (first founded for the 1986 divorce referendum, and linked with a similar organization in Britain). It has a low public profile, and its main activity is providing information and arguments for its members through a quarterly newsletter, *Response,* and a journal, *Family Bulletin.* The Responsible Society has an avowedly anti-feminist agenda, and *Response* carries, as a regular item, a survey entitled "The Onward March of Irish Feminism." The organizations on whose activities it reports include the government-sponsored National Women's Council (formerly the Council for the Status of Women) and Women's Aid, the organization that assists victims of domestic violence. It quoted approvingly from a hostile newspaper account of the 1995 Annual General Meeting of the CSW:

> "It had a definite 'women's group look'. For example there was a strong tendency to dress butch and many could have been described as 'Big Mamas'. Put it like this, as I surveyed the unglamorous girls, I just craved a bit of high-heeled and articulate. The core of the CSW seems to be ageing feminists and lesbians." [11]

Women's Aid, it wrote, "while it has an undoubtedly charitable function is driven by feminist ideology and tends to grossly exaggerate domestic violence." [12] Subscribers to *Response* and members of the Responsible Society and the Irish Family League, with which it shares many members, formed the core of the several hundred activists in the divorce campaign.

Another organization that played an important role behind the scenes in the divorce debate was the Public Policy Institute of Ireland (PPII), a right-wing Catholic think tank that has links with Opus Dei, the Catholic lay organization. Among its board members are William Binchy, a professor of law and the major spokesman and advocate for the Anti-Divorce Campaign (ADC); Ger Casey, an academic philosopher and leading member of the rival No-Divorce Campaign (N-DC); and Mrs. Monica Barber, who spoke frequently during the campaign as "an ordinary housewife" against divorce. One of its founding members is Mark Hamilton, a member of Opus Dei and the author of *The Case against Divorce,* a book that provided many of the arguments against divorce in both 1986 and 1995. He was an important intellectual force in the campaign and, although he did not play any public role, he gave a number of talks to meetings of activists. In his book he argued that the availability of divorce destabilized marriage and led to an increase in marriage breakdown. This was based on linking the statistics for divorce in a number of countries, especially the United Kingdom, with the liberalization of legislation.

However, his book also carried an undercurrent of misogyny, conveying a picture of women as either predators or victims: "The increase in the number of older persons looking for second partners following on divorce leads to pressures on persons in existing happy marriages. Also young eligible women can successfully set their sights on older men with secure financial prospects."[13] This passage contains a number of extraordinary assumptions. First, "older" married men are seen as only tenuously committed to their marriages, vulnerable to the the temptations of a circling band of predatory females. Second, according to this picture, not only are young single women predatory, they also aspire to dependency on a man "with secure financial prospects."

Hamilton situates his opposition to divorce within the framework of opposition to the ethos of the individual, which he sees as pervading Western society. "This ethic is primarily permissive in that it supports the autonomous claims of the individual over and above any other claims society might make for the general welfare of its members."[14] This leads to selfishness, he writes. "Trading on 'my right to do what I want,' the husband who abandons his middle-aged wife to make way for somebody more attractive is a classic, and common, example of selfishness."[15] According to this picture, divorce is the device whereby fickle men abandon their devoted and faithful spouses. However, according to both Irish and international statistics, among those who initiate divorce proceedings women outnumber men by about three to one. While the reasons women do so may vary, and infidelity is undoubtedly one reason, that so many women initiate proceedings contradicts the passive picture painted by Hamilton and his colleagues in the anti-divorce lobby.

The PPII also presented a critique of the Report of the Second Commission on the Status of Women. Called *Women Scorned*, it was presented by Monica Barber at a press conference on 29 March 1995. At this press conference it was stated that four members of the board of the PPII were members of the Opus Dei, and that the PPII's objectives involved conducting research on matters of public policy "on the basis of the Natural Law and Christian principles."[16] This document questioned the whole basis of the Commission's report, especially its concern with women's access to, and treatment in, the world of work. It criticized what it saw as the modern emphasis on economics—and, in particular, the battle of women to secure economic independence.

Its opening paragraph closely mirrored the views of Mark Hamilton:

> An increasingly consumerist culture and the ever-demanding financial needs of the interventionist state have led Western Europeans to focus more on their own perceived needs than on those of others. . . . At the same time we are uncomfortable with the ill fruits of this liberalism: family breakdown, urban violence, wasteful comsumption, sexual irresponsibility and increasing personal unhappiness. We may realise that the worthwhile pursuit of freedom has been sidetracked by individualism. We might like to hear more talk of duties and less of rights. But we are slowly becoming more entangled in the web of individualism. . . .
>
> Many political feminists have unfortunately allowed themselves to be too influenced by individualism and its associated liberal economic thinking, allowing personal gain to become the motor which drives everything. . . . While it is the case that some women may wish or need to work outside the home, political feminists go further and claim that the issue is one of liberation from economic dependence and that it is imperative that the woman escape from the home, make her own private contribution to the needs of the economy and receive payment in return. Other considerations regarding the role of woman—for example, child-bearing, providing a supportive home environment for the family—are seen as obstacles to her well-being.[17]

Barber stated here: "The contribution made by married women to home life is the single most significant factor influencing the quality of life in Ireland today."[18] A happy home life for the breadwinner was an important contributing factor to the quality of life in the workplace, and therefore the taxation system should favor wives working full time in the home.[19] Referring to divorce, the book stated: "Full-time work in the home is a very uncertain option for women in a state where divorce exists. Fear of financial dependence on the State following on a divorced husband remarrying undermines a woman's freedom to give herself to the upbringing of her family."[20] According to William Binchy during the referendum campaign: "Divorce undermines altruism in marriage, through one spouse making sacrifices in their career for the sake of the family."[21]

These views were echoed by the PPII submission to the Joint Oireachtas Committee on the Family in May 1995. It said that "the aim
of public policy should be to strengthen the family and marriage on
which it is based and to defend it against attack." In particular, "the
State should financially encourage one parent to work full-time in the
home. Attention must be paid to the question of wholetime employment and the reintroduction of meaningful child tax allowances as
ways to support marriage." [22] While not specifying which parent
should work full time in the home, the implication of the document is
clear—it is in the best interests of society, children, men, and women
that married women, especially those with children, work full time in
the home, and are supported by their husbands, and by the state,
through tax relief. Financial independence for married women was
seen as, at best, an unavoidable by-product of the need for some
women to contribute to the family income, but as essentially undesir-
able in the idealized version of the nuclear family it advocated. The
well-being of society depended on women's embracing a passive,
home-bound role and on men supporting them financially and emo-
tionally. The presence of women in the workforce and an emphasis on
women's economic independence, transformed women into predators
of married men and undermined the stability of marriage. If sanctioned by divorce, this would further encourage more women to seek
economic independence as a safety net against the danger of abandonment.

Documents like these represented the intellectual cutting edge of
the campaign against the introduction of divorce. They were based
on a well-worked-out and coherent philosophy, and drew widely on
international research and the work of conservative think tanks in
Britain and the United States. While they had an intimate connection
with the conservative currents in Catholic social teaching, they were
by no means exclusively Catholic, and the arguments were all couched
in secular terms.

The government position, however, was presented in entirely prag-
matic and statistical terms. Of course, as its spokespeople acknowledged, no one claimed that divorce was a good thing per se.
Nonetheless, it made little attempt to present its case in terms of a
vision of a society that would be better if people were accorded the
right to divorce and remarry, or in terms that promoted marriage as a

loving commitment between equals rather than as a collection of duties and obligations between individuals of widely different degrees of power.

The main government document, *The Right to Remarry,* indicated that the growth in the number of people separating was the basis for the need to change the Constitution. But it prefaced its proposals by reiterating its commitment to the family: "The Government is strongly committed to protecting the Family and the institution of marriage. A considerable number of legislative and administrative measures are now in place to help protect the Family, to prevent marriage breakdown as far as possible and to minimise the trauma of marital conflict. . . . Central to the Government's position on divorce is the need to protect the Family and the institution of marriage, while at the same time providing remedies for the increasing number of cases of irretrievable breakdown." [23] Yet many of those working in the field of child welfare and family therapy knew that the services were woefully inadequate.

The document went on to outline the various pieces of legislation that had been introduced to protect the family and ease the position of those who had separated since the defeat of the 1986 divorce referendum. The invocation of the "18 pieces of legislation" was one of the main planks of the government campaign for many weeks. Other than advocating the legalization of divorce, it did little to address the concerns of people about the nature of Irish society in the future, and about the growing problem of family breakdown.

Ten days before the referendum, at the government press conference held to promote a "Yes" vote, the Taoiseach, John Bruton, addressed this question in the following way: "The Irish people want a society confident enough of its own traditional strengths of family and faith to be caring enough not to deny by law a second chance to those whose lives have been scarred by the trauma of marriage breakdown, and whose beliefs allow them to remarry." [24] This appeal came as support for a "Yes" vote continued a long and steady fall, and a few days later the government began to panic and went on the offensive. On RTE radio the Sunday before the vote, John Bruton made a more emotional appeal, urging voters to embrace a compassionate and pluralist vision of Irish society, while assuring them of his own personal commitment to his Church's teaching and to support for the family. [25]

The lack of vigor in the government's campaign did not surprise many of those campaigning for a change in the law. Having anticipated something like this, a group of individuals and organizations that had been seeking change for some time had come together over the summer and set up the Right to Remarry Campaign. This consisted of family lawyers and civil rights campaigners like the Irish Council for Civil Liberties (ICCL), and women's organizations like the National Women's Council and Women's Aid. It also included the veteran campaigners of the Divorce Action Group.

As early as 1979 the ICCL had argued for the removal of the ban on divorce in a book written for it by law professor William Duncan.[26] As well as arguing that the number (relatively small in 1979) of marriage breakdowns in itself required a legal remedy, Duncan summed up the ICCL and liberal position: "Politicians and people have a duty to consider whether the law forbidding divorce which may at present reflect their moral viewpoint should be changed because, without adequate social justification, it limits the freedom of others to act according to the dictates of their conscience."[27] But this element of the debate was never developed.

Of course, not all debate during the campaign was conducted at such a cerebral level. Fear and loathing were also present. Some of the rhetoric at public meetings organized by one wing or the other of the anti-divorce lobby revealed the wellsprings from which it drew some elements of its active support—the currents of misogyny lying deep in Irish society. For example, the No-Divorce Campaign, a more aggressive campaigning organization than the Anti-Divorce Campaign, had among its central core of activists one Clem Loscher, who was the author of an unpublished book on the "X" case, in which he argued that the fourteen-year-old girl at the center of this sexual abuse and abortion controversy was the author of her own misfortune, and had had an affair with a neighboring boy. His publishing project fell apart when the man accused of raping her, whom Loscher had defended, changed his plea to guilty after two years of protesting his innocence.[28]

At a public meeting in Thurles, Co. Tipperary, on 28 September addressed by Nora Bennis of the Limerick-based Solidarity movement and Rosemary Swords of the Anti-Divorce Campaign, various speakers, including two priests, referred repeatedly to alleged immoral behavior on behalf of those advocating divorce. Special odium was reserved for lawyers.[29] At this and other public meetings a sad picture of Irish marriage often emerged—one where couples felt they were bound together, not by mutual love and commitment, but by legal ties and social pressures that made escape from an unsatisfactory marriage difficult. Remove such legal bonds, it was suggested, and these marriages, without the buttress of the law, would fall apart.

Another train of thought was also revealed: men were weak and easily seduced and the world was full of seductresses; while nothing could be done about this state of human frailty, society should not endow, with the blessing of married respectability, a union based on the seduction of a weak man by an attractive and scheming "other woman." This revealed that the main targets of the misogyny were young working women presumed to be sexually active, and, therefore, sexual predators of married men. This sometimes extended to young married working women, expecially those with children. Not only were the latter neglecting their children, they were also rejecting the division of labor—and their consequent dependence—within the family, which, it was argued, lies at the core of social stability.

The other side of this argument was the portrayal of women as dependents and victims, potentially abandoned by faithless spouses. In a properly ordered society, the argument went, women who opted for the role of full-time homemaker—the desired role for women— would be rewarded with security and an assurance of permanent support from their partners. But men are weak, and easily lured from the path of duty and responsibility. When society allows divorce, it promotes the predator female at the expense of the dutiful wife, and it rewards the man who abandons his reponsibilities in order to pursue the pleasures of sex. These two female models—the faithful wife and mother, devoted only to her home and family, whose satisfaction lies in providing for their well-being, and the sexually active predatory working woman, whose priorities are self-gratification through career, money, and sex—ran like a red thread through the debate.

This is illustrated in a briefing document for activists by one of the two anti-divorce lobby groups, the Anti-Divorce Campaign, which listed twenty-six reasons why the amendment should be rejected. Some of these relate to divorce on principle, others to "no-fault divorce" as proposed by the government, and some to the specific text of the proposed amendment. While a divorce law based on "no-fault divorce" (where the person seeking a divorce does not have to prove a marital offense on the part of the other spouse) was sharply attacked, this did not lead the anti-divorce lobby to support the possibility of a fault-based divorce law. Nonetheless, it reveals the campaign's preoccupation with the plight of the middle-aged dependent wife.

Among the reasons the document listed as to why the amendment should be rejected were: "it does not oblige the courts to take the conduct of the spouses into account in granting the divorce or in deciding custody, maintenance and the division of property and other assets, . . . it does not require the court to ensure that a woman with children who has not brought about the marriage break-up should not be compelled against her will to leave and sell the family home, . . . it does not require the courts to refuse to grant a divorce where one spouse still wants reconciliation and believes it possible." In an explanatory note it adds: "the irresponsible spouse abandoning his [sic] wife and family would be regarded by society and the law as exercising a civil right when he set up a second home and demanded the sale of the original family home to give him the money to buy a home for his new family."[30] This view was expressed much more succinctly by the No-Divorce Campaign in its dramatic campaign slogan, erected on hoardings around the country: "Hello Divorce, Goodbye Daddy," the brainchild of the media-conscious leader of the N-DC, Peter Scully.

The ADC briefing document objected to the four-year living-apart provision in the constitutional amendment on the grounds that, again, it facilitated a man setting up a second dependent family. "A man would start a second relationship, then desert his wife and children, knowing that in four years' time he will qualify for his divorce. By then he may have a few children, so he can claim in court that he is unable to pay adequate maintenance to his wife and children. The judge will have to take account of that because the logic and thrust of divorce is that this man is exercising a socially recognised and supported civil right in setting up that second family."[31] In an appeal to the tax-paying electorate, it again cites the case of the irresponsible man who abandons his wife and family. "It will force taxpayers to pick up the tab for irresponsible men who default on their financial obligations to their first family. In effect, the taxpayers are forced to take on the financial responsibilities for their first families."[32] The

N-DC topped this with an advertisement stating baldly: "You will pay 10 per cent more tax."

Underlying this argument is the concept of marriage as a set of obligations between provider and dependent (conveying social status on both), rather than as a relationship between equals. Much was made in the course of the debate of the possibility of being "divorced against your will," as if people could be forced to stay married, in any real sense of the word, against their will.

The emphasis on the plight of women working full time in the home, in the event of divorce, struck a chord with the electorate. Ireland has a very high, if declining, proportion of married women working full time in the home, with over 60 percent of all married women not engaged in paid work outside the home. This rises with age, for various reasons, but mainly because both legislation and social attitudes strongly discouraged married women from working outside the home until relatively recently.

So the picture of a middle-aged woman working full time in the home for ten, fifteen, twenty or more years, whose children were growing up, whose chances of re-entering the workforce, even if she wanted to, were slim, corresponded to a widespread social reality. In the event of divorce, she would be vulnerable to a decrease in standard of living, possible dependency on social welfare, and, if the children were grown up, loss of the family home in the division of assets. (In Ireland the courts, in the case of marriage breakdown, have tended to leave a mother and young children in the family home.) It is not surprising, therefore, that the arguments of the anti-divorce lobby struck a chord with this group, as was shown in successive opinion polls.

But not all women in this position opposed divorce. Further, this group does not represent all Irish women, and is declining as a proportion of the female population. Yet there was almost no challenge to this picture of Irish marriage, and the anti-divorce lobby was able to take its opponents onto this ground for debate, where they were very much on the defensive. The question of women's dependency in marriage was not seriously challenged by spokespeople for the government.

The Right to Remarry Campaign contained a number of individual activists, particularly women, who had been prominent in previous campaigns on divorce and abortion. The National Women's Council and Women's Aid were both specifically involved in campaigning for women's rights. In the course of the campaign, Women's Aid drew attention to the plight of abused women who wanted to extricate themselves from marriages to violent men.[33] While this was a powerful argument, it tended to reinforce the image of women as victims, albeit victims who had come to the point of rejecting their victimhood. The response of the anti-divorce lobby was to ask if the violent husband should have the right to inflict his behavior on a second wife.

The National Women's Council was the one organization to challenge the picture of all women as the dependent wife threatened with desertion by her husband, which had become the norm during the debate. In a press statement issued on 2 November 1995, the president of the NWC, Noreen Byrne, said:

> . . . there is anger at the depiction of women by the opponents to divorce. . . . They are attempting to frighten women by reinforcing inequality and vulnerability. . . . And now women who are abused and beaten are being asked to act as jailer to a violent husband as though this will protect other women. These images are an abuse of women. These arguments require that women must be dependent victims. They are arguments which women should reject—for themselves, their daughters and for all women.[34]

In any case, the fears expressed by the anti-divorce lobby were not founded on the real experience of family breakdown in Ireland, where this group (a family with the man employed and the woman working full time in the home), which makes up the majority (though not a large majority) of families, is underrepresented in the statistics for marriage breakdown.

Different surveys have been used to attempt to establish the extent of marriage breakdown, the most important of which are the census and the annual Labour Force Survey, which now list those married but separated as a distinct category. However, these are not further broken down. In 1994, sociologists Tony Fahey and Maureen Lyons sought to do this in a major survey of family law clients of solicitors in Ireland. Their findings were published shortly before the divorce referendum. The survey covered not only those who sought legal separations, but also those who sought legal remedies to the problem of domestic violence. Irish law provides for the offending spouse to be barred from the family home through a simple procedure in local district courts. This is quick and inexpensive, and the survey found that it was the preferred solution to violent family discord for those on low incomes.

One of the areas investigated by Tony Fahey was the employment status of the partners in families involved in marriage breakdown. In 80 percent of cases one or both partners were in paid employment. This included 21 percent in which the man was in paid employment and the woman engaged in "home duties"—the "conventional" family in Ireland—and 13 percent where the woman was employed and the man unemployed—not the "conventional" family. In 11 percent of cases the man was employed and the woman unemployed, indicating that she had recently worked and was eligible for unemployment assistance. In 35 percent of cases both were in employment—a family pattern that is much smaller in the population as a whole. The 20 percent of couples not in employment included 6 percent where both were unemployed, and therefore drawing social welfare in their own right, and 10 percent where the man was unemployed and the woman described as engaged in "home duties," thereby corresponding to the traditional division of labor within the family, even while the man was unemployed. The remaining 4 percent included students and those on other forms of social welfare benefit.[35]

About 64 percent of married women do not work outside the home. Therefore the proportion of "conventional" families, with male breadwinner and dependent wife, 31 percent, who feature in the marriage breakdown statistics falls far below their proportion in the population as a whole. On the other hand, the proportion with the woman working (48 percent) or unemployed, and therefore drawing unemployment benefits (17 percent) was greatly in excess of the national average at 65 percent. Fahey also found that the vast majority of initiators of legal action were women.[36]

It would appear, therefore, that economic independence for women —whether through employment or social welfare—was a major contributing factor for women seeking a legal solution to their marital difficulties. The phenomenon of a married man leaving his dependent wife for someone else, though it certainly happens (and some of the women who sought separations undoubtedly did so for this reason), was not the norm. The phenomenon of the working wife is growing in Irish society; this suggests that more and more women will feel that they have an alternative to tolerating a bad marriage.

Over the past two decades in Irish society the roles played by men and women, and the form of the family, have been changing. For example, from a negligible base in the 1970s, by 1993 the number of working women with children was 36.8 percent of all women working.[37] The increase was even more dramatic in the 25–35 age group, that most likely to have young dependent children. From 1985 (the year before the last divorce referendum) to 1993, the number of working mothers with children under age ten rose from 18 percent to 30 percent, still low by European standards, but showing the increase in rate of participation in the workforce.[38]

Furthermore, Ireland has one of the highest figures in Europe for single mothers, with 9,664 nonmarital births in 1993. This represents one in five of all births, almost exactly the same figure as for Britain.[39] Some of these are only nominally single; they live with partners, some of whom are married and separated and have been unable to remarry until now because of the ban on divorce.

There are 115,200 lone parents in Ireland, 91,000 of them lone mothers.[40] This includes those who are widowed, separated or divorced, as well as those who are single. Forty-five thousand of these have young children, and 39,384 receive the Lone Parents' Allowance of £79.70 (for one child; it rises with more children). In 1991 10.7 percent of all families with children were headed by a lone parent, and this has undoubtedly risen in the past five years with the rise in nonmarital births.

If we add to this the number of married couples where the wife is working (about one in three, higher in the younger age-groups), and where the husband is unemployed (about seventy thousand),[41] then the number of families that have a male breadwinner and a wife working full time in the home, while still a majority, exceeds all other kinds of families by only the narrowest of margins. It can no longer be considered the norm, and social policy based on this as the norm is likely to exclude a large proportion of the population.

Nor is this family model seen any longer as the ideal by many women, though there is no doubt that they still place a high value on marriage, child rearing, and the family as such. The views of Irish women on feminism and the role of women were sought in a rather sketchy survey carried out by the Marketing Research Bureau of Ireland in 1992. This looked at the way a sample of Irish women between the ages of 25 and 64 viewed their role in Ireland today. Questions were asked under the headings of Feminism, the Role of Women Today, Family Life, Issues of Concern to Women, Women's Group Activities, and Concerns Regarding Divorce. There was no examination of women's experience of work, or of how they reconciled these demands with those of their families, but such a complex area does not yield to examination by the multiple choice approach of opinion polls.

It is significant that the majority of women surveyed, 74 percent, viewed motherhood and providing for a family as the most important roles for women.[42] This was not equated with the role of wife or housewife, however, which fell under a different category, and was favored by only 27 percent. Unfortunately, the survey did not inquire as to whether these roles were considered compatible with working outside the home. So the poll did not clarify the views of Irish women on whether married women or mothers should work exclusively in the home or should combine this with work outside the home. But it did find that while only a third shared the responsibility for earning the household income, over half felt that this should be the norm, perhaps reflecting the difficulty experienced by many women in combining work with caring for children in the absence of acceptable child care.

However, the fact that the most admired group of women were office cleaners (working anti-social hours, and therefore, it can be assumed, managing to combine this with domestic responsibilities) and the most admired individual was President Mary Robinson, who has combined a career with motherhood, suggests that such a combination was viewed favorably. After these two very different role models, the mothers of respondents were named by the same number of individuals as had named broadcaster Marian Finucane (who combines her high profile job with marriage and motherhood), followed by a number of other media and political personalities, the majority of whom are mothers.

In another survey, conducted by the Institute of Advertising Practitioners in Ireland, and reported in the *Irish Independent* on 10 November 1995, just two weeks before the divorce referendum, 77 percent of those polled (men and women) agreed with the statement, "A woman with small children can work full-time outside the home and still be a good mother." Only 35 percent agreed with the statement, "A woman's life is fulfilled only if she can provide a happy home for her family."[43]

The 1992 Market Research Bureau of Ireland (MRBI) poll found that the majority of respondents also felt that household tasks should be shared between spouses, while only a minority reported that this actually happened in their lives. Therefore it appears that, while family life, and especially motherhood, is seen as highly important for women, the combination of family responsibilities with work outside the home had come to be seen as normal for women by a majority of people in the 1990s.

The social base for the ideology of the anti-divorce lobby had, therefore, been eroded. Social, attitudinal, and legislative changes had brought about a situation where lone parents made up a significant, and no longer stigmatized, minority, where many married women with children worked outside the home and favored a sharing of responsibility in providing for the family and in domestic tasks between partners. The presentation of female dependency as either the ideal or the norm was no longer acceptable.

Many young women were undoubtedly influenced in this by the experiences of their own mothers, who had endured less than satisfactory marriages, including physical abuse, without any possibility of getting out of them. At the same time they admired their mothers' devotion to their children, and motherhood and strong family ties continue to be regarded as of great importance both to individual women and to society as a whole.

What has changed is how people perceive these values. For example, a survey of lone parents in a deprived area in north Dublin found that "a universal aspect" of the decision of young pregnant single women to keep their babies was the support of their mothers.[44] It also found that material assistance from relatives formed a significant part of their support system. In popular culture a picture of this kind of support was shown in the Roddy Doyle novel, *The Snapper,* later made into a film of the same name. Thus, in a subversion of the usual counterposition of "conventional" and "single-parent" families, the formation of a "single-parent family" was, to a large extent, dependent on the existence of a "conventional" family, often an extended one of grannies and aunts and uncles, as well as an immediate family of parents and siblings.

This raises a question that received little discussion in the course of the divorce debate. While "family values" were invoked by the anti-divorce lobby, and frequently cited by respondents in opinion polls as the reason for their opposition to divorce, there was little discussion as to what this meant, or what "the family" consisted of. The pro-divorce lobby also proclaimed its attachment to "the family," and there is no doubt that such an attachment is part of public opinion across the political spectrum. Indeed, the pro-divorce lobby invoked "the family" in support of its campaign, with the main government party, Fine Gael, using a poster showing a woman alone with children, and posing the question "If she was your daughter, would you give her a second chance?"

As statistics and a growing volume of sociological data show, the family is changing in Ireland. However, the extent to which the nuclear family—two parents and a number of children, an autonomous unit in society supported by a working man—was ever the norm is debatable. In the 1940s and '50s, looked to nostalgically by those who promote this view, large numbers of people did not marry at all, and Ireland had one of the lowest, and latest, marriage rates in Europe, and therefore a very low rate of family formation. This means that today, one in four elderly men and one in five elderly women are single.[45] Social welfare was woefully inadequate, and widowhood often brought destitution. When a parent died, children were placed in orphanages, which, it has recently been revealed, were harsh, unloving, and sometimes abusive. Emigration often divided families, with the father emigrating, leaving his family behind, and usually (though not always) sending money home to support them. The family was then, to a great extent, a single-parent family, with all responsibility resting on the mother. Other family members assisted where they could, and the role of the extended family was important.

Solidarity among family members, the support of parents, siblings, uncles, and aunts, and, indeed, the wider community, were all necessary to survival, and were also an essential part of social life. (Of course the family could also be repressive and claustrophobic, and many emigrated to escape it.) But far from the norm was a cosy, idealized and autonomous nuclear family consisting of two parents and a number of children. Therefore, the changing form of the Irish family over the past twenty years to encompass lone parent families and, with the increase in marriage breakdown, step-families, has not involved a major break with "family values." Since individuals can still call on solidarity from parents—especially mothers—and from siblings and the broader network of the extended family, the family remains of central importance, a source of strength and support that is widely valued.

Social and demographic change, rather than ideological challenge to the anti-divorce arguments, led to the narrow victory for the proponents of change. But these changes have occurred without much discussion of their implications for the role of women or for public policy. Public policy has tended to respond to the latest problem in a piecemeal fashion, without giving any thought to the long-term implications, although the recently established Commission on the Family might present a coherent policy.

The divorce campaign revealed the poverty of the thinking on the side of the government, which had proposed the constitutional change. It was obvious that the anti-divorce campaigners had a clear vision of the kind of society they wanted, the desired role of women in it, and the need to subordinate individual happiness to the presumed social stability provided by indissoluble marriage. But it was equally obvious that the government did not.

As Irish society changes—with the grip of religion weakening, the growth in male unemployment, the rise in female employment, and the fundamental shift in sexual mores and attitudes toward personal rights and liberties—a huge vacuum appears at the level of public policy and official ideology. At the moment the only thing that appears to fill it is the consumer-driven ideology of Western capitalism, with its lack of concern for the vulnerable in society and its insensitivity to the social solidarity that holds society together. The divorce debate, and the high "No" vote recorded, showed the deep unease that exists with this vision of the future and the widespread desire to stem its advance. But the inability of the government or any of the major political parties to marry their support for constitutional change with a vision of society that would combine individual rights with support for social and family solidarity leaves the future development of family policy in Ireland uncharted territory, where the only maps are the ones provided by those who still promote female dependency.

Notes

1. Donald Taylor Black, *Hearts and Minds* documentary, Radio Telefis Eireann, 13 December 1995.

2. Ibid.

3. While regular attendance at religious services is still important for almost 80 percent of the population, this number falls dramatically in deprived areas and among the young.

4. Council of Europe, *Recent Demographic Developments in Europe 1995,* 149. Births outside marriage accounted for 22 percent of births in 1995. This shows an increase of over 2 percent since 1993, when it was 19.8.

5. Ibid. This is a fall of about 36 percent since 1980, when it was 3.24. It is also below the replacement level of 2.1.

6. In 1993 there was a scandal concerning a priest, Father Brendan Smyth, who had systematically and extensively abused children, and whose extradition was sought from the Republic to face charges in the North; and in 1995 it was revealed that some members of the Sisters of Mercy had systematically physically abused children in orphanages run by the order.

7. Mags O'Brien, ed., *Divorce: Facing the Issues of Marital Breakdown* (Dublin: Basement Press, 1995), 22.

8. *The Right to Remarry: A Government Information Paper on the Divorce Referendum* (Dublin: Stationery Office, 1995), 5.

9. Second Commission on the Status of Women, *Report to the Government* (Dublin: Stationery Office, 1993), 29.

10. This was not sufficient for her election, however. The Irish system of voting, proportional representation, allows voters to vote for candidates in the order of their choice. If their first choice is not elected and is eliminated from the count, the vote is transferred to the second choice on the ballot paper, and so on, until it contributes to someone being elected.

11. "The Onward March of Irish Feminism," *Response* 14, 2 (Summer 1995): 19.

12. Ibid., 3 (Autumn 1995), 23.

13. M. Hamilton, *The Case against Divorce* (Dublin: Lir Press, 1995), 20.

14. Ibid., 59.

15. Ibid., 60.

16. "Report Faulted for Ignoring Women in the Home," *Irish Times* (30 March 1995).

17. Public Policy Institute, *Woman Scorned* (1995), 11–12.

18. Ibid., 44.

19. Ibid., 47.

20. Ibid., 59.

21. William Binchy, press conference of Anti-Divorce Campaign, Davenport Hotel, 21 November 1995. Comments noted by the author.

22. Public Policy Institute of Ireland, *Submission to Oireachtas Committee on the Family* (May 1995), 2.

23. *The Right to Remarry*, 6, 7.

24. John Bruton, press statement, 15 November 1995.

25. John Bruton, interview on *The Week,* RTE Radio, 19 November 1995.

26. William Duncan, The Case for Divorce in the Irish Republic, ICCL, Dublin, 1979.

27. Ibid., 32.

28. In February 1992 news broke of an injunction being granted to the government in a closed session of the High Court to prevent a 14-year-old girl, a victim of rape by a family friend, from going to England for an abortion. The ensuing controversy put the recently passed anti-abortion amendment to the Constitution (through which the injunction was granted) under close scrutiny. Within weeks the Supreme Court had reversed the High Court decision on the grounds that the girl's life was in danger because of the suicidal tendencies provoked by her condition. This qualification of the anti-abortion clause in the Constitution remains law in Ireland although a campaign exists for a new referendum to tighten up this "loophole."

29. "Bleak Picture of Marriage Given at Divorce Meetings," *Irish Times* (30 September 1995).

30. Joe McCarroll, "26 Reasons Why the Divorce Amendment Should be Rejected" (talk at Anti-Divorce Campaign, Cork, 4 October 1995).

31. Ibid., 3.

32. Ibid., 4.

33. Women's Aid, Press Release, 2 November 1995.

34. National Women's Council, "Women's Council Endorses Yes Vote on Restrictive Divorce Proposal," press release, 2 November 1995.

35. T. Fahey and M. Lyons, eds., *Marital Breakdown and Family Law in Ireland,* (Dublin: Oak Tree Press, in association with the Economic and Social Research Institute, Dublin, 1995), 52.

36. Ibid., 66.

37. V. Richardson, "Reconciliation of Family Life and Working Life," in *Irish Family Studies: Selected Papers,* ed. Imelda Colgan McCarthy (Dublin: Family Studies Centre, University College, 1995), 131.

38. Ibid., 132.

39. Department of Social Welfare, *Statistical Information on Social Welfare Services* (1993).

40. Council of Europe, *Recent Demographic Developments in Europe* (1995), 149.

41. There were some 70,000 recipients of the adult dependent allowance among those on unemployment benefit and unemployment assistance in 1993.

The vast majority of these recipients were wives of unemployed men. Department of Social Welfare, *Statistical Information on Social Welfare Services,* 1993, 7.

42. Marketing Research Bureau of Ireland [MRBI], *Mna na hEireann: An MRBI Perspective on Women in Irish Society Today* (Dublin, 1992).

43. *Irish Independent,* 1995.

44. A. McCashin, *Lone Mothers in Ireland* (Dublin: Oak Tree Press in association with Combat Poverty Agency, 1996), 131.

45. T. Fahey, Economic and Social Research Institute, talk given to National Economic and Social Forum, Dublin, 29 April 1997. Reported by the author as "Time mothers gave to children gave the ground for boom, gathering told," *Irish Times,* 30 April 1997, 3.

Language, Stories, Healing

I GREW UP in Dublin, speaking only English, but Irish was there around the edges. *"An bhfuil na leabaí réidh?"* my father used to ask my mother in the evening, when my sisters and I were small: "Are the beds ready?" I didn't know then, and I don't suppose he ever knew, that the plural of *leaba,* "bed," is not *leabaí* but *leapacha.* He had grown up in Foxford, Co. Mayo, an old garrison town whose people prided themselves on their good English and felt little in common with the Irish-speakers who still lived in the surrounding countryside. My mother's Irish was better, but at her national school in Co. Cavan, just across the road from the farm where she grew up, she had been taught a northern dialect that few people in Dublin understood. Dad used his smattering of Irish to communicate with her in code and start the process of putting us to bed without alerting us. She answered him in English, and it worked for a while.

At school, Irish was compulsory—and confusing. What did it mean, to call this set of unfamiliar sounds and meanings Irish? We lived in Ireland; we were Irish. England was elsewhere, the other. So surely the language we spoke all day should be called Irish? Learning what the school called Irish was easy, though, with endless repetition; and sometimes it was fun. Like learning to dance, it was a series of clever tricks; paces I could be put through. It was rhymes and spellings and tables to chant in comforting unison; a special language for that place: *"Dún an doras,"* "Close the door," *"Téigpií a chodladh,"* "All go to sleep." Fifty children put their heads down on their folded arms and pretended to be asleep. Nothing that happened in Irish was real.

We learned about the work of the blacksmith, haymaking, a day on the bog; our schoolbooks were full of rural images. But where we lived there were no donkeys or turf bogs, and no potato fields, although a woman who lived near us did keep hens. We played on a concrete-paved lane behind our row of redbrick houses and hit tennis balls against the peeling paint of garage doors, or lost them in the nettles. We were three miles from the center of Dublin, but farmers drove flocks of sheep down from the mountains along our main road, and the local butchers drove cattle up the same road to their slaughter-houses.

Like my parents, our teachers had grown up in small towns or in the country and still pined for things rural, or at least presented them-selves to children as doing so. They showed us Dublin as a hostile place, makeshift and artificial, where we would always have to be on our guard. Products of De Valera's Ireland, they warned us about the corruptions of the modern world embodied in everything that came from England. Religion and Irish were to be talismans against all that.

At home there was no talk of ideology, but my parents loved the country. Reserved, shy, and apolitical, my father was much moved by the romantic nationalism that endowed landscapes of grass and mountain and water with mystery and meaning, and denied the reality of the urban. He chafed at the difficulty of maintaining a family in lower-middle-class respectability in Dublin, and he remembered his own childhood as a time of walking and cycling the country roads around Foxford, fishing the River Moy, and rowing on Loughs Conn and Cullen. His accent changed when he pronounced those place-names: became rounder and fuller as he seemed to taste the word "Lough" on his tongue.

My mother made bread every day, marmalade from Seville oranges every January, jam every summer. She walked briskly and enjoyed fresh air. She didn't want to talk about her childhood. Memories were quickly dismissed. All our grandparents were dead, and I was hungry for stories.

Sometimes on Sundays our family went out for picnics, to the sea-side or the mountains. Sitting on a rug beside the big reservoir, Dad told us about the valley that had been flooded to store water for the city, and he explained that its name, Poulaphouca, *Poll an Phúca*, meant "the *Púca*'s water-hole." The *Púca* was a sort of boogeyman, he told us, who lived around there somewhere. We were eating sand-wiches, our backs to some blackberry bushes, and I can still see their curving, prickly branches against the blue sky as I looked back over my shoulder, fascinated and terrified. Poulaphouca had been a valley where people lived and farmed. Now it was lost and gone forever, overwhelmed by the wateriness of its name, but the mysterious *Púca* still haunted it. Or maybe I have invented those blackberry bushes.

We did pick blackberries for jam in late summer every year, but much later, studying folklore, I learned that, though the *Púca* is man-shaped in my father's native Mayo, in other parts of the country it is a sort of horse that fouls the blackberries every year at Halloween, making them unfit to eat.

Words and names in Irish were doorways into stories. Ardee in County Louth was *Áth Fhirdia*: the place where the hero Cú Chulainn killed his boyhood companion Ferdia in single combat at the ford. Kildare was *Cill Dara,* the oak church built by St. Brigid in the sixth century. These stories were in our school reading books, which I read from cover to cover as soon as I got them. Children's books were scarce. Whenever I was sick in winter, I spent the days in my parents' bedroom. My mother brought me hot drinks and clean handkerchiefs —old, soft worn ones that had been my father's—and I spread my coloring books and jigsaw across the double bed. Left alone, I used to explore the bookcase, full of fly-blown hardbacks that no one ever read, and copies of *Hobbies Weekly,* bound and covered in wallpaper by my father. I read the plans for model aeroplanes and wooden toys; I read *David Copperfield* twice, and James Thurber's *The White Deer* many times. I read incomprehensible novels on thick spongy paper in the uniform hardback covers of The Book Club, and then I found *The Golden Legends of the Gael,* by Maud Joynt, and I read and read and reread it. It was printed on cheap wartime paper, already brittle and yellow when I was seven. I wrote my name on it, my address and my age, and when its cover came off I mended it with the bright blue sticky tape that Dad had brought home from somewhere.

The Golden Legends of the Gael was just as good as Grimm's *Fairy Tales,* with shape-changing, color and magic, love, sorrow, and battles; but it was about Ireland: about kings and queens, poets and warriors who lived here long ago, and it told the stories with a wealth of vivid detail that our school readers sadly lacked. Much later I learned that Maud Joynt had been a celticist, a contemporary of William Butler Yeats, and that the stories I had read were scholarly translations of medieval manuscript sagas.

One of them told about Nuada, a king who lost an arm in battle. The physician, Dian Cécht, made him an artificial arm of silver, which could imitate the movements of a real one, and from it he was known as Nuada Silverarm. But Miach and Airmed, son and daughter of

Dian Cécht, were even more skilled than their father. They could tell by the smoke that rose from a house whether anyone was sick within, and what remedy was needed. Miach found the severed arm and reconnected it, using the words of a special healing charm, but this made his father so insanely jealous that he murdered Miach. From his grave grew 365 herbs, one for every joint and sinew of his body, and Airmed collected them and arranged them on her cloak according to their healing properties. Again, jealousy made Dian Cécht violent, and he scattered the herbs. The text adds that this is the reason nobody now knows the virtues of plants unless the Holy Spirit has taught them.

Lost and gone forever: the knowledge of herbs; the farms of Poulaphouca; the heroes of old. The elegiac tone was everywhere. Or maybe I was listening out for it. Eldest of my family, living in an old house, with few other children as neighbors, I lived a lot in books and acquired a taste for gloom quite early.

The story of Airmed and Miach had said that Airmed's knowledge was lost. The only way to learn things now was to be taught by the Holy Spirit. Many of those Old Irish tales take that attitude: written by monks, they are ambivalent about the pre-Christian traditions they relate. Their message is hard on girls and women: it makes us troublemakers, irrelevant, defeated. The Holy Spirit was on the side of men, of schools and churches. "Unless a man be born again," our catechism told us, "of water and the Holy Ghost, he shall not enter into the Kingdom of Heaven." So it was not enough to be born of woman. Born a girl, you had no chance at all.

Outside school and that book of *Golden Legends,* the written word dealt almost exclusively with England. The Enid Blyton mysteries and boarding-school books we borrowed from the library were set there, and so were the comics: the *Bunty* and the *Judy,* the *Beano* and the *Dandy.* Nowhere in them were children taught by nuns, as we were. Nowhere was Ireland or Irish mentioned. Instead children learned French, from teachers called *Ma'm'selle;* they drank ginger beer; they met the vicar, and the vicar's wife, and helmet-wearing policemen called P. C. Something-or-other. No priests, no *gardaí,* no changing baby brother's nappies, no going to mass, no first communion, no going to the toilet. Instead there were owls hooting, and hedgehogs

drinking saucers of milk, and girls learning ballet and grooming po-
nies.

Stories set in Ireland were few and far between, and invariably
rural. To be properly Irish, it seemed, you should be barefoot, poor,
and pious, and preferably the child of a widow. The short stories of
Patrick Pearse were all about such children, and when we read some
of them in Irish in our last year of primary school, it seemed that
where we lived was a frighteningly narrow place. On one side was
England, a collage of godless, sooty factories, great houses, and impos-
sibly snobbish boarding schools; but rural Ireland was equally exotic:
sunlit and numinous, green and blackberried, forgiving and pure. The
further west one went, the purer it got, apparently, so that the Conamara *Gaeltacht,* or Irish-speaking district, of Pearse's stories was a
place where being good was easy, and love was everywhere. I wanted
to go there.

A year after starting secondary school, I spent a month in Conamara, at a government-subsidized "Irish College," a summer language
school, and found that nobody was barefoot. This was not, after all,
the simple romantic life of Pearse's stories, but it did have another
kind of magic.

We stayed in the dormitories of a boarding school and attended
classes in Irish every morning, learning vocabulary and some grammar
by memorizing songs and stories, blessings and curses. In the after-
noons we walked in straggling gangs to swim at a beach two or three
miles away, constructing elaborate friendships and flirtations as we
went, and wearing holes in our thin summer shoes. In the evenings we
dressed up, in our own or each other's clothes, put on what makeup
we could find, and walked again, to the hall in the village for a nightly
céilí. Every summer as a teenager I went back to Irish College. We
were away from our parents; away from the rigid decorum of our
single-sex schools; away from paved streets and brick walls and the
disapproving eyes of adults. The teachers who supervised us were
young, and mostly male, and they were on holiday too. Like us, they
played ball games, and swam and sang and danced, and when thir-
teen-and fifteen-year-olds fell in love, as they did every year, and went
everywhere hand-in-hand, they smiled.

That combination of fresh air, sunshine, and adolescent sexuality was inseparable from the air that smelled of seaweed and turf smoke, and the shadows the little flat-bottomed clouds cast on the landscape of green and brown and blue; and its language was Irish. Back at school in Dublin, the Irish-language syllabus was as boring as ever—pallid and pedestrian by comparison with English and History—but pronouncing its complicated consonants and seductive diphthongs the Conamara way, I could imagine myself back in a world of stone walls, beaches and grass, long songs sung unaccompanied, placenames packed with stories, and adults who let us dance till we were red in the face and drenched in sweat, instead of treating us as children or nuisances.

Nostalgia for summer hooked neatly into the earlier escapism of the *Golden Legends of the Gael*. The cold Holy Spirit androgyny, which school seemed to require as a corollary to cleverness, contrasted strongly with the frank acceptance in the *Gaeltacht* that a female body could house a mind. The resourceful Airmed with her cloakful of healing herbs seemed more at home there than in Dublin.

THE RIGID polarization of my imagined environment into materialistic Dublin and spiritual *Gaeltacht* didn't survive the sixties. About the time I started university, new violence in Northern Ireland was helping to discredit the romantic nationalism I had grown up with. I did Celtic Studies with a few like-minded souls, but other people our age who rejected the authoritarianism of their schooling were turning firmly away from Irish tradition as they immersed themselves in left-wing politics.

We loved our subject: reveled in the study of early Irish, picking texts apart as though with scalpels; but often we found ourselves typecast as owlish, irrelevant, and reactionary. At parties people would hear the word "Irish" and grow glassy-eyed, visibly making assumptions about our politics, social attitudes, and religious beliefs. For a long time too, any identification with Irish was suspect, at home and abroad. Friends whose passports showed their names in Irish were detained at British ports for days and nights without explanation or apology.

Revisionism threw out quite a few healthy cultural babies with the ideological bathwater. Most painfully for me, feminism and an interest in Irish appeared to be mutually exclusive. The majority of the women doing such exciting work in challenging the authoritarian structures of our society didn't want to know about Irish. They associated it with the most repressive and fatalistic aspects of our culture. Almost axiomatically, the *Gaeltacht,* so often invoked by patriarchal nationalists, symbolized all the forces that had kept women subservient to men.

Peig Sayers, the Kerry storyteller and verbal artist whose autobiography had been on the school curriculum for generations, became a joke. Invariably photographed wearing a shawl, she was resoundingly rejected as a role model for modern women. Her independence, her strength, wit, and insight, might almost never have been. Airmed, spreading her cloak and arranging the healing herbs upon it, was never mentioned.

Jumping through the hoops of scholarship, I resigned myself to this division. On one side I kept the rigorous study of language and the meticulous reading of texts; on the other side were identification with women, my own sense of self. But it is not possible to stay divided like that, and as I grow older, I find myself less and less willing to separate the things I believe in from the things I know. My love of stories makes a sort of bridge, heals the rift. I work on traditions about women and girls: I read the oral poetry and stories of the Irish language, listening for the voices of real women. I write fiction that tries to make an insistent account of individual experience sound through the neutral, laconic narratives of folktale, or through the registers of English spoken unselfconsciously in Ireland.

We have urgent need of stories in Ireland at the moment, as our society comes to terms with painful memories. All at once, it seems, we are trying to cope with the famine of the mid-nineteenth century, when a million people died of fever or starvation and another million emigrated; with twenty five years of violence in Northern Ireland, followed by the sudden possibility of peace, and then more violence; and with a heartbreaking series of revelations about betrayal of trust, about domestic violence, and about cruelties secretly inflicted on women and children. The old narratives will no longer serve, and it is not just politicians and journalists who are struggling to make sense of it all. Religion used to offer answers and explanations, but more and more it is artists who confront the broken certainties that lie all around. The literature and oral tradition of the Irish language were

used for so long in the service of self-righteous patriarchal nationalism
that for years the most creative and radical minds in the country
wanted nothing to do with them. But that is changing. Filmmakers,
painters, and poets are finding ways of expressing what was done and
what was felt, using the threads of what we already had, but could no
longer see. More and more, as silenced voices speak, the need for
different kinds of language is being acknowledged.

Irish is a language that was almost lost. A hundred years ago,
children were sent to school with tally sticks on strings around their
necks. Every time a child spoke Irish, her stick was marked with a
notch by teacher or parent, and punishment doled out accordingly. In
this century, memories of that pain persist. Some revivalists expressed
their love of the Irish language and its literature as contempt for
English; some teachers enforced its study with just as much cruelty as
had been used to stamp it out. Many of those whose vision of the
world was broader retaliated by repudiating everything Gaelic.

For a hundred years after the famine, Irish people behaved as
though they could afford only one language; as though they had to
choose between Irish and English: material poverty translated into
cultural frugality. One book I read as a child told how a fox whose
leg was caught in a trap would gnaw off its own foot in order to be
free. The cruelty perpetrated in the name of language on the children
who wore tally sticks was that sort of desperate measure: a grim
hacking off of part of the cultural body; a self-mutilation designed to
end a greater pain.

"All their wars are merry, and all their songs are sad," wrote G. K.
Chesterton, and indeed there is no shortage of sentimentality in what
passes for Irish oral tradition. But alongside and underneath the facile
expression of sadness runs an idiom that knows about the experience
of pain, and about living through and overcoming it rather than wal-
lowing in it. In my own work I come back again and again to one
story, which I give here in my own translation. It was told in Irish in
1938 by a master storyteller, Éamon a Búrc from Conamara, recorded
and written down by a professional folklore collector, preserved in an
archive, and published in a scholarly edition more than forty years
later.[1]

A Young Woman Taken by the Fairies

Long ago here in Conamara there was a couple who married. They had two sons and a daughter: two fine men, and no woman in the country was more beautiful than the girl when she grew up. One day, one of the young men went out to the hill to cut a load of heather, and as he set about cutting, he noticed very fine heather growing on a cliff. Up he went to the top, cutting away, when suddenly a voice said out of the cliff, "What are you doing there?"

"Cutting heather," said the young man.

"I'm telling you," said the thing in the cliff—the person—"you'd better leave it, if you know what's good for you!"

He stopped cutting. But on his way home with the load on his back he tripped, and a woman's voice spoke behind him:

"You've not heard the last of this, you know. We're not finished with you by any means. You've let the rain in on us from every side and left us in a terrible state."

He threw down his load and ran, leaving it there. He came home and told his story. When his father and mother heard what had happened, they said he had had no business staying in that place once he heard the first voice.

"I left the load behind," he said, "right where I fell, where the woman spoke to me."

"Well, then," said the father and mother, "leave it there!"

And he did; they never moved it.

Well and good. They had cows out on the hill, and every morning they used to go out to milk them, the sons taking turns. Then one day they were both away from home on some business, something they had to do one day. And the day was growing late, evening was falling, and the father told the young woman to go out and milk the cows. She didn't want to. She said it was getting late.

"Hurry up," said the mother. "Don't let it get any later."

The sun was still fairly high. She took her can and her *naggin* measure—that's what they used in those days—and out she went. The place she came to was a sort of marsh, boggy marginal land, with the cows standing on the side of a grassy little hill in the middle. She put down the can, left it there and set off, milking the cows into the naggin. Whenever the naggin was full she would carry it over and pour it into the tin can. She went on like that, naggin by naggin, until the can was full: a great big can full to the top with milk.

She turned around to drive the cows ahead of her, and suddenly she couldn't see the can; she had no idea where in God's name she was. She kept stumbling; evening was coming; the day had darkened up with fog, and if she was there till now she couldn't find the can, or the naggin, from the moment she left it out of her hand. She went on until night fell, falling and stumbling in the black darkness among hills and mountains and bogs, and going up to her waist in rivers, with no idea where in God's name she was, until she saw a light in the distance:

"I declare to goodness," she said, "that must be someone's house. I'd be better to head there than die here, for certainly if I keep walking like this, taking the knocks I'm taking, and wet to the skin as I am, there'll be no life left in me by morning."

She made for the house where she saw the light, barely able to move her legs one in front of the other, her clothes were so wet and so full of mud. When she entered the house, she saw people moving around, and food and drink on a table set in the middle of the floor; a red-haired woman serving the food, and a black-haired woman by her side. But as soon as the black-haired woman saw the young woman approaching, she came to the door and told her not to eat any food whatsoever that might be offered to her until she herself divided it and gave it to her:

"For the sake of all you ever saw or ever will see, don't you taste a bite of the food the red-haired woman is serving till I come and tell you to eat. You can eat then and it will do you no harm."

When the young woman entered the house she was called by her own name and surname and made heartily welcome. And it wasn't long before a fine woman like a queen came in from the other room, a beautiful woman, and she too made her welcome and ordered the red-haired woman to set out a supper for this woman who had just come in. The red-haired woman set to work. But while the food was being prepared, the black-haired woman quietly shook her head to tell her she shouldn't go to the table or eat anything. The red-haired woman laid out the food and told her to sit down. She said she wasn't hungry, that she wouldn't eat anything until morning.

"That's very strange behaviour," said this red-haired woman. "Eat.

It's good for you. Everyone knows that a person who's been walking since morning needs food by now."

"I don't," said the earthly woman, "I can't eat anything."

The mistress came in again—the mistress of the fairy fort, for that's where she was—and told the woman to set out food for her.

"I've already set it out for her," said the red-haired woman, "but she wouldn't eat."

"Set it out for her again until she eats," said a big fat woman who had come in from the other room. "My instructions. Tell her she has to eat it."

The red-haired woman set food out for her, but she said she wouldn't eat it; she wasn't hungry and she couldn't possibly eat.

"You may as well eat," said the red-haired woman. "Talking won't do any good. You have to eat; it's sinful for a person to fast when there's so much food and drink here for anyone who wants it."

"I don't want it, thank you very much and long life to you," said the earthly woman.

The red-haired woman kept at her for a while after that, trying to persuade her to eat.

"No," the young woman kept saying, "I can't."

And every time the red-haired woman ordered the earthly woman to eat, the dark-haired woman would pass through the other side of the house and shake her head, telling her not to. Finally, when she still wouldn't eat, the red-haired woman gave up:

"Maybe if Bríd set out food for her she'd eat."

Bríd was the dark-haired woman.

"Set out food for her," said the queen of the fairy fort, putting her head out the door of the other room. "You, Bríd."

Bríd got up and set food and drink before her. She ate then, and when she had eaten she felt better. But Bríd—the woman they called Bríd—whispered to her as she sat at the table:

"For the sake of all you ever saw or ever will see, don't taste any bite in this place but what I set in front of you, for if you do you'll never be able to leave."

Well and good. The next day the same thing happened. The red-haired woman set out food for her but she wouldn't eat. And when the next day came and she didn't come home to her family, they went to the hill to look for her, but found no sign of her. All that night and all the next day her two brothers searched. They found the can full of milk on the patch of grass on the bog, with the naggin laid down beside it. Of course they took the milk home, I suppose, though they hadn't much interest in it, they were so upset about their sister. They didn't know where in the name of God she'd gone. Six days that week they searched for her, every day that she was missing, until they decided she must have done away with herself—thrown herself into a lake or river and drowned. There was no sign of her anywhere. But all the time she was held in the fairy fort. Six days and six nights, and they didn't stop or sleep all that time, day or night, but mourned and searched for her all over.

That went on until the sixth night. She was kept indoors, and while she was inside, Bríd—the woman they called Bríd in the fairy fort— was standing at the door. She saw a man approaching.

"Goodness," she said, "here's Seán Rua coming."

And the earthly woman didn't know who Seán Rua was, but in he came. And who was he—he'd been dead a certain length of time— but a first cousin of her own! He came into the fairy fort and stood with his back to the fire, looking at his first cousin who was being kept there.

"What brought you here?" he asked, taking her by the shoulder and shoving her toward the door.

She told him she didn't know.

"Get out right now," he said, "and go home."

"She will not," said the red-haired woman.

The queen herself came out and told the young woman not to leave, but she said she would, and a fight broke out then between Seán Rua, with Bríd helping him, and those others. They were killing each other.

"We'd better send her home," said the queen.

They grabbed her and threw her out onto the ground. Seán Rua and Bríd went with her some distance from the house, until she was fairly close to her own home. But no sooner had Seán Rua and Bríd left her than she fell down right beside the house and a sharp spine, like a big needle, was driven into her knee. She kept walking, though her knee was very sore, and sure enough, she made it home. When she came in, she didn't mention it, but they asked what had happened to her, and blessed her and praised her and gave her butter and salt and every other sort of thing they could. She told them the story from start to finish and their conversation didn't touch on falls or injuries or anything of that kind from then until morning.

But when morning came there was a terrible pain in her knee, and by the next afternoon it was so bad she couldn't stand on the floor. By the third day she had to stay in bed altogether; they had to make up a bed for her by the fire; people had to nurse her, while she moaned and screamed—screeching at the top of her voice with pain.

The knee swelled. Doctors came to her. The priest came to her, trying to cure her. They tried everything: plasters and poultices and herbs, but nothing could be done for her, until she'd been there three months and the leg had swelled so much and grown so big that no one could lift it. It was swollen right up to the top of her thigh.

She spent almost a year lying on her back in bed, screaming all the time with pain. No one could lay a finger on her she screamed so much with pain and agony, until one night an old woman—an old beggar-woman—came in and sat by the fire.

"Is it any harm to ask what ails the woman who's screaming?" she asked.

"No harm at all," said the mother of the young woman, and told her what I've told you: all that had happened to her, how she had been taken into the fairy fort and made her way home, and how she had gone out milking in the first place.

"Hm," said the old woman.

"And the first thing she felt was when she fell down and something like a sharp spine went up into her knee and the knee swelled up. There's no cure for her, and I'm afraid there won't be until she dies."

"If it was daylight," said the old woman, "I could do something. We'll have to wait till daylight."

Next morning, as soon as day dawned, the old woman got up and went out before the sun was up, and whatever secret communication she had with herbs, she went out and the herb told her—she brought it in between two fingers—it would work.

"Now," said the old woman, "off you go to where the bonfire is" —it was around St. John's Eve, so there was a bonfire in the village. She told them to go to the bonfire site and look for some trace of bone, even ashes, and to bring home some of the burnt embers from the fire:[2]

"And mix them with this herb here and put them on her knee

between two cloths," said the old woman. "If that won't cure her, I don't know what will."

The mother and the two brothers went out and did everything as the old woman had told them. The old woman had collected the herb for them, so they mixed up the bones that were burnt to ashes and embers from the bonfire with the herb, wrapped it in cloth, and laid it all between two cloths on her knee.

"Don't move that now," said the old woman, "until tomorrow morning. Whatever pain or torment she suffers until then, don't lay a finger on her, and I guarantee she'll be healed by morning as soon as the sun rises. Goodbye to you now," she said. "I'm leaving."

"Oh," said the woman of the house, "you can't be."

"I am," she said. "I'm not staying here any longer."

She went out.

"You know," said the father and the sons, "you should give that old woman something."

But when the woman of the house went out after her a few minutes later, to pay her something, she couldn't see her anywhere.

"I don't know where in the name of God she went," she said.

But from the moment the plaster, or poultice, was put on the young woman's knee, there never was such horror under the sun as the pain she felt, or the way she screamed until day broke. They did as the old woman had said however. Before sunrise in the morning they went to her, and when they took away the rags and lifted off the plaster that morning, a needle as long as your finger, or longer, came out of her knee along with the cloth, for every man to see. From that moment on she improved. By the end of a week she could sit by the fire; at the end of a month she could move around the house, and after three months she was as well as she had ever been.

That's no lie. It happened here in Conamara in the old days.

The blessings of God and the Church on the souls of the dead, and may we and the company be seventeen hundred thousand times better a year from tonight![3]

I AM FASCINATED and moved by this depiction of a young woman's unhappiness: her ill-treatment by adults, her bewilderment and pain, her resistance expressed through rejection of food, and her final release through the wisdom of an older woman, a stranger to her family, who knows the virtues of herbs. I read it as metaphor for things that can occur in any age, in any society, whether rural or urban. It happens that the language of this story is Irish, and that its setting is Conamara: landscape of small lakes and hilly bog land. Its terms of reference, often trivialized and denigrated in literate culture, are familiar in Irish oral tradition: fairy people live near humans, hidden and unseen, often underground, and if they are offended, they will seek revenge.[4] They abduct children and young women, sometimes leaving changelings in their place. Their world is seductive and rich, but illusory, and anyone who eats their food is lost to normal life forever.

Stories like these deal with ambivalence and paradox, with transitions in human life and situations that are beyond human control. Their protagonists stumble into a world where everything is other, and emerge either mutilated or enriched. Fairy legends like this one are meditations on change, reassuringly rooted in the past. Their association with intimately known landscapes helps listeners to remember, and often to believe them, yet their psychology is timeless. Many, if not most, are about women and children.

For me, the compelling strangeness of this story and others like it is one of the rewards of knowing Irish. The vivid descriptions of a hidden world where the normal is turned inside out give access to a psychic and imaginative richness that is specially valuable because so little known. As Irish society painfully confronts an avalanche of revelations of child sex abuse, incest, and teenage pregnancies hidden and repudiated, stories like this can perhaps offer the possibility of healing.

Notes

1. Told in Irish by Éamon a Búrc, Cill Chiaráin, Carna, Co. Galway, and recorded on Ediphone by Liam Mac Coisdeala (29 September 1938). Mac Coisdeala's transcription, entitled "Bean Óg a Tugadh sa mBruíon," is in the Irish Folklore Collection archive at University College Dublin (ms. IFC 529: 304–317). Edited by Peadar Ó Ceannabháin in his *Éamon a Búrc: Scéalta* (Dublin: An Clóchomhar, 1983), 267–73, it is here translated by Angela Bourke. See also my "Fairies and Anorexia: Nuala Ní Dhomhnaill's Amazing Grass," in *Proceedings of the Harvard Celtic Colloquium* 13 (1993): 25–38.

2. For magical uses of embers from a bonfire, compare Mary Carbery, *The Farm by Lough Gur* (1937; reprint, Cork: Mercier, 1973), 163.

3. For permission to publish the translation of Éamon a Búrc's story, I

thank Professor Bo Almqvist, Department of Irish Folklore, University College, Dublin, where Liam Mac Coisdeala's manuscripts are held, and Peadar Ó Ceannabháin, editor of the Irish text. A somewhat shorter version of this essay first appeared in French translation as "Langue, Histoires et Guérison," in *Désirs d'Irlande,* ed. Catherine de St. Phalle and Paul Brennan (Arles: Actes Sud, 1996), 63–75.

4. For a discussion of fairy-belief in oral narrative as a vernacular cognitive system, see my essays "The Virtual Reality of Irish Fairy Legend," *Éire/ Ireland* 31, 1 and 2 (1996):7–25; and "Reading a Woman's Death: Colonial Text and Oral Tradition in Nineteenth-Century Ireland," *Feminist Studies* 21, 3 (Fall 1995): 553–86.

Notes on Contributors

GUINN BATTEN is assistant professor of English at Washington University in St. Louis. Her book, *The Orphaned Imagination: Melancholia and English Romantic Poetry*, is forthcoming from Duke University Press. She has also published several articles on contemporary Irish poetry, and is an advisory editor for Wake Forest University Press's Irish Poetry series.

ANGELA BOURKE is a statutory lecturer in the Department of Modern Irish, and director of the M. Phil. Program in Irish studies at University College, Dublin. She has also taught at Harvard University, Boston College, and the University of Minnesota. She is the author of *Caoineadh na dTrí Muire: Téama na Páise i bhFilíocht Bhéil na Gaeilge* (1983), as well as a short-story collection, *By Salt Water* (1996), and numerous articles and reviews.

ANTHONY BRADLEY is professor of English at the University of Vermont. He is author of a critical introduction to Yeats's plays, *William Butler Yeats* (1980), and editor of *Contemporary Irish Poetry* (2nd edition, 1988). He has also written numerous essays and reviews, and is at present working on a study of literature and politics in contemporary Ireland.

CAROL COULTER is a journalist with the *Irish Times*. She won the National Media Award for Campaigning Journalism in 1990 and is the author of *The Hidden Tradition: Women, Feminism and Nationalism in Ireland* (1993); *Web of Punishment* (1991), and *Ireland between the First and the Third Worlds* (1989). She is also a general editor of the magazine *The Irish Reporter* and is currently working on a book on the recent divorce referendum in Ireland.

ELIZABETH BUTLER CULLINGFORD is professor of English at the University of Texas at Austin and author of *Yeats, Ireland, and Fascism* (1981) and *Gender and History in Yeats's Love Poetry* (1993). She has written numerous articles on contemporary Irish poetry, drama, and culture, and is currently working on Irish film.

MARY E. DALY is chair of the Combined Departments of History at University College, Dublin, a member of the Royal Irish Academy and president of the Economic and Social History Society of Ireland. Her books include *Dublin, the Deposed Capital: A Social and Economic History, 1860–1914* (1984); *The Famine in Ireland* (1986); *Industrial Development and Irish National Identity, 1922–1939* (1992); *The Buffer State: The Historical Roots of the Department of the Environment* (1997), and *Women and Work in Ireland* (1997).

ADRIAN FRAZIER teaches at Union College, New York, and is the author of numerous articles on contemporary Irish poetry and the Irish Literary Revival. His *Behind the Scenes: Yeats, Horniman, and the Struggle for the Abbey Theatre* was published in 1990. He is writing a biography of George Moore for Yale University Press.

DILLON JOHNSTON is the founder and director of Wake Forest University Press, which publishes books by Irish and French poets. He is the author of *Irish Poetry after Joyce* (1985, revised 1997). Professor of English at Wake Forest University, he is currently working on a book entitled *The Economy of Modern British & Irish Poetry.*

MARGARET MACCURTAIN, former lecturer in Irish history, holds a Senior Honorary Fellowship in the Women's Education and Research Centre in University College, Dublin. A founding member of the Irish Association for Research in Women's History, she is co-editor and contributor to *Women in Irish History* (1978) and *Women in Modern Ireland* (1991). She is a contributing editor to *The Field Day Anthology of Irish Writing* (volume 4), to be published in 1998.

LUCY MCDIARMID is author of *Saving Civilization: Yeats, Eliot and Auden between the Wars* (1984), *Auden's Apologies for Poetry* (1990), and co-editor of *Lady Gregory: Selected Writings* (1995) and *High and Low Moderns: Literature and Culture 1889–1939* (1995). A former Guggenheim fellow, she is professor of English at Villanova University and president of the American Conference for Irish Studies (1997–99). The essay included here forms part of her next book, *The Irish Art of Controversy.*

MAUREEN MURPHY is professor of curriculum and teaching at Hofstra University, New York. She is the editor of Maire MacNeill's *Maire Rua, Lady of Leananeh* (1990), Sara Hyland's *I Call to the Eye of the Mind, A Memoir* (1996), and Asenath Nicholson's *Annals of the Famine in Ireland* (1997). She is working on a study of Irish domestic servants in the United States, to be called *Hope from the Ocean.* She is a former president of ACIS.

ANTOINETTE QUINN is a senior lecturer in the School of English and a member of the executive committee of the Centre for Women's Studies at Trinity College, Dublin. She is the author of *Patrick Kavanagh, Born-Again Romantic* (1991), editor of *Patrick Kavanagh: Selected Poems* (1996), and is currently completing a biography of Patrick Kavanagh. She has also published a number of essays on Irish women's writing.

CATHERINE B. SHANNON teaches Irish history at Westfield State College and the University of Massachusetts. She held a senior fellowship at the Institute of Irish Studies at Queen's University, Belfast, and is the author of *Arthur J. Balfour and Ireland, 1874–1922* (1988), and articles on Irish women. Active in Irish cultural organizations, she was the first woman to be president of the Charitable Irish Society of Boston, the oldest Irish organization in America.

MARYANN GIALANELLA VALIULIS is a lecturer in women's studies and academic coordinator of the Centre for Women's Studies at Trinity College, Dublin. She is the author of *Almost a Rebellion: The Irish Army Mutiny of 1924* (1985) and the award-winning *Portrait of a Revolutionary: General Richard Mulcahy and the Founding of the Irish Free State* (1992). She is currently completing a study of the reconstruction of gender ideology in the Irish Free State.

MARGARET WARD is a feminist historian specializing in studies of Irish women and nationalism and contemporary Irish feminism. She is the author of several books, including *Unmanageable Revolutionaries* (1983), and *Maud Gonne: A Life* (1990). Her latest book, *Hanna Sheehy-Skeffington: A Life,* is forthcoming from Attic Press. She is currently research fellow in history at Bath Spa University College.

Index

Addams, Jane, 68, 78, 79
AE. *See* Russell, George
Ahern, Nuala, 269
Akenson, Donald, 85, 96
Allen, Theodore W., 185 n. 75
Allgood, Sara, 43
Andrews, J. H., 183 n. 39
Armstrong, Laura, 29
Arnold, Matthew, 160, 162, 163
Arsenius, Mother, 105

Banotti, Mary, 269
Barber, Monica, 280, 281, 282
Barrington, Ruth, 112
Batten, Guinn, 6
Beale, Jenny, 104
Beer, Ann, 238 n. 21
Beere, Thelka, 265
Behan, Brendan, 166; *An Giall/The
    Hostage,* 166, 172–73
Benedict XV, 251
Bennett, Louie, 4, 60–81
Bennett, Ronan, 184 n. 64
Bennis, Nora, 279, 285
Bernard, Mother Agnes Morrogh, 94
Bettleheim, Bruno, 98
Bhreathnach, Niamh, 269
Binchy, William, 280, 282
Blackwell, Sir Ernley, 127, 128
Blake, William, 216, 217, 244 n. 89
Blom, Ida, 117
Bloom, Harold, 22
Bock, Gisela, 111
Boland, Eavan, 187–89, 190, 198–200;
    "Degas's Laundresses," 188–89, 190;
    "The Journey," 200; *Object Lessons,*
    198; "Oral Tradition," 199
Boucicault, Dion, 5, 160–62;
    Arrah-na-Pogue, 160, 161; *Robert
    Emmet,* 161; *The Shaughraun,* 161,
    164, 165
Bourke, Angela, 4, 101 n. 29

Bradshaw, Brendan, 103
Bruton, John, 284
Bryson, Norman, 190, 198
Burton, Joan, 269
Butler, Mary, 41, 48–49
Byrne, Noreen, 289

Cahill, Eileen, 238–39 n. 21
Cairns, David, 182 nn. 4, 5
Carbery, Ethna. *See* Johnston, Anna
Carr, Marina, 271
Carson, Ciaran, 203–4
Carson, Michael, 151
Casement, Roger, 6, 11, 127–53,
    154 n. 7, 231
Casey, Eamon, 150
Casey, Ger, 280
Chardin, Jean Baptiste, 198–99
Cixous, Hélène, 217
Clark, Alice, 106
Clarke, Austin, 252
Clarke, Kathleen, 110
Clear, Catríona, 107, 111, 246, 255 n. 2
Cohen, Ed, 8
Cole, Donald, 90
Colum, Padraig, "She Moved Through
    the Fair," 205
Condren, Mary, 81 n. 4
Connery, Meg, 68, 69
Connolly, James, 71, 72, 73, 74, 76,
    262
Corcoran, Mary P., 100 n. 4
Correggio, 191, 192, 193, 194, 197
Cosgrave, William, 77
Costello, John, 263
Coulter, Carol, 1, 4
Craft, Christopher, 8, 34 n. 16
Crilly, Anne, 182 n. 5
Cullingford, Elizabeth Butler, 5, 12, 29
Cummings, Pauline, 271
Curtis, L. P., 159, 183 n. 35
Curtis, Maurice, 112

Daly, Mary E., 4–5
Deane, John F., 237 n. 9
Dégas, Edgar, 188–89
Dellamora, Richard, 8
Deneham, Susan, 270
Despard, Charlotte, 77
de Valera, Eamon, 77, 107, 108, 129, 134, 143, 249, 257, 258, 261, 262, 263, 300
Devlin, Anne, *Ourselves Alone,* 170–72
Diner, Hasia, 85
Dinneen, Father Patrick, *An Tobar Draoideachtha,* 43
Dixon, Catherine, 249–50
Docherty, Thomas, 239 n. 21, 241 n. 33
Dockrell, Mrs., 110
Dollimore, Jonathan, 8
Douglas, Alfred Lord, 36 n. 50; *The Spirit-Lamp,* 28
Douglas, Mary, 130, 133
Dowling, Linda, 8
Doyle, Avril, 269
Doyle, Roddy, 293
Duffy, Rita, 271
Duncan, William, 285

Eagleton, Terry, 162
Edge, Sarah, 185 n. 81
Eliot, T. S., 217
Ellis, Havelock, 8
Evans, Richard J., 104, 120 n. 12

Fahey, Tony, 246, 255 n. 2, 289, 290
Fanning, Mrs. C., 110
Fanning, Ronan, 103
Fay, Willie, 45–46
Finucane, Marian, 292
Fitzgerald, Eithne, 269
FitzGerald, Garret, 266
Flaherty, Mary, 266
Foley, Carmel, 267
Foster, R. F., 29
Foucault, Michel, 2; *History of Sexuality,* 8
Fox, R. M., 77–78
Frazier, Adrian, 5, 7
Freud, Sigmund, 188, 194, 214, 215

Friedan, Betty, 105
Friel, Brian, *Translations,* 160, 161–62, 169–70, 183 n. 39

Gaffney, Maureen, 270
Gardiner, Frances, 107, 109
Garvin, Tom, 108
Geary, Nevill, 28
Geoghegan-Quinn, Máire, 266
Gibbon, Monk, 142, 143, 145
Gibbons, Luke, 129
Glenn, Alice, 266
Gonne, Maud (MacBride), 3, 4, 39–55, 58 n. 38, 77, 140, 141; *Dawn,* 3, 39, 40, 51–55, 56 n. 2; *A Servant of the Queen,* 52, 59 n. 60
Gore-Booth, Eva, 132
Gould, Cecil, 209 n. 15
Gould, Warwick, 29
Graves, Robert, 232
Gregory, Lady Augusta, 22; (with W. B. Yeats) *Cathleen ni Houlihan,* 32, 39, 44, 45, 47, 48, 49, 54, 55; *The Gaol Gate,* 55
Grennan, Eamon, 195
Griffith, Arthur, 42, 48, 49–50, 57 n. 17, 58 n. 47
Gwynn, Edward, 11–12

Haberstroh, Patricia, 211 n. 45, 238 n. 21
Hamilton, Mark, 280, 281, 282
Hardinge, William Money, 13
Harkin, Margot, *Hush-a-Bye-Baby,* 170
Harkin, Patricia, 113
Harney, Mary, 266, 269
Hazelkorn, Ellen, 64
Hearn, Dana, 81 n. 5
Hepburn, Audrey, 252
Herr, Cheryl, 183 n. 10
Hogan, Edmund, 247, 251
Hollander, John, 187
hooks, bell, 185 n. 76
Hopkins, Gerard Manley, 217
Hoy, Suellen, 246–47
Hufton, Olwen, 102, 106
Hughes, Ted, 191
Hussey, Gemma, 266

Hyde, Douglas, 159
Hynes, Garry, 271

Irigaray, Luce, 217, 241 n. 42

Jackson, Charles Kain, 28
Jackson, Thomas, 222, 237 n. 11
Jacob, Rose, 76
James, Henry, 12
Jay, Martin, 197–98, 202, 203
Johnson, Lionel, 9
Johnson, Thomas, 77
Johnson, Toni O'Brien, 182 n. 5
Johnston, Anna (Ethna Carbery), 47,
    58 n. 36
Johnston, Dillon, 6
Jordan, Neil, 5; *The Crying Game,*
    173–76, 184 n. 64; *Michael Collins,*
    160
Joynt, Maud, *The Golden Legends of
    the Gael,* 301–2
Jung, Carl Gustav, 217, 237 n. 10

Kapferer, Jean-Noël, 129
Kavanagh, Patrick, "Pygmalion,"
    206
Keaney, Teresa, 251
Kearney, Richard, 182 n. 5
Kellogg, David, 237 nn. 9, 11
Kelly, John, 29
Kennedy, Patrick, 98
Kennedy, Robert, 117–18
Kenny, Mary, 273 n. 18
Kiberd, Declan, 34 n. 1, 183 n. 16
Kickham, Charles, 89
Kinsella, Thomas, 6, 203, 212–36,
    237 n. 9, 242 n. 52; "All is
    Emptiness . . . ," 212, 215, 221;
    "Ballydavid Pier," 222, 223, 224, 231;
    "Ely Place," 232; *From Centre City,*
    224; "Good Night," 233; "Hen
    Woman," 218, 221, 229; "His Father's
    Hands," 213; "Invocation," 215;
    Madonna and Other Poems, 224; "The
    Messenger," 217, 224; "Minstrel,"
    218, 233; "Model School Inchicore,"
    233; "Morning Coffee," 224, 231;
    "Out of Ireland," 215, 233; "Phoenix
    Park," 223, 224, 233; *Songs of the*

Psyche, 220; *A Technical Supplement,*
    232; "Worker in Mirror, at His
    Bench," 214, 220
Koestenbaum, Wayne, *Double Talk: The
    Erotics of Male Literary Collaboration,*
    31
Kristeva, Julia, 214, 217, 238 n. 16,
    241 n. 38, 243 n. 76

Lacan, Jacques, 207–8, 214, 216, 218,
    225, 237 n. 9
Lane, Hugh, 11, 36 n. 50
Lee, Joseph, 105, 106, 273 n. 11
Lee, Vernon, 12
Leerson, Joseph Th., 182 n. 5
LeGuin, Ursula, 255
Leland, Mary, 271
Lemass, Séan, 113, 257, 263
Lesthaeghe, Ron J., 118
Levenson, Leah, 65
Lloyd, David, 184 n. 64
Loftus, Belinda, 182 n. 5
Longley, Edna, 183 n. 39
Loscher, Clem, 285
Lowell, Robert, *Life Studies,* 219
Luddy, Maria, 65
Lynch, Jack, 266
Lynch, Patrick, 260
Lyons, Maureen, 289

MacBride, John, 50, 55
MacBride, Maud Gonne. *See* Gonne,
    Maud
MacBride, Sean, 55
MacCana, Proinsias, 182 n. 5
MacColl, René, 141, 142
MacCurtain, Margaret, 2, 3, 88, 99, 105,
    152
MacDonagh, Thomas, 69
MacNeill, Eoin, 72
Mageean, Deirdre, 96–97
Maher, Mary, 273 n. 18
Malone, Bernice, 269
Mannin, Ethel, 138
Manning, Maurice, 109
Markievicz, Constance, 70, 73, 108–9,
    266
Marshall, Catherine, 63–64
Marshall, Lewis, 17, 18

Martin, Marie, 250, 251
Martyn, Edward, 20–21, 23–29, 33,
    36 n. 63, 38 n. 84, 45; *The Dream
    Physician,* 28–29; *An Enchanted Sea,*
    28; *The Heather Field,* 28; *Maeve,* 28;
    "Pericles," 25; "Pheidas," 25
McAuley, Catherine, 245
McCartan, Patrick, 138
McCormack, William, 237 n. 11
McDiarmid, Lucy, 6
McGinley, P. T., *Eilis agus an Bhean
    Deirce,* 43
McGuckian, Medbh, 6, 150, 152,
    157 n. 68, 187, 204, 212–36,
    239 n. 24; "Blue Vase," 229; "The
    Book Room," 255; "Breaking the
    Blue," 219; "Brothers and Uncles,"
    228, 232; "Clotho," 232, 233; "A
    Conversation Set to Flowers," 225; "A
    Dream in Three Colours," 234; "Echo
    Poem," 227; "First Letters from a
    Steamer," 229; "Four O'Clock,
    Summer Street," 226, 230; *Marconi's
    Cottage,* 225, 229, 234, 235;
    "Marconi's Cottage," 225, 228;
    "Minus 18 Street," 218, 225; "No
    Streets, No Numbers," 218, 225, 226,
    227, 229, 230; *On Ballycastle Beach,*
    225, 229; "On Ballycastle Beach," 230;
    "On Her Second Birthday," 235;
    "Open Rose," 234; "The Rosary
    Dress," 230; "Shaferi," 227; "She
    Which Is Not, He Which Is," 217;
    "Sky in Narrow Streets," 218; "Stone,"
    228; "Teraphim," 232, 234; "Through
    the Round Window," 225, 227; "The
    Time before You," 214; "To the
    Oak-Leaf Camps," 229; "Vibratory
    Description," 212
McGuinness, Arthur, 238 n. 21
McGuinness, Frank, 5; *Carthaginians,*
    173–74; *Someone Who'll Watch Over
    Me,* 176–81, 185 n. 84
McKenna, Patricia, 269
McKillen, Beth, 81 n. 5
McLaren, Angus, 117
McManus, Liz, 269
McMillan, James, 105

McQuaid, John Charles, 114
Meehan, Paula, 187; "The Statue of the
    Virgin at Granard Speaks," 187;
    "Zugswang," 187
Mellows, Liam, 77
Miller, Kerby, 85, 99
Milligan, Alice: *The Deliverance of Red
    Hugh,* 43; *The Last Feast of the
    Fianna,* 43
Mitchell, B. R., *International Historical
    Statistics: Europe 1750–1988,* 115
Mitchell, W. J. T., 201
Mokyr, Joel, 115
Moloney, Frances, 251
Moore, George, 8–33; *Confessions,* 19;
    A Drama in Muslin, 13; *Flowers of
    Passion,* 18; *Hail and Farewell,* 17, 26–
    27, 28; *A Mere Accident,* 13–16
Mosse, George, 10, 46
Muldoon, Paul, 150–51, 203; "Ireland,"
    127, 130
Murphy, Cliona, 61, 81 n. 5, 82 n. 16
Murphy, Maureen, 5
Murphy, Richard, "Casement's Funeral,"
    143–44, 148, 149

Nagle, Nano, 105, 245
Nairac, Robert, 170–72, 184 n. 49
Nandy, Ashis, 182 n. 4
Natterstad, Jerry, 65
Norris, David, 176
Newman, Nina Casement, 133, 134,
    138
Nicholson, Asenath, 88
Ní Chuilleanáin, Eiléan, 187–208; 253;
    "Acts and Monuments of an Unelected
    Nation: The *Cailleach* Writes about the
    Renaissance," 202; "All for You," 196;
    "The Architectural Metaphor," 194–
    96; *The Brazen Serpent,* 192, 196;
    "Daniel Grose," 196, 201; "Fireman's
    Lift," 192–94, 196; "Following," 205;
    "Home Town," 196; "J'ai mal à nos
    dents," 253; *The Magdalene Sermon,*
    206, 256 n. 14; "Man Watching a
    Woman," 189–90; "Passing Over in
    Silence," 189, 206, 207; "Pygmalion's
    Image," 206; "The Real Thing," 200;

"River, with Boats," 188; "Vierge Ouvrante," 189, 206–7; "A Voice," 204–5
Nic Mhathuna, Una Bean, 275
Ní Crohan, Máire, 88–89
Nic Shuibhlaigh, Maire, 43, 46
Ní Dhomhnaill, Nuala, 101 n. 29, 202
Ní Shuilleabháin, Éilís, 91
Nolan, Janet, 85
Norris, David, 132, 176
Noyes, Alfred, 133, 134, 137, 138, 139, 140, 141

O'Brien, George, 113
O'Casey, Sean, 166; The Plough and the Stars, 167
Ó Conaire, Padraig Óg, 90
O'Concannon, Tomás, 87
O'Connell, Daniel, 107
O'Connell, Marie, 246
O'Connor, Emmet, 109
O'Connor, Sinéad, 132, 150
Ó Corráin, Donncha, 106
Ó Crohan, Tomás, 88, 89
Ó Direáin, Máirtín, 86
O'Dowd, Liam, 272 n. 4
Ó Dubhghaill, Séamus, 91
Offen, Karen, 60
O'Hara, Daniel, 237 n. 9
O'Hara, Patricia, 273 n. 13
O'Kelly, Emer, 151
O'Leary, Philip, The Prose Literature of the Gaelic Revival, 1891–1921, 91
O'Reilly, John, 279
O'Riada, Sean, 233
O'Rourke, Mary, 269
O'Toole, Fintan, 274 n. 36
Owen, Nora, 269

Parnell, Charles Stewart, 107
Pater, Walter, 8, 12, 13, 14, 15, 16, 19, 23
Pearse, Patrick, 69, 78, 79, 159
Pettitt, Lance, 185 n. 72
Pinchbeck, Ivy, 106, 107
Pius X, 246
Pius XI, 247, 253
Pius XII, 247, 248, 253, 254
Porter, Susan, 238 n. 21

Quinn, Antoinette, 3
Quinn, Maire, 43, 47–48

Raffalovich, Marc-André, 19, 27
Reed, Carol, Odd Man Out, 175
Richards, Shaun, 182 nn. 4, 5
Richtarik, Marilynn, 183 n. 39
Robinson, Mary, 132, 261, 262, 263, 264, 267, 271, 292
Roche, Anthony, 184 n. 40
Rogers, Mollie, 251
Rose, Kieran, 145, 150
Rosenberg, Carolyn, 237 n. 10
Rudkin, David, 129; Cries from Casement as His Bones Are Brought to Dublin, 144, 146–47, 148–49
Russell, George (AE), 31
Ryan, Father Liam, 260
Ryan, Louise, 81 n. 5
Ryan, Mary, 251

Sailer, Susan Shaw, 239 n. 21
Sayers, Peig, 99, 305
Scully, Peter, 287
Sedgwick, Eve Kosofsky, 19, 164–65, 171
Shannon, Catherine, 1
Shaw, George Bernard, 5, 10, 15, 132, 139, 140, 159, 169; John Bull's Other Island, 162–66
Sheehy, Eugene, 73
Sheehy-Skeffington, Francis, 63, 65, 68, 70, 73, 75
Sheehy-Skeffington, Hanna, 4, 60–81, 108, 132, 141; British Militarism As I Have Known It, 74
Sinfield, Alan, 9
Smyth, Ailbhe, 102, 273 n. 18
Smyth, Father Brendan, 277, 296 n. 6
Stenbock, Count Stanislaus Eric, 24, 36 n. 63
Strong, Eithne, 202
Stuart, Francis, 140
Swanton, Daisy, 76–77
Swanwick, Helena, 78–79
Swinburne, Algernon Charles, 11, 18, 35 n. 43
Swords, Rosemary, 285

Synge, John Millington, 4, 48, 49, 51, 56 n. 6, 58 n. 38, 86; *In the Shadow of the Glen,* 39–40, 47–51, 53

Taylor, Mervyn, 271
Tennyson, Alfred Lord, 34 n. 16; "On One Who Affected an Effeminate Manner," 13
Thane, Pat, 111
Thomson, Sir Basil, 142
Toíbín, Colm, 274 n. 36
Toomey, Deirdre, 29
Travers, Pauric, 273 n. 14

Ua Tuatháil, Lorcan, 89

Valiulis, Maryann, 121 n. 27, 272 n. 4
Vellacott, Jo, 65, 66

Walsh, Archbishop, 27
Walsh, Brendan, 116, 118
Walsh, Eleanor, 219, 223
Walshe, Eibhear, 150
Ward, Margaret, 3, 104
Ward, Peter, 275

Watt, Stephen, 182 n. 9, 183 n. 22
Wellesley, Dorothy, 138
Whitman, Walt, 238 n. 12
Wilde, Oscar, 8, 9–10, 11, 21, 33, 145
Wills, Clair, 238 n. 21, 243 n. 75
Wilson, Chris, 118
Wrigley, E. A., 115–16, 117
Wyer, Teresa, 110
Wyse-Power, Jenny, 110

X, 1, 268, 285, 297 n. 28

Yeats, John Butler, 50
Yeats, William Butler, 22, 29–32, 33, 42, 50, 134, 135, 136, 137, 138, 139–40, 141, 145, 159, 216, 217; *Autobiography,* 22; (with Lady Gregory) *Cathleen ni Houlihan,* 39, 44–47, 53, 54, 55; *The Countess Cathleen,* 26; (with Moore) *Diarmuid and Grania,* 31; *Fairy and Folk Tales of the Irish Peasantry,* 98; *On Baile's Strand,* 231; (with Moore) *The Tale of a Town,* 31; *Where There Is Nothing,* 31

The authors are grateful for permission to use the following material under copyright:

From *Object Lessons: The Life of the Woman and the Poet in Our Time*, by Eavan Boland. © 1995 by Eavan Boland. Reprinted by permission of W. W. Norton and Company, Inc., and Carcanet Press.

From *Outside History: Selected Poems, 1980–1990*, by Eavan Boland. © 1990 by Eavan Boland. Reprinted by permission of W. W. Norton and Company, Inc., and Carcanet Press.

From *Blood and Family* and *From Centre City*, by Thomas Kinsella. Reprinted by permission of Thomas Kinsella and Oxford University Press.

From *Poems, 1956–1973*; *Peppercanister Poems, 1972–1978*; *Madonna and Other Poems*, by Thomas Kinsella. Reprinted by permission of Thomas Kinsella and Wake Forest University Press.

From *Marconi's Cottage* and *On Ballycastle Beach*, by Medbh McGuckian. Reprinted by permission of The Gallery Press and Wake Forest University Press.

"Ireland," from *Why Brownlee Left*, by Paul Muldoon. Reprinted with the permission of Wake Forest University Press and Faber and Faber, Ltd.

From *The Brazen Serpent*, by Eiléan Ní Chuilleanáin. Reprinted by permission of The Gallery Press and Wake Forest University Press.

From *The Magdalene Sermon and Earlier Poems*, by Eiléan Ní Chuilleanáin. Reprinted by permission of The Gallery Press and Wake Forest University Press.